# DATE DUE

| 24 XII 08 | | | |
|---|---|---|---|
| | | | |
| | | | |
| | | | |
| | | | |
| | | | |
| | | | |
| | | | |
| | | | |
| | | | |
| | | | |
| | | | |
| | | | |
| | | | |
| | | | |
| | | | |
| | | | |

Demco, Inc. 38-293

# Bernadette of Lourdes

# Bernadette of Lourdes

*Her Life, Death and Visions*

THÉRÈSE TAYLOR

BURNS & OATES
*A Continuum imprint*
LONDON • NEW YORK

**Burns & Oates**
*A Continuum imprint*
The Tower Building
11 York Road
London SE1 7NX

370 Lexington Avenue
New York
NY 10017-6503

*www.continuumbooks.com*

First published 2003

**British Library Cataloguing-in-Publication Data**
A catalogue record of this book is available from the British Library.

ISBN 0–86012–337–5 (hardback)
      0–86012–338–3 (paperback)

Every effort has been made to contact the copyright holders of material featured in this book. The publisher welcomes any queries from those copyright holders we may have been unable to contact.

Typeset by BookEns Ltd, Royston, Herts.
Printed and bound in Great Britain by MPG Books Ltd, Bodmin, Cornwall

# Contents

# List of Plates

# Abbreviations

AC       *Archives Cros.*

AD       *Archives départementales* (Hautes-Pyrénées), Tarbes.

AG       *Archives de la Grotte*, Lourdes.

AN       *Archives nationales,* Paris.

AML      *Archives municipales de Lourdes.*

BVP      René Laurentin, *Bernadette vous parle*, vols 1 and 2, Lethielleux, Paris 1972.

ESB      André Ravier, ed., *Les Ecrits de Sainte Bernadette et sa voie spirituelle*, Lethielleux, Paris 1980.

LDA      René Laurentin et al., eds, *Lourdes, Documents authentiques*, vols 1–7, Lethielleux, Paris 1958–66.

Logia    René Laurentin, and Sr Marie-Thérèse Bourgeade, eds, *Logia de Bernadette. Etude critique de ses paroles de 1866 à 1879*, 3 vols. Lethielleux and Oeuvre de la Grotte, Paris 1971.

PON      *Procès ordinaire de Nevers*, 1909–1911, Archives of the Sisters of Nevers, St Gildard.

Procès   Tauriac J.-M., and J. Aubery, *Procès de Bernadette. Documents authentiques*, Libraire des Champs-Elysées, Paris, 1958.

RdAM     Hommage à la bienheureuse Bernadette Soubirous, *Revue d'ascétique et de mystique* 10 (1929). Printed testimonies from the Cros archive.

RdC      *Registre des contemporaines.* November 1907. A preliminary enquiry for the canonization. Archives of the Sisters of Nevers, St Gildard.

Témoins  Cros, Léonard, and P. M. Olphe-Galliard, *Lourdes 1858. Témoins de l'événement* Lethielleux, Paris 1958.

# Introduction

In 1892 Émile Zola wrote that: 'A life of Bernadette, made by a mind like mine, and fully documented, would be the most interesting story in the world. But a history, not a novel.'[1] Having written this, Zola went on to write a novel. There is no scholarly biography of Bernadette, either in French or in English. This is surprising, as she is a well-known figure, both in the Catholic world and beyond it.

Although Bernadette Soubirous has escaped the attention of historians, Saint Bernadette of Lourdes is the subject of a vast devotional literature. There are numerous hagiographic works, and many of them are well-researched and beautifully written. There are also document collections which have been assembled by the Catholic Church. Lourdes scholarship is indebted to Père Laurentin for his edited collections of primary sources and his careful studies – of the apparitions at Lourdes, of all authentic quotations of Bernadette's words, and of all extant photographs of her – and to Père André Ravier for his collections of her letters, the notes of which place each document in its immediate context. These volumes appeared during the 1960s and 1970s. The clerical scholarship has been scrupulously accurate, non-sentimental and aware of historical context. But it has not been accompanied by a complete scholarly biography.

Even before the Lourdes documents were edited and printed, several Lives of Saint Bernadette appeared which met high standards of religious scholarship. Père Trochu's *Sainte Bernadette de Lourdes* appeared in 1956, and has stood the test of time. This is a masterpiece of religious biography, explaining how Bernadette lived and why she became a saint. The major and minor themes of her life are set out effortlessly, although not all would agree with the writer's serene view of Bernadette's life as an unbroken spiritual ascent. Insights into the sadness and difficulties of Bernadette's life were more clearly expressed in Père Petitot's 1935 work, *Histoire exacte des apparitions de N. D. de Lourdes à Bernadette.*[2]

Despite the value of these writings, and many other books about Bernadette, the need for a scholarly biography is evident. The purpose of the religious writers is to assess the reality of the apparitions at Lourdes, to persuade the reader of their significance, and to relate the life of Bernadette in terms that make her a figure of spiritual inspiration. The purpose of this book, and any other historical life of Bernadette, is to put her within the context of her time, to describe the social forces and specific events which were important, and to trace her individual life. I do not assert the reality of the visions, and can offer no new information which would help the reader to make up their mind about this. It makes no difference to this biography

1

whether or not the reader believes Bernadette was genuine, mistaken or fraudulent in her claims. The point is that various claims were made, by Bernadette and those around her, and a narrative evolved from them. A chain of events was then set off which made her one of the most famous women in France.

Because I do not seek to set Bernadette forth as a moral example, I concentrate instead upon her historical existence, and I hope to interest the reader in this. Exactly what did happen to a girl who became famous as a visionary? This is an important story, even for those who do not read church history. Bernadette is remarkable for her contact with the significant themes of nineteenth-century France. She was one of the few peasant women who became a public figure, and she did so at a time when the peasantry were ideological and artistic symbols in an industrializing society. Bernadette lived during the era when Millet exhibited in Paris salons, when rural resorts were professionalized into a tourist industry, and when the pre-modern past was enlisted into the political discourse of both the left and the right. She was also a display of youth, purity and virginity in a society which had become obsessed with categorizing women in sexual terms. In a sense, she was a living myth.

This life of Bernadette brings in many features which are usually ignored in religious works. I describe the secular history of Lourdes, as a town facing numerous problems, but also with certain advantages. The myth of Lourdes as a pristine or remote village is firmly laid to rest, and a different representation is offered. I also look at all forms of supernatural belief, and give them impartial consideration as sources for the Lourdes apparitions. Beliefs about witches, fairies and ghosts are obviously very important to the story of the Lady of the Grotto.

As a work of history, this biography is obliged to attempt to provide a rational answer to a difficult question. Why did Bernadette attain such a special status? Why is she uniquely celebrated? After all, it is not uncommon for Catholic women and girls to claim to see visions. Bernadette was not even the only visionary in Lourdes, much less in France. My account gives an explanation which depends upon contingent factors – the situation of Lourdes, the power of the media, and the attractions of Bernadette's persona.

All biographies are written of their own time, as well as that of their subjects. A late twentieth-century theme which has strongly marked my work is an awareness of celebrity. Celebrity is a public status which makes a person the focus of obsessive love, curiosity and adulation. We are more aware of this now than ever before, but the beginnings of media-driven fame had first appeared in the 1860s – exactly the era when the Lourdes visions became known. Bernadette became a well-known individual because of the printed media and photographic prints. She had an image, and a public identity, quite separate from her own life, and these autonomous forces came to dominate her individual existence. Bernadette was an early traveller on a path which has since been followed by many. When reading this book, one will be reminded of other women who have caught the public's eye, and have been celebrated for their feminine qualities. Bernadette's life is not simply a religious story.

One can see clear prefigurings of the public gaze which fixed upon people such as Marilyn Monroe and Diana, the Princess of Wales.

Much of Bernadette's life was spent coping with irrational sensationalism. She coped well, and emerges as a person of dignity. From quite an early age – as only an adolescent girl – she is remarkable for her refusal either to engage with fame or to fashion herself according to public responses. Bernadette was loved by innumerable people who did not know her. Their fascination with the holy young girl of Lourdes created a situation which restricted her life and distanced her from her own people. Like most people with admirers, she had no real friends. Bernadette's calm response to celebrity status, and her acceptance of the lonely life it imposed upon her, are qualities which have rarely been discussed by religious writers. I do not agree with the Catholic authors who claim that Bernadette is a particularly good example for girls, or for women in general. The circumstances of her life were so peculiar that it is difficult to draw a lesson from them. But I would maintain that she is an excellent example for those few people whose lives oblige them to exist in the public eye. She seems to have had an inner centre of balance, untouched by the hysteria of shared enthusiasms.

Among the new material included in this book are full details of the astonishing way that church historians persecuted Bernadette during her last months of life. Writers such as André Ravier and René Laurentin have mentioned that the historians of the Grotto made many demands upon Bernadette, even when she was very ill, but the full story of these inquisitions has not been told. It is not important to the hagiography of Lourdes, except in so far as it shows the trials from which Bernadette's virtues emerged triumphant. But it is very important to an historical account such as this one, which aims to give consideration of all factors which were significant in her life. The endless interrogations about every detail of the visions ate away at Bernadette. Along with tuberculosis, they are one of the things that killed her.

It is my belief that Bernadette's life had three levels. There was her life as an individual, her life as a celebrity, and her spiritual experiences. This last aspect has already been examined by writers qualified in theology. I consider only the first two factors, and I do not think that this biography exhausts either of them. Different interpretations of her life could be offered by other historians, and I would be especially interested to read an account of Bernadette from someone like Isaure Gratacos, fluent in the indigenous language and culture of the Pyrenees, as I am not. Much more could be said about Bernadette's fame and reputation, and I hope that in future she will be included when scholars talk about representations of women in nineteenth-century France. In this purpose, my work resembles that of Rachel Brownstein, who has studied the actress Rachel (a contemporary of Bernadette) and has considered both the life and the legends which existed around her.[3]

I first learnt the story of Bernadette, in its most legendary form, when I was a schoolgirl in the 1960s. I was acquainted with holy books and lives of the saints, which often included the pristine tale of the asthmatic, poverty-stricken girl who saw the Virgin Mary and gave the world the shrine of Lourdes. It was obvious, even then, that there must have been a whole other story to tell from her point of view. I would like to put such an account on paper, but I do not think that I have done so. I wonder if anyone could.

René Laurentin has cited the saying, which is found in many books about Lourdes, that Bernadette is 'the most hidden of the saints'.[4] There are numerous records of Bernadette's life, but they record Bernadette being displayed by others, being circumspect in response to them, or repelling attention. She never had any inclination toward self-representation, or confidences, or communicating her version of events. Unlike most saints, she was not famous for what she said or did, but for what others saw in her.

Even before she became a visionary, Bernadette's life had been one of change and upheavals. Her family had once been prosperous, but the family inheritance, a Lourdes mill, was lost by her parents. They did not have the management skills of the family's previous generation. Bernadette was the eldest child, and could probably best remember the early years of comfort and then the downward spiral of slum lodgings and unpaid rents. At the age of thirteen, she was sent to live as an unpaid child-servant in a nearby village, as her parents could not afford to keep her. But the post was unsatisfactory, and Bernadette returned home in February 1858. A few weeks later, on a cold February day, she went wood-gathering, and saw a beautiful 'White Lady' standing in the Grotto of Massabielle. This was the beginning of the visions, which eventually caused thousands to flock to the Grotto where they watched her experience trances and emerge with messages from the White Lady. Eventually, these apparitions were accepted by the Church as genuine appearances of the Virgin, and Bernadette was a figure of admiration all over the Catholic world. She had only eighteen visions, over a few months in 1858, but they altered her status for ever.

Was she genuine? This was the question people never ceased to ask, and they demanded of Bernadette that she confirm their faith and make the supernatural real. Those who visited Bernadette during her years of fame were impressed by her indifference to public opinion. To a priest in the 1860s, her statement that 'if anyone does not want to believe me, then they are free to do so, it does not concern me'[5] seemed evidence of her modesty. One might wonder if this was not merely the literal truth, and if, as many of her actions indicated, she was unconcerned about the fate of the story of the apparitions. Yet it is also possible that she was aware that her impassive demeanour was part of her credibility, and that she reacted skilfully to people's need to believe her. An early observer precisely noted the sources of charm and plausibility in her manner when he wrote that he was struck by the 'form of indifference with which she spoke; the natural charm which I nevertheless found in her narration; the assurance and her answers; the naivety of her reflections'.[6]

Another observer found these recitals rather suspect. Frère Léobard, a resident of Lourdes, said that he had considered her closely and often asked himself 'if she was not rather an adroit actress rather than a sincere visionary'.[7] The Police Commissioner made the same point during the period of the visions, in 1858, and put a more openly hostile construction on it: 'Bernadette is very intelligent: she understands the important role she plays for the public, and she appreciates the benefits (*douceurs*).'[8]

The Police Commissioner may have been making a genuine point, for it seems impossible that any genuinely naive and innocent peasant could have played the role of naivety and innocence as effectively as Bernadette did during the stressful years after 1862. Trapped by her family's obligations and her own renown, she battled amid public exploitations and failing health to preserve her own identity. It is conceivable that during the controversy over the Grotto she had enjoyed a respite from the powerlessness and unimportance which had been her sole experience of life until 1858. Yet, having become a renowned person, she made no move to use her status or improve her situation. She left the development of the Grotto to those who took responsibility, and showed no inclination for the type of promotions which the church authorities organized around her after 1860.

According to my reading of events, the conclusive turning-point of Bernadette's life was not the visions in 1858. Although these changed other people's view of Bernadette, she herself refused to change her way of life. She remained with her family, and – when not interrupted by visitors – worked each day in ordinary tasks. Having left school, she even had some paid employment as a servant. But the feckless habits of her parents, and their inability to manage their finances, led to her exile from home. Just as they had sent her to Bartrès as a child in 1857, they were obliged to send her to the Lourdes convent as a sixteen-year-old in 1860. The Catholic Church took over the custody of Bernadette, and her life on public display began in earnest. Whatever the 'benefits' of being a visionary in 1858, they vanished quickly enough, and Bernadette's quality of life had deteriorated disastrously by the time she left Lourdes in 1866.

At Nevers, Bernadette was exiled from the Pyrenean culture of her home, her childhood and her visions. Yet she made the difficult transition to her post-1866 life as a Sister of Nevers with unfaltering perfectionism. At the convent, she was offered a sanctuary from the public, in return for a strict and repressed existence among women from much more elevated social backgrounds than her own. With notable fortitude, and in an environment where her every fault was noted, Bernadette faced boredom, isolation, snubs, and the exacting standards of the religious rule. In 1872, she developed a rare and agonizing variety of tuberculosis which infected the marrow of her bones rather than her lungs. Her stoic attitude did not alter throughout the long illness, which finally ended her life in 1879.

Bernadette's only advice to the historians of Lourdes was to mind that they did not write too much. 'Out of the wish to embroider things, one disfigures them.'[9] Bernadette's passivity was one of the reasons why a very strong public image could be constructed around her. In refusing to interact with her fame, she did nothing to contradict it. Her retiring nature also makes her very different from the other women who entered the historical record through French Catholicism. In particular, the other young woman saint of the nineteenth century, Thérèse of Lisieux, found posthumous fame through an autobiography which vividly communicates her childhood memories and interior feelings. This is in complete contrast to Bernadette. Bernadette wrote as little as possible, although her collected letters, notes and *récits* of the visions do fill a respectably sized single volume.

In recent years, the apparitions at Lourdes have attracted attention from scholars. Thomas Kselman's *Miracles in Nineteenth-Century France* put visionary experiences at the centre of a firmly historical work. Previous to this, the writings of Edward Berenson, James McMillan, and other historians, have shown that religion needed as much attention from historians of Europe as from those of the Third World, where it is a more acknowledged focus of study. Most recently, Ruth Harris's *Lourdes: Body and Spirit in the Secular Age*[10] has provided a detailed history of the shrine, and has fully contextualized the pilgrimage movement as part of the history of France. French historians have already published works in which Lourdes was considered as a part of larger pictures. Jean-François Soulet's *Les Pyrénées au XIXe siècle*[11] is a marvellously rich history, Isaure Gratacos's folklore studies of women in the Pyrenees are profound,[12] and specialized tourist studies such as Michel Chadefaud's[13] are also important.

The appearance of these works has further motivated me to publish a scholarly life of Bernadette. It is an anomaly that all of these academic scholars are obliged to rely upon hagiography whenever they give an account of the girl whose experiences triggered the phenomena of Lourdes. Bernadette was not a visionary who preached or proclaimed a message. She was a disadvantaged person – poor, young, and rural – who captured the imaginations of those who lived far from her. It was they who made most of the significant moves in the history of Lourdes. But she was, still, important to the story which grew beyond her. Without Bernadette, there would be no shrine at the Grotto.

# NOTES

1.  Émile Zola quoted by Jacques Noiray, 'Zola et Bernadette. L'image de Bernadette Soubirous dans *Lourdes*', in Pierre Delay, ed., *Littérature – Région – Religions* (Bordeaux 1988).

2.  Père Henri Petitot, *Histoire exacte des apparitions de N. D. de Lourdes à Bernadette* (Paris 1935).

3.  Rachel M. Brownstein, *Tragic Muse: Rachel of the Comédie-Française* (North Carolina 1995).

4.  René Laurentin, *Vie de Bernadette* (Paris 1977), 9.

5.  E. Boyer, *Une visite à Bernadette et à la Grotte de Lourdes* (Tarbes 1866), 27.

6.  A. Clarens, *RdAM*, 14.

7.  Frère Léobard, *RdAM*, 31.

8.  Police Commissioner to the Préfet, 7 April 1858, *LDA* 2, no. 122, 146.

9.  Bernadette, quoted, *LDA* 2, no. 10.

10. Ruth Harris, *Lourdes: Body and Spirit in the Secular Age* (London 1999).

11. Jean-François Soulet, *Les Pyrénées au XIXe siècle*, 2 vols (Toulouse 1987).

12. Isaure Gratacos, *Fées et Gestes, Femmes Pyrénéennes: un statut social exceptionnel en Europe* (Toulouse 1986).

13. Michel Chadefaud, *Lourdes, un pèlerinage, une ville* (La Calade 1981); *Aux origines du tourisme dans les pays de l'Adour* (Pau 1987).

## PART I

# Lourdes
## The Making of a Shrine

**CHAPTER 1**

# Like Any Town
## Lourdes Before the Apparitions

> Like any nation, or any town, Lourdes has a legendary past and an historic past.
>
> Gustave Bascle de Lagrèze, *Chronique de la ville et du château de Lourdes*, 1845

Saint Bernadette is now a well-known figure and Lourdes is a much-visited place. The shrine at the Grotto, with its sacred spring, is a byword for miracles. Millions of pilgrims, including invalids seeking a cure, flock there from all over the Catholic world. They come to venerate the place where Our Lady appeared to a holy young girl, a pristine figure, whom even sceptics acknowledge was sincere and untouched by self-interest. Most people, whether Catholic or not, have seen some representation of Lourdes, such as statues, pictures, plaques, or the 1950s Hollywood film, *Song of Bernadette*.

Among Catholics, and among those who have heard the story of Our Lady of Lourdes, the town is usually imagined to have been a remote village, which suddenly took on a new identity when Bernadette had her visions. As to when these visions took place, the image is misty. Quite frequently, even those who are well read in religious history will suppose them to have been a medieval event. As Alan Neame, a modern writer, found when he was researching this topic, many people are astonished to hear that Bernadette was a contemporary of Queen Victoria who lived in the age of the railway. 'Oh, they exclaim, I thought that Bernadette lived in the middle ages, in the dark ages, in the fairy tale ages.'[1] She steps into popular consciousness as a resident of some distant part of France, who became a saint because the Virgin Mary appeared to her. There are sound reasons for this legend of distance and antiquity, which will be explained in this book. The first task, in giving an account of Bernadette's background, is to explain the lively, remarkable, and sometimes sordid history of Lourdes during the nineteenth century.

The local historian of Lourdes wrote in 1845 that: 'Like any nation, or any town, Lourdes has its legendary past and its historical past.'[2] The truly surprising aspect of this statement is that it was printed in a book more than a decade *before* the visions at the Grotto. Before the celebrated visions, Lourdes already had an historian, was the subject of a book, and had a varied past which, as he notes, included many supernatural legends. Many historical factors were to contribute to the dramatic events of 1858, when the population of Lourdes outfaced both the disapproval of the secular authorities and the reservations of the clergy to make the Grotto of

Massabielle a shrine. The shrine of Lourdes sprang from the crises of the nineteenth century – the decline of traditional rural life, unemployment, rising populations and the confrontation between the world of tradition and modernity.

## Culture, economy and society in the Hautes-Pyrénées

During the nineteenth century, Lourdes was a medium-sized town on the border of France. It was within the département of Hautes-Pyrénées, in the mountain range on the border with Spain. This département had been made by combining several regions: a fraction of the Pays Basque, and also Béarn, Comminges and Bigorre. The indigenous populations of these last three areas each spoke their own varieties of Occitan (*langue d'oc*), the language of southern France. Hagiographic texts have often described Bernadette Soubirous as Basque,[3] but this is inaccurate. Lourdes is within the Bigorre region.

During the 1850s, the very decade when Bernadette beheld a beautiful *Dame* who spoke to her in Occitan dialect, this ancient language was being routed by the advance of standard French. It was regretfully reported by a local antiquarian that 'every day it [i.e. Occitan] tends to disappear in our towns, retreating before the advance of French culture'.[4] Bernadette (b. 1844) was to belong to the last generation of Bigourdanians which included people who spoke *only* the indigenous language. In later years a number of educated visitors were to ask her how the Virgin Mary could possibly have spoken 'that wretched language'.[5] Like many Pyreneans, Bernadette was attached to her heritage, and had only learnt to speak French as an adult. She replied defiantly to such remarks, defending her own language as equal to any other.[6]

The decline of the indigenous language was only one of the wholesale changes of the nineteenth century. A series of economic depressions and natural disasters followed one another from the 1800s to the 1850s. The harvests of potatoes and cereals failed repeatedly because of new horticultural diseases. Human beings were also afflicted by pestilence in the form of cholera epidemics and tuberculosis. Industrial manufacturing in the cities undermined local crafts, and primary products were difficult to market. It was harder to gain a living in time-honoured ways, there were fewer opportunities and more competition. The unemployment and collapse of prices felt throughout France from 1847 to 1852 also took a prolonged toll. A pattern of emigration began wherein the most enterprising members of the communities sought their fortunes elsewhere, and this was to continue into the twentieth century.

Until a general upturn after the 1860s, the only flourishing sector of the local economy was tourism. The beauty of the mountains and the existence of spas brought large numbers of visitors to the area during the 'season' of May to September. Travelling in the mountains and 'taking the waters' were a social rite of purification, socialization and healing for the European upper classes and those who strove to imitate them. Some tourists also liked to visit the local Marian shrines, which had been the subject of pilgrimage since the sixteenth century.

Throughout the nineteenth century France had a series of wars, revolutions and coups which brought various governments to power. By 1851 the country was governed by Louis Napoleon III (nephew of the famous Napoleon) who overthrew the existing constitution and founded an autocratic regime. His rule was to last for twenty years, an era known as the Second Empire. The institution of the Second Empire in 1851 was met by violent protests in some parts of rural France, but only scattered dissent in the Hautes-Pyrénées. People may have been indifferent, or they may have been intimidated. The Sous-Préfet at Bagnères noted that as soon as arrests began, there was a 'general panic' among protesters.[7] The only issue which consistently roused the Pyreneans to active protest at this time was the Forestry Code. This was a law which forbade wood-gathering in the state forests, and it directly impinged upon the standard of living of the poor. Every turbulent change of government was an opportunity to assert local rights to wood-gathering, and to burn the legal registers which listed offenders.[8]

Although the Hautes-Pyrénées was one of the more peaceful areas, the state officials of the province partook of the pervasive Second Empire attitude which saw subversion everywhere. Government officials were usually ardent supporters of the officially sponsored idea that in 1851 France had faced a choice between anarchy and legitimate authority. They stated their forebodings in obsessive terms, and their fears were not allayed by peaceful appearances. As Howard Payne has written, the Procureur at Nancy spoke for many when he said, 'one feels that order exists only on the surface'.[9] His counterpart in the Hautes-Pyrénées had conceded some months before the coup that 'the country continues, in general, to be *rather calm*, at least in appearance'.[10] He then qualified this already cautious statement with the observation that a great number of people in St Palais were in possession of pocket pistols.[11]

In the winter of 1854, after a very poor harvest and a cholera epidemic in the Hautes-Pyrénées, the Procureur Général noted with relief that disorder had been prevented. He attributed this to two causes, 'the vigilance . . . and the severity of the magistrates' and the giving of charity, which he described as always generous in this region.[12] The giving of charity is often mentioned by the middle-class residents of Lourdes when they recalled the time of Bernadette's visions.[13] They invited the children of the poor to dine in their kitchens and maintained traditions such as that the first item of clothing made in a household would be donated to someone who needed it. These people were 'middle class' only in terms of their level of education and adherence to French norms of respectability. They did not command large incomes, but even when they themselves were struggling with debts they accepted without question the duty to give alms.[14] It was the larger proprietors who found this type of charity onerous. One owner of a *grange* solicited the local politicians to open a workhouse in Tarbes because of the presence of numerous beggars during the famine year of 1854.[15] He claimed that they were professional mendicants who should inspire no pity. It seems that these people regarded him with an equal hostility, for his property had been ravaged by fire after his wife had refused shelter to a beggar.[16]

The dismissive attitude of this proprietor, and the consequent episode of revenge, contrasts with a statement from the same era from the Lourdes Municipal Council. In December 1853, the councillors agreed that the severity of the times was placing 'the workers in a state of suffering' and that it was a matter of urgency to provide relief for the poorest families.[17] Some residents of the Hautes-Pyrénées with an interest in economics called not for workhouses and state repression but for the provision of credit facilities, protection of local markets, and the introduction of modern manufacturing into the area.[18]

The social structure of the indigenous people of the Hautes-Pyrénées was distinctive and has led to the area being described as 'matriarchal'.[19] In the central and western zone of the Pyrenees the local laws of marriage and inheritance, which prevailed formally until 1791 and regulated customs until much later, conferred a high status upon women.[20] Like men, Pyrenean mountain women were not subject to strict sexual repression, and were not necessarily expected to be virgins when they married.[21] Pyrenean women did not lose their own property upon marriage, and were entitled to equal inheritance with male members of their families. Whoever was first-born in a family was the 'heir' and had greater rights than the younger siblings. In the Occitan regions of the Hautes-Pyrénées, this meant that an eldest daughter had rights over her younger brothers. Only the Basques reserved the rights of inheritance for the males. An Occitan heiress, when married, was superior to her husband.

How different this was to general French attitudes may be judged by the nearly anguished reactions of scholarly commentators who happened to come to the Pyrenees. One writer who studied the area in the 1850s almost shuddered at these horrid customs. As he explained, the situation of women in marriage is known to everyone, and understood, but in the Hautes-Pyrénées it is reversed: 'in an abnormal manner, to the detriment of a man who is linked with an heiress'.[22] He cited the views of other scholars, and said that there was a general agreement that 'a society which gave women such a degree of influence and power, could, for that reason alone, be accused of barbarism'.[23] Another writer related an awful tale where an unwanted government official, posted to the valley of Ossau during the eighteenth century, was murdered by local women. He noted in the 1860s that they were 'those women whom we still see now, while the shepherds are absent on the high pastures. The women take on heavy duties, holding a child in one hand, while working the land with the other.'[24] In the 1850s these coarse, self-reliant, mountain women, who made their own rules, were beginning to vanish. They were evolving into more mannered types, more likely to have received some schooling and more likely to have worked for wages at some time in their lives. They travelled from the remote villages and pastures to work as servants and field hands. Sometimes they moved permanently to the towns, and their daughters lived different lives.

The mid- to late nineteenth century was a period of flux when the traditional Pyrenean sexual morality was rejected by the middle classes, and was effectively combated by a numerous and dedicated clergy. The idea that it did not matter if a single woman was pregnant, provided that she married eventually, and that sexual relations could be freely indulged on certain days of the year (an echo of pre-Christian fertility rites) was consistently condemned by the literate. The peasantry eventually got the message, although some remote areas only caught up as late as the 1920s.[25] In the more frequented areas, and the larger towns, French standards of respectability held sway among the middle classes, and the respectable poor, by the 1850s. This was partly the work of priests, schoolteachers, civil servants and other authority figures. It may also have been due to a change in population patterns, the decline in the traditional subsistence lifestyle, and the spread of a money economy. Women's conformity with norms of chastity and fidelity was necessary, if each family was to remain ordered and provide for itself.

## The town of Lourdes

In 1858 Lourdes was a town, rather than a village, with a population of 4,000.[26] Despite the hard times experienced by the Pyrenean population as a whole, Lourdes was a place where opportunities were being created. It had medieval monuments, modern residential areas, and both slums and prosperous quarters. Its commanding position at the entrance to the Lavedan valley had made it an important place during medieval times. It is from this period that Lourdes has its most striking historical monument, an eleventh-century fortress with sheer stone walls which rise dizzyingly from the highest point of the town. The fortress is now a museum, but was still used as a posting-place for soldiers during the nineteenth century.

The population had doubled since the French Revolution, and it was from this time that the town had risen in importance. The municipal council was energetic and ardently promoted local interests. Even during the disruptive time of the Revolution civic pride had maintained itself, and it was during these years that permission was received for Lourdes to commence construction of a 'Town Hall worthy of its ambitions'.[27] These ambitions maintained themselves, and in 1804 Lourdes became the *chef-lieu de l'arrondissement*. A Procureur Impérial was therefore resident in the town, accompanied by a small staff of public servants.

In 1858, Lourdes was the site of both Pyrenean and external commerce, being the location of the local fortnightly markets, and also a stopping-point for the tourists to the Hautes-Pyrénées. It possessed several quarries which were mined for marble and slate. The municipal council claimed in 1854 that more than 1,200 workers were employed in local industries.[28] Proudly describing their town as one of 'the most industrial' of the département, the Lourdes Council claimed that they had an incontestable right to be part of the railway system.[29]

When Louis Veuillot, a leading Catholic journalist from Paris, visited Lourdes in 1858 he realized that he was not on a hardship trip to a rude village: 'there are lovely houses, good restaurants and cafes, and people who have the latest journals available to them'.[30] These observations show the existence of both a prosperous sector of the community and an inclination for reading and information. Already, in 1855, the town maintained four schools. Jean-Baptiste Estrade, who came to the town during the 1850s as a taxation administrator, found the local inclination for education prodigious.[31]

A local newspaper, *Le Lavedan*, was published in the town to serve Lourdes and the surrounding area. Other Pyrenean newspapers, such as *L'ère Impérial*, printed in Tarbes, were sold in Lourdes, and the leading Paris newspapers were also available. Lourdes was relatively well served with news and anecdotes. *Le Lavedan* was edited by the brothers Cazenave, a lively family who sought out every item of interest which they could find. Their standpoint was socially progressive, with an undertone of republican politics. A police report to the Sous-Préfet of the area noted that the home of the Cazenave brothers was a meeting-place for republicans, and one could guess as much from reading their paper.[32] The articles in their paper showed them to be admirers of modern inventions, hopeful of social change, interested in the outside world, and cool toward the Catholic Church. *Le Lavedan* performed the function of a local newspaper, by recording market days and recent events, such as the case of a man from Lourdes killed in a drunken brawl.[33] It also, more ambitiously, informed its readers of current trends in social ideas, for example by reprinting a statement from the socialist thinker Proudhon, on the question of women's rights.[34] The most distant parts of the world were not too far for this newspaper, and articles were carried even on such esoteric information as the marriage customs of Australian Aborigines.[35]

Closer to home, and closer to controversy, were stories of Algeria, one of the first French colonies, acquired in 1830. France had been involved in arduous warfare during the 1840s, and was opposed by a legendary Arab resistance leader, Abdel-Kader, who was finally taken prisoner in 1847. *Le Lavedan* reported on the career of Abdel-Kader in surprisingly idealistic terms. They described him as a 'Hero of the African war' and a 'lion' among his people.[36] There also were articles describing the Islamic religion and the life of Muhammad.[37] The fascination with Abdel-Kader may have been due to the fact that this interesting person was resident in the Hautes-Pyrénées. In 1848 he had been held at Pau, and the citizens of Lourdes unsuccessfully petitioned the French government, asking that he could be transferred to their castle, where, in their opinion, he would be 'better' accommodated.[38] They were unsuccessful, and therefore Lourdes remained, as yet, without any resident celebrity.

The newspapers were read by literate residents of the Hautes-Pyrénées, and a significant number of these consumers of the written word organized themselves into literary circles and historical societies. Lourdes gained occasional mention in their publications as a 'truly historic town'.[39] It even had an historian of its own. In 1845 Gustave Bascle de Lagrèze published the *Chronique de la ville et du château de Lourdes*, a small leather-bound volume. Lagrèze, who lived in Tarbes, was a civil servant, and the author of a number of monographs about local history and government administration. Like many literate men, he enjoyed the academic study of folklore and traditional beliefs, and could see that these were aspects of a way of life disappearing during his lifetime. For some reason, his attention was drawn to Lourdes, where he may have had friends in the local literary circle. He thought the place worthy of some attention, but not an overwhelming amount. In a self-deprecating introduction to his book he noted that: 'I am the first historian of Lourdes; it is quite likely that I will also be the last.'[40] In his book he recounted the medieval legends and historical episodes in which Lourdes had featured, and also gave a genial account of its current fortunes.

The people of Lourdes related stories, and commemorated events, which usually involved them bravely facing up to bullies and outsiders. Their history included wonderful incidents, such as withstanding a siege by Crusades from Spain, and refusing to co-operate with Roger de Montfort, a detestable outsider, who came to persecute the Cathars during the Middle Ages. Both the Virgin Mary and her old adversary Satan had also played a role in history, and had appeared to people of the Pyrenees at crucial moments.

To the educated, these beliefs were an aspect of rustic charm, but for many Pyrenean people, they were deadly serious. The real elements of reverence, awe and terror were not well conveyed when folk beliefs were written down. A shocking incident which showed the savage edge of Pyrenean culture occurred in April 1850, when a woman was burnt as a witch in the commune of Pujo. Jeanne Bedouret, aged sixty, was accused by her neighbours, who believed that they were cursed by her spells. A man and a woman violently assaulted her, inflicting fatal burns. When the perpetrators were brought before the court at Tarbes, the Procureur found them to be 'victims of their profound ignorance'.[41] They received only light sentences. This may have been the last witch-burning in the whole of France, and it indicates with what tragic force supernatural tales were believed the Pyrenees.

No such violence against sorceresses seems to have taken place in Lourdes, but it is a documented fact that various witches were known in the area, and that they were approached by people who wanted charms and cures for illness. There was a saying in the Pyrenees that all the women in Lourdes were witches. If so, they had it all their own way, and intimidated other people rather than being victimized by them.

The living heritage of supernatural beliefs attracted scholars to the Hautes-Pyrénées, most importantly Eugène Cordier. He was a folklorist, and his work was a precursor to the modern discipline of ethnography. He came to the area in 1852, and made several lengthy stays, including a sojourn in Lourdes. Although Cordier admired the sublime poetry of many Pyrenean tales, he deplored the ignorance and superstition of his informants, and looked forward to the day when 'legends, fictions, and all types of errors, will leave the memory of the people, to forever be consigned to the grave domain of history'.[42]

Eugène Cordier is an important source for the history of Lourdes, because he stayed in the town during the early 1850s, and wrote, although he did not publish, an account of the area. He was not favourably impressed by the common people of Lourdes, who struck him as a collection of vagabonds, with children who begged shamelessly and women who constantly went into the forests, illegally collecting wood. In his eyes, they lacked charm, although he was happy to view some of them. He described the wood-gathering women:

'some were very old, others were almost children. Several were young and pretty, and scantily dressed.'[3] The path being always muddy, they had their skirts hitched up to the knee – an unbridled exposure by nineteenth-century standards. He believed that these women had no morals, and that in the forests they were inclined to show 'deplorable licence'.[44] He was told that the youngest and most beautiful of them were available for only 3 or 4 *sous*, to be enjoyed under the trees, but later learnt from soldiers who had propositioned them that in fact some of the women would indignantly refuse any intimacies, despite their bare legs. They were, however, of a coarse nature, and alien to civilized ways. He was told that: 'They like that free life', they liked to work for their living in the woods, 'because there they have liberty.'[45] The men of the town impressed him no better, and he found that the only respectable aspects of their lives were the social organizations such as 'solidarities', which he attributed to the influence of the Church rather than local inclination.

Eugène Cordier's description is fascinating because only a few years later some of the wood-gathering girls of Lourdes were to enter history, playing a vastly different role from the dissipated characters which he portrayed. Cordier's description of the women is revealing of himself. He is outwardly disapproving, but his description of the youth, beauty and slatternly ways of the Lourdes women, and his speculations about their couplings in the forest, have a distinctly lascivious tone. People from metropolitan France often imagined peasant life to be more traditional, in the sense of more moral and innocent, than that of the towns. A scholar of folklore, and even a tourist who ventured out to the remote provinces, could be better informed. One wonders if such men were really so dismayed by rural lewdness as they claimed to be.

When the media of the Hautes-Pyrénées reported on crime Lourdes was frequently mentioned. Violent crime was common in the mountain communities. Even women engaged in public brawls, and murders were committed over everyday disputes such as the sale of land, or the theft of a sheep. In 1849 Lourdes was jolted by the 'Bordebat affair', in which a man was at first thought to have committed suicide, but was later found to have been murdered by his wife, Catherine Bordedebat, and her lover, Jean Gesta. They were found guilty of the murder, and a large crowd were attracted to 'enjoy the hideous spectacle' of their execution.[46] The most disturbing killings were those without any apparent motive. In July 1850 M. Lapène suddenly killed his pet piglet with an axe, then attacked his young daughter and his wife. The girl died, the wife was gravely injured, and he hanged himself. A journal from another town wondered what 'fatality it is which seems to weigh on the town of Lourdes, to the point of making it the theatre of suicides and frightful dramas'.[47] Government officials, such as Procureur Dutour of Lourdes, claimed that the abuse of alcohol was frequent in the region. If so, this would be a cause of some of this violence. The editor of *L'Echo des Vallées* suggested that people were being deprived of work and resources, and thus were being driven to suicide 'so deplorably frequent in our time'.[48] Visitors to the Pyrenees also took their own lives. To the dismay of locals, who included witnesses to their deaths, individual tourists sometimes drowned themselves by plunging into the lake at Lourdes, and into the Gave river.[49]

Although the poor lived in squalor in the old part of town, Lourdes had many new buildings, and some examples of this nineteenth-century architecture still survive. Buildings presently preserved such as the Lourdes library, which once was Curé Peyramale's presbytery, show that in the decades before 1858 many people lived and worked in buildings which had met contemporary standards of style and convenience. A gracious structure was also raised by the Sisters of Nevers, a nursing and teaching order which came to the town in 1834. These religious were colloquially known in Lourdes as the *Dames de Nevers*. They had only one other convent in the Hautes-Pyrénées, which was a hospital and boarding school in the fashionable spa-town of Bagnères.[50] In Lourdes the Sisters ran a boarding school patronized by the middle classes and a day school and hospital which were charitable establishments.

Despite all of the respectable and flourishing activities, Lourdes had a reputation as a city of mavericks. Its name is featured surprisingly often in administrative archives, and frequently in unfavourable terms. An 1853 police report on political unrest showed only a scattering of rebellious people in other towns, most of whom were judged to be 'not important'.[51] By contrast, Lourdes had 27 known malcontents, many of whom were noted to be 'very bad' or 'very audacious'.[52] They represented a full spectrum of political opinions, from royalists to socialists, but the majority were 'democrats', i.e. republicans who resented the 1851 *coup*. Elsewhere in the Hautes-Pyrénées, the people of Lourdes were the subject of jests and criticisms; for example the term 'Lourdes cuisine' was used to describe ill-prepared food.[53] Although visitors to the town were met with many suitable conveniences, those who stayed for any length of time, like Eugène Cordier, tended to find reason to complain. The people of Lourdes seemed rude and self-interested. The Catholic episcopal authorities, who were responsible for sending parish priests to Lourdes, learnt to dread the very mention of its name.

In contrast to its prosperous sector which built and published, Lourdes had a relatively large population of poorer people, who had the culture of peasants or villagers, but were resident in a town. Following an environmental pattern often seen in nineteenth-century towns, the poor quarters of Lourdes were in a low-lying area which had been the old city before modernization and expansion.

The dissonance between the town and part of its population was commented on by one municipal councillor who said in 1862 that everyone knew that the bulk of the population of Lourdes 'is composed of workers, and with only a few exceptions nearly all their resources are their own hands, which perform their daily toil ... The town, by contrast, has considerable revenues.'[54] This is a recipe for class conflict, yet friction between the middle class and the poorer neighbourhoods seems to have been rare. Rather, the common people of Lourdes were antagonistic in their relationship with authorities from the outside world. In defence of their own customs they could be particularly troublesome, and during the restoration of the Catholic Church from the 1830s to the 1850s the people of Lourdes irritated the secular authorities and were sometimes a serious problem for the Church. Lagrèze, in his tactful history, noted that Lourdes had gained a list of liberties as early as 1138. Equating this feudal concept with later calls for liberty, he cheerfully suggested that: 'Our town must have conserved a germ of republican sentiment from ancient times.'[55] Without necessarily being republicans in terms of a developed political ideology, the people of Lourdes seem to have cultivated a self-image which stressed independence, dissent and an inclination to make one's own rules. An outside observer acidly commented in the early nineteenth century that the inhabitants of Lourdes were 'delivered up to themselves' and 'easily inclined to wrongdoing'.[56]

Their own oral history claimed that even after the terrors of the thirteenth-century Albigensian crusade, the defeated Cathar heretics were sheltered in the Lourdes fortress.[57] The truth of this story cannot be determined,[58] but it is significant that in the mid-nineteenth century the people of Lourdes still wanted to claim that they had supported these distant heretics. The idea was not suggested to them by the modern re-evaluation of the Cathars by romantic French writers, for Lagrèze recorded this story in 1845, well before this interest made itself felt.[59] The Cathar heresy died only slowly throughout the Pyrenees. As late as the nineteenth century a man in Foix (Ariège) was refused burial in a Christian cemetery because the Curé knew that he was reputed to be one of the 'perfect' (i.e. a Cathar).[60] However, the Lourdes story does not seem to have been motivated by an informed inclination for Cathar beliefs, but only a natural sympathy for heretics and a local patriotism which claimed that 'the inhabitants of Lourdes do not hold their beliefs cheap, and they do not abandon their grievances and their weapons quickly'.[61]

Many clerics and government officials would have attested to the truth of that statement. Even the Catholic journalist Louis Veuillot, who took a deliberately affable view of the people of Lourdes, conceded that they were 'a people very strongly attached to their beliefs ... even to their superstitions'.[62] Funerals brought out the worst examples of Lourdes superstitions and truculence; but the rites of death were not the only point of contention. The recalcitrant spirit of this otherwise undistinguished town came to the attention of the authorities during the episcopate of Antoine-Xavier de Neirac (1757–1833), Bishop of Tarbes during 1823–33. This prelate was an ardent royalist who had spent the Revolution in seclusion. From 1823 onward, he tried to enforce the politics of the Bourbon restoration, although he acknowledged that the population of the whole area were 'dead to any religious or monarchical sentiment'.[63] Nowhere more so than Lourdes, which leads the list of five Pyrenean parishes which revolted against episcopal authority during Mgr de Neirac's tenure.[64] The problems began when he attempted to replace Curé Condat of Lourdes, a long-established priest who had signed the oath of the civil constitution during the Revolution. This provoked such vociferous protests from the Lourdes community that the *affaire Condat* reverberated as far as the ministries in Paris. From 1826 to 1830, when Curé Condat died, the parish of Lourdes was in revolt against canonical authority. The defiant Curé informed the episcopal authorities that he had never regretted his adherence to the principles of the civil constitution and that he refused to vacate his parish church. Mgr de Neirac sent a replacement to the town, and this priest was greeted with 'scenes of protest which were so unexpected and violent that, despite the witnesses, one can hardly believe it'.[65]

During the time that the Bourbons were restored to the French throne, the Catholic Church began a huge effort to re-educate the French people into a stronger and regularized religion. This usually met with a certain amount of passive resistance. The situation in Lourdes was uncommon because of its open belligerence and the length of the dispute, which was not resolved until 1831, six months after Curé Condat's death. In 1832 the Bishop of Tarbes informed the Minister of Cults that until recently 'Lourdes was in a state of trouble and disorder, no Catholic priest dared to show his face there.'[66] His favoured candidate for the curacy, M. Langa, had worked in the town and had 'the goodness to re-establish order and tranquillity, and to make religion loved and respected'.[67] One wonders how happy and successful M. Langa had really been, as he had responded to the offer of the curacy with a formal declaration that he would never accept it.[68]

Lourdes should have been a desirable parish. During an era when priests found it difficult to gain places which offered a reasonable standard of remuneration and amenities, Lourdes offered both. Supported by a large congregation, the Curé of Lourdes lived in comfort and was assisted in his duties by vicars. He did not suffer the solitude and poverty frequently seen in rural parishes, including many of those nearby in the Hautes-Pyrénées. What he did have to endure was a talkative and meddlesome population, firmly attached to their own parochial ways. In 1831 the Préfet had been obliged to intervene in a quarrel between the locals and a M. Langa, who had refused a funeral to an indigent who had died in the parish. As the Préfet irritably observed, it was fortunate that the Bishop had given a quick authorization in this case, 'because without that there probably would have been uproar in Lourdes, where heads are rather hot'.[69] Between the 1830s and the 1850s the religious situation became much more tranquil, especially after the end of Mgr de Neirac's episcopal tenure in 1833. But the Bishops of Tarbes always knew Lourdes for a troublespot.

The bad harvests of 1853–4 caused great suffering in the Pyrenees, and this was aggravated by the cholera epidemic of 1854. The worst outbreaks were in 1832 and 1854, the disease still being a threat at other times.[70] Lourdes suffered much less than many other areas. The disease arrived late, in one of its reprises, and did not begin until the autumn of 1855.[71] Because of the cooler weather, late in the year, it did not rage in its most toxic form. Despite this relative good fortune, the people of Lourdes were horrified by the epidemic. The Garrison Sergeant remembered that most government officials fled the area, leaving the Police Commissioner, one Health Officer and himself to continue their duties, 'in the midst of the terrible dangers of cholera'.[72]

Lourdes shared the moral norms and population averages of the Hautes-Pyrénées. As many as a third of the individuals in the poorer classes would remain unmarried and childless. Married couples had numerous children, and methods of limiting births, aside from abortion, seem to have been unknown. Women lived longer than men did, and in 1856, Lourdes had 210 widows and 120 widowers.[73]

In its employment patterns the population of Lourdes was much more varied than the mountain villages, as the town had a comparatively well-developed secondary economic sector. The electoral list of 1858 gave the details of 1,077 individuals and their professions.[74] This list shows that 76 men were employed in administration, with a further 43 employed by the army. The liberal professions were followed by 66 men, of whom 15 were listed as retired. The 408 unskilled manual workers were the most numerous group, followed by commerce, 213, and artisans, 193. The electoral list only gives details for men, but the testimonies of the Lourdes apparitions state the employment of many female witnesses.[75] Women were particularly active in the merchant sector classed as *Petit Commerce*.[76] Such employment was often seasonal and insecure.

Not all means of earning money were openly acknowledged. The Hautes-Pyrénées had one of the highest ratios of prostitutes per head of population of all the départements of France.[77] This has been attributed to the rise in destitution, the presence of military garrisons and the tourist trade. Lourdes had an acknowledged problem with commercialized sexual relations and its inevitable aftermath, the spread of syphilis. A local doctor claimed that because of the spread of venereal disease[78] Lourdes should have an officially supervised brothel. By 1858 the municipality of Lourdes was contributing 5 per cent of the cost of treatment for female syphilis patients at the hospice at Tarbes.[79] It was considered to be in the interests of the town that they could send their infected women elsewhere for treatment.[80] The municipality declined an offer to provide the same service for syphilitic men, stating that it was acceptable that they be treated at the hospice in Lourdes.[81]

This one example shows that the costs of sexual activity were unevenly borne. The Lourdes authorities shared the common nineteenth-century attitude which banished women as the carriers of venereal disease while men were merely seen as suffering from it. The surviving 'matriarchal' codes of Pyrenean society had a limited practical effect during the modern era. Slightly fewer than 10 per cent of the children who received free primary education in Lourdes were of illegitimate birth and were being raised by single mothers.[82] Even more numerous were the children conceived out of wedlock, to women who later married, while an unknown number of pregnancies were terminated.

The state officials tried to limit the crimes of abortion and infanticide, which were judged to be 'all too frequent in this area'.[83] The Procureur Général hoped that 'well-founded charges will guarantee repression'[84] which indicates that he felt that he could not rely upon common moral sentiment to condemn such proceedings. In 1854, the Procureur Général noted that 'I have grounds to congratulate myself, in the interests of the vindication of society' after successfully bringing Anne Peyret of Lourdes to trial for infanticide.[85] She was sentenced to eight years hard labour. During the same era, other women were charged with procuring and performing abortions, a risky operation usually undertaken in secret by midwives. It seems that the measures of repression did not alter attitudes, although they doubtless intimidated women who were already battling for survival. The documents on the Lourdes miracles were to show that women of the poorer classes would openly acknowledge that even the drastic recourse of infanticide was a realistic option when faced with a sickly, burdensome child.[86]

Women of the poor quarters of Lourdes, who accompanied Bernadette during the first days of her visions, were described by some respectable observers as a shocking collection of prostitutes, unmarried mothers and drunkards.[87] These were hostile opinions, but not entirely unfounded. Such ill-educated women, who depended upon folk beliefs for inspiration in a harsh world, would receive the news of an apparition of a mysterious White Lady (*Dame blanche*) with enthusiasm. These women may not have been pious, but they were believers.

## The Grotto of Massabielle

Like Lourdes, Massabielle has an identifiable history prior to the apparitions of 1858. This rock outcrop on the left bank of the River Gave was a short walk from the town of Lourdes. It was part of a chain of grottos, some of which opened into deep caverns within the mountains. The grottos were sufficiently notable that the local historian wrote about them and said that the 'human mind has always been struck by the spectacle which they present'.[88] To the educated, such striking natural formations were interesting and brought forward scientific exploration and scenic appreciation. To the common people, they were typical sites for the supernatural. As the nineteenth-century anthropologist André Lefèvre wrote: 'There is hardly a single French province which does not have trees, grottos or dolmens which are haunted by fairies. One hears of fairy pillars and rocks, fairy nooks, fairy wells, lakes, houses and chambers of fairies, wraiths and sorcerers.'[89]

Superstitions concerning Massabielle give evidence of both a sacred and demonic reputation. Massabielle was a haunted place and a holy place. When describing this area, Lagrèze noted that 'the belief in fairies and sorcerers is dear to our mountain people'[90] but did not record exactly what stories the grottos inspired. The interests of local scholars, and of tourists to the area, had led to the exploration of some of the grottos. In one deep cavern not far from Massabielle, the *Grotte de Saint-Pé*, the explorers were astounded to come upon a wall, of ancient appearance, constructed by human hands. They opened the wall and water gushed out. As a scholarly provincial journal commented to its readers: 'one could explore a subterranean cavern where, for centuries, no living being has penetrated'.[91] Rather gruesomely, bones were also found in the cave. Lagrèze described the finding of bones in several grottos. Some were of an unknown animal 'of a huge species' while in deeper caverns the calcified bones of humans were found.[92] As Lagrèze wrote, this was a great subject for hypothesis, for those who were savants and those who were not. The stories of these grotto explorations would have circulated in Lourdes, and the macabre findings in the *Grotte de Saint-Pé* may have contributed to an oral tradition that human sacrifices had once been offered in the grotto of Massabielle.[93]

When he first visited Massabielle in 1858, the Mayor was to comment that it was a picturesque area which was doubtless visited by tourists during the season.[94] He was correct in this assumption, and many years afterwards one of these visitors was to make a claim which casts a curious light on Bernadette's experiences in the Grotto. The *Archive* of the Grotto preserves a letter written by J. Latour de Brie on 30 May 1879. His family was visiting the Pyrenees in 1856–7, when he was twelve years old. According to de Brie, he went walking along the River Gave with his brother and another child and explored the grotto of Massabielle. They crawled into the large oval niche in the wall of the rock, where they discovered many little statues of the Virgin Mary, buried in the sandy floor. He stated that at least one of the images was of the standard 'Miraculous Medal' type, but he could not remember the others: 'the design meant little to us, what struck us as being strange, and beyond explanation, was the existence of these images in such a place'.[95]

This is also what perplexes an historian, and it is extremely difficult to assess the story which de Brie recounted. It may be a fabrication, inspired by the subsequent fame of the Grotto. In later years, many people were to make claims such as that they had heard prophecies that 'you will see miracles in that Grotto'.[96] However, de Brie's story was not an obvious attempt to link himself to the miraculous history of the Grotto, nor was he trying to debunk the later events. He wrote his account for a priest and simply concluded that it was 'a faithful account of my little story, ... I would be happy to think that the memory of it will not be lost'.[97]

His story is not impossible in itself. In 1858 various people were able, albeit with difficulty, to climb into the niche of the Grotto where, according to Bernadette, the beautiful *Dame* stood. It leads on to deeper caves, where one of the rock formations resembles a white statue of a woman.[98] The sight of this object sent a group of Lourdes women fleeing in awe, declaring that they had seen the Virgin Mary, after they had ventured to explore the niche in May 1858. If someone had been there in earlier years, they might have been impressed by this natural formation, and have made gestures of worship such as bringing statues to the site. In other Pyrenean locations, stones which had a resemblance to female forms were identified with either fairies or the Virgin Mary, and were the subject of veneration.[99]

If the Grotto at Massabielle was the site of some form of worship of the Virgin Mary prior to 1858, Bernadette's visions would suddenly be given a clear history, but conclusive evidence is lacking. Latour de Brie's letter remains uncorroborated by any other document, and among all the voluminous testimonies later collected from Lourdes residents, no-one mentioned the statues at Massabielle which he claimed to have encountered. There were reports of it as haunted, with ghostly cries frightening people who had sheltered in the cave during rainstorms. However, Lourdes tradition did link the area to the Virgin Mary. It was claimed that in the eleventh century Lourdes had been dedicated in feudal vassalage to Notre-Dame de Puy, and that every year green herbs from the fields around Massabielle were gathered to be offered to this ancient icon.[100] The idea that 'the herb of the field'[101] was in some way sacred to Mary may have inspired the message which Bernadette was to receive from her vision: 'Go and eat of the grass which is there'[102] on the occasion that the sacred spring was uncovered. This message has remained without explanation. It scandalized many educated observers and puzzled even Bernadette's admirers.

Unlike tourists, local people were ignorant of the picturesque and described the appearance of Massabielle in somewhat unfavourable terms. The area was wild and desolate and it was used as a common where pigs were pastured. The Garde Champêtre said that he had never gone to the Grotto prior to the apparitions: 'that was an entirely wild and empty area'.[103] There was a saying in Lourdes that if someone was particularly uncouth, they must have 'got their education at Massabielle'.[104]

The Grotto of Massabielle was at the base of a steep slope covered in brush and trees. This wild forest was part of public land, and the common people had always gone there to collect firewood. During the nineteenth century, it was made illegal for them to do so, because the French Government passed a Forestry Code in 1827 which made all wood on public land the property of the state. This legislation caused daily and irreconcilable conflict between Pyrenean people and the authorities. Local people were informed that if they needed wood they should buy it for cash, an impossible demand which they fiercely resisted.

Pyrenean resistance to the Forestry Code was led by the *demoiselles*, men who dressed as women in order to raid the forests. Their costume was based on regional carnival customs. It was partly a disguise and partly a statement of community resistance which hearkened back to the traditional reversals of wrongs which were enacted during the carnival. By dressing as women, and adopting the name *demoiselles*, these men were also offering homage to the traditional nature spirits, the *dames blanches* who were called *demoiselles* (*demaiselas* in Occitan) and who lived in the forests.[105] The state authorities responded to the *demoiselles* by banning the use of fancy dress and disguises, stationing guards with orders to arrest transgressors, and levying fines from offending communes rather than individuals.[106]

Physical threats against the Pyrenean Forest Guards seemed to have increased during the 1850s, possibly because of the bad harvests and general distress of the decade. Lourdes saw its share of such incidents, as in November 1852, when a Forest Guard was shot and wounded.[107] Earlier that year a fire had ravaged twelve hectares of the commune's forest, which was attributed to 'the vengeance of forest offenders'.[108] In April 1851 two Forest Guards of Lourdes were dismissed because they had entirely failed to check daily thefts of wood from the forest of Subercarrère.[109] It was repeatedly urged that they be replaced by men who were strangers to the locality,[110] a telling indication of communal pressure. Such an approach may have been effective, as in January 1853 the Forest Guard threatened to use his firearm against two men when they were caught stealing wood in the Lourdes forest.[111] Various forms of sanctions and resistance were to continue until the early decades of the twentieth century, but the 1850s stand out as a markedly dark period of violence and arson in the conflict over the forests.

The Catholic clergy responded by trying to preserve peace and legality. In many sermons, priests informed their congregations that theft from public lands was the same as a theft from private property. This point was never well accepted by Pyreneans, who tended to consider that public lands were their own, and even that the only theft was on the part of the Paris authorities. The parish priests of mountain villages faced another problem in promoting the message of legality and firewood. As a villager commented: 'even M. le Curé is obliged to buy stolen wood, seeing that there is no other'.[112]

This struggle over the forests was a moral protest against the decline of the indigenous culture, and also a battle between the Pyrenean imagination and modern rationality. The release from social restraints during the Carnival season, and the myths of the forest, were the recourse of hard-pressed Pyreneans confronted with oppressive regulation from the outside world. The early history of the visions at Lourdes is intimately connected to the battles over the Forestry Code. When Bernadette went with two other girls to Massabielle on 11 February 1858 her errand was to gather wood so that her mother could cook their midday meal. It was *jeudi gras*, the concluding day of the Carnival season. The girls returned with their faggots, and also with a story that a white figure, which they termed a *demoiselle*, had appeared to Bernadette. Within a few months the people of Lourdes were going at night to smash barricades which the authorities had erected to keep them out of the Grotto. The early recitals of the visions reverberate with both the myths and the practical struggles of the nineteenth-century Pyrenean forests.

## Visions of the Virgin

In common with most of Catholic France the Hautes-Pyrénées had numerous Marian shrines, the two best-known being Garaison and Bétharram. They were surrounded by smaller but still well-patronized shrines, such as the Notre-Dames of Héas, Bourisp, Médoux, and Arrens. Many of the shrines had well-known foundation stories which document the local patterns of Marian devotion and link them to Catholic legends throughout Europe. Several Pyrenean shrines had statues which had been miraculously 'found' when oxen refused to plough a particular site, and others had 'recalcitrant Virgin' statues which would resist removal from their open air shrines. Any attempt to place them in churches led the statue to fly back to its original location. Scholars state that these legends, which are found all over Europe, relate to the incorporation of pagan sites into Christianity.[113]

An eminent Pryrenean figure was Notre-Dame de Garaison, whose legend exactly prefigures that of the apparitions at Lourdes. In 1500, a poor shepherdess named Anglèse Sarazan[114] had a vision of the Virgin Mary while she tended her flocks. The people of the village of Monlong believed her story after they found that Anglèse's meagre portion of black bread was miraculously changed to bountiful servings of the finest white bread. In accordance with the vision's instructions, a chapel was raised at the site (Garaison), which also had a spring. Thus far, the story of Garaison is not very different from that of many local shrines, but it was to gain an exceptional degree of outside recognition. In 1537, the shrine of Notre-Dame de Garaison was already so well established that it was served by a resident group of clergy. This is an entirely different status from the solitary peasant oratories found at most country shrines. In 1600, Garaison was visited by Étienne Molinier, a priest who became a fervent devotee. He wrote a book, *Le Lys du val*, which was first printed in 1630 and ran through innumerable editions. Sensational reports of the miracles at the shrine were printed in Paris, and pilgrims flocked from all over France. All the scholars who have contemplated Pyrenean religious history have acknowledged that Garaison is a clear predecessor of Lourdes.

The individual history of the visionary, Anglèse Sarazan, offers a sixteenth-century version of the hagiography of Bernadette. From being an innocent and poor shepherdess, she became venerated by numerous pilgrims, but she left the area and entered a Cistercian convent. She lacked the dowry and education judged necessary for admission as a nun, and tradition related that the superiors refused to admit her to vows, keeping her as a novice for six years.[115] Accepting these trials with humility, she persisted in the religious life and was aged in her nineties when she died on 30 December 1582.

Anglèse's longevity is a point of difference from the short life of Bernadette, who died as a Sister of Nevers at only thirty-five. Otherwise they are remarkably similar historical characters. Bernadette's life story bore many motifs of the sixteenth-century legend, such as working as a shepherdess, eating black bread, and the finding of a holy spring. Historically verifiable elements from Bernadette's life also match Anglèse's story, for when Bernadette entered a convent in 1866, she was treated with disdain by her religious superiors, who tested her humility in many ways. To judge by a seventeenth-century painting of Anglèse, who is depicted wearing a white capulet and tending her lambs, they even physically resembled each other.[116] This may have been because all local girls tended to be small and dark, and wore the regional costume. As soon as the news of the Lourdes visions began to circulate in the Pyrenean society of 1858, various miracle stories associated with Anglèse Sarazan were recounted in reference to Bernadette.

It seems that Bernadette herself never visited the shrine at Garaison, but she had been taken to Bétharram, the shrine of the 'Madonna Who Saves'. It is only fifteen kilometres from Lourdes. This shrine, which was of great antiquity and fame, probably dates to the eleventh century. There were various legends associated with its foundation. When French newspapers began to report the events at Lourdes in 1858, they located the town by informing their readers that it was near Bétharram, for this town was known beyond the locality.

Aside from the centuries-old fund of Marian miracles provided by Pyrenean religious history, the populations of the nineteenth century were entertained by newer stories of apparitions of the Virgin which were popularized through the French media. Between the 1830s and the 1870s France experienced a series of renowned Marian apparitions.

In November 1830, Catherine Labouré, a novice in the Rue du Bac Paris convent of the Daughters of Charity, had a vision in which the Virgin Mary appeared to her and asked that a special medal be struck in her honour. The medal began to circulate in 1832 and was received with great enthusiasm. The hagiography of Lourdes claimed that Bernadette, when describing Our Lady of Lourdes, had stated that she was 'like the Miraculous Medal but without the rays'.[117] This statement has been accepted by scholars and cited as evidence of how the Miraculous Medal had penetrated even a distant provincial area such as Lourdes.[118] However, a study of the original documents shows that Bernadette's statement is drawn from an interview of 1859 in which a Miraculous Medal was shown to her, and she was asked to agree that it showed a resemblance to her vision.[119] She replied that her vision did not have 'those' – the rays of light from the hands. However, the Miraculous Medal would almost certainly have been known in Lourdes, with its simple but memorable design and the wonderful claims associated with it.[120]

Even more sensational were the visions at La Salette, in September 1846. Two children herding sheep, Maximin Giraud and Mélanie Calvat, returned from their pastures in the Hautes-Alpes with a story that they had met the Virgin Mary, who had given them a long prophetic message. Dismayed by the irreligious behaviour of the French people, the Virgin had threatened that crops would fail and natural disasters would occur. This attracted mass attention, and pilgrims began to arrive at La Salette. The failure of the harvest in 1847 and the revolution of 1848 appeared to confirm the Virgin's prophecies. The two visionaries became very famous, but showed signs of instability. Mélanie Calvat entered and left several convents, then began to write florid religious pamphlets full of prophecies. Maximin Giraud initially was associated with right-wing extremists, but then drifted away from this to take up a wandering life marred by quarrels and unpaid debts. The disconcerting character of the two visionaries of La Salette was only just becoming evident at the time of the Lourdes visions. In 1858 most French Catholics still accepted the story of La Salette as it was first known, a simple fable of innocent children reporting a prescient prophecy.

Not all visionaries of doubtful sincerity escaped detection. In late 1850 and early 1851 the French newspapers were preoccupied with the case of Rosette Tamisier, a peasant in a small French alpine village of Saint-Saturnin (Vaucluse). She claimed to have been the subject of various miraculous graces. Crowds of pilgrims began to visit the village, but her claims were detected as fraudulent. She presented her followers with a holy picture of Christ, which was alleged to shed blood, but it was seen to have been tampered with. Rosette Tamisier's visions were rejected in an Episcopal Inquiry by the Bishop of Avignon. She was convicted of fraud and imprisoned by the secular authorities. Several of the state officials who served in Lourdes in 1858 inevitably recalled the case of Rosette Tamisier when Bernadette Soubirous began having visions.[121]

Events such as Rosette Tamisier's rise and fall, La Salette, and the Miraculous Medal visions, were written about and became famous. But these were the exceptions. Most visionary episodes, which occurred so frequently in rural France, were celebrated only by their immediate communities. An example can be found in the tiny commune of Nouillan (Hautes-Pyrénées). This village was in an unfrequented valley where, as late as 1860, the remains of pagan votive altars could be seen.[122] In June 1848 three young girls

28

reported that they had seen the Virgin Mary beside a spring. She had requested the restoration of her ruined chapel. The vision was investigated and approved by the Bishop of Tarbes, and an oratory was established.

The visions at Nouillan remained unknown to the outside world and have attracted only slight comment because of their resemblance to the events at Lourdes, which took place ten years later. Only when something about a vision, its site, its visionary or its message was able to coalesce with general preoccupations did a Marian apparition become famous. The most extraordinary example of this is the case of Lourdes in 1858.

# NOTES

1. A. Neame, *The Happening at Lourdes* (London 1968), 57.

2. Gustave Bascle de Lagrèze, *Chronique de la ville et du chateau de Lourdes* (Pau 1845).

3. A mistake which, surprisingly, is repeated even in the documents of her canonization, where her character is sometimes described in terms of its 'Basque' features. Marie Jeanne Garnier, *PON*, Sessio C, 1144.

4. Gustave Bascle de Lagrèze, *Essai sur la langue et la littérature du Béarn* (Bordeaux 1856), 4. This situation applied to the areas of Occitan dialects. In the Basque and Catalan areas the indigenous languages were far stronger and remained totally dominant even in the 1890s.

5. M. de Resseguier Conseiller Général and former Deputy of the Basses-Pyrénées, quoted in the testimony of Jules Marie Le Cerf, *PON*, Sessio XLIII, 585.

6. Ibid.

7. Report by the Sous-Préfet of Bagnères, 12 Jan. 1852, *AD*, I M 215.

8. T. W. Margadant, *French Peasants in Revolt: The Insurrection of 1851* (Princeton 1979), notes this tendency for mid-century political protest to be concentrated on the forestry issue in the mountain areas.

9. Quoted by H. Payne, *The Police State of Louis Napoleon Bonaparte 1851–1860* (Seattle 1966), 29.

10. Procureur Général Moulon to M. le Garde des Sceaux, 17 Mar. 1851, *AN*, BB 30 384, registre 3. Emphasis in the original.

11. Ibid. St Palais is in the vicinity of Bayonne.

12. Procureur Général Falconnet, 15 Jan. 1854, *AN*, BB 30 384, registre 3.

13. Mme Jacomet and Mlle Estrade, *Témoins*, 77, 84.

14. See letters of Adelaide Monlaur. On 18 May 1858, and other occasions, she wrote that she had been conversing with visitors who came seeking alms. At this time, her father was borrowing money from his brother-in-law in order to maintain their household. See letter of 9 Apr. 1859, *AG*, A8.

15. 'La mendicité et le vagabondage leurs abus et leurs dangers nécessite d'en obtenir l'extinction dans le département des Hautes-Pyrénées.' Société académique des Hautes Pyrénées, *Bulletin* 4/1–3 (May 1854–5), 4–29.

16. He bitterly concluded that 'J'en fis, en vain, mon rapport à la justice.' Ibid. Arson was a weapon of the disaffected poor, also used with impunity against state forests. 4 June 1852, *AN*, BB 30 384, registre 3.

17. 'Délibérations', 29 Dec. 1853, *AML*, D9, 375. This was organized through the 'dèpenses supplémentaires' and the exact sum allocated is not recorded.

18. I. Gratacos, *Fées et Gestes, Femmes Pyrénéennes: un statut social exceptionnel en Europe* (Toulouse 1986), 10–14.

19. Neame, *Happening at Lourdes*, 14.

20. Gratacos, *Fées et Gestes*, 10–14.

21. See Ch. 10, 'Les femmes et la sexualité', Gratacos, *Fées et Gestes*, 129–38. These tolerant moral standards seem to have been more common in mountainous areas which experienced low population growth. See H. G. Rosenburg, *A Negotiated World: Three Centuries of Change in a French Alpine Community* (Toronto 1988), who points out that 'neither submissiveness nor virginity' were required of women in the French Alps or in Scandinavia, 27–8.

22. Eugène Cordier, *Le Droit de famille aux Pyrénées* (Paris 1859), 29.

23. Ibid., 33.

24. L. La Caze, *Les Libertés provinciales en Béarn* (Paris 1865), 21.

25. i.e. the sexual licence of the *veille de Saint-Jean*. Gratacos, *Fées et Gestes*, 125.

26. According to the municipal records, in 1858 the population was 4,135. It had doubled from 2,300 in 1789. 'Population de la ville de Lourdes', *AML*.

27. P. Lafourcade and G. Marsan, *Lourdes autrefois de 1800 à 1930* (St Etienne 1988), 17.

28. Council minutes of 9 July 1954, cited by M. Triep-Capdeville, 'Le premier train et ses tribulations', *Bulletin des Amis de Nay et de la Batbielle* (1982), 27.

29. They began lobbying in 1854 and achieved a railway line in 1869. Ibid.

30. L. Veuillot, 'La Grotte de Lourdes, 1858', *Mélanges religieux, historiques, politiques et littéraires*, 2/4 (Paris 1860), 344.

31. J.-B. Estrade, *Les Apparitions de Lourdes, souvenirs intimes d'un témoin* (Lourdes 1920; f.p. 1899), 16.

32. June 1853, *AD*, I M 215.

33. *Le Lavedan* 8/1 (5 Jan. 1856), 1.

34. Ibid. 9/4 (5 Jan. 1857), 1.

35. Ibid. 8/1 (5 Jan. 1856), 1. This researcher was bemused to find a number of articles on Australia in the Lourdes newspaper. Either this was a particular hobby of the proprietors, or there was an interest in this nation by prospective immigrants from the Pyrenees.

36. Ibid. 6/39 (28 Sept. 1854), 1.

37. 'Mort de Mahamet', an extract from a history book, ibid. 6/43 (26 Oct. 1854), 2.

38. 'Request by the citizens of Lourdes ...', 29 June 1848, *AD* 1 M 213.

39. A. A., 'Lourdes', *Revue d'Aquitaine* 1 (1857), 151.

40. G. Bascle de Lagrèze, *Chronique de la ville et du château de Lourdes* (Pau 1845), ix. In 1875 Lagrèze reprinted this work and stated that in retospect he was amazed at his choice of town: 'J'avais parlé d'une petite ville ignorée; cette ville est aujourd'hui célèbre', *Le Château de Lourdes et la Grotte de l'Apparition* (Tarbes 1875), v. Lagrèze was a native of the Pyrenees who worked as a government official and resided in Tarbes. He was a member of local scholarly organizations and published many works on the language, history and current affairs of the Pyrenees.

41. M. le Procureur de la République, quoted by E. Cordier, *Les Légendes des Hautes-Pyrénées* (Tarbes 1986; f.p. Lourdes 1855), 81–2.

42. Cordier, *Légendes*, 64.

43. Fonds Eugène Cordier, *AD* Tarbes.

44. Ibid.

45. Ibid.

46. *La République* 293 (28 Feb. 1850), 3.

47. *L'Echo des Vallées* (4 July 1850), 2.

48. Ibid. (20 July 1854), 1.

49. *Le Lavedan* 24 (15 June 1854), 1.

50. Liste des Etablissements de la Congrégation, *Calendrier des Soeurs de Nevers* (1861).

51. *AD*, I M 215, Arrondissement d'Argeles, June 1853.

52. Ibid.

53. N. Rosapelly, *Traditions et coutumes des Hautes-Pyrénées* (Pau 1990), 230.

54. Unnamed councillor recorded in the minutes, 18 Mar. 1862, *AML*, D10.

55. Lagrèze, *Ville de Lourdes*, 109.

56. Rosapelly, *Traditions et coutumes*, 230.

57. Ibid., 45.

58. In historical terms, it is far from unlikely. During the eleventh century both the holders of the Lourdes fortress and the Archbishop of Auch were under suspicion of being sympathetic to the heretics. See Gilbert Garrigues, 'Conséquence de la croisade albigeoise en Bigorre', *Cahiers d'études cathares* 2/55 (1972), 55–7.

59. Much of the restoration and display of Cathar relics in the Pyrenees has been fuelled by this modern interest, but it only became significant after 1900. J. Sturrock, *The French Pyrenees* (London 1988), 162.

60. Ariège is where one might expect to find such a survivance, as it was the Cathar heartland. The separate grave of this man, Ferrocas, can be seen to this day. Possibly he was merely a recluse or peasant holy man whose status the *Curé* misunderstood. B. Duhourcau, *Guide des Pyrénées mystérieuses* (Paris 1985), 433.

61. Lagrèze, *Ville de Lourdes*, 45.

62. Veuillot, 'La Grotte de Lourdes', 354.

63. Mgr de Neirac, 1823, quoted by J.-B. Laffon, *Le Monde religieux Bigourdan (1800–1962)* (Lourdes 1984), 296.

64. The parishes were Lourdes, Sinzos, Lhez, Burg and Chatel. J.-B. Laffon, 'Le rétablissement et l'essor du diocèse (1823–1875)', J.-B. Laffon, ed., *Le Diocèse de Tarbes et Lourdes* (Paris 1971), 140. The other four became defiant in 1830, inspired by the political changes and also, perhaps, the example of Lourdes.

65. Chanoine L. Dantin, *L'Évêque des Apparitions. Mgr Laurence Évêque de Tarbes, 1845–1870* (Paris 1931), 60.

66. Bishop of Tarbes to the Minister of Cults, 7 Jan. 1832, *AN*, F19 3042.

67. Ibid.

68. Ibid.

69. Préfet of the Hautes-Pyrénées to the Minister of Cults, 4 Nov. 1831, *AN*, F19 3042.

70. It was the 1854 epidemic which was the most pronounced in the Pyrenees. See table 3, 'Proportion de communes infectées par département', P. Bourdelais and J.-Y. Raulot, *Une peur bleue: histoire du choléra en France* (Paris 1987), 100.

71. Laurentin, *Vie*, 21.

72. Joseph-Adolphe d'Angla, *Témoins*, 65.

73. Bernard Billet, 'Lourdes et les Lourdais au temps de Bernadette', Musée Pyrénéen, *La vie quotidienne dans les Hautes-Pyrénées au temps de Bernadette* (Pau 1979), 10.

74. 'Professions à Lourdes en 1858', the municipal electoral list reprinted, Musée Pyrénéen, *Vie quotidienne*, 23.

75. Antoinette Peyret, *couturère, Témoins*, 229; Antoinette Tardhivail, *marchande*, 231; Fanny Nicalou, *institutrice*, 113; Basile Castérot, *aubergiste*, 163.

76. Billet, 'Lourdes et les Lourdais', Musée Pyrénéen, *Vie quotidienne*, 24.

77. In 1856, 79 *filles publiques* per 100,000 inhabitants, twice the national average. Soulet, *Pyrénées*, 2. 412. These figures were compiled by the French government authorities, who registered known prostitutes and *maisons de tolérance*. The actual numbers of women who engaged in commercial sexual relations on an occasional basis would be even higher.

78. Doctor quoted, ibid., 2. 42.

79. A contribution of 100 francs per annum. 21 Mar. 1858, *AML*, D9, 519–20.

80. Ibid.

81. 'Hommes syphilitiques', 10 Sept. 1865, *AML*, D10, 150.

82. See list of indigent children to be admitted to the *école communale*, 11 out of 136 were identified as illegitimate. 8 Apr. 1852, *AML*, D9.

83. Procureur Général Falconnet, describing the case of *la femme* Lamarque who had been arrested in Tarbes for arranging an abortion for another woman. 15 Feb. 1854, *AN*, BB 30 384. This issue was of course not restricted to the Pyrenees, and may have been generally increasing at this time. B. le Clère and V. Wright, *Les préfets du Second Empire* (Paris 1973), 56, cite the Préfet at Aveyron complaining of rising numbers of abortions and infanticides.

84. Ibid.

85. Procureur Général Falconnet, 10 July 1854, *AN*, BB 30 384.

86. Testimony of Croizine Bouhohorts, who affirmed that her women neighbours thought that she should bring about the death of her chronically sick child. L.-J.-M. Cros, *Histoire de Notre-Dame de Lourdes* (Paris 1925), 1. 405.

87. Police Commissioner, Report to Prèfet Massy, 19 Apr. 1858, *LDA* 2, no. 164, 204–5. Also the opinion of Dominiquette Cazenave, *RdAM*, 169.

88. Lagrèze, *Ville de Lourdes*, 150.

89. André Lefèvre quoted by M. le Dr Lafforgue, 'De quelques superstitions et usages populaires dans la région de Bagnères', *Explorations Pyrénéennes, Bulletin de la Société Ramond* 2/10 (April–June 1905), 79–80.

90. Lagrèze, *Ville de Lourdes*, 145.

91. A. A., 'Lourdes', *Revue d'Aquitaine* 1 (1857), 152.

92. Lagrèze, *Ville de Lourdes*, 153–5.

93. This rumour is repeated in Lourdes and has appeared in several modern sources, e.g. C. C. Martindale, SJ, *Bernadette of Lourdes* (London n.d.), 11.

94.    Letter from the Mayor to the Préfet, 4 Mar. 1858, *AML*, D45.

95.    Letter of J. Latour de Brie, 30 May 1879, *AG*, A21.

96.    The father of a Pyrenean schoolteacher quoted by Adelaide Monlaur to her cousin, 8 Mar. 1858, *AG*, A8.

97.    Letter of J. Latour de Brie, 30 May 1879, *AG*, A21.

98.    A picture of this stalactite is reproduced in R. Laurentin, *Bernadette vous parle* (Paris 1972), 151. An accompanying note makes the firmly asserted, but unprovable, claim that Bernadette had never penetrated the caverns to see this form.

99.    See the stone *'era dama blanca'* illustrated in figure 7, Gratacos, *Fées et Gestes*. Also an account of 'La pierre de l'enchanteresse', Duhourcau, *Pyrénées mystérieuses*, 190.

100.   Cros, *Histoire* 1. 18–19.

101.   'Legende de Mirat', quoted ibid., 19.

102.   Quoted by Laurentin, *BVP*, 1. 80.

103.   Pierre Callet, *Témoins*, 44.

104.   Saying of 'les gens du peuple' quoted by Elfrida Lacrampe, *Témoins*, 107.

105.   The cultural history of this revolt has been carefully examined in F. Baby, *La Guerre des Demoiselles en Ariège (1829–1872)* (Montbel 1972).

106.   J. M. Merriman, 'Demoiselles' in Merriman *1830 in France* (New York 1975), 100.

107.   6 Nov. 1852, 'Rapport spécial et entièrement du Procureur Général Falconnet', *AN*, BB 30 384.

108.   4 June 1852, Procureur Général Falconnet, ibid.

109.   'Gardes forestiers', 15 Apr. 1851, *AML*, D9 244–6.

110.   Ibid. The requirement that they be strangers to the locality is recorded twice in the minutes.

111.   Jan. 1853, 'Rapport spécial et entièrement du Procureur Général Falconnet', *AN*, BB 30 384.

112.   Pyrenean villager quoted by Soulet, *Pyrénées*, 2. 504.

113.   Ralph Gibson, *A Social History of French Catholicism 1789–1914* (London 1989), 137.

114.   Or perhaps Anglèze de Sagasan. This version of her name would seem to be a later refinement, which has added aristocratic overtones. X. Ravier, *Anglèze Sagasan et la chapelle de Garaison* (Pau 1983).

115.   G. Bernoville, *De Notre Dame de Garaison à Notre Dame de Lourdes. Jean-Louis Peydessus, Apôtre marial de la Bigorre, 1807–1882* (Paris 1958), 40.

116.   'Notre-Dame de Garaison, peinture sur bois, anonyme, XVIIe siècle'. plate VI, Georges Frechin and Jean Robert, *Pèlerins et Pèlerinages dans les Pyrénées Françaises* (Lourdes 1975), 9. This painting shows Anglèse Sarazan beholding the apparition and it is similar to, but of more artistic individuality than, the nineteenth-century depictions of Bernadette at the Grotto.

117.   Quoted by Barbara Corrado Pope, 'Immaculate and powerful: The Marian revival in the nineteenth century', C. W. Atkinson et al., eds, *Immaculate and Powerful: The Female in Sacred Image and Social Reality* (Boston 1985), 176.

118.   Ibid.

119.   The actual interview with Bernadette was conducted by the Abbé Duboé. He began by asking if the pose of the apparition had been: 'Comme dans l'image de l'Immaculate Conception?' – 'Oui, M. l'abbé.' – 'Est-ce qu'elle était comme lorsque elle a apparu à une

fille de la Charité?' – 'Je ne sais pas, M. l'abbé.' – 'Et est-ce qu'elle avait des rayons à ses mains?' – 'Non, M. l'abbé.' 12 Aug. 1859, Visites à Bernadette, *AG*, A9.

120. One of the prayers recited by Bernadette's family was *O Marie conçue sans péché priez pour nous qui avons recours à vous* which was printed on the Miraculous Medal.

121. 'Je n'avais aucune confiance dans les choses qui se passaient à la Grotte, parce que je me souvenais de l'affaire Rose Tamisier, qui, peu auparavant, avait fait grand bruit.' Raymond Prat, Clerk of the Tribunal at Lourdes, *Témoins*, 72–3. References to the 'affair Tamisier' are also found in the correspondence of the officials.

122. Louis d'Argos wrote of these altars, quoted by M. Colinon, *Guide de la France religieuse et mystique* (Paris 1969), 465.

# CHAPTER 2

# An Ignorant Young Girl
## The Childhood of Bernadette, 1844–1858

My name is Bernadette Soubirous, I am about thirteen or fourteen years old, from Lourdes, I know neither how to read nor write and have not made my first communion.

Bernadette's statement to the Police Commissioner,
21 February 1858

When he first heard of the visions at Massabielle, an officer of the local garrison claimed that he had asked himself: 'Is it possible that the Blessed Virgin would appear to such a vagabond? I mean vagabond in the sense of an indigent, a nobody, the daughter of a disreputable family.'[1] This girl, whom he described quite accurately, was Bernadette Soubirous, the future Saint Bernadette of Lourdes.

Bernadette was not initially destined for the state of indigence in which she lived at the time of the visions. Her mother's family had once been prosperous and settled as the proprietors of a mill, but after her parents took possession of their inheritance the business failed and they suffered the fate of downward mobility.

The 'matriarchal' social structure of the Hautes-Pyrénées determined that the eldest child of the household, whether boy or girl, was the heir. Within the traditional communities, where scarce material resources were carefully managed and social pressure was a powerful force, the marriage of two eldest children was virtually forbidden. Such a marriage would raise a practical difficulty concerning which house should be the residence of the couple, and a more important problem of imbalance, with the concentration of wealth in few hands. Many Pyrenean tales related the melancholy fate of two eldest children, united by love but separated by the duty of inheritance. An eldest child could only marry a younger child. Junior siblings could marry the younger children of other families, but there was the effective deterrent that they would only unite their poverty. Often they stayed single, and remained in the family home, helping to raise their nephews and nieces. The heir always had authority, and would often direct the younger siblings' lives, telling them if they could marry, sending them out to work, and even confiscating their wages. The name of the house was interchangeable with the family name and therefore a man would use his wife's name if he married an heiress.

In larger towns, such as Lourdes, traditional restrictions were breaking down during the nineteenth century, but were still acknowledged as the ideal way to live. Pyrenean lore required deterrents to the temptations of romantic

**Plate I**   François Soubrious and Louise Castérot. © *Photos Viron, Lourdes*

disobedience, and young people were warned that couples who wed in defiance of social sanctions headed onto the road to ruin. According to a local proverb such marriages 'unite hunger and thirst'.[2] One such couple was François Soubirous and Louise Castérot, the parents of the future visionary of Lourdes. They married in January 1843, in defiance of the local customs of succession, and their subsequent disastrous history would have satisfied the worst expectations of a Pyrenean moralist. During the lifetime of Bernadette's parents, both the Castérot and the Soubirous families altered the traditions of inheritance in order to accommodate love matches and convenient household arrangements. In material terms, the results were unfortunate.

## Childhood and education in a Pyrenean town

In the classic fashion of her society, Bernadette was always regarded as the child of her mother's family. The Castérots, bearers of an old Lourdes name, were the proprietors of the Boly Mill. Justin Castérot died from an accident in a cart in 1843. His sudden death left his widow and four daughters with the problem of running the mill, and therefore a marriage was speedily arranged with a journeyman miller, François Soubirous. He was the younger son of a local family. François Soubirous came from a respectable family who had aspirations to join the middle classes. Some of his siblings had extended schooling and became public servants and teachers. But he was inclined to a simple life of outdoor labour, and had never learnt to read. He worked in flour mills up and down the Gave river.

François Soubirous was a peaceful, humble man. He had the Pyrenean virtues of generosity, piety and contentment in a simple way of life. But he had little ability in managing an enterprise, or in organizing himself without

36

direction from an employer. When he came to the mill he apparently had the strength and skills which the Castérot women needed. The limitations of his feckless nature were not yet conspicuous, and throughout all of his younger years, when he was directed by his mother and then his mother-in-law, he maintained a good standard of living. Soon after his introduction to the Boly Mill, he flouted custom and announced his preference for Louise Castérot, the second daughter, over the eldest, Bernarde.

François Soubirous seems to have wanted to marry for love, and to have a wife with a soft nature like his own. Louise Castérot was an attractive and affectionate girl. The later history of Bernarde Castérot shows her to have been active, resourceful and bossy. She would not have suited François Soubirous so well at a personal level, and he was a person to follow his own inclinations. He and Louise married in the face of opposition but stayed on in the Boly Mill – a household soon racked by arguments. The eventual right to inherit the mill was transferred to Louise Castérot, as she was married to a man with the necessary expertise to run it. In the meantime, the mill was still managed by the family matriarch, the widow Claire Castérot. This careful housewife directed the work at the mill and negotiated with customers. She seems to have accepted Louise's marriage as an inevitable compromise. Not surprisingly, Bernarde Castérot never liked her brother-in-law, who had effectively jilted her. Perhaps as a gesture of reconciliation, the first child of François and Louise was named Marie-Bernarde, in honour of her Aunt Bernarde, who was also her godmother. Marie-Bernarde, soon familiarly known as Bernadette, was born on 7 January 1844 and baptized two days later.

The baby Bernadette cried continually throughout her baptism. This was regarded with exasperation by some, who said that she was a nuisance, but as a good omen by more tolerant observers who recalled the handy superstition that a child who cried a great deal during baptism was thoroughly cleansed from original sin. Bernadette returned to an auspicious atmosphere at the Boly Mill. She was exempt from the tensions in her family, and, as the only baby among adults, she attracted love and care, especially from her Aunt Bernarde. The happy situation continued until Bernadette was sent to a wet nurse. It was an unusual step for a member of the peasant classes, and was due to a domestic accident. A candle fell onto the bodice of Louise Castérot, ten months after Bernadette's birth. She burnt her breast and could no longer feed the infant. A woman called Marie Lagües, who lived at the nearby village of Bartrès, offered her services. Her own baby had recently died, so she was able to feed Bernadette, and received five francs per month, paid in flour. Bernarde Castérot took her niece to Bartrès, and stayed with her for some weeks, while she became accustomed to the new faces.

Bernadette did not return home until she was two years old. She returned in 1846, at the time of the birth of her sister, who bore the unexpectedly grandiose name of Marie-Antoinette (familiarly known as Toinette). A baby boy had been born during her absence, but he had lived only a short while. The idyllic days of her infancy were over, she was now among other children; and among adults who were constantly quarrelling with each other. Her character and appearance can only be deduced from descriptions of her at an older age. She would have been small and dark, as she was to be all her life. She came from a region where the average height, recorded among the men conscripted for national service, was below average. The French are not a tall people, but even by their standards, the Bigourdanians were of short stature. Bernadette was actually tiny, even as an adult, and grew only slowly. She had large eyes and a full mouth, pretty features as an adult, and no doubt appealing as a child. Her family was very fond of her, she was a favourite with her Aunt Bernarde, and was also remembered at her foster home. As soon as she could be instructed, she was given tasks to work on. As the eldest daughter, she was constantly minding the other children, and had authority over them.

In 1848, when Bernadette was four years old, the uneasy household dissolved itself. That year Bernarde Castérot had given birth to a child out of wedlock and seems to have had some difficulty in bringing her suitor to the altar. She went briefly to live in Tarbes, possibly to contact his family. Her mother, Claire Castérot, took her remaining unmarried children and moved out of the Boly Mill. There were to be further illegitimate births among them, as Basile Castérot gave birth to a daughter and could not marry until the father, Pierre Pène, returned from military service three years later. Bernarde Castérot eventually also married the father of her child and set up a successful business, a tavern in Lourdes. It was later remembered by locals that Bernadette's aunts were all much better placed in life than the Soubirous family.[3]

The popular culture of the Pyrenees was tolerant of illegitimate births, especially if the situation was regularized by a subsequent marriage. Nevertheless, the Castérot sisters were of sufficient social standing to feel the disapproval of the Christian and middle-class morality which was expanding its hegemony over their society during this period. Both Basile and Bernarde Castérot were expelled by the Curé from the *congrégation* (the Children of Mary) because of their illegitimate children.[4] Membership of this group, organized in most French parishes, was a mark of respectability and social status. They were not crushed by this rejection. Bernarde Castérot, in particular, enjoyed a reputation as a woman with a successful business and a forceful personality. Louise Castérot does not seem to have been a member of the Children of Mary, although her life was without the blemish of immorality. After the births of her children her life was taken up with family responsibilities and financial failure, which was to alienate her from the genteel social activities of the town. The other Castérot sister, Lucile, was the youngest member of the family. She married, did not work outside the home, and was a lifelong *congréganiste*. Less is known of her than of the other sisters, and she died young, in 1870, before testimonies were collected.

After 1848 Louise and François Soubirous were left at the Boly Mill without the supervision and criticisms of their relatives. They had a disastrous habit of extending credit to idle individuals, who would often be invited to share their hospitality with drinks and snacks at the mill. The standard of housekeeping declined, and the mill was no longer an orderly and impressive place of business. The style of the Soubirous, which attracted the worst type of non-paying customers, alienated the respectable clients. Soon they had financial troubles. Probably the Soubirous were also hampered because they would have been obliged to pay Bernarde Castérot a sum of capital, in place of her inheritance rights over the property, but the people of Lourdes saw their business problems as a personal failing. As one relative pointed out, if François Soubirous had displayed 'some proper conduct, the Boly Mill could have belonged to him. The Castérots, his mother and father-in-law, had been there for thirty years.'[5] In 1854 they were unable to meet the annual lease payment of 130 francs and they were obliged to leave. They left with many debts and were regarded with scorn. They were compared to others. Bernarde Castérot was 'a neat hardworking woman, she could not put up with their disorder: she did not like François, and the whole family saw nothing in the Soubirous.'[6]

While the material fortunes of the Soubirous family had declined, their numbers had grown. Eventually, they were to have nine children, and six of these had already been born by 1855, when they lost the Boly Mill. Bernadette was then ten years old, and was one of four surviving children. Her sister, Toinette, was eight years old, her brother Jean-Marie was four, and there was also Justin, a new-born baby.

As a ten-year-old, Bernadette would have been well able to understand the change in fortunes which took place when her family left the mill. She also would have been old enough to feel the social ignominy of belonging to a degraded family. It is possible that she also understood that it was her future, her inheritance, which had vanished, because she was the eldest daughter, the *héritière* (heiress). It would be interesting to know if in 1855 Bernadette appreciated the bitter fact that she was the heir to nothing. It is possible that she did not appreciate the long-term factors. Recollections of the young Bernadette give the impression of a dreamy and careless child, who was not noticeably different from her feckless parents. In the fashion of many disadvantaged children, she may have taken her family's view of the world as her own, sharing their unrealistic hopes and accepting their excuses. However, she would not have been able to avoid hearing criticisms of her parents, as she was often in contact with her aunts and other relatives who were willing to voice their opinions of Louise and François Soubirous.

These critics included Jeanne Védère, a cousin on the Soubirous side of the family, who was one of the few family members to record their impressions at length. She was fourteen years older than Bernadette, and the daughter of Thècle Soubirous, François's sister. The Védère family lived in Momères, and were distant from the rough life in the old quarter of Lourdes. Thècle Soubirous had married well, her daughter was a schoolteacher, her son a military officer. When Jeanne Védère visited the Soubirous mill she was not impressed, for the atmosphere was disorderly. She complained to Bernadette that too many people were visiting and being entertained there. Bernadette replied that Jeanne Védère should speak to her parents about it, for she herself 'did not dare to do so'.[7] In saying this, Bernadette was probably refusing to play the role of a messenger of other people's complaints. Jeanne Védère had her criticisms, but she seemed almost surprised when in later years she was asked how Bernadette had felt about her parents. To her, the answer was self-evident: 'as children always do, she loved her parents a lot, she respected them, she was very obedient'.[8]

Bernadette never said anything about any of this, even in later years when her words were recorded and remembered. A reconstruction of her attitudes can be no more than speculation. Most religious writers have simply depicted her as always poor, and as naturally accepting of this situation. Poverty was extolled by conservative writers as a state blessed by God, and fitting to Christian humility, therefore Bernadette's story was all the more clear and holy if she was described as a child of the poorest quarters of Lourdes, who did not wish to be anywhere else: 'The attribute of holiness belongs, not to the poverty which was Bernadette's by birth, but to the spirit of detachment which was hers by grace. If she was holy, it was not because she had lived in a slum, but because she had not rebelled against the decree of God which put her there.'[9] This quotation is from a much later period, and reflects the story of Lourdes as it was built up over time. During Bernadette's own lifetime, such statements would have scandalized many members of the Castérot family, who would have indignantly pointed out that poverty was not Bernadette's 'by birth', but by the circumstance of having improvident parents. The way that they squandered their chances, during their children's early lives, is a much more involved and excruciating story than that of simply being born into poverty. Bernadette grew into a resigned woman, with little appetite for material goods, and years later she told a childhood friend that: 'When one desires nothing, one will always have what one needs.'[10]

The only anecdote which she ever related about her childhood was an innocuous comic story. The husband of Bernarde Castérot, her uncle Jean-Marie Nicolau, had visited the shrine at Bétharram, and had returned with a ring which he gave to Bernadette as a gift. She put it on with difficulty, because it was too small for her finger, and then could not remove it. It eventually had to be filed off, and since then, she commented with a laugh, 'I have never wanted a ring.'[11] This story would have related to her life between the ages of four and fourteen, when she was often staying with her Aunt Bernarde.

Henceforward, she would always be poor, although late in 1855 the Soubirous family had another chance at prosperity, as they inherited 900 francs on the death of Claire Castérot, Louise's mother. This was the last of the money earned during the prosperous days when the Boly Mill was under Castérot management. But this money, a considerable inheritance by the standards of the time, vanished in only a few months. François Soubirous took a lease on a farm property near Lourdes, apparently without understanding the terms of the contract. Predictably, this impulsive and optimistic venture into an activity in which he was not skilled soon dissipated the second inheritance. Even relatives on the Soubirous side of the family thought that François had done poorly. His sister's husband, who was probably reflecting on how he would have liked to have had such a legacy, commented: 'He is not provident: in his place, I would manage my affairs better than that.'[12] It was also said that, despite his poverty, François Soubirous frequented taverns, played cards and was generally lazy.

**Plate II**  The interior of the cachot. © *Francis Trochu*

They returned to Lourdes, and François Soubirous obtained work, when he could, as a labourer. 1855 to 1857 were years of economic depression. There were poor harvests, high bread prices and destitution among the working classes of Lourdes. All across the Hautes-Pyrénées, those who had the security of an income, however small, were asked in the churches to give

41

charity to the poor. Bread and clothing were collected, and Curé Peyramale himself would give up his Sunday dinner to the miserable people whom he saw at Mass. The secular authorities were also active, as the Municipal Council asked its members for donations, which were distributed as a form of unemployment relief. There was no help from outside the area. The Paris government was not willing to bring down grain prices by state regulation, and workers were told to work harder. The bad conditions motivated the French government to beware of socialist and anarchist agitators. They strengthened the security forces, and a few extra men in the provinces did get the benefit of employment as gendarmes and guards. There was no spending on social security.

The situation of the Soubirous family worsened. They moved from one wretched lodging to another. In 1857 they finally had to beg for free lodgings from André Sajoux, a cousin of Louise. He was embarrassed by their request, but felt obliged to give in to it, as they would otherwise have been left on the street. The place where they asked to live was a stone room on the lowest level of the Sajous's house. This cramped, damp area looked out onto an overflowing cesspool. It was known as *le cachot* (the dungeon) because it had been used as the town prison, before it was judged too unhealthy for this purpose even by nineteenth-century standards of incarceration. In later years, people in Lourdes often called Bernadette 'Bernadette Boly' and 'Bernadette Savy', after the Boly Mill where she was born, and the Savy Mill which her parents had briefly leased. But amid such a reversal of fortune, there was nothing left to her of these former homes, except their names. A walk from the Boly Mill, Bernadette's birthplace, to the *cachot*, the nadir of her family's life, is only a short distance. But it represents such a change of living conditions. The mill was a large building, and a place of work, income and life. The *cachot* was a dungeon.

In this less than ideal home the Soubirous family were to experience cold, hunger, unemployment, alcoholism and infestations of lice. Even their few pieces of furniture, inherited from the Castérot family, had been seized by a landlord in lieu of rent. Their destitution was conspicuous among their relatives, and André Sajoux found their situation beyond description: 'They were so poor, I cannot say how bad it was.'[13] Another cousin, on the paternal side, said that the poverty which she had seen in their dwelling 'was so great, that they had absolutely nothing'.[14]

Despite all of these disadvantages, they were remembered as an affectionate family. Corporal punishment was the rule in their milieu, but François and Louise were not described as cruel parents. André Sajoux stated that although they corrected their children sternly 'as the common people do'[15] they did not ill-treat them and there was never any animosity in the household. Another reflection on the family's methods of child-rearing was provided by Bernadette's aunt, Bernarde Castérot, who said that 'their mother brought them up well, without sparing the rod; and I also used a cane to keep my own children in line'.[16] Even the relatives of François Soubirous, who were inclined to criticize Louise and point out that she was a bad housekeeper, stated that 'she was a good Christian, kind natured and hard working. She brought up her children well.'[17]

Even when hungry, the Soubirous children would not beg for food, and their clothes, although worn, were clean. Toinette Soubirous recalled that their mother combed the children's hair every evening.[18] Their neighbour explained that they did have lice, but that this was only because of the state of their unsanitary dwelling.[19] They were not among the shameless and importunate poor, the very dregs of Lourdes society, beggars, thieves and prostitutes. The Soubirous children were not as carefree as those who had never had anything to lose. This is reflected in minor aspects of anecdotes about them, such as that on the day of the first vision, when Toinette was wading across the Gave river, and Bernadette called out to her not to raise her skirt. This is in contrast to the folklorist Eugène Cordier's description of the labouring Lourdes women exposing their legs, unconcernedly, while children wheedled for a few coins. Bernadette would have seen such women, and may also have seen the wealthy male tourists who looked at them. Even in 1858, as a member of a destitute family, she still maintained a different way of living, and she would have learnt such standards from her mother. This is relevant to the impression which Bernadette was later to make on the outside visitors, who flocked to Lourdes during her visions. Many were charmed by her peasant dress and her poverty. This vision of rural unsophistication was attractive because, as so many admirers said, she was clean, neat and dignified, despite her circumstances. They did not realize that she had fallen from her original social position and was thus *déclassée*. She lived in want, but with the style of a respectable person.

Poverty aggravated Bernadette's poor health, but she had been noticeably ailing even in better days, during 1850. Louise Castérot called upon the services of a midwife when Bernadette's health began to deteriorate at the age of six.[20] The midwife recommended home-made medicines, which provided some relief, but Bernadette had developed asthma. This is a chronic condition and she took up her lifelong identity as a sickly person. She was not the only such member of her family – only four of her nine brothers and sisters were to survive until adulthood. Four died as infants, while her brother Justin died in 1865 at the age of twelve. Presumably he shared her weak constitution. The recollections of Toinette Soubirous indicate that the surviving younger siblings were stronger than Bernadette: 'she had a bad chest, she ate very little'.[21]

In 1855 Bernadette was among those who caught cholera when the epidemic reached Lourdes. As a girl between the ages of five and fifteen she was in a group which showed a statistically high mortality rate from cholera,[22] yet she survived. Her mother said that the disease left her even 'more feeble and sickly' than before.[23] Her digestive system had been damaged by the violent purging. According to her sister she could not digest maize, but would vomit after eating it.[24] This was a real problem as maize porridge and rye bread were both staple foods of the poor. Bernadette received a few precarious privileges because of her semi-invalid state. Her parents would try to provide her with white bread instead of black bread or porridge; and unlike most poor children, who had bare feet in sabots, she had a pair of stockings.[25]

No-one had much to say about Bernadette as a child. Basile Castérot said simply that her niece had been 'little and timid. I do not know that she had any faults.'[26] From early in life, she was very quiet and self-contained. Toinette recalled that when she and Bernadette were twelve and thirteen both their parents went out to work during the day. 'We were together in the house, and she never bickered with me, but I often did with her. I was jealous because it seemed to me that she worked less, and that my brothers loved her more than me, and that despite this I have to look after them when I would have liked to have left the little ones and gone out to amuse myself.'[27] Other accounts say that it was Bernadette who had primary responsibility for the younger children, and that this took up most of her time. Toinette remembered that Bernadette usually knitted and sewed. After commenting again on Bernadette's weak chest and poor appetite, Toinette concluded that she 'never told our father or mother that I had hit her'.[28]

The family arguments were remembered more mildly by Bernadette. She said that she and her sister 'would argue quite often, but not to the point of fighting'.[29] According to Bernadette, they would contradict each other; neither ever wanted to give in. Bernadette stated that she sometimes smacked her brother, but that he never hit her. Obviously her authority as the eldest child was acknowledged. Both Toinette and her brothers said that Bernadette would scold them if they went to sleep without saying their prayers. 'What would become of you if you were to die?'[30] It was normal to threaten children with the possibility of their deaths.

It was a harsh world, and whenever witnesses reviewed their brief memories of Bernadette's childhood, they seem to gravitate naturally towards the subjects of death, illness and corporal punishment. Bernadette emerges from these anecdotes as a dutiful girl, mild-natured but able to exert power. She was timid with adults, but not with other children. Isabeline Aguillon, who lived as a child on the Rue de Petits Fossés, knew both Bernadette and her sister, 'who did not resemble her at all'. Toinette was heedless, and Bernadette would often call her to order: 'God knows she never failed to do it ... she was severe toward her sister, for whom she was responsible ... and treated her brothers the same way. – That was typical of Bernadette, she believed in discipline.'[31] Isabeline stated that she liked Bernadette, but could recall few of her conversations, for Bernadette was someone who listened without speaking.

While Bernadette bossed the younger children, she herself was dominated by adults. Bernarde Castérot, who often lodged Bernadette in her own home and employed her in the bar, said that her niece was good humoured and docile, 'when scolded, she never answered back'.[32] Many witnesses agreed that she was not intelligent, 'Bernadette, people say, had a very weak mind.'[33] This is a quotation from one of the local police force, who had good reason to dislike Bernadette and all her relatives, but it is in keeping with much other evidence. Although skilled at manual tasks, Bernadette found it difficult to acquire learning, either at school or at home. People who saw Bernadette during Sunday church services recalled her as being inattentive, 'like the other children, she would be constantly turning her head to look about her'.[34] A more critical note was sounded by the Sisters who conducted the Lourdes school. Bernadette did not distinguish herself as an ideal pupil during her infrequent attendance. One of her former teachers was quoted as saying that 'Bernadette as a child had none of the attractions of a person destined to have visions, rather, she was quite inattentive and particularly wayward.'[35] Bernadette's later role as a visionary could be analysed as the spectacular result of a desire to escape from her family circumstances. Yet in her early years she imitated the improvident ways of her parents, rather than reacting against them. When serving drinks in her aunt's bar, she would give free glasses of wine to her acquaintances as a gesture of friendship. 'Come, have a glass, my aunt isn't looking.'[36]

In March 1857, François Soubirous was arrested and charged with the theft of two bags of flour which had disappeared from a local bakery. The proprietor stated that he knew no ill of François, whom he sometimes employed on a casual basis, but suspected him of this theft simply because of his poverty.[37] He was held in prison and following an investigation was cleared of this charge only to fall under suspicion of having stolen a wooden board which he apparently intended to use as firewood. He was eventually released for lack of evidence, but in the eyes of the local authorities, he was marked ever afterward by this further disgrace. When he was arrested, poor Louise Castérot had 'cried like a child'.[38] She was a humble, unimpressive woman, crushed by life's burdens. During the family's downward spiral, she had acquired a reputation as a heavy drinker.

Pierre Callet, a Field Guard (*garde champêtre*) of Lourdes who had known the family since his childhood, later told Père Cros that 'François was an idler and a drinker, his wife drank too and they could not succeed because of that, mainly because of that, they were good people.'[39] He had seen Louise Castérot drunk in her kitchen while she entertained guests at the mill, using bad language. Basile Castérot sadly remembered that Louise had not liked drinking when she was young, 'that habit came to her after marriage'.[40] Her brother-in-law termed her a 'wretched woman' who would sell anything, even her own linen, in order to buy drink. He said that he had forbidden his wife, Lucile Castérot, to have anything to do with her.[41]

Louise Castérot's drinking was a problem to the extent that it fractured family bonds and made some of her relatives ashamed of her. But, in a town like Lourdes, not everyone was too dismayed. Quite tolerantly, a local Gendarme recalled her as an 'honest girl. Later, she became a drunkard, but she did not get drunk every week, not even every fortnight, and there never was any public scandal in the street.'[42] Isidore Pujol explained that Louise Castérot 'working very hard, exhausted, and however still obliged to feed her infants from the breast, felt herself in need of being fortified by something, and a drop of wine revived her'. He knew this lifestyle very well: 'I knew the Soubirous before the apparitions: my mother and Bernadette's mother used to work together, and, equally poor, they lived their lives in common.'[43] People tended to think of heavy drinking as normal, if their own wives and mothers had the same problem. André Sajoux, when commenting that Louise would drink until she was unconscious, added that his wife also would take to wine: 'it was a fault of hers'.[44] Despite her youth, Bernadette also was described as fond of white wine. 'I never heard anything said against Bernadette,' commented the wife of the Police Commissioner, 'except that she drank.'[45] This sounds alarming, but there are no accounts of Bernadette ever being intoxicated. She liked wine, and would join in social drinking.

After 1855, the Soubirous family were in a social stratum wherein no-one was expected to conform to respectable norms of behaviour. Although they tried to retain a proper appearance, their forays into alcoholism were simply seen as characteristic, rather than shocking. Sergeant D'Angla later explained, 'the Soubirous family were not well-known, and they were extremely poor, so that the irregular life of the aunts, and the mother's taste for wine, did not raise much comment'.[46] Joseph-Adolphe d'Angla was the Garrison Sergeant (*maréchal des logis*) at Lourdes, and was therefore responsible for the Gendarmes of the area.

It was necessary for Bernadette to play the role of a substitute mother for the younger children, as in their poverty Louise Castérot was obliged to work outside the home, harvesting in fields and washing in laundries. Basile Castérot claimed that this necessity was forced on Louise because François Soubirous was lazy: 'he did not exert himself for every type of work; Louise did: one must live'.[47] Acting on this imperative, Louise Castérot would go into the local forests and gather faggots of wood to sell to the more fortunate. Her daughter Toinette said that she only did so when the family were entirely without food.[48] Her activities did not go unnoticed. As the Sergeant d'Angla coldly commented: 'I knew the Soubirous before the apparitions, as people without resources, and as marauders.'[49]

When not infringing the letter of the law by snatching wood in the forest, Louise Castérot exerted herself in the backbreaking labour of the fields. Romaine Mingelatte, a woman who had employed Louise during the harvest of 1855, recalled that the baby (Justin) was in the care of Bernadette, who could be seen carrying him out to be nursed in the meadow. Bernadette, who was then eleven, had a woman's responsibilities, and a woman's clothing. Her hair was always covered by a scarf, and her body by a long dress. Bernadette's clothing had been bought second-hand, and she probably only had the clothes that she stood up in. But it was essential, even for the young and poor, to cover the female body. 'She had a shawl over her shoulders; because girls wore a shawl, every day, from the age of eleven or twelve. It was crossed over the chest and fell down the back. I think I remember hers as black. Naturally, she had a long dress. Have you seen that statue of her in front of the hospice?' exclaimed Romaine Mingelatte 'They have given her a short dress, that is an error.'[50] The statue in question still stands, and shows her in a dress which reached the lower calf of her leg. If this dress is considered 'short', the real one must have reached her feet. Her legs were always covered, and so also was her hair.

Bernadette was always veiled. Pyrenean women did not appear in public with their heads uncovered, and we do not possess a single picture or description of Bernadette which represents her hair. Her head was covered by a cotton scarf folded into a triangle, knotted at the back of the head. Over that, went a shawl. Pyrenean women liked to have a special kerchief of silk, for Sundays, but such ornaments were not seen in the Soubirous family.

Bernadette did have a capulet, which is a hooded woollen cape. It is a traditional part of the Pyrenean costume and dates back to the fifteenth century, at least. The capulet was worn for warmth when going outside, and was also drawn forward over the head on special occasions, such as when paying a formal visit. Bernadette's capulet, worn and patched, had been bought from a second-hand clothes stall.

The woman who employed Louise Castérot to harvest her field remembered Bernadette as a stalwart little figure, tired from carrying her baby brother but able to keep going. Her face was 'round and pretty, with beautiful soft eyes'.[51] The description of her face would indicate that she was not wasted with hunger, although food was often short at home. This informant added that the women in the fields received 20 sous per day and a laundress earned 10 sous.[52] René Laurentin, citing *l'Indicateur des Hautes-Pyrénées* of 1856, gives the figure of 523 francs per year 'to live at the absolute minimum, that is to say, not to die'.[53] The Soubirous, a family of six, were struggling to survive, although it may also be true, as their neighbour later commented, that as soon as Louise Castérot had a few sous she would buy wine.[54]

In these circumstances Bernadette's formal education was virtually non-existent, although free education for the poor was provided in Lourdes. Throughout the 1850s an average of 130 children per year were admitted to the Lourdes communal schools as indigents. None of the names of the Soubirous children appear on these lists, although some of their neighbours, such as Julian Gesta, are noted.[55] A small but appreciable number of children would be further sponsored for education at the Ecole Supérieure, and ten children were so admitted in 1856.[56] In addition, the *Frères de l'Instruction Chrétienne* had been appointed to open a primary school in Lourdes in 1854, at the expense of the community. The Brothers' school was to be a matter of dispute between anti-clerical and Catholic factions on the Lourdes Council. However, there was almost no dissent from the general principle stated by the Mayor in 1859, 'that the Brothers' school has been founded on the principle of gratuity, and this in itself is of immense benefit for the population'.[57] The Sisters of Nevers also conducted a primary school for the children of the town and a *pensionnat* for older girls. Their school was divided between free and paying classes. The Sisters ran the school at the Hospice that had been their original establishment, and therefore attendance at this school was popularly termed 'going to the hospice'.[58]

None of these opportunities for receiving instruction were of any benefit to the young Bernadette Soubirous. Until the age of fourteen she was not only less educated than most other children in the town but was even disadvantaged in comparison to her own sister and brothers. Jean-Marie (b. 1851) and later Justin (b. 1855) would attend the Brothers' school while Toinette (b. 1846) attended catechism classes with the Sisters of Nevers. Toinette was a lively and hardy child, nicknamed by companions 'Gendarme'. She was later quoted as saying that 'I was not a girl, but a demon, and I knew nothing, but as far as the Catechism was concerned, I was always in the top rank.'[59] Having learnt the catechism, Toinette was able to make her First Holy Communion on the feast of Corpus Christi, Sunday 14 June 1857.

The First Communion was an important event in a child's life and was regarded as an indispensable ritual, even in parts of France where the practice of Catholicism was at a low level. It was not until the late nineteenth and early twentieth centuries that a 'rival' for the first communion appeared in the awarding of the Primary School Certificate.[60] As Ralph Gibson explains, the reason for the near-universality of first communion 'was not a religious one. It was, for all French men and women, the obligatory rite of passage into adulthood. It was partly that you could not normally get a job without it, but also, more generally, that you simply were not considered an adult until you had made your first communion.'[61] For Bernadette, this important ceremony was indefinitely delayed because she had been unable to attend catechism classes. Later accounts claimed that she had cried when she saw her younger sister join the solemn procession while she remained among the onlookers, and that her mother had promised her that she would have her turn soon.[62]

Bernadette was so entirely lacking in formal education because of her position as the eldest child and substitute mother for the little children. Her aunt, Bernarde Castérot, explained that Bernadette went rarely to school, 'her occupation of looking after the children did not permit her to go there often'.[63] This pattern was often seen in large families of few resources, where the eldest girl was obliged to second her mother. This was taken for granted; for instance, a biography of the Breton holy woman Marie-Julie Jahenny (b. 1850) noted that she was the eldest child in the family and: 'for such there was no question of school'.[64] Having fallen behind in her education, Bernadette found it difficult to learn, and was outpaced by younger children. Even if she had been able to attend the classroom regularly, the results may not have been spectacular. Unlike many of the unlettered people around her, and unlike her own dynamic sister Toinette, she had a poor memory. Even later in life, when intensive attempts were made to educate her formally, progress was slow.

Catechism, so important in the life of a French child, was by modern standards hardly a form of education at all, because it consisted of rote learning which did not even require minimal literacy. Children unable to read would be laboriously taught to memorize the catechism. Many of them may have accomplished this well, because in non-literate societies people have good skills in memorizing quotations. It was a tradition in France that one could recall until one's dying day the questions and answers of the catechism.

In the absence of formal education, Bernadette learned all she knew from her immediate environment. Despite their irresponsible ways and their decline in society, the Soubirous were a family who maintained their religious faith. Among their neighbours' recollections of drunkenness and domestic disorder, it is also mentioned that the family could be heard saying their prayers together every evening. In the words of one Lourdes resident, the Soubirous 'were Christians, as everyone was then'.[65] Bernarde Castérot stated that as a small child her niece Bernadette had a rosary: 'she rarely went to school, because of work and poverty, not enough to gain any education, so the rosary served as her schoolbook'.[66] She therefore knew the Lord's Prayer and the Hail Mary. Her family also recited the prayer revealed through the 'Miraculous Medal' visions of 1830, *Oh Marie, conçue sans péché, priez pour nous* (Oh Mary, conceived without sin, pray for us who have recourse to you). Toinette stated that Bernadette had once visited the local shrine of Bétharram, and had brought back a rosary for her which had cost two sous.[67] Long before 1858, Bernadette was habituated to visions, shrines, miracles and the overwhelming importance of the Virgin Mary among common Catholics.

Bernadette lacked religious instruction but not information about the practice of the Catholic faith. Likewise she was without secular education but was not entirely unskilled. The daily work at home was the type of activity which would occupy her foreseeable future. Unlike her mother, she had a natural sense of order and was very adroit. Toinette Soubirous recalled that 'Bernadette did spinning, knitting and patchwork: she was always very good at all forms of dressmaking.'[68] In later life, aside from her full time 'career' as a visionary, the only paid work Bernadette would ever do was to work as a nursemaid and to embroider articles for sale. She had assimilated the skills for these simple professions by the age of fourteen, outside of school.

After Toinette Soubirous had made her first communion in 1857 she no longer attended school, and it seemed that Bernadette would be free to attend catechism classes. These expectations were not fulfilled because at this time Marie Lagües of Bartrès asked the Soubirous family if Bernadette could be sent to stay with her. This was the woman who had once been Bernadette's wet nurse, and she had maintained links with the Castérot family. When she offered to take the eldest child out of their household Bernadette's parents accepted with alacrity. According to Bernarde Castérot they replied: 'We would willingly give you Bernadette, and if you like, two others with her.'[69] Marie Lagües did not want any other of the Soubirous children, and Bernadette went alone to live at Bartrès in 1857.

## The shepherdess of Bartrès

Bernadette's life at Bartrès is the starting point of legends about the Lourdes visionary, and there are several genres of primary source material concerning this time of her life. One is the literary works produced by early visitors to Lourdes such as Henri Lasserre, author of *Notre-Dame de Lourdes*. These works are infused with the aesthetic of romantic pastoralism, and her life at Bartrès provided an opportunity for writers to describe her as the innocent young shepherdess in the green fields. A second genre, equally mythic but actually generated from the inhabitants of rural France, was the miracle stories which emanated from the people of Bartrès after the Lourdes apparitions. People of the area said that she had miraculous powers. Thus the waters of a flooded stream had parted to allow her to cross with a flock of sheep, and she could multiply loaves of bread. Such tales are inevitably generated by the traditions of popular religion. When asked about such stories Bernadette scornfully replied, 'there is no truth in any of it'.[70] Interspersed with such tales are details of material life offered by people who had known Bernadette and were interviewed during the 1870s. Their memoirs leave an incomplete but negative picture of an oppressed child-servant. In Bernadette's words, 'my wet nurse was not always kind'.[71]

Marie Lagües and her family were in many ways a reverse image of the Soubirous. The family were known as one of the 'most prosperous and most respected of Bartrès', and they exemplified the positive stereotype of the peasantry.[72] The Lagües family were pious, frugal, hardworking and respectable – and they had reaped their reward. Marie Lagües's brother had become a priest, a significant achievement of upward mobility. Their gable-roofed stone farmhouse, which incorporated a barn, still stands on the outskirts of the village of Bartrès. It is a solid and imposing structure which is now a memorial to Saint Bernadette. Despite the respect in which they were held, there is a note of reserve in memoirs of the Lagües family which suggests that they were harsh and exacting. Jean Barbet, the schoolteacher at Bartrès, described the family as follows:

> She [i.e. Marie Lagües's mother], Jeanne Aravant, née Bernata, was a good housekeeper, dedicated to hard work and piety. She was also charitable and kind to the poor; her father, Denis Aravant, was rather selfish and narrow-minded. Her husband, Basil Lagües, who came from Poueyferré, was a good man, but without any education; ... pious like her mother, Marie Lagües was rather cold and 'a bit parsimonious'.[73]

Bernadette had often visited Marie Lagües's home as a guest, as Bartrès is only about one hour's walk from Lourdes. Bernadette, always accompanied by a younger sibling, would walk over to Bartrès on the feast of St John the Baptist, which is the town's festival. She would return with little treats from the Lagües household, such as potatoes or a piece of cake.

Bernarde Castérot said that Marie Lagües, maintaining an affection for Bernadette, requested that she 'keep her at her home and give her the job of caring for the children and a flock of sheep'.[74] Marie Lagües herself said that she had several very young children in 1857, and only one servant, Jeanne-Marie Garros: 'this was not enough for all the work, therefore I sent Jeanne-Marie to Lourdes to ask for Bernadette, who would look after the children or herd sheep and some cows, always near to the house'.[75] Marie Lagües, like Bernarde Castérot, remembered that Louise Castérot offered to send other children as well. Indeed, as Toinette had now completed her education, she was more fit to be employed than her own older sister. She was also stronger. However, it was only Bernadette who Marie Lagües wanted. Other girls could have been found, more useful than this puny asthmatic, but it was Bernadette who was called for.

The relationship between Marie Lagües and the future saint was ambiguous, as some witnesses record that she loved Bernadette, others that she hated and ill-treated her. The motives for this alleged hostility are almost preposterous; it was said that she always bore a grudge against Bernadette because she had been fed on the milk which had been destined for her dead son, Jean.[76] It was the death of this infant which had left her free to take on the nursing of the Soubirous baby in 1844. Since then Marie Lagües had given birth to another son, also called Jean, who had also died. A third son, again christened with the ill-fated name, was two years old when Bernadette entered the household, and one of her tasks was to care for him. He was sickly and died in 1857, during Bernadette's sojourn. Evidently these bereavements roused Marie Lagües's emotions, and Bernadette seems to have been the target of simultaneous love, hatred and blame. Others assign the responsibility for rumours of ill-treatment to the father of the household, Basil Lagües. Joseph Vergès, who was a priest at Bartrès after the Lourdes apparitions, said that he had heard that: 'If Bernadette's wet nurse was affectionate to her, the husband was harsh.'[77] The other servant, Jeanne-Marie Garros, would have known the whole story, but only made the circumspect remark that she herself never had any cause to complain of Bernadette, who was 'well treated and well loved by almost everyone'.[78] The word 'almost' is conspicuous in that sentence, but it stands without a full explanation.

It seems odd that, so many years after Bernadette's infancy, Marie Lagües would continue to be identified as a wet nurse, but this is consistently found in the memoirs of every witness. She is constantly termed *la nourrice* (the wet nurse), although at that time she was Bernadette's employer. In contrast with many people of her generation, she did not like to recall her memories of the visionary, whatever they were. In her old age she left Bartrès, went to live near Tarbes, and remained 'very uncommunicative'.[79]

Bernadette's position as a former nursling who returned as a servant, and the forbidding characters of the Lagües family, are akin to the stories of provincial France from the pens of writers such as Flaubert and Balzac. There are the rigid exteriors of social conduct and the passionate, irrational influences of hidden emotions. The history of the relationships within the Lagües home is irretrievable, but it is reliably recorded that Bernadette soon wanted to leave. Her total stay at the Lagües household was between six months and a year, and she would have returned home for a visit at least once, as she was in Lourdes in June 1857 when Toinette had her First Communion. She was expected to stay longer at Bartrès, but for some time she had been asking to be sent home.

Contradictions about the situation at Bartrès extend even to Bernadette's own statements. When Bernadette was in her thirties, some of the Sisters in her convent, who had evidently heard rumours of her early life, asked Bernadette if she had been mistreated at Bartrès. Bernadette told them, quite definitely, that she had not been. However, her cousin, Jeanne Védère, had received different confidences. Bernadette stated that her wet nurse had been unkind to her, and one day, when she was with Jeanne Védère in Lourdes, her memories of Bartrès were raised by a chance meeting with a priest. He stayed only a few moments, speaking to Bernadette in a most friendly manner, and she explained to Jeanne Védère that this was the brother of Marie Lagües, who had visited the household during his vacation in 1857. Bernadette spoke warmly of this man: ' "he was so good to me at Bartrès! I liked him a great deal! He came to stay for several days during his vacation. For as long as he was there, he took my part and I had nothing to suffer, but then she who was unkind to me went back to her previous ways." [80] Jeanne Védère asked Bernadette why she had not complained to her father, but Bernadette appeared resigned, and said ' "Oh no, I thought that this was as God willed." [81] She then asked Jeanne Védère not to speak of this to anyone, which she did not do until after Bernadette's death.

The priest described here was the Abbé Aravant, who became a Curé in a parish of the Hautes-Pyrénées. When asked about these events he remembered Bernadette's early sojourn in his household, as a baby in 1844, but claimed that he had been absent from Bartrès in 1857. Apparently he no longer remembered the brief visits, which had been such a welcome change of atmosphere for Bernadette. It is possible that this was a disclaimer on his part, the historian who approached him commented dryly that possibly Abbé Aravant 'had forgotten, or wished to forget' the visit of 1857.[82] After all, the questions raised by Bernadette's favourable recollection of him were troublesome for the reputation of his family. Rather than entering into the question of Bernadette's life at Bartrès, Abbé Aravant found the opportunity to say that at Lourdes Bernadette had been 'unhappy and neglected' in poverty.[83] He suggested that it was a favour on the part of his relatives to take her into their home.

In mentioning the disadvantages of Bernadette's earlier situation in Lourdes, Abbé Aravant was delicately raising a relevant point. Even if Bernadette was unhappy at Bartrès, she may have been in better material circumstances than were offered in her own home. It was also natural that members of the Lagües household would seek to preserve the reputation of their family, and to deny that there was any persecution of their one-time servant girl, who was so unexpectedly transformed into the saint of the area. It is less clear why Bernadette would deny her unhappiness in their household, but as we have seen, she was unwilling to speak about it, and confided these hardships only to Jeanne Védère – and then only in the most general terms. The harshness of Marie Lagües may have been irregular, and unpredictable, which would make it difficult even for Bernadette herself to give a coherent account of whether she was liked or disliked. It is also quite possible that Bernadette was humiliated by her situation at Bartrès, and preferred to deny her memories of unhappiness, especially before outsiders. It also reflected badly upon her own family, to whom she was loyal. There remains the possibility that Bernadette's ill-treatment at Bartrès was not so very bad after all, and was certainly sufficient for a stoic girl to tolerate. The evidence against this is that as early as 1858 people in Lourdes had heard that Bernadette had been treated with 'little consideration' in her former foster home.[84] Nineteenth-century standards of behaviour were not lenient, especially toward young people engaged in labour. A great degree of harshness would have to be exercised, if it was to be even noticed, much less remarked upon and remembered.

The tasks assigned to Bernadette were looking after the children and shepherding a flock of sheep. Marie Lagües had five children between the ages of two and eleven. The care of children was a task in which Bernadette had experience, but herding sheep was a different matter. As she had been born in a mill, raised in cramped urban conditions, and employed in her aunt's tavern,

Bernadette had no experience of rural life. She was not really a *bergère* in the Pyrenean meaning of the term, for she did not take the sheep into the high mountains and live with them while they pastured.[85] Like many children, Bernadette simply took the sheep during the day to nearby fields. Child labour was so inexpensive that this form of herding cost less than fencing the land. Her work as a shepherdess was to be the foundation of the iconography of Saint Bernadette, as images of pastoralism were influential artistic and literary motifs of the time. The innumerable descriptions of her on the hills at Bartrès bear only a tenuous relationship to the historical record of her employment and are significant rather to the later story of the cultural appetites which drew her into fame. An example of the literature which, from the 1860s onwards, described Bernadette's life at Bartrès is given in *Notre-Dame de Lourdes*:

At that school of innocence and solitude, the poor shepherdess learnt, perhaps, what the world has forgotten: the simplicity which is so pleasing to God. Far from all impure contact, conversing with the Virgin Mary, passing her time and her hours in offering wreaths of prayers as she said her rosary, she conserved her absolute sincerity and her baptismal purity.[86]

How vividly this prose expresses the images which Bernadette's later admirers were to attach to her! In this paragraph one has a complete view of Catholic romanticism of rural life. And how easily the oppressions faced by Bernadette are glossed over. Despite this author's visits to Lourdes and to Bernadette, he has avoided informing his readers of anything about her actual situation at Bartrès. For one thing, Bernadette's attendance at a school of 'innocence and solitude' was a difficult situation of no benefit to her, as she dearly wished to be at the catechism class. If she could have been there, she would have enjoyed the company of other girls, and would have been advancing in the proper ranks which her society valued. On the hillside at Bartrès, she was out of place, and moving further into a social limbo.

Shepherding sheep was usually not an onerous task, the major difficulties of the job being exposure to all weathers and loneliness. After Bernadette had returned to Lourdes, on the day of the first vision, her mother suggested that she should not go out because of the cold. She replied: 'I always went out at Bartrès!'[87] Despite her fragile health and her asthma, she seems to have coped well with the outdoor conditions. The solitude may have been the most difficult trial of her employment. It must certainly have been a great change for Bernadette, who until then had always been surrounded by other people and had never spent long periods of time outdoors. Even those who lived the traditional rural lifestyle found the long watches in the empty fields a lonely task. A printed recollection of a child shepherd stated that at times 'fear and sadness overtook me, and I started to cry, to cry without reason, for hours on end'.[88]

Religious writers have supposed that the isolation must have been very good for Bernadette: 'It was providential that ... the work assigned to her obliged her to spend many hours in solitude – it is then that God "speaks to the heart" '.[89] By contrast, the sceptical commentator Émile Zola suggested that 'the solitude of the meadows' where Bernadette would pray the rosary 'repeated until the point of hallucination' must have unbalanced her mind, so that she began to imagine herself as the heroine of marvellous religious stories she had heard.[90] The notion that Bernadette passed her time in the fields reciting the rosary is a convention of literature on Lourdes. However, as Abbé Laurentin, a careful modern scholar, has pointed out, there is no evidence that Bernadette did recite the rosary while she minded her flock. Her child companion at Bartrès stated that she did not recall having seen Bernadette with a rosary and, when questioned, Bernadette also said that she could not remember.[91] Her reputation was that she was pious, but only 'as we all were in the village. She did not pray more than anyone else.'[92] Jeanne-Marie Caudeban said, 'I saw Bernadette keeping the flocks, and I stayed with her to keep her company, as far as Arriouan. I do not remember that she had rosary beads; but she had several medals or images of the Virgin Mary, and she did not want to give me any of them. I never saw her at catechism or confession. She was good-natured, simple and tranquil.'[93]

In later years Marie Lagües, who did not like to say anything on the subject, was interviewed by the indefatigable Père Cros (with his status as a Jesuit priest, and his mission to write a history of the shrine, he insisted upon receiving testimonies). She had no criticisms to make and described Bernadette as being 'gay and lively, despite the fatigue caused by her short, laboured breathing. She never complained of anything or anyone, she was always obedient and never answered back. She never gave us any trouble: she took whatever was given to her and she always appeared contented.'[94] But it is possible that she found the life physically difficult, especially as she could not cope with a normal diet. Even years later, when Bernadette was dying in her thirties, well tended in a convent infirmary, she would often vomit after eating. If no regard was given to her diet at Bartrès, and there was no reason why it should have been, Bernadette may have been nearly starving in the midst of plenty.

The memoirs of the Bartrès schoolteacher stated that it was a local custom to make bread 'of pure wheat for the older masters' and bread 'half wheat and half maize' for the young and the servants.[95] He included this in his text without explanation, and it would appear to be an irrelevant detail, but the making of bread was part of the Pyrenean oral history of Bernadette's life at Bartrès. Only a few pages later, Barbet's memoir fondly recalled that the housewives of Bartrès would give Bernadette white bread, cooked food and fruit as she took her flock to the fields.[96] These are obviously gilded memories, by which informants could both show their charity and establish a link with the most famous person ever to reside in Bartrès. However, these anecdotes may also be literally true, and the list of foods is significant – they are all delicacies – more easily eaten than black bread and raw food, which are perfectly nourishing for a normal person, and which may have been all that the Lagües family saw fit to offer Bernadette. Amidst these recollections Jean Barbet also included the standard miracle story of Bartrès, which claimed that a stream parted so that Bernadette could pass through with her flock, and that she would come inside dry from thunderstorms.[97]

It is interesting to compare Barbet's text with a series of letters, contemporary with the Lourdes apparitions, which recorded much of the oral communication in the district. In March 1858, only six weeks after Bernadette's return from Bartrès, the miracle story of the flock and the stream was current as Lourdes rumour. This early version included a few details concerning Bernadette's employers. As Bernadette approached a flooded, raging stream, 'the husband of her wet nurse, who saw her approaching from a distance, began to curse and swear with great anger'.[98] He was amazed that his flock arrived without harm: 'it is said that the waters parted to give her passage'.[99] Here one can see the remnants of an actual incident which has been given a mythic explanation. The guiding of a flock of sheep is not always an easy task, and if the unskilled Bernadette directed them to ford a stream, she would have appeared to have acted rashly. If she then managed, against the odds, to send them through without any becoming scattered or drowned, it might well appear remarkable. At a third or fourth telling, it could be said to be a miracle. One notes, in this story, that Bernadette's employer was furiously angry and cursed at the sight of his incompetent worker. This, alas, has no element of the fabulous. It is an aspect of the story which has a ring of truth, although it may be somewhat exaggerated.

Such was the story conveyed in a letter from Lourdes in 1858. However, in a following missive the correspondent retracted the miracle of the stream. She did this in terms so definite that it seems likely that Bernadette herself had provided the curious with a clear refutation: 'it is said that this is not true'. [100] In addition, Lourdes hearsay provided some details about Bernadette's life at Bartrès. Her admirers stated that she had cared well for the flocks but that 'that poor child was very badly treated there; because she was given black bread made especially for her, of the worst type, but the child remained always obedient'.[101] Jean Barbet would not have been aware of these particular letters, which did not appear in print during his lifetime, but it is likely that he encountered these same Lourdes rumours from the oral sources which they reflect. His assurances that the making of coarse bread for the young is a Bartrès custom is probably an implicit reply to allegations that Bernadette was malnourished and despised in her foster home. In a way, both the criticisms and the justifications are valid. From the perspective of the thrifty Lagües household, there was no reason why the young should be indulged with white bread. If Bernadette obediently took whatever was given to her, she was following the proper ways for one of her station, and she evidently did not expect anything better. She was either too obedient, or too timid, to complain.

These stories, with their recurrent motif of black and white bread, entwined the material aspects of Bernadette's biography with the religious folklore of the province. They hearken to the legend of Anglèse Sarazan, an archetype visionary of the Hautes-Pyrénées, who triumphed over the scornful when her bread was miraculously transformed from a small black piece to bountiful white loaves. In a recent book on French visionary religion, Thomas Kselman has reprinted one of the early Lourdes accounts of the 'miracle of the stream' and has analysed this as a story which allowed for the triumph of the humble.[102] Such satisfying narrative conclusions are the purpose of miracle stories in general. Bernadette made an effort to deny the Bartrès miracle stories, and in the face of her direct denials, fabulous elaboration could not multiply. As an historian, one would wish that she had gone further, and told of her actual experiences in Bartrès, but this did not happen. Confronted with miraculously saved flocks, she stated that there was no truth in the story, but she did not go on to describe how her shepherd life had really been.

It had been agreed between Marie Lagües and the Soubirous family that Bernadette would attend catechism and ordinary school classes at Bartrès. As Jean Barbet explained: 'whether through negligence or through "parsimony" the Lagües forgot that part of their promise'.[103] When at the end of her life Bernadette was asked about this aspect of her life at Bartrès she recovered her memory, which was so dead to the images of pastoralism, and replied: 'I scarcely ever went to school, and when I did I learnt nothing.'[104] Sometimes Marie Lagües would attempt to teach Bernadette the catechism in the evenings, after the day's work was completed, but she did not find an apt pupil. Bernadette had no ability to learn the French text, and Marie Lagües would become so impatient that she would throw the book in the corner. The Abbé Aravant remembered his brother-in-law telling him that: 'She was docile, affectionate, good ... but she made us lose hope when we tried to teach her the catechism or prayers.'[105] In defence of the Lagües family, it has to be said that Bernadette was always to be a slow learner with a poor memory; but in defence of Bernadette, it was also true that it would have been difficult for her to apply herself to memorizing a text taught by an inexperienced teacher, after working all day.

Aside from formal religious instruction, Bernadette would have gathered information about the supernatural through folktales. Both at Lourdes and at Bartrès she would have continued to hear the stories which are part of the heritage of Occitan speakers. As Émile Zola found when he visited Lourdes, the whole area is 'pious and superstitious, with haunted places, and constant stories of werewolves and sorcerers'.[106] A boy who had known Bernadette slightly later told Zola that he remembered her only as being 'a child like the others'.[107] On one occasion he had accompanied her on the walk to Bartrès, and on the route they passed a house with an evil reputation. It was said that a sorcerer lived there. Bernadette appeared to be very nervous, and took a long detour in order to avoid the house. She evidently took magical powers seriously. In other circumstances – even unpleasant times such as when she was berated, rejected, or put to work – she remained tranquil. This boy's account of her fear as she passed the witch's house is a rare moment of emotion from the placid Bernadette.

The inability to learn the catechism and make her First Communion remained as an insuperable barrier between Bernadette and adult life. The situation at Bartrès was sufficiently bad that, despite her passive and laconic nature, she was roused to speech, and then to action. When shepherding the flock, she saw a person from Lourdes passing on the road, and sent a message to her parents: 'Tell them that I am unhappy here. I want to go back to

Lourdes to prepare for my First Communion; tell them to come and get me.'[108] Bernadette also sent a message by Jeanne-Marie Garros, when she went to Lourdes, 'Bernadette asked me to tell her mother to come and take her. Louise did not come.'[109] The motives of the Soubirous parents are easy to comprehend. While they would have wished for Bernadette to make her First Communion, and to live at home, they could not afford to remove her from a situation which was, in material terms, satisfactory. In the face of her parents' silence, Bernadette took the initiative. Early in 1858 she gathered her few belongings to return to Lourdes without warning. The Lagües family were displeased and told her to 'come back tomorrow without fail'.[110] She did not return until a brief visit several days later, when she told them that she would be staying at Lourdes to make her First Communion.

During her stay in Bartrès Bernadette made the acquaintance of the Abbé Ader, parish priest of the town. This man was possibly of great influence in the genesis of the Lourdes apparitions; memoirs of her life in Bartrès credit him with several predictions which seem either prophetic or suggestive of the visionary role she was shortly to assume. Abbé Ader conducted the catechism class which Bernadette rarely and unfruitfully attended. The schoolteacher, Jean Barbet, and others in the town, claimed that he had commented on her charm and innocence, then made the startling comment: 'Look at that little girl; when the Blessed Virgin appears to someone, she would choose a child like that.'[111]

The Abbé Ader, who died in the early 1870s, was never interviewed on the subject of Bernadette, and all information is from his former parishioners. He himself left Bartrès in November 1857, before Bernadette returned to Lourdes, in order to enter a Benedictine monastery. Jean Barbet explained that Abbé Ader had a great enthusiasm for the apparition of Our Lady of La Salette, and was sure that Maximin and Mélanie must have been 'good, simple and pious like her (Bernadette)'.[112]

The people of Bartrès had a natural tendency to produce apocryphal narratives which linked their town to the subsequent dramas at Lourdes. A claim that their priest had prophetically recognized Bernadette's destiny is within this genre of legend-making. Alternatively, it is quite possibly true that this priest, who had a reputation for great piety and idealism, had noticed Bernadette and complimented her for an assumed resemblance to the visionary children of La Salette. If he did so, he could well have introduced a suggestion into the mind of the discontented young girl. Émile Zola found in the Bartrès story a rational explanation for the entire subsequent history of Bernadette. He had no doubt that the Abbé Ader would have made such a statement and also that he would have recounted the story of La Salette to his impressionable listener:

Without doubt, Bernadette would have passionately listened to this glorious tale, with her silent air of a dreamer awakened, then she would have carried this into the empty fields where she passed her days, to relive it while following the flocks.[113]

The clerical authorities who were to investigate Bernadette's life at Bartrès anticipated the reasoning of interpreters such as Zola. Less naive than Abbé Ader's former parishioners, they were uneasy about this story of the prophecy. In the process of inquiry for Bernadette's canonization, Jean Barbet's son gave a welcome assurance, which was accepted as an unquestionable fact, that neither his father nor the priest ever spoke of these matters in Bernadette's presence.[114] It was also claimed that Bernadette denied having ever heard of the children of La Salette before 1858, and could not even remember the name of the Curé of Bartrès, when she was questioned about him at the end of her life.[115]

Another possible contribution by Abbé Ader to the Lourdes visions was that he had a great reverence for making the sign of the cross. He reproved his parishioners for their careless manner in doing so, comparing their gestures to flicking off flies, and would show them a better way, instructing them to 'Do it as I do.'[116] After the apparitions, Bernadette's distinctive and graceful manner of signing the cross was noted by observers, who attributed it to the vision's heavenly example. It seems far more likely that this kindly priest, anxious to instruct his flock, was the source of her impressive style. If she learnt this from him, what else may she have picked up? Abbé Ader was a dreamer, he was soon to abandon the more comfortable life of a parish priest for the rigours of a Benedictine monastery, which he then was obliged to leave for the sake of his health. Abbé Ader was also a devotee of striking tales about the Virgin Mary appearing in the fields of nineteenth-century France. He may have had a profound effect on Bernadette. By the time that organized historians were questioning her in detail about her early life, she was 35 years old, and dying from a protracted illness. She had always had a poor memory, and seemed to have washed away the recollections of her Pyrenean childhood, having taken up a new way of life elsewhere. She stated that she knew nothing of the parish priest at Bartrès, and no further information is available.

Before her sojourn in Bartrès, Bernadette had experienced little contact with priests. Those in Lourdes were aloof authority figures. In the case of Curé Peyramale, who roared out angry sermons, they were intimidating as well. However, the brother of Marie Lagües, who played the touching role of being Bernadette's only friend during his infrequent visits, introduced her to a much closer view of clerics. Abbé Ader may also have personally impressed her, although in later life she claimed not to have remembered him. At thirteen, Bernadette was desperate to pass through the rituals of the catechism class and join the other grown-up girls at the communion rail. She had every reason to pay attention to anything the priest may have said, when she was lucky enough to be able to get away from her duties and attend a class. It is frustrating for the modern scholar that Abbé Ader died before the early historians of Lourdes began to conduct their interviews. We do not know if he really said that she looked like a visionary, or even if he remembered her. As Alan Neame, a modern scholar, wrote in 1968: 'Bartrès is Bernadette's prehistory. Bartrès, key to all that is susceptible of rational explanation in this strange story. That key is lost.'[117]

## A lady in white

The Soubirous family may or may not have been pleased to see their eldest daughter return home early in 1858. Their material situation was no better, and Bernadette returned to the *cachot*, where she shared a bed with her sister. In one aspect her life improved, as she was able to begin attending ordinary classes at the school of the Sisters of Nevers. She was also enrolled in the catechism class of Abbé Pomain, vicar of Lourdes. It is possible that her family contemplated returning her to Bartrès when she had achieved the formality of her First Communion. This is especially likely as agriculturalists such as the Lagües had more need of labour mid-year than at the end of winter, when Bernadette returned home. However, the shadow of Bartrès, and other aspects of ordinary life, were to be swept away by the events which began on 11 February 1858, two weeks after her return home.

The story, as told by Bernadette's sister, began on a note which was characteristic of the lives of the Pyrenean poor. That morning, when preparing the soup, 'Bernadette said: My God! We have no more wood.'[118] Their mother sent Bernadette and Toinette out in search of wood, accompanied by their neighbour's child, Jeanne Abadie. They left Lourdes and followed the Gave river, gathering wood and bones on their way. Bones were useful because they could be sold as fertilizer. A local woman who encountered them on their way advised them to go to the meadow of M. Laffitte, who had recently cut trees. Bernadette rejected this suggestion, in order 'not to be taken for thieves'.[119] She may have been justifiably cautious, or she may have been expressing a customary moral distinction that taking wood from private land was theft, whereas wood on common land was common property. They went on, the town was now out of sight and they were crossing meadows at the edge of the forest. Then they arrived at a point where the hills by the river began to extend upwards, nearly as steep as cliffs. There was a hollow in the base of the hill, at the very point where a mill-stream joined the Gave river; it was the Grotto of Massabielle.

The girls wanted to go onto the hill above the Grotto where there was a good chance to find fallen wood for a faggot. They may also have been seeking bones in the Grotto itself, which was full of debris washed up from the river. In order to reach the Grotto, they would be obliged to wade through the water. They had crossed streams earlier in their journey, but that was in the more populated areas, where little wooden footbridges had been placed. The younger girls took off their sabots and crossed the stream, but Bernadette hesitated. She was wearing stockings, and could not so quickly approach the water. She was also daunted by the cold. The others had crossed with the icy water up to their knees, as Bernadette recalled: 'they went through the water. They began to cry. I asked them why they were crying and they said that it was cold.'[120] The girls were bickering, and Bernadette called out to Toinette to 'lower your skirt!' while she was wading through the water. She then annoyed the others by suggesting that she should be helped across, either by them throwing stones for her to step on, or carrying her. Jeanne Abadie exclaimed '*Pét dé périclé* (Blast of thunder!) come across like us.' Bernadette told her not to swear, although, as Toinette commented years later '*Pét dé périclé* is not serious swearing.'[121] They dismissed her and went on in search of wood.

Left to her own devices, Bernadette walked up and down the bank, seeking a better place to cross. There was none, and she returned to the Grotto, and sat down to take her shoes off. She was lowering one of her stockings when she experienced her first encounter with the supernatural. According to her later statement to a church inquiry: 'her attention was caught by a sound of rushing wind, which made the trees rustle. She looked at the poplars which bordered the Gave, but they were still. She was occupied with taking off her second stocking when the same sound occurred, and then she turned to the opposite side, towards the Grotto, where she noticed a movement in the branch of a wild rose, at the opening of an oval niche.'[122] This niche was an oval hollow in the wall of the Grotto, a sort of cave within a cave. Although it was a natural formation, it could almost have been made for its current purpose – as an alcove to display a statue. While it appeared to be a shallow cavity, the shadowed back wall opened into a passage into the side of the mountain. According to Bernadette, from this dark alcove came a dazzling light, and a white figure.[123]

When the other girls returned shortly afterward they found Bernadette kneeling on the rocks, staring at the niche. Her appearance was strange – she was rigid and pale. Toinette was frightened and exclaimed that she might be dead. Jeanne reassured her, with the practical observation that 'if she were dead she would be lying down'.[124] They called Bernadette, then threw several stones at her, which she did not appear to feel. Suddenly Bernadette looked about her and recovered her normal appearance. She picked up her shoes and waded through the millstream to her companions, commenting that the water was not cold but was as warm as dishwater. Then she asked them if they had seen anything, but they told her that they had not.

During their return to the house Bernadette told her companions that there had been a beautiful white figure in the Grotto. Upon seeing her she had taken out her rosary beads, but her hand was frozen, unable to make the sign of the cross until the Lady also did so. Bernadette's initial accounts of the apparition were brief and vague. She stressed the adjective 'white' and referred to the apparition as *aquero*, a Bigourdanian word meaning 'that', as if she was not sure if it was an individual or an object. One of the most precise explanations from her early impressions was given by the Abbé Pomain, who quoted her as saying 'I saw something white, which had the appearance of a lady.'[125] According to an 1858 visitor to Lourdes, when people came to question Bernadette for the first time about what she saw, she replied, 'something white'.[126] However, soon stories were to circulate in the town that the apparition was of a young lady dressed in white with a rosary and a blue sash, and this is in accordance with Bernadette's subsequent, more detailed descriptions of the vision. It may have taken some time for Bernadette to organize her perceptions of what she saw during the trance into a coherent description. Eventually the apparition was to take on the appearance of the Virgin Mary, as she was known through religious art.

Her companions on the day of the first vision were interested, but they were not overwhelmed by the revelation that Bernadette had seen a white lady in the Grotto. Toinette accused her of trying to scare them: 'You told me this in order to make me afraid, but I can laugh at it, now that we are out on the road.'[127] Bernadette fell silent and quickly carried her faggot home on her head. Toinette was astonished by her stamina as Bernadette was usually easily exhausted but, on this day, outpaced her companions and even offered to carry Toinette's faggot as well.[128]

In its first appearances, Bernadette's vision was an ambiguous visitor from the other world. A tale such as this belonged to the dark and the forests, but could be laughed off in daylight on the road. It is notable that Bernadette was immediately transformed, physically and in terms of her relationships to others, from the time when she first fell into a trance. The first vision took place at a moment when she had just been rejected by her companions, Jeanne Abadie having refused to help her through the water. After awakening from the trance, Bernadette suddenly needed no assistance from anyone and the erstwhile puny child performed wonders of determination and self-confidence from this time onward. The trance, as far as can be determined, was genuine and was characterized by insensibility. Bernadette's companions long remembered her indifference to the cold millstream, because it seemed to them to be so strange. The inability to feel heat and cold is a recognized symptom of trance states and would appear in a more dramatic form during later visions. This is apart from any argument as to whether Bernadette's visions were 'real' in the sense of being genuine mystical experiences or not. Trances, and various forms of suspended consciousness, have been observed and documented in many cultures and are within the range of explicable human experiences.

When Toinette returned home she told her mother about what Bernadette had claimed to see. The story was received very unenthusiastically by the Soubirous parents. Louise Castérot exclaimed '*Praoubro de ioù*! (Poor me!) What are you saying?'[129] and was so angry that she beat both girls with a cane. She told Bernadette that her eyes must have deceived her, but when Bernadette protested that she had seen clearly, Louise obviously became touched by fear. She said: 'We must pray to God, it is perhaps the soul of one of our relatives in purgatory.'[130] François Soubirous likewise wavered between blaming his daughter for disturbing the household with a ridiculous story and uneasily believing that the apparition in the Grotto might really be something from another world. Toinette recalled his reaction: ' "Already, at your age, you have begun to say silly things!" He thought that the lady was something evil.'[131]

Peace was not to be restored to the household that evening. When they said their prayers together, Bernadette suddenly burst into tears and was sent to bed. Worried by these unexpected events, Louise visited two women neighbours and discussed the matter with them. They agreed that the story was probably a child's illusion. The next day Toinette told several other children of the happenings and word began to spread within their small community. Bernadette herself told Abbé Pomain, when she went to confession that week, only a few days after the first vision. Upon opening the grille for the next penitent, the priest was unable to see her small figure, but heard a voice, in Occitan dialect, telling him that she had seen 'something white' which may have been a Lady, at the Grotto of Massabielle. In later days, Abbé Pomain had the honour of being able to say 'I was the first priest to hear the story of the apparitions,' but, as he honestly noted, at the time he had 'not given any importance to what had been said to me'.[132] Only one element of her story struck him. That was her description of the sudden sound of the air moving, which had preceded the apparition. These words stayed in his mind, and he could quote them in Bernadette's original patois many years later. This Occitan phrase by an ignorant girl recalled to the priest's mind holy statements in the Latin Vulgate – the sound of rushing wind which preceded divine apparitions at Pentecost and in the book of Elijah. Even the faintest possibility of an action by God could not be ignored by a cleric. He asked Bernadette her name, and asked her permission to relate this story to the Curé. He needed her permission, of course, as otherwise he could not repeat anything which a penitent had said. To have a priest ask her permission for anything would have been a new experience for the downtrodden Bernadette, and she gave it readily. In fact, the secrecy of the confessional had already been breached, because Elénore Pérard, a woman of Lourdes who was waiting next for the confessional, had accidentally overheard. Lourdes was not a good place for keeping anything confidential. A few days later, Abbé Pomain mentioned it to Curé Peyramale, who, like himself, attached little importance to the odd story.

It is not clear why Bernadette would recount this event in the confessional. It was not a sin, and therefore need not be confessed, although of course Bernadette may have been too uneducated to know this. After he realized who she was, Abbé Pomain made a point of questioning her in the catechism class, and found that her mind was 'a blank sheet as far as doctrine was concerned'.[133] Her parents, or other elders, may have told her to tell the priest, in the hope of settling the issue.

As far as the clergy were concerned, the matter rested there, but more susceptible people in Lourdes were curious, especially the little girls who knew Bernadette. After Mass the following Sunday, 14 February 1858, a group of girls gathered around and successfully importuned the Soubirous parents to allow her to return to Massabielle with them. Against his better judgement, François Soubirous told them that they could go, but he would give them only a quarter of an hour. Both Toinette and Bernadette were rather hesitant, according to Marie Hillet 'they did not want to, they said "We are already unlucky enough." '[134] She thought that they were recalling their father's arrest for theft, but they may have been intimidated by their mother's use of the cane. Marie Hillet was evidently a girl who learnt more at catechism classes than Bernadette. When the Soubirous sisters asked her what she would do if the apparition was evil, she came up with the idea of testing it with holy water and a special prayer. The Lourdes children were now a sizeable group. They returned to the church to get some holy water and no doubt worked themselves into a state of agitation even before arriving at Massabielle.

At the Grotto Bernadette immediately knelt on the ground and said that she could see *aquero*. Marie Hillet recommended that Bernadette throw holy water at the vision, while pronouncing a formula of prayer which repelled devils: 'If you come from God, advance, if you are from the devil, get thee hence.' Bernadette began to do so, somewhat unwillingly. Her appearance began to disquieten her impressionable companions. She had a fixed stare and seemed entirely altered.[135] The brisk Marie Hillet was not helpless, and decided to act, saying 'Wait, wait, I will get your White Lady!'[136] She threw drops of holy water at the niche. At this moment Jeanne Abadie arrived late and ran to the top of the Grotto, overlooking the entire scene. She was annoyed that the others had not waited for her and in recompense threw a large stone at them. The stone shattered on the ground without harming anyone, but to the children it seemed that something had fallen from heaven at the very moment that they cast holy water at the mysterious apparition. They all began to cry and were not reassured when Jeanne Abadie appeared and told them that she had thrown the stone. Bernadette was now in a trance – an unexpected and frightening state – in which she was apparently unable to notice what was happening around her. In Jeanne Abadie's words:

> Bernadette was in a trance. We were about a dozen girls, all of the same age and all from poor families. Bernadette resembled an angel, but we believed her to be dead and at the sight of her we all cried. One of the girls went running to Lourdes, to tell Louise that I had killed Bernadette.[137]

Others ran to a nearby mill to get help from its residents, the Nicolau family. Antoine Nicolau, like so many young men of France on a Sunday, was dressing to go to a tavern. He rushed to the Grotto and there found Bernadette, kneeling on the ground, apparently unaware of her surroundings. Tears ran from her eyes and she was smiling. He remembered her face as 'more beautiful than anything I had ever seen'.[138] Whether because of her appearance, or because of the general atmosphere of panic, he too was shaken by the sight: 'I felt both fear and happiness, and for all of that day, my heart turned over every time that I thought about it.'[139] Unable to rouse her, he picked her up and carried her away. She remained in the same state for some time, and those present claimed that she continued to believe herself in the Grotto and seeing the apparition after her arrival at the Nicolau mill. Bernadette did not remember the journey but always maintained that the vision was over and that: '*Aquero* had already disappeared at the moment when I was going to ask her if she came from God or from the devil.'[140]

The eventful day seemed to be a debacle. Louise Soubirous arrived at the mill, so angry that she had to be restrained by others from hitting Bernadette with a stick. Some of the people at the mill were struck by 'the child's beauty at that moment ... the light in her gaze',[141] but not everyone took a positive view, and one young man kept exclaiming: 'That child will go mad.'[142] Toinette Soubirous also thought so and told Marie Hillet: 'It is because of you that my sister has become an imbecile.'[143] Another witness had an entirely different attitude. As they carried Bernadette to the mill 'a man from

Batsurguère' who passed them on the road said: ' "Don't be scared, it is nothing" as he went on his way.'[144] At every point in the story of the Lourdes visions, while many people are moved, enraged or struck by events, there is an occasional witness who can see nothing noteworthy. Bernadette slowly recovered her senses, and this episode was to be unique, as never again was she shaken out of her trances.

These events no doubt spread the early story of the apparition still further in the community, although nothing had yet happened to put Bernadette and her visions in a favourable light. Antoine Nicolau recounted the story to Bernarde Castérot that afternoon, in the public-house of which she was proprietor. It was the first that Bernadette's aunt had heard of the visions, and the point which struck her was that this had taken place in an area of such ill-repute, Massabielle: 'My God! What was the little one thinking of, why did she go there?'[145]

It would have been natural for people to assume that the apparition was diabolical in origin, and Bernadette herself clearly feared that it might be.[146] In possibly meeting Lucifer in one of his guises she had not undergone an unusual experience. Pyrenean folklore was full of accounts of his visits and this was something which it had in common with Catholic popular culture throughout France. As the famous statement by the early sociologist of religion Gabriel le Bras confirmed: 'When I was a child, the devil was a familiar character. I have known men who fought with him, I know houses where he knocked on the door.'[147] The way in which the apparition had disappeared before holy water, and the symptoms of Bernadette's trances, were consistent with both learned and popular lore concerning the devil. This suggestion was made, and continued to be made in the future, yet the most favoured early hypothesis about the identity of the apparition concerned other supernatural beings, either a ghost or a fairy.

The fairy mythology has been so influential and durable in the Pyrenees that Isaure Gratacos chose to entitle her contemporary ethnographic study of Pyrenean women *Fées et Gestes* (Fairies and Legends).[148] This scholarly work briefly reviews Bernadette's visions and investigates a claim which one finds hinted at in various sources – that the apparition in the Grotto could have been a fairy (a *fée* in standard French, or *hada* to use the Bigourdanian word). Exact primary source material on this question is scarce. The clerical investigators who generated the original documents of enquiry on Lourdes neither enquired about nor recorded elements of the local fairy folklore. It was part of the mentality of the nineteenth-century Catholic Church that they ignored all varieties of mythology other than their own. Yet, as Isaure Gratacos writes, the Grotto of Massabielle is still known, among some older people of the area, as the '*tuta deras hadas*'[149] (cave of the fairies).

According to Isaure Gratacos's analysis, the visions at Massabielle and the nature of the Grotto conform exactly to the characteristic elements of 'fairy caves' found throughout the Pyrenees. She points to three particular factors which identify such sites: the discreet distance from the town (within walking distance but out of sight of any dwelling), the presence of flowing water, and *Paléolithique Supérieur* archaeological debris within the cave.[150] Moreover, the term *dama* or *demaisela* (*demoiselle*), often used by Bernadette to describe her vision after it began speaking to her, was a commonly used term to designate the *hadas*.[151] The alternative term was *les dames blanches*[152] (the white ladies), and again one finds this in the early sources. Bernadette said that Marie Hillot, one of her companions, had called the apparition *ta Dame blanche* (your white lady) during the second visit to Massabielle.[153] Everything about the early story of the visions resonated with the animist, semi-pagan beliefs of peasant Europe. It is quite probable, as Isaure Gratacos suggests, that many elements of this folklore were edited out of the primary recitals when they were translated into French.[154]

Fairy beliefs no doubt provided Bernadette and her community with suggestions about the possibility of encountering *dames blanches*. These beings lived in the woods and caves, always appeared to be white, and in keeping with what Bernadette always insisted about the apparition, they were small and young. None of this existed in opposition to Christianity. As far as the Pyrenean popular imagination was concerned, no distinction was made between various forms of the supernatural, and a powerful or impressive *fée* could simply be identified with the figure of the Virgin Mary whom she both shaped and mirrored. The continuum in popular belief between Blessed Virgins and Fairy Queens must have made the orthodox narration of the origins of the Lourdes story by the Church somewhat easier. It was a matter of selection rather than recreation. Although ignored by clerical writers, the traditional view, which did not separate religious visions from fairy sightings, has been documented and has persisted in the lives of the Pyrenean people until the present era. One of Isaure Gratacos's informants, who had been asked about fairies, replied that at 'the fairy grotto' at Sauveterre her father had seen 'a beautiful lady dressed in blue and white; so pretty, pretty! And she smiled at him. Then he said to her: Come here! but the beautiful lady had vanished. Oh that was the Virgin, ah yes, my father said that it was the Virgin.'[155] White ladies, who have the fairy tendency to appear and enchant, then to vanish, while also having a religious costume and identity, haunt the grottos of the Pyrenees.

Whether fairy, devil or Virgin Mary, Bernadette's *Dame blanche* seemed destined for oblivion after the second apparition. Bernadette's cousin, Jeanne Védère, said that 'her mother renewed the prohibition against going to the Grotto. She understood very well that her daughter had seen something, but she did not think that it was the Immaculate Virgin!'[156] Her mother's warnings to stay away from Massabielle were reiterated with threats of another beating, while Bernadette seems to have also been frightened by her insensibility and her companions' panic after the ill-fated visit. Antoine Clarens quoted Bernadette as saying that she had not recovered her senses for a long time after the second apparition and had returned home 'quite convinced, for my part, that I had made an eternal adieu to *aquero*'.[157] However, as Bernadette explained: 'If I did go back, it was because of the repeated and pressing requests of Madame Millet and Mademoiselle Peyret of Lourdes. Encouraged by the idea of being accompanied by grown-ups, I went with them, the Tuesday afterwards.'[158]

These two ladies had become interested in Bernadette's vision and wanted to accompany her for a further visit because of another hypothesis concerning the identity of the apparition. For those who did not give the apparition a religious or fairy identity, the possibility that it was a ghost still remained. This had been the first supposition of Louise Castérot, who had thought of her own deceased relatives. Other people of Lourdes were soon to find a different candidate for the subject of Bernadette's vision.

Élise Latapie, a young woman of Lourdes, had died the previous year. She had been a socially prominent person, very charitable, and active as the president of the Enfants de Marie. By the standards of the area she was wealthy, being able to leave a legacy of 1,500 francs for the erection of a chapel in the local prison. Five months before the commencement of Bernadette's visions, the Curé of Lourdes gave an account of the death of Élise Latapie in his regular correspondence with the Bishop of Tarbes. This letter provides some details which indicate why public opinion would identify the Massabielle apparition as Élise. She had died after several months of illness and had spent the final stage at the local hospital. Her piety and resignation are described in detail by the Curé, who evidently found her an inspirational figure. 'This death has made a most profound impression in the town ... in the eyes of all, she was a saint.'[159]

Peyramale recorded what he termed a 'strange incident'[160] which took place shortly before her death. Élise Latapie requested that while still alive she be arranged for 'her last toilette'.[161] Specifically, she wanted to be dressed in the white robe of her Children of Mary costume. The staff at the hospital would not agree to her request to arrange her so in preparation for death, but she was at least able to state her wishes for the disposal of her corpse. 'She wanted to be in the grave, and in death, as she was during her life.'[162] It was this costume which linked her to the apparition in the Grotto. When stories began to circulate of mysterious sightings of a young lady in a white robe, Antoinette Peyret, a dressmaker who had worked for Élise Latapie, and Mme Millet, a prosperous widow, discussed the possibility that this could be the ghost of their former companion. As Antoinette Peyret explained:

> I thought that when a Lady appeared, with a white robe and a blue girdle [and a rosary], that it was our Superior of the Enfants de Marie, Élise Latapie, dead for several months. We have, in fact, a blue ribbon and a medal, and we carry a rosary from our waists on our days of Consecration and funerals.[163]

Peyramale's account of Élise Latapie's strange request to be effectively laid out before she was dead indicates some anxieties surrounding her which would have easily given rise to stories of her ghost returning to reiterate her last wishes. Another possibility is that despite the glowing terms of the Curé's letter, there were indefinite rumours which besmirched Élise Latapie's reputation and suggested that she may have died with an unquiet conscience. As Mlle Emmanuelle Estrade told Père Cros: 'Many years ago I received a confidence in regard to Mlle Latapie, but I must not recount it, on pain of sin

... Perhaps you, mon père, are aware of the matter which was spoken of.'[164] Whatever the content of such speculations, Antoinette Peyret and Mme Millet were to judge it worthwhile to accompany Bernadette to the Grotto and attempt communication with the apparition.

Mme Millet was a former servant who had risen in society by the scandalous route of marriage to her employer. In 1858 she was a middle-aged widow and if not generally well regarded she was at least prosperous. A local government official was to describe her as of doubtful morality, and as the type of person whose 'idle curiosity leaves her open to all sorts of impressions and subject to any caprice'.[165] When the story of the apparition at Massabielle reached her ears she requested that one of her maids find Bernadette after school to bring her for a talk. When first approached, Bernadette said that she could not visit. However, Mme Millet was in a position to make requests that prevailed; she sometimes employed Louise Castérot as a washerwoman. The servant later returned with a different message: that her mother had agreed that she should visit Mme Millet. The interview roused Mme Millet's interest still further, although Bernadette spoke of the apparitions as a past episode. To the suggestion that they go together to the Grotto Bernadette replied that she had been forbidden to visit it ever again, but Mme Millet knew that this could be arranged: 'Yes, yes! We must throw light on this. ... I know your mother well. She would not know how to refuse me.'[166] She was quite right. Louise Castérot was not going to offend someone who was paying for her labour.

The ladies had arranged to meet Bernadette early on the morning of 18 February 1858. They arrived prepared. Mme Millet brought a candle which had been blessed and Antoinette Peyret brought a pen which she had inherited from her father. It was hoped that the apparition would provide written instruction concerning its wishes. It is evident that they did not see such an attempt at mediumship as incompatible with Catholicism, in fact they expected their communications to give rise to devotions of the most orthodox kind. As Antoinette Peyret explained: 'I thought then that if she (Élise) had need of Masses, she would write her request: I have always had a great devotion for the souls in purgatory.'[167]

When the three women arrived at the Grotto they knelt together on the ground and began to recite the rosary. Antoinette Peyret stated that as soon as they began to pray Bernadette exclaimed: ' "She is here." We said to her: "Be quiet, recite your rosary." '[168] On this occasion neither of the witnesses could see any change in Bernadette's features when she regarded the apparition. After reciting the rosary they rose to their feet and Antoinette Peyret instructed Bernadette to ask the Lady what she wanted, and to convey these wishes in writing.[169] Bernadette advanced toward the niche, indicating with a gesture of her hand that the others should stop when they began to follow her.

The two women watched her proffer the pen, then stand in silence. Becoming impatient Mme Millet exclaimed: 'Bernadette! Ask of her what I told you!'[170] Antoine Clarens quoted an account from Bernadette of this third vision:

'Could you please', I said to the vision, 'put in writing what you want from me.' For the first time, I heard her voice which said to me: 'It is not necessary that I write anything down. I do not promise to make you happy in this world, but in the next. Have the goodness to come here each day for a fortnight, and I will be very pleased.' At my reply: 'I will come', the Vision rose toward the roof of the Grotto and vanished.[171]

As stated above, this was the first time that Bernadette reported any speech from the apparition, and she conveyed the words to her two companions as she heard them. They replied with questions, and when they entered into communication with the mysterious being the power relationship between the visionary and her audience was temporarily altered in Bernadette's favour. They asked if they might approach and Bernadette told them that it was permitted.[172] They then approached the niche, but the vision had ended, the entire episode having taken just less than half an hour.

Bernadette told Antoinette Peyret that the Lady had looked at her and smiled. Antoinette Peyret 'at that time felt no particular emotion; but later she said that she lived on the memory of that smile'.[173] Bernadette was eventually to be known as a conduit of heavenly favours, but this was virtually unforeseeable during the meeting at the Grotto that morning. On the way home they asked if the vision had resembled Élise Latapie, and Bernadette replied 'No.' Mme Millet was the first person on the historical record to have then asked the fateful question: 'And what if it were the Blessed Virgin?'[174] Her remark was received in silence by the others. Antoinette concluded:

> I did not think that there was anything Satanic involved, but neither did I think that it was the Blessed Virgin, and I remained sceptical for a long time. As we went back, we said to Bernadette: 'If you are lying, God will punish you!'[175]

The experiment tried by Mme Millet and Antoinette Peyret had clear precedents. Many people of the Pyrenees had been attracted by stories of communication with ghosts. Jean-François Soulet cites the *Echo des Vallées* of 1845 which reported that in Lourdes a ten-year-old girl claimed to have been visited by her recently deceased aunt who transported her to another world. Very soon the home of this girl was visited by crowds of people, anxious to hear her story and to learn if their departed relatives wanted Masses said for them.[176] Antoinette Peyret's beliefs were shared by others, including those close to Bernadette. Basile Castérot testified at Bernadette's canonization that: 'I did not believe that it was the Blessed Virgin who was appearing to her.' She stated that M. Pomain, the Vicar of Lourdes, had asked her who she thought 'that Lady' was and that she replied:

> 'I think that it is a soul in need of prayers, who has come to take refuge there.' M. Pomain smiled at me, saying: 'No, it is not that, later on it will be known, but now we must have patience.' ... As for Bernadette, she did not know either: she greatly desired to see the Lady again, always saying 'She is

so beautiful!' If anyone said to her that this might be the Blessed Virgin, she would reply: 'I know nothing about it.'[177]

According to Bernarde Castérot, neither she nor Bernadette knew the identity of the Lady until the declaration, 'I am the Immaculate Conception', which did not take place until 25 March, during the sixteenth vision. In the meantime, Bernadette was captivated by the apparition. She described it as extremely beautiful and was determined to keep her promise and return every day to the Grotto.

The story of the visions was now circulating freely in Lourdes, inciting the curiosity of many people who were socially more powerful than the Soubirous family. They included the local priests, who wondered if it might be a case of fraud, or some other problem for the Church, and the state officials, who anticipated trouble as soon as they heard of crowds gathering at the Grotto of Massabielle.

Writers of the religious history of Lourdes have always treated the first three of Bernadette's visions separately from those that followed. These encounters, which took place on 11, 14 and 18 February 1858, have been considered as an inauguration of '*la Quinzaine sacrée* (the holy fortnight)',[178] the dramatic and public series of subsequent visions.

Whether to a secular or theological writer, 11 to 14 February is a distinct era. During this time the visionary episodes were equivocal because the nature of the apparition fluctuated according to the ideas of whoever heard the story. They were private events, which are documented only by personal memoirs and which had not yet connected to the public structures of the society. Each expedition to Massabielle was a journey of exploration, from which the participants came away frightened, puzzled or intrigued. The communication between Bernadette and her contemporaries was setting the parameters of what could appear to her during the trances, but the situation remained open-ended until Bernadette heard the apparition speak to her on 18 February. Once the visionary reported that she had received a mystic command to return to the Grotto every day for a fortnight the events had acquired a pattern and a purpose. Until then, they were haphazard. There were various possible conclusions to the story, all far more pedestrian than what was to follow. A later report by the medical authorities of Lourdes suggested that during the early days, 'that strange apparition' so little preoccupied Bernadette that had her friends not urged her to return to the Grotto, 'it is likely that she would have been left with only a vague memory of it'.[179]

Bernadette's interlocutors questioned her and shaped her replies into descriptive statements. The stories which were then edited obviously came from the ideas of the spectators as much as those of the visionary. The necessity to explain this scenario to the people from the outside world, and therefore to translate it into French, required further evolutions, which could be termed distortions. The memoir of Antoine Clarens, a Lourdes school-teacher, was to be criticized for this reason in the 1870s, by the early historian Père Cros. Cros pointed out that the long speeches attributed to Bernadette in

Clarens's memoir are far from being 'the literal speech of the Visionary'.[180] The same could be said for all the other documentary material, but this process of translation and mutation is itself part of the story of the Lourdes legend, not an accretion on it.

An example of these explanations and exchanges, which relates to the period of the first visions, was given by Siste Damien, who taught at the Lourdes Hospice. She learnt of the events at the Grotto after the second vision, when the schoolchildren were talking about the marvellous events. The young nun was kinder and more light-hearted than most adults, she listened to them. According to Sr Damien's testimony they invited Bernadette to tell what she had seen, but she declined: 'I, she said, I do not know how to speak French.'[181] The children, 'always avid to recount wonders', gave their amused teacher a recital of their supernatural adventures.[182] Bernadette listened 'and sometimes in her patois, she corrected them. "That is not as I told you, she said to them, it was like this." '[183] Sr Damien suggested that they not tell anyone else, or they would surely be laughed at. The alchemy of communication amid unequal power relationships is made evident in this testimony. Language barriers, cultural standards, and individual temperaments shaped what could be said and what could be understood. Sr Damien's account is representative of numerous occasions throughout Bernadette's life, when she would allow other people to tell her story for her. Her intermittent corrections to their versions were much less than a controlling role. Bernadette lacked either the ability or the inclination to create a complete story from the apparitions. However, she was always to be surrounded by people, whether schoolchildren in 1858 or educated literary men in the 1860s, who were, in their own way, 'always avid to recount wonders'.[184]

Mme Millet has never been granted an illustrious role in the history of Lourdes, but her fleeting and early intervention was probably very important. It is apparent that she was a significant influence in the process by which Bernadette's 'something white'[185] became a 'young girl, dressed in white'.[186] The supposition that the being who appeared at the Grotto might be the former superior of the Children of Mary introduced an element of orthodox religion, which, until then, had been conspicuously lacking.

In February 1858 Bernadette was an outwardly unimpressive individual. She had plenty of social disadvantages, and was a Catholic who could not receive Holy Communion, for she knew almost nothing about her faith. She knew very little about the outside world, either. At the beginning of Lent, in mid-February 1858, Bernadette Soubirous was still the poor girl whom her neighbours barely noticed. But she had encountered a supernatural being and a small group of people were curious enough to accompany her daily to the Grotto. The mundane period of her early life had come to an abrupt end. Within days, her visions would change the history of her town.

# NOTES

1. D'Angla quoted, Cros, *Histoire*, 1. 214. He uses the word 'drôlesse', also 'fille de rien', which I have translated as vagabond and nobody.

2. 'Amassar era ham tab era set, unir la faim et la soif.' Gratacos, *Fées et Gestes*, 90.

3. An observation made by many people, e.g. Marie Fourcade, *Témoins*, 239.

4. Laurentin, *Vie*, 77.

5. Dominique Vignes, the husband of Lucile Castérot, Louise's younger sister. *Témoins*, 157.

6. Ibid.

7. Jeanne Védère, *Témoins*, 182.

8. Ibid.

9. L. L. McReavy, *Bernadette, Child of Mary* (London 1933), 124.

10. Bernadette quoted by Julie Garros, *BVP*, 1. 17.

11. Sr Marie Bernard quoted, Trochu, *Sainte Bernadette*, 44.

12. Jeanne Védère quoting her father's words, Cros, *Histoire*, 1. 47.

13. Quoted by H. Petitot, *Histoire exacte des apparitions de N.-D. de Lourdes à Bernadette* (Paris 1935), 16.

14. Jeanne Védère quoted, Cros, *Histoire*, 1. 52.

15. André Sajoux quoted, Cros, *Histoire*, 1. 51.

16. Bernarde Castérot, *Témoins*, 160.

17. Jeanne Védère, *Témoins*, 182.

18. Marie-Antoinette Soubirous, *Témoins*, 216.

19. André Sajoux, *Témoins*, 167.

20. Testimony of Louise Soubirous, *ESB*, 36.

21. Marie-Antoinette Soubirous, *RdAM*, 154. Bernadette's sister and her two brothers respectively died at the ages of 46, 68 and 72.

22. See the statistical tables provided by P. Bourdelais and J-Y. Roulot, *Une peur bleue. Histoire du choléra en France 1832–1854* (Paris 1987), 110–11.

23. Testimony of Louise Soubirous, *ESB*, 36.

24. Marie-Antoinette Soubirous, *RdAM*, 154.

25. Ibid.

26. Basile Castérot, *Témoins*, 164.

27. Antoinette Soubirous, *Témoins*, 214.

28. Ibid.

29. Bernadette Soubirous quoted, Laurentin, *Logia*, 2. 275.

30. Bernadette quoted by Antoinette Soubirous, *Témoins*, 214.

31. Isabeline Aguillon quoted by E. Guynot, *Bernadette d'après ses contemporains* (Paris 1978), 18.

32. Bernarde Castérot quoted, Cros, *Histoire*, 1. 54.

33. Joseph-Alolphe d'Angla, *Témoins*, 65.

34. Jeanne Fourcade quoted, Cros, *Histoire*, 1. 54.

35. Sr Marie Gérault quoted by Sr Emilie, *PON*, Sessio XXXIX, 539.

36. Zola, *Mes Voyages*, 97.

37. Report of the Procureur Impérial, 31 Mar. 1857, quoted by Laurentin, *Vie*, 26.

38. André Sajoux, *Témoins*, 167.

39. Pierre Callet, *Témoins*, 45.

40. Basile Castérot, *RdAM*, 165.

41. Dominique Vignes, *Témoins*, 157–8.

42. Bernard Pays quoted, Cros, *Histoire*, 1. 46.

43. Isidore Pujol quoted, ibid.

44. André Sajoux, *Témoins*, 168.

45. André Sajoux, *Témoins*, 168. Mme Jacomet, *Témoins*, 77.

46. Joseph-Adolphe d'Angla, *Témoins*, 65.

47. Basile Castérot, *RdAM*, 165.

48. Marie-Antoinette Soubirous, *RdAM*, 154.

49. Joseph-Adolphe d'Angla, *Témoins*, 61.

50. Romaine Mingelatte-Poueyto quoted by Guynot, *Contemporains*, 10.

51. Ibid., 9.

52. Ibid., 10–11.

53. Laurentin, *Vie*, 21.

54. André Sajoux, *Témoins*, 167.

55. 8 Apr. 1852, *AML*, D9, 302.

56. 9 Oct. 1856, *AML*, D9, 481.

57. 19 Sept. 1859, *AML*, D10, 22.

58. Marie-Antoinette Soubirous, *RdAM*, 154.

59. Toinette quoted, 'Temoignage sur Bernadette par soeur Saint-Sardos, fille de la charité à Tarbes', *AG*, A21.

60. See Jean Mellot, 'Rite de passage et fête familiale. Rapprochements', J. Delumeau, *La Première Communion. Quatre siècles d'histoire* (Paris 1987), 187.

61. R. Gibson, *A Social History of French Catholicism 1789–1914* (London 1989), 166.

62. Trochu, *Saint Bernadette*, 55.

63. Bernarde Castérot quoted, Cros, *Histoire*, 1. 54.

64. P. Roberdel, *Marie-Julie Jahenny, la stigmatisée de Blain 1850–1941* (Montsûrs 1987), 28.

65. Simon Philippe Viron, *PON*, Sessio LXXVIII, 926.

66. Bernarde Castérot, *Témoins*, 160.

67. Toinette Soubirous, *Procès*, 31.

68. Ibid., 19.

69. Bernarde Castérot, *Témoins*, 160–1. Marie Lagües recalled exactly the same words from Louise Castérot, quoted Cros, *Histoire*, 1. 57.

70. Bernadette quoted by Jeanne Védère, *Témoins*, 181. Jeanne Védère comments that she asked Bernadette about such stories, many variants of which are found in the early records. According to several informants, Bernadette denied these and other tales of miracles.

71. Ibid.

72. J. Barbet, *La Dame plus belle que toute* (Paris 1957; f.p. 1901), 19.

73. Ibid.

74. Bernarde Castérot, *Témoins*, 160.

75. Marie Lagües cited by Cros, *Histoire*, 1. 57.

76. Laurentin, *Vie*, 28.

77. Joseph Zéphyrin Vergès, *PON*, Sessio LXX, 845.

78. Cros, *Histoire*, 1. 58.

79. Zola, *Mes Voyages*, 96.

80. Jeanne Védère cited, Cros, *Histoire*, 1. 60–1.

81. Ibid.

82. Ibid., 59.

83. L'abbé Aravant, *Témoins*, 172.

84. Frère Léobard's memoir cited by Cros, *Histoire*, 1. 61.

85. A task usually performed by men, but sometimes by women and girls. H. Fedacou, *Henri Fedacou raconte la vie montagnarde dans un village des pyrénées au début du siècle* (Tarbes 1984), 89.

86. Lasserre, *Notre-Dame de Lourdes*, 14.

87. Marie-Antoinette Soubirous, *RdAM*, 155.

88. Guillaumin, 'Vie d'un simple', quoted by Heywood, *Childhood in Nineteenth-Century France* (Cambridge 1988), 52.

89. Trochu, *Saint Bernadette*, 27.

90. É. Zola, *Lourdes* (Paris 1895), 101.

91. *BVP*, 1. 20.

92. Zéphyrin Lagües quoted; ibid., 19.

93. Quoted by Cros, *Histoire*, 1. 59.

94. Marie Lagües quoted, Cros, *Histoire*, 1. 58.

95. Barbet, *La Dame plus belle*, 20.

96. Ibid., 23.

97. Ibid., 22.

98. Adelaide Monlaur to her cousin, 21 Mar. 1858, *AG*, A8.

99. Ibid.

100. Ibid., 8 Apr. 1858.

101. Ibid.

102. T. Kselman, *Miracles and Prophecies in Nineteenth-Century France* (New Jersey 1983), 108.

103. Barbet, *La Dame plus belle*, 24.

104. Bernadette quoted, Cros, *Histoire*, 1. 62.

105. Quoted in Cros, *Histoire*, 1. 58–9.

106. Zola, *Mes Voyages*, 91.

107. Ibid., 90.

108. Cros, *Histoire*, 1. 60.

109. Ibid.

110. Marie Lagües quoted, *BVP*, 1. 24.

111. Abbé Ader quoted by Antoine Emile Barbet, whose testimony was a reading from Jean Barbet's notes. *PON*, Sessio LXXII, 860.

112. Ibid.

113. Zola, *Lourdes*, 100.

114. Antoine Emile Barbet, *PON*, Sessio LXXII, 859.

115. Trochu, *Sainte Bernadette*, 32.

116. Barbet, *La Dame plus belle*, 24.

117. Neame, *The Happening at Lourdes*, 66.

118. Bernadette quoted by Marie-Antoinette Soubirous, *RdAM*, 155.

119. Bernadette quoted, ibid.

120. Bernadette Soubirous, written account of 1861, Cros, *Histoire*, 1. 71.

121. Marie-Antoinette Soubirous, *RdAM*, 155.

122. Episcopal Statement, quoted by Cros, *Histoire*, 1. 75.

123. Bernadette Soubirous, statement to the Procureur Impérial, 21 Feb. 1858, quoted by Cros, *Histoire*, 1. 76.

124. Ibid.

125. L'abbé Pomain, *Témoins*, 265.

126. 'Relation d'une visite faite à Bernadette à la fin de juillet 1858, par un jeune avocat de Dijon', *AG*, A9.

127. Marie-Antoinette Soubirous, *RdAM*, 157.

128. Ibid.

129. Louise Castérot quoted by Marie-Antoinette Soubirous, *RdAM*, 158.

130. Ibid.

131. Marie-Antoinette Soubirous, *RdAM*, 158.

132. Abbé Pomain, *Témoins*, 265.

133. Ibid.

134. Marie Hillet quoted, *Témoins*, 228

135. The testimonies of her companions are reassembled at Cros, *Histoire*, 1. 149–50. See also Marie Hillet, *Procès*, 31.

136. Quoted by Clarens, *RdAM*, 11.

137. Jeanne Abadie, *Procès*, 32.

138. Antoine Nicolau, *Témoins*, 32.

139. Ibid.

140. *Procès-verbal* of the interrogation of Bernadette by Commissioner Jacomet, 21 Feb. 1858, *LDA* 1, no. 3, 163.

141. Barbet, *La Dame plus belle*, 46.

142. Ibid.

143. Toinette Soubirous quoted, *Témoins*, 228.

144. Ibid.

145. Bernarde Castérot quoted by Antoine Nicolau, *Témoins*, 112.

146. As the documents of the episcopal inquiry noted, 'Bernadette had, more than once, heard talk of appearances of evil spirits', quoted Cros, *Histoire*, 1. 137.

147. Gabriel le Bras, quoted by J. Devlin, *The Superstitious Mind* (New Haven and London 1987), 122.

148. Gratacos, *Fées et Gestes*.

149. Ibid., 55.

150. These factors are listed ibid., 54. Fossilized bones and other archaeological remains from the Grotto of Massabielle, and other caves in the region, were deposited in the Muséum d'Histoire Naturelle de Toulouse by Edouard Piette, a nineteenth-century natural scientist.

151. Ibid.

152. Ibid., 25.

153. Bernadette quoted by Clarens, *RdAM*, 11.

154. Gratacos, *Fées et Gestes*, 54.

155. Marie Dumail quoted, ibid., 53.

156. Jeanne Védère, *Témoins*, 190.

157. Bernadette quoted by Clarens, *RdAM*, 11.

158. Ibid.

159. Letter from Abbé Peyramale to Mgr Laurence, 26 Oct. 1857, *LDA* 1. 143.

160. Ibid., 144.

161. Ibid., 143.

162. Ibid.

163. Antoinette Peyret, *Procès*, 37.

164. Emmanuelle Estrade, *Témoins*, 99.

165. Report of Procureur Impérial Dutour to Procureur Général Falconnet, 1 Mar. 1858, *LDA* 1, no. 11, 176.

166. Mme Millet quoted, *BVP*, 1. 44.

167. Antoinette Peyret, *Procès*, 37.

168. Ibid., 38.

169. Ibid.

170. Mme Millet quoted, *BVP*, 1. 46.

171. Bernadette quoted by Clarens, *RdAM*, 12.

172. *Procès*, 38.

173. Bordenave, *Sainte Bernadette*, 28.

174. *BVP*, 1. 48.

175. Antoinette Peyret, *Procès*, 39.

176. Soulet, *Pyrénées*, 2. 358.

177. Basile Castérot, *PON*, Sessio LXII, 757.

178. 'Ainsi allait s'inaugurer la Quinzaine sacrée', C. Yver, *L'Humble Sainte Bernadette* (Paris 1933), 107.

179. The *rapport des médecins* quoted, Cros, *Histoire*, 1. 139.

180. Cros, *Histoire*, 1. 154. Antoine Clarens spoke to Bernadette in late February and wrote an account of events in March 1858. Clarens's memoir is therefore one of the very early sources. Like all the memoirists, he quotes all the participants in the French language rather than Occitan.

181. *Sr* Damien, *RdC*, 1.

182. Ibid.

183. Ibid.

184. Ibid.

185. *Procès-verbal* of the interrogation of Bernadette by Police Commissioner Jacomet, 21 Feb. 1858, *LDA* 1, no. 3, 161.

186. Report from Procureur Impérial Dutour to Procureur Général Falconnet, 1 Mar. 1858, *LDA* 1, no. 9, 175–6.

# CHAPTER 3

# The Fortnight
## Daily Visions from 18 February to 4 March 1858

As soon as she arrived, Bernadette knelt and made the sign of the cross. After two decades of the rosary, her eyes turned toward the niche, an expression of joy came over her face, a transformation ... I was impressed as much as if I had seen the Blessed Virgin.

Antoinette Tardhivail, a witness to the apparitions

Bernadette obeyed the *Dame*, and went daily to the Grotto between 18 February and 4 March 1858. During these days, later termed the 'great fortnight', events took place which made Lourdes famous. She was accompanied by ever increasing crowds and the whole region was enthralled by stories that a girl was seeing visions at the Grotto of Massabielle. Bernadette was to experience a total of eighteen visions, most of which took place during late February and early March 1858.

Most of Bernadette's visits to the Grotto took place early in the morning. She would rise at dawn, and leave to go to the Grotto as soon as she was dressed. Upon arrival she would kneel on the ground, her eyes fixed on the niche in the wall of the Grotto, and would silently pray her rosary. After the third vision, she always brought a lighted candle. Bernadette was surrounded by crowds, and everyone knew when the apparition appeared to her because she would fall into a trance. She claimed that she spoke aloud to the apparition and seemed surprised that the people around her could not hear her voice.

The state officials of Lourdes utterly disapproved of these unexpected events. In turn the Gendarmerie, the Police Commissioner, the Procureur Impérial and the Préfet began to concern themselves with Bernadette's visions, and they tried to halt them. They wanted Bernadette to stop making a spectacle of herself. To them, her actions suggested either madness or an attempt at a fraud. Even more strongly, they wanted to stop the manifestations of popular religion at Massabielle.

The apparitions were to cause a tumultuous disruption of the entire Lourdes community. As in most French provincial towns of the era, conflicts and communications were a question of individual social relations. People lived on terms of familiarity which made personalized intercourse between members of the small middle class almost obligatory. People such as the Curé, the Police Commissioner, and the local bureaucrats all dined together. As Mme Jacomet tersely recalled, after 'that business at the Grotto, our friendship was broken'.[1] During the 'fortnight' of 1858, before such bonds were broken, the relationships of these individuals influenced the unfolding of events. The clergy, the state functionaries, and their various friends, informally sought each other's opinions concerning the news of the Grotto. The middle classes did not only confer with each other, but with their inferiors. The common folk of the town, especially the women, were the main source of miracle stories. Most Lourdes ladies learnt of the events through conversations with their domestic servants, or with poor women who came to their door seeking alms.

Many of the people of Lourdes who went to the Grotto during the visions were later interviewed by Père Cros, who worked from 1875 to 1880 gathering research for his extensive three-volume history of the apparitions. Their statements and memoirs are preserved in the Cros archive and have been partly reproduced in several documentary collections. A smaller number of the surviving witnesses to the apparition also offered their recollections when they were interviewed for the *Procès* of Bernadette's canonization in 1911.

These are valuable sources, although there is the inevitable issue that people's memories were subject to forgetfulness and revision during the twenty years that elapsed between the events and Père Cros's path-breaking research. This problem is known in any oral history project and is particularly marked with events such as those at Lourdes. The actual apparitions were unexpected and occurred amid rumours, conjecture and controversy. People had to interact with the stories they heard, accepting and rejecting different aspects according to their own standpoint, if they were to make any sense of them at all.

The process of selection, elaboration and amendment is vividly enacted in one of the most interesting contemporary records of the apparitions, which are the letters of Adelaide Monlaur.[2] Adelaide Monlaur, a 23-year-old woman, lived at the village of Angles, three kilometres from Lourdes. She lived alone with her father, the village schoolteacher, and most of her days were spent in small duties and local gossip. She was somewhat above the social level of the village women, and decidedly superior in education, but she spoke the local dialect and shared the local beliefs. In her own words, she was 'bored at Angles',[3] where she was used to 'having almost nothing to do'.[4] One of her few diversions was to write to her cousin, a young priest who had recently been employed as a tutor by an affluent family. In a series of lengthy letters during 1858–9, Adelaide Monlaur reported the events at Lourdes, the apparitions, miracles, rumours and controversies which swept the town. She was not the only one writing letters. Another source, even more voluminous than these letters and equally vivid and contemporary to events, are the numerous documents from the state officials who reported to each other on the situation at Lourdes throughout 1858.

The most keen observer of Bernadette and the Grotto was Dominique Jacomet. He was a conspicuous figure in Lourdes, where he had been Police Commissioner for five years. At 37 years old, he was in his prime, and was a handsome, intelligent man. Born in the town of Argelès (Hautes-Pyrénées), he was the son of an unwed mother and had known disadvantage in his youth. He rose by taking advantage of public education and was a good student at the College of Argelès. He was a Catholic, and on good terms with the local priest, but was not notably pious. To judge by reports in *Le Lavedan*, he was a good friend of the brothers Cazenave, who edited the local paper and interested themselves in republican politics, literature and the outside world. Dominique Jacomet was married, and had several children. Despite his limited means – he had only his modest salary and no private income – he had adopted a nephew and raised the child as his own.

The Police Commissioner in Lourdes was somewhat at odds with his surroundings. His superior, Procureur Dutour, judged him to be worthy to be employed in a town with 'a more numerous population, and a less modest position'.[5] The people of Lourdes were in awe of him. As the Field Guard Callet explained:

> We never had anyone like him in the town; he ran things very well, and yet he was not harsh in pressing charges against people; but when he so much as took a step, it was intimidating. He had such charm. When he went to Court, he was not afraid to speak to the lawyers: he would argue back at them, laughing ... You would have thought him a Crown Prosecutor ... A handsome man, very gracious, lighthearted, a face which was pleasing, especially wearing his uniform ...[6]

The Police Commissioner at Lourdes did not conform to a stereotype of the provincial policeman, who was an ignorant reactionary. The humble Gendarmes and Guards, who were used to inconsiderate authority figures, were amazed that he would speak to them as equals and provide them with meals on long watches. As one can see from Callet's description, Commissioner Jacomet was a glamorous figure in the limited society which surrounded him. Probably because of this, both he and his wife were the subjects of gossip and speculation. The Field Guards claimed that Jacomet sometimes went out late at night, and implied that he may have been seeing someone. He and his wife entertained an old acquaintance from Argelès, and stories circulated of drinking and card parties. But there were no serious attacks on his reputation. Even those who disagreed with him, because of his opposition to the shrine at the Grotto, remembered him warmly as a person of exceptional ability and integrity.

Commissioner Jacomet wrote several reports about events in the Grotto, and also kept a notebook in which he jotted accounts of events. His reports are lively and revealing. He recorded all the information that he could, and was very sceptical of the motives of those who talked of miracles in the Grotto. His distinctive figure became part of the drama of the apparitions, and he several times offered his arm to ladies of Lourdes returning from the Grotto.

## Visiting the Grotto

The news that a girl had seen a mysterious *Dame blanche* (white Lady) at Massabielle had already begun to circulate in Lourdes during the period of the first three ambiguous apparitions. Frère Cérase, who worked in the Lourdes school during 1858, recalled of the early stage of the visions, the 'first story was already known, and each interpreted it in their own way; some saying that it was the Virgin Mary appearing on a rock; others believing that it was a soul from purgatory, asking for prayers'.[7]

From 19 February onwards, Bernadette was accompanied by one of her aunts each time she visited the Grotto. Her parents and siblings seem to have been there occasionally. In addition, there were increasing numbers of observers drawn by interest in the story. How many attended the commencement of the fortnight is not known, but Henri Lasserre, who had interviewed the participants, estimated that on the 19th 'one hundred people were found before the Grotto at the time Bernadette arrived. The day after, there were four or five hundred. Several thousands were counted by Sunday morning.'[8] On 1 March 1858 the Procureur Impérial explained that after Bernadette had experienced six visions, 'it was not a little group of people who followed Bernarde [sic] to the Grotto: it was a massive crowd'.[9] These crowds concerned the Police Commissioner and his superiors. They were not noisy or violent, but they were uncontrolled. They flowed around Bernadette, joining her as soon as she left her house and following her to the Grotto. Within days, it was not possible to get a good place at the Grotto unless one had already gathered there in the pre-dawn hours. People spent the night waiting. The only person guaranteed of a place was the visionary, who would nudge past masses of witnesses in order to take her place before the cavity in the rock. Everyone wanted to be within sight of her when the *Dame* appeared.

Almost overnight, Bernadette had become famous in her region, and within a few weeks newspapers in Paris would begin printing stories about the events in Lourdes. She did not communicate with the crowds who surrounded her, but merely returned home from the Grotto and resumed her usual daily round. She worked at domestic tasks and attended catechism classes. Her family was obliged to put up with a great deal of disruption.

The Soubirous parents were left, without authority, to live amid the consequences of their daughter's activities. Poor and disreputable, even within the circle of their own family, they were too dependent upon others to be able to dismiss interference by their more prosperous relatives and fellow citizens. Louise Castérot lamented her unhappy position to many of the people who came to her home in search of Bernadette. One has the impression that she was complaining to anyone who would listen. She told Mlle Estrade: 'I am her unfortunate mother ... you can see what is happening, the police threaten to put us in prison; some laugh at us, others complain against us.'[10]

Adelaide Monlaur visited Bernadette's home in April 1858. She was a total stranger to the family, and turned up because of her interest in the visions. Adelaide Monlaur came from a small village, and had face to face contact with the Pyrenean poor, but even so she was shocked by the misery of the Soubirous dwelling. 'They are so poorly lodged!' But they would accept no alms, from her or anyone. The schoolteacher's daughter was refined enough to impress them, but understanding enough for them to talk to. Louise Castérot told her that the family had suffered dreadfully from 'all the threats which have been made against them' and that 'sometimes she would have preferred to see her little one dead, rather that enduring these painful ordeals which she has caused them'.[11] As an example of the jibes Louise Castérot heard, some people made jokes to the effect that if Bernadette was a saint she should cure her father, who had lost the sight of one eye. This type of comment would wound any family, and even worse were the terrifying police officers with their threats of prison. Bernadette, meanwhile, continued to be oblivious, visiting the Grotto daily, apparently living for the sight of the beautiful white *Aquero*.

Visitors must have added to the stress which the Soubirous parents were feeling, although women such as Adelaide Monlaur may have at least provided sympathy for Louise Castérot. François Soubirous met visitors less often, because he was absent at work. Despite all the uproar, the precarious financial position of the Soubirous family had improved slightly. One notices that the documents written during March and February 1858 describe Bernadette as being at school during the day, her father at work, and her mother and sister at the *cachot*. The miserable period when François Soubirous was entirely unemployed was finally over. He was in work at the time when Bernadette's visions had commenced, and through the following months he was able to get day work as a labourer, while his wife could at least stay at home rather than working in the fields. All of their children remained at home, including Toinette, who would have been sent elsewhere as a servant if matters had been desperate. By mid-1858, the whole town of Lourdes was enjoying some prosperity. The destitution caused by the poor harvests of 1853 and 1855 was finally lifting. Moreover, Lourdes was a market town, and it had never had such influxes of visitors as it was getting now. The winter was over, and there was enough money circulating to employ the cheap labour of men like Bernadette's father.

One resident, Jean-Baptiste Estrade, remembered the first stirrings in Lourdes being marked by activity and excitement among the poorer women, which then spread more widely: 'The common women whispered to each other, at first, of the news; but these confidences were not slow to enter into the public domain, and became the subject of numerous conversations.'[12] Jean-Baptiste Estrade was a civil servant who worked in taxation. He was unmarried and lived with his sister, who like himself later provided a written memoir of the apparitions.

Mlle Estrade recalled that a local woman met her at their door and declared that 'a girl has said that she saw a beautiful lady, so beautiful that it is supposed to be the Blessed Virgin, or perhaps the soul of Mlle Elise Latapie'.[13] Further stories reached Mlle Estrade during following days, and she soon told her brother that 'It is no longer something to laugh at' – no doubt this had been his first reaction – 'the stories of the apparition have come to the attention of serious people and our neighbour, Mme Millet, has accompanied the visionary to the Grotto'.[14] Mlle Estrade resolved to visit the Grotto and, although he greeted the story sceptically, her brother was at least curious.

Before they joined the stream of common people gathering daily at the Grotto the Estrades were offered a different point from which to observe events. On 21 February the Police Commissioner decided to call Bernadette in for an interview. Mme Jacomet informed Mlle Estrade of this event, as the two families lived in adjacent dwellings. Ceding to his sister's 'requests and friendly insistence'[15] Jean-Baptiste Estrade agreed that they would visit their neighbour and be present during the informal interrogation, which took place in Jacomet's parlour on Sunday 21 February 1858.

This encounter between the Police Commissioner and Bernadette was the first time that her recital would be transformed into a written form. Commissioner Jacomet took notes of her replies to his questions and fashioned them into a written statement.[16] The Estrades also reconstructed records of the interview in their memoirs, and their later accounts of the questions and answers tally closely with the Commissioner's contemporary statement. Bernadette also wrote a brief account of this meeting in the *Récit des Apparitions* of 1866.

According to the Estrades' accounts Bernadette was calm in manner, with a voice which was loud but pleasant in tone.[17] They remained discreetly at the back of the room and could not observe her well as she was 'wrapped in the traditional capulet of the Pyrenees' or, in Mlle Estrade's opinion, 'hidden in an unattractive hood'.[18] By means of numerous direct questions the Police Commissioner extracted a story of the apparitions from his passive witness, and from this conversation he then wrote a narrative, in the first person, of the events. The statement described how the three girls went to Massabielle, where Bernadette beheld a dazzling light, and a beautiful white thing, which was like a girl. This white object had been there again, on other occasions, and had asked Bernadette to return every day for a fortnight. There are two points where Bernadette's statement of February 1858 differs from the later narratives of Lourdes. Faced with the Police Commissioner she prudently stated that their errand had been 'collecting bones'[19] rather than gathering wood. Like everyone in the Pyrenees, she would have been aware that any mention of wood-gathering would have led to allegations of theft.

Bernadette's statement nominated the vision first as 'something white' and then as '*aquero*' (that).[20] This must have been an issue of contention between herself and the Commissioner. Mlle Estrade recalled the question and reply '– You say that it is the Virgin Mary who appears to you? – I do not know if it is her: she has not said it to me.'[21] The Police Commissioner's question was natural. In his draft statement, Jacomet did write 'the Virgin' when describing the appearances and actions of Bernadette's vision. However, in the final version, it is referred to as *aquero* throughout. In this fair copy *aquero* is italicized and written large. The single Bigourdanian word appears as an anomaly which disrupts the page of slanted French writing. The ambiguity may have puzzled the Commissioner, but he did record Bernadette's own terminology.

Commissioner Jacomet questioned Bernadette concerning many points and tried to trap her into contradictions in her description of events. Bernadette later wrote that she had 'replied sharply ... Then, he started to get angry and kept saying it was so, and I always kept replying that it was not.'[22]

Stalled in his attempt to discredit the story of an apparition of 'something' which had the form of a young girl, Jacomet impatiently told Bernadette that he knew her statement was 'a made-up story' and threatened her with prison. According to Jean-Baptiste Estrade's account, he said:

> 'You hope to trick me as you did the simple women of your *quartier:* you are too stupid to succeed, and your sweet ways are not enough for it. Enough of these jokes: I will send for the Gendarmes, prepare to go to prison.' Bernadette remained impassive.[23]

This stand-off was resolved by the arrival of Bernadette's father. The Police Commissioner threatened that as Bernadette was a minor, her parents could be prosecuted: 'If she continues these pious farces at Massabielle, I will arrest you and prosecute you according to the full force of the law.'[24] François Soubirous was abject before such an authority figure and he assured the Commissioner that both he and Bernadette's mother were against the whole thing.[25]

Because of their poverty, the Soubirous parents were consistently suspected of having arranged the visions in order to benefit themselves. They did not have Bernadette's disinterested and serene manner which attracted a qualified respect even from hostile officials. As the Procureur Impérial wrote in his report of 1 March 1858, Bernadette 'has absolutely not seemed, and still does not seem to this day, to hope personally for any material benefits ... Her parents are less immune from suspicion: their past behaviour, leading to their present conduct, permits one to presume that the motives which inspire them are far from pure.'[26] This report went on to note that Louise Castérot was known to be a heavy drinker, and François Soubirous's arrest on suspicion of theft was also inevitably cited as relevant information.

When François Soubirous attended the interrogation of 21 February 1858, he 'timidly showed his face'[27] and agreed to everything that was demanded of him. Bernadette remained calm and gave no undertaking that she would not return to the Grotto. Her attitude was unexpected. Contemporary writers described the quailing demeanour of the poor as a natural feature of their condition. Henri Lasserre, when writing of the nervous reaction of Bernadette's companions as they first heard her story on their return from Massabielle, stated that 'they were afraid, the children of the poor are always fearful. That is all too explicable: misfortune comes at them from all directions.'[28]

There was another possible reaction, which stood in contradiction to that of the cringing individual. This was the anti-authoritarian solidarity of the disadvantaged when they formed a group. The quick arousal of the defiance of a crowd was the nerve-racking possibility that made the officials of the mid-nineteenth-century French state so fearful, despite their apparently overwhelming power. There was a resentment which always seethed, and put a great number of people unthinkingly in opposition to them. As a French priest wrote in 1856, when describing the lower-class populations of the towns: 'Unfortunately, in their eyes the authorities are always wrong, and they never fail to side against the local officials.'[29] This was a sentiment which a girl in Bernadette's position could count on.

Estrade noted that the 'detention of the girl had caused some agitation'[30] and that a crowd gathered outside Commissioner Jacomet's residence. This crowd would no doubt have grown larger and more hostile as an hour and a half passed.[31] In her account of this event she did not mention her father's reaction to the Commissioner but she did write that:

> From time to time, I heard kicking at the doors and windows and voices calling out: 'If you do not let her out, we will break the door down.' ... So much for the first time that I was obliged to appear before those gentlemen.[32]

Her calm certainty brought her through this occasion. The interrogation would be followed by others, but each would follow the same course, the visionary obdurate, the official frustrated, and the people of Lourdes gathering angrily outside.

Some of the Commissioner's questions and comments show that he believed in a type of conspiracy behind Bernadette. He asked her, 'Is there not someone who has taught you the statement which you just gave us?'[33] and he later told Jean-Baptiste Estrade that: 'It is not from her. There is a snake in the grass.'[34] Yet the description she gave of the vision was quite simple, and not beyond the creative powers of an ordinary girl:

> She wore a white robe, gathered at the waist with a blue ribbon. Her head, up to the forehead, is covered with a white veil which falls down her back. Her feet, which one can barely see under the hem of the robe, are bare, but each is ornamented with a bright yellow rose.[35]

This could be a description of any statue of the Virgin in a village church, and Bernadette herself was later to say that the vision was 'like the Virgin of the parish'.[36] The statue which Bernadette apparently referred to was differently coloured, but had the same dress and pose.

Bernadette's early recitals were probably impressive and unexpected because of her manner of delivering them. She was remembered as being 'little and shy'[37] prior to the visions. Her reversal of character was striking. Bernadette's neighbours observed that 'That child was previously very timid, but now she is not; she speaks out with an energy and clarity which is astonishing.'[38]

When speaking about the unknown being of Massabielle, Bernadette had taken up a role that made her the focus of her community's vital interest in the supernatural. She had passed from the unimportant sector of life, in which she had engaged in futile struggles to make her First Communion and earn her living, into the extraordinary and supernatural, where adults hung upon her every word in reply to their questions. Many people also enjoyed supporting her during confrontations with the authorities, and she was the occasion, not the cause, of the outpouring of much existing resentment.

A minor anecdote of Bernadette's defiance, and the satisfying spectacle which it provided to those around her, was given by Julie Garros, a schoolchild at the Hospice. She recalled that early in 1858 one of the teachers, Sr Anastasie, cornered Bernadette in the schoolyard and exclaimed: 'Ah! you have not yet finished with your carnival?' Bernadette's response, 'No, my dear Sister, not yet,' was astonishing to the children around. Julie Garros explained that: 'We were surprised by that answer because we knew Bernadette to be timid, but we were very pleased by it, for we heartily detested Sr Anastasie.'[39] During the time of the apparitions, the weakest members of the Lourdes community had the rare chance to defy authority. At the lowest level of society there was an overt enjoyment of such a display, which, in its temporary inversion of authority, did resemble the carnival to which Sr Anastasie contemptuously compared it.

During the carnival season prior to Lent, the energies and dreams of the poor were awakened amid traditional festivals of rebellion, and the bounds of reality, dignity and order were fragile. Both the state officials and the church authorities of the Pyrenees disliked carnivalesque behaviour and considered it to be a pretext for disorder and immorality. The first of Bernadette's visions had taken place on *jeudi gras*, the last day of the festivals which preceded the season of repentance, and this alone would have roused the suspicions of the religious authorities. Several of the Sisters, and also Curé Peyramale, complained of Bernadette's behaviour as an 'unworthy Carnival'.[40] The carnival was succeeded by Lent during the fortnight, but, as will be shown later, the penitential practices of popular religion were no less an affront to educated sensibilities than their festivals.

Bernadette had need of her 'impassive assurance',[41] because criticisms and even blows came down on her from all sides, not only from those in authority. Even among those who accompanied her to the Grotto, there were many drawn simply by curiosity as their judgements of events vacillated. One Sister recalled that some of the other children at school mocked Bernadette, and that they went so far that the teachers had to punish them.[42] A woman who worked as a servant in the town stated that when she first heard of Bernadette during the early apparitions, 'people said that she was bewitched and insane'.[43] Sophie Pailhasson, another resident of Lourdes, went to the trouble of waiting outside the school to confront Bernadette and slap her, exclaiming '*Drôle! Drôle!*'[44] Many years later, when outrage had given way to veneration, Sophie apologized for this incident and Bernadette replied that she had forgotten it.[45] She was to be apparently impervious to the disapproval of others during the entire time of the visions.

Commissioner Jacomet had succeeded at least in intimidating Bernadette's parents. During the days following 21 February they would not talk of the apparitions nor permit people to see Bernadette. They forbade their daughter to visit the Grotto, but when she left home to go to school she changed direction and ran through the town, already attracting a following of curious people, and took up her usual pose when she arrived at the Grotto. However, 22 February was to be one of the few occasions on which the *Dame* did not appear. Bernadette knelt and recited her rosary but left half an hour later, visibly disappointed.

Three Gendarmes were present at the Grotto during Bernadette's visit of 22 February. One was stationed there and two others had followed her through the town. People at the Grotto blamed the Gendarmes for the non-appearance of the apparition. The Sergeant of the Garrison was irritated by the allegation that his presence might have deterred an appearance of the Virgin Mary. He later said that he had told Bernadette: 'If you were not a little idiot, I say again, you would know that the Virgin has no fear of Gendarmes because she is without reproach.'[46] Despite this failure, Bernadette was determined to continue to keep her promise to *aquero* and visit the Grotto daily. Her parents discovered that it was useless to try to prevent her. As her mother lamented to Mlle Estrade 'she is not usually disobedient, but she told me that she felt herself pushed to go by something that she could not explain'.[47]

Aside from this mysterious compulsion, Bernadette had received advice from alternative authority figures who told her that she would not be prevented from visiting the Grotto. Her aunt, Bernarde Castérot, said that she could go, and like Mme Millet, she volunteered to continue to accompany her. The attitude of these women did not originate from a religious conviction that the Virgin Mary was appearing at Massabielle. They were filled with awe and dread, but acted as if the apparition's request for daily visits was an imperative. Bernarde Castérot explained that she had not known what to think, but had often exclaimed: ' "May the Lord keep us from evil!" We had to await the end of the fortnight to discover what it would be.'[48]

Not all women took this view. Fanny Nicolau, a Lourdes schoolteacher who sometimes employed Louise Castérot as a laundry-woman, was so convinced that Bernadette's visits to the Grotto would lead to trouble that she went to the Soubirous's home to warn them that these activities must cease. There she was met by the *femmes du quartier* and she quoted them as exclaiming to her: ' "Who are you to forbid that little one from doing her duty? The Lady told her to come for a fortnight." I said to them: "Will you go to prison for her?" '[49] However, people around Bernadette had already perceived that charges would not easily be laid.

On 23 February, the day following the disappointing non-appearance of the apparition, Bernadette returned to the Grotto. A crowd awaited her. Aside from the Gendarmes, there were a number of ladies, among them Mlle Estrade, and a small group of professional men such as the local doctor. These people were distinct in their clothing, their attitudes and their manners from the peasant devotees.

Mlle Estrade had been visited on the previous evening by a group of ladies who formed the project of visiting the Grotto. They needed Jean-Baptiste Estrade's escort, for unlike the women of Bernadette's class they did not have freedom of movement. As Mlle Estrade explained: 'at that time it was not respectable for ladies to venture out, during the hours of darkness, on the streets'.[50] Her brother did not want to join this party of ladies. He knew that he would be noticed: 'at that time all eyes were fixed on the Grotto, and I feared the ridicule'.[51] As a man, he took it for granted that he could go where he wished, but he feared that he would be laughed at if he was seen to be caught up in the visions of a peasant girl. Jean-Baptiste's intentions were changed both by his sister's pleas and by an unexpected recommendation by Curé Peyramale, whom he met that evening. The Curé had already forbidden any of the clergy to visit the Grotto, but he wished the Estrades to report on events to him: 'I would not be annoyed if some serious people were witnesses of what is going on.'[52]

The Estrades and their friends arrived at Massabielle at about 6am, shortly before Bernadette appeared. Jean-Baptiste Estrade was relieved to find that some of his social equals had likewise been drawn to Massabielle:

At one corner of the Grotto was a group of gentlemen of Lourdes, conversing in an animated fashion. They were, among others, M. Dozous, the doctor, M. Dufo, lawyer, M. de Lafitte, former military officer, and the Captain who at that time commanded the citadel. I went to join the gentlemen and took part in their conversation. Naturally, the question of Bernadette was being discussed: some of them saw this as a case of illness; others, as an optical illusion; ... No one dreamt of the possibility of supernatural intervention; that was a possibility out of season or reason.[53]

Dr Dozous, one of these gentlemen who were present, later claimed that he had gone to the Grotto 'with the secret hope of destroying, with only a word in the name of science, all that puerile edifice of pathological mysticism'.[54] Among such men, an attitude of superiority was obligatory. Jean-Baptiste Estrade wrote that upon his arrival he saw many 'common women kneeling in prayer. I could hardly repress a smile at the facile faith of these good Christians.'[55] According to Estrade's memoir, these sentiments were to be swept aside shortly after Bernadette arrived. She knelt on the ground in prayer, her manner as normal as if she were in the parish church, and then went into a trance. In his memoir, Jean-Baptiste Estrade wrote of her appearance as extremely moving:

Suddenly transformed, Bernadette was no longer Bernadette ... she was like an angel in prayer, reflecting in her features all of the glory of the heavens. ... Her head bowed with an ineffable charm. Everyone understood that the Blessed Virgin was there. The entire crowd fell, by instinct, to their knees ... We, positivists of the first rank, so proud until that moment, we knelt like children.[56]

Jean-Baptiste Estrade recalled that as they returned to the town Dr Dozous 'invited us to moderate our initial enthusiasms: he told us that there were real illnesses which could cause such a change and that the line which separates the natural and supernatural was very difficult to draw'.[57]

Mlle Estrade spoke to Curé Peyramale and assured him that her brother had been 'very moved'[58] during the events at the Grotto. Another priest, at that time in the junior position of a vicar, was given an account by his sister, Mlle Pène. Deprived of the sight of the visionary herself, Abbé Pène seems to have projected the allure of her glamour onto his informant. Years later he wrote that he could still recall the sight of his sister when she returned from Massabielle: 'she seemed to have come from another world, and she spoke to me of the scenes at the Grotto with such a tone of conviction, that I in my turn was very moved'.[59] Such news spread. Dominiquette Cazenave recalled that she had no intention of going to the Grotto until she was impressed by the words of Dorosie Tarbès, a retired schoolteacher, whom she met on the route to Massabielle. 'I said to her, "You as well, Dorosie?" She replied: "I was like you, but I have seen; believe me, there is something to it." '[60]

## Penance, penance, penance

The same events, and the same reactions, were repeated the following days. Bernadette again knelt before her invisible lady, to the awe and wonder of most spectators. She would pray, stare and sometimes move her lips in communication with the *Dame*. Although Bernadette seemed oblivious to her surroundings, she became agitated if people touched the rosebush, and members of the crowd would tell others not to go too near it. Bernadette said that the *Dame* was standing above the plant, which grew out of the niche, and that she was afraid that the apparition would fall.

The size of the crowds which gathered had continued to increase. By 24 February the small group of literate and 'respectable' people was augmented by Fanny Nicolau, the Lourdes schoolmistress. Despite her initial attitude of disapproval, she had been prevailed upon to go to the Grotto by her maid servant, who had protested that 'all of our neighbourhood goes to the Grotto at Massabielle, we are the only ones not going!'[61] Fanny Nicolau found: 'That change in the physiognomy (of Bernadette) was very striking, I burst into tears. M. Dufo (a Lourdes lawyer), who was only a few steps away from me, could not stay, he was so overwhelmed.' [62] Fanny Nicolau watched Bernadette closely and noticed that her colour fluctuated. At times she was absorbed in the vision and appeared transformed. During other intervals she returned to normal and was aware of her surroundings. This would happen if she moved about and no longer fixed her eyes on the niche.

It was during this vision, the eighth time that Bernadette had seen the apparition, that she began to perform penitential exercises. She heard *aquero* say, *'Penitenço ... Penitenço ... Penitenço'* (penance, penance, penance) and she also heard an exhortation to kiss the ground and pray for the conversion of sinners. It was the season of Lent, when repentance was enjoined on the faithful, and these messages added to the religious identity of the apparition. Bernadette had not yet given any name to her vision. Most people around her proceeded on the assumption that this was an apparition of the Virgin Mary and, by conveying messages of such overt piety, Bernadette edged closer to conceding this vital point.

The performance of penitential acts was a standard part of Catholic devotional practice, but the forms and understandings of penance were very varied. In this, as in so many aspects of the faith, the popular and institutional forms of religion were at odds during the nineteenth century. Educated clerical norms tended to advocate individual acts of penance which required a moral self-scrutiny. Popular religion maintained an older tradition of external gestures performed in public by individuals or groups as a part of rituals of repentance, pilgrimage and celebration. Penance, therefore, was already a contested practice with competing ideas of what could be considered suitable, genuine and holy. Bernadette's gesture of kissing the ground was not among the repertoire of folk beliefs which preserved the norms of the Middle Ages. As a corporeal penance, kissing the ground was an orthodox Catholic gesture common to all classes and much practised in religious houses. Despite this, the particular context of Bernadette's action, kissing the muddy earth of an unsanctified open area, was the type of thing which could repel educated observers. During the next vision, she was to strain the tolerance of her audience much further.

On 25 February, the crowds gathered at Massabielle were so large that for the first time witnesses record that it was difficult to find a place to stand. The Estrades were present and they had persuaded their friend Mlle Elfrida Lacrampe to accompany them. She had not wished to attend 'one of those *séances* of Bernadette'[63] and she was never to be fully convinced of the truth of the apparitions. Jean-Baptiste Estrade finally convinced her to visit the Grotto by a comparison which he often made in regard to Bernadette. He claimed that even the celebrated actress Rachel had never made on stage 'poses as beautiful at those of Bernadette at the Grotto'.[64] Already, less than two weeks after the carnivalesque beginnings, the visions were being appreciated according to the norms of cultured entertainment. Elfrida Lacrampe's first sight of Bernadette was as she walked toward the Grotto: 'The way in which she presented herself slightly displeased me: in pushing through the crowds who had preceded her to the Grotto, she said, several times, and in a voice which I found impatient: "Let me through! Let me through!" ' Worse still, Elfrida Lacrampe noticed something which others did not. When Bernadette lifted her rosary to begin her prayers, she crossed herself with the crucifix, but she held it wrongly – head downward: 'That is a terrible and a forbidden thing.'[65] Presumably, it was an error on Bernadette's part. It is one of those hints of the malevolent, like the disappearance of the Lady when Marie Hillet threw holy water, which can be found in stories of the Lourdes apparitions.

On this occasion, as during the third vision in the company of Mme Millet and during the earlier attempt at penance, Bernadette did not fall into a profound trance. Rather than remaining in rapt immobility as she recited the rosary, she was engaged in attempted activities and her appearance was not transformed. She began walking about on her knees and went so far into the Grotto that she was in a narrow space between the rock roof and the damp earthen floor. She kissed the ground several times then turned again to look up at the niche with her face 'all muddy'.[66] To the astonishment of the crowd, she picked some grass and ate it, smeared mud over her face, then, after three unsuccessful attempts, swallowed some mud. Her aunts, Basile and Lucile, were distressed by her actions and wiped her face. Jean-Baptiste Estrade wrote that a 'feeling of sadness spread among the onlookers'[67] and people said that she was insane. Elfrida Lacrampe refused to believe 'that the Blessed Virgin presided over such bizarre actions and, it seemed to me, in human terms, to be all quite ridiculous'.[68] Everyone present seemed disconcerted as 'nothing, it was said, had gone as normal'.[69] They looked differently at the visionary: 'her prestige was gone'.[70] Bernadette remained indifferent to her surroundings and returned to her usual place to pray for a short while before leaving.

Jean-Baptiste Estrade wrote that the Grotto emptied much more quickly than on previous days. Bernarde Castérot remembered that people from the crowd mocked them: 'we went away quickly to escape the crowd; people reacted to us as if we were a laughing stock'.[71] Estrade returned home, sadly reflecting on the shocking possibility, 'Bernadette insane!'[72] He was shaken in his beliefs but acknowledged that it 'was painful, nevertheless, to detach myself from my sweet illusions'.[73] He was unable to leave it at that. Once lured into belief, it was difficult to abandon it. On the same afternoon he sent for Bernadette, to question her, and found her 'as she always was, with her air of tranquillity, confident and pleasant'.[74] The jeers from the erstwhile sympathetic crowds had left her unmoved, just as she had been before their extravagant admiration. Bernadette explained that the apparition had pointed to the ground and had told her to drink of the water of the spring, to wash in it and to eat the herb that grew there. This was the area where she had scraped the earth and, after three attempts, had gathered enough muddy water to swallow. From that time onwards she would explain her actions with the words: 'The vision told me to do so, for penance.'[75]

The news of the visionary's ridiculous antics on 25 February seems to have circulated slowly. Although the Grotto was deserted that day, with only 'some women, with persistent faith, continuing to say their rosary',[76] another large crowd gathered on 26 February, the day following the fiasco. The floor of the Grotto, always muddy, was now flowing with water. On 26 February, Bernadette visited the Grotto but did not have any vision. As on 22 February she prayed the rosary, then left disappointed. At some time during that or the following day it was noticed that the water in the Grotto was part of a constant stream. The *Dame*'s instructions to Bernadette suddenly took on a meaning, and Massabielle was graced with a frequently found amenity of shrines to the Virgin Mary – a holy spring.

Bernadette's manual excavation had taken place at the site of a mountain spring. It had always existed, because water flowed on the floor of the Grotto, but it appeared to increase in volume and regularity from that time onward. This may have been because the flow was clarified as local people dug around the source and cleared the stony ground. The uncovering of the spring was of course seen as a miracle. The debacle of 25 February was reversed. Henceforward, when Bernadette would kiss the ground, the crowds would do so as well. But no-one, then or since, took up the practice of eating grass at the Grotto. Bernadette herself only did it on the day when the *Dame* asked her to.

On the afternoon of 25 February, Bernadette was told to present herself before the Procureur Impérial,[77] who occupied a house and office in the better area of Lourdes. Louise Castérot accompanied Bernadette during the interrogation, and their neighbour André Sajoux waited outside. The

Procureur questioned her at length and tried to claim that there were discrepancies between her answers to him and her earlier *procès-verbal*. Bernadette replied that 'I told him that I had recounted the same things and if the Commissioner was deceived, it was too bad for him.'[78] She could hear the noise of a crowd outside, who had gathered to call for her release. André Sajoux claimed that 'M. Dutour said to her: "It is only beasts who want to eat grass!" Bernadette smiled, and did not reply to him.'[79]

Procureur Dutour was obliged to ascertain Bernadette's plans, and to understand what her own reasons were for acting this way. He argued with her, but did not prevail. His own account of the conversation is as follows:

—Do you have the intention to go to the Grotto every morning? – Yes Monsieur: I have promised to go there for a fortnight.
—But you have been told that this vision is a dream, an illusion; you should not pay attention to such nonsense. The Sisters, who instruct you and who are very pious women, have told you so: why not follow their advice? You would avoid all of this trouble. – I feel too much joy when I visit the Grotto.
—Take care: there are people who suspect that you and your parents want to exploit people's credulity. I could think so myself: your family is poor; since your visits to the Grotto, you have been given all sorts of comforts which you never had before, and you are hoping for more. I must tell you that if you are not sincere in this story of apparitions, or if you or your parents get any profits from it, you will be exposed as a fraud and will be prosecuted and severely condemned. – I expect no profits in this life.[80]

This conversation is quite typical, in that the official had a great deal more to say than Bernadette. Her replies are brief and cold. The official's description of her family is contemptuous, and the tone very threatening. It is understandable that the Soubirous refused every offer made to them, even gifts of traditional charity which they were entitled to. Suspected of fraud, Bernadette refused the slightest present. When a neighbour offered her the last of the old season's apples, she declined it. No wonder, when one considers the words of the Procureur.

Procureur Dutour looked thoughtfully at Bernadette, and he later wrote an account which showed a certain amount of respect. 'As far as Bernadette Soubirous was concerned, she had a very simple style, common even, at first glance. There was nothing about her face which attracted attention. No artifice in her clothing: very clean, which indicated self-respect despite her poverty – that was all.' He found her way of speaking sincere, and when she spoke of 'uncommon thoughts' her features had a striking charm. All that he could see of her was her face. She wore a headscarf 'which covered half her brow, and which was folded around her hair so closely that nothing but the shape of her head could be seen'.[81] Over this went a shawl, and he thought that her clothes were so heavy that they must have made her laboured breathing worse.

Finally, the Procureur threatened to put Bernadette in prison, and her mother burst into tears. Bernadette had a ready reply. 'I consoled her, saying:

"You are too good to cry because we are going to prison, because we have done no harm to anyone." '[82] The Procureur then offered Bernadette and her mother chairs, as they had remained standing for more than an hour. Louise Castérot accepted his offer, but Bernadette was contemptuous. She exclaimed, 'No, we would dirty it!' and sat on the floor.[83] This reply was preserved and delightedly repeated by the common people of Lourdes. 'I, who was so naughty,' she said remorsefully many years later, when she recounted this event as a Sister in a prestigious convent.[84] At the time she had no regrets and remained defiant. Eventually the Soubirous women were allowed to leave, and they were taken by André Sajoux to a local café where they drank wine and gave their supporters an account of their experiences.[85]

Bernadette probably refused the chair because she sensed the Procureur's scorn for her mother and herself. Despite his memory of her fine gaze and clean hands, he was not won over by this slum child. And he knew what to think of her family and friends. When M. Dutour wrote his report he noted the poor reputations of her parents and added that the sight of these 'miserable people, their language, above all their standards and their reputation were of such a nature to destroy any charm, and to inspire, not only doubt but also disgust'. They were, he wrote, poor intermediaries for the Virgin Mary 'who is regarded as the Being of perfect purity'.[86] The state officials were developing an animosity for the devotees of the Grotto, and this emotion, as individual as the charm and interest found by the Estrades, was to be a factor in later events.

The Procureur Impérial warned Bernadette that she should cease visiting the Grotto, but as his own report stated, he was 'very soon convinced'[87] that he would not be able to stop her by any means short of incarceration. This would be difficult to justify as he had no evidence of fraud. He conferred with the Police Commissioner, who also consulted the Mayor, and it was decided that 'one must wait'.[88] Extra policing was to be arranged for 4 March, 'the day of the last visit ... and at the same time market day in Lourdes'.[89] The Procureur Impérial grimly concluded his letter with an assurance that if 'firmness should be necessary ... I would find it consistent with my sense of duty'.[90] Stories had arisen that some marvellous event would conclude the fortnight. The state officials wondered if there might not be rioting, looting and disorder.

On 27 and 28 February, Bernadette continued to follow penitential exercises at the Grotto, walking on her knees and kissing the earth, as well as praying the rosary and contemplating the apparition. The finding of the spring had vindicated her actions, and after 25 February many members of the crowd would kiss the ground when she did. Despite this, her gestures were still disagreeable to an educated eye. Antoine Clarens, a teacher in the municipal elementary school at Lourdes, visited the Grotto for the first time on 27 February, and his reactions mirror those of Jean-Baptiste Estrade. He was amazed by the transformation of Bernadette's features when she entered a trance. She was unrecognizable with her 'indefinable smile, her strange pallor, ... you would have said that she was no longer of this world'.[91] While she remained kneeling in prayer and absorbed by the vision she seemed divine, but this was disrupted by her crawling around the Grotto and throwing herself forward to kiss the ground. Antoine Clarens drew back: 'I had been strongly impressed by her first pose. Her comings and goings, made with great activity, were very disagreeable to me.'[92] In common with the Estrades, he sought out Bernadette to clarify his opinions by hearing an account from her. He was impressed by her recital and claimed that it would convert anyone: 'go and hear her, you who show cynical attitudes'.[93] As the Procureur Impérial wrote on 1 March 1858, many people believed her to be mentally ill, 'but the number is very great, and growing, of people of all social ranks, who believe her to be in direct communication with the Divinity'.[94]

It is difficult to estimate the effect of Bernadette's penitential exercises on the whole of her audience, as it was chiefly the middle-class individuals who left records of their reactions to events as they happened. It seems that everyone was surprised and recoiled from her mud-covered face, so different from the reports of her beauty during ecstatic trances. People of Bernadette's own class had rather relaxed standards of hygiene and decorum, while they were also often tolerant of apparent insanity in visionaries. Yet in this case the entire crowd seems to have been struck by a reversal of feeling. Madeleine Barbazat, an old friend and drinking companion of Louise Castérot, said that she had only attended two of Bernadette's visions, and that it 'gave me a pain in the heart to see her, in ecstasy, rise and descend from her knees, often in the mud'.[95] Even the visionary herself probably found these actions a painful effort. In later years, when Bernadette described the famous scene of the finding of the spring she added an unusual note of self-explanation and commented that it had cost her dear to swallow water so impure that it was virtually mud, 'the water was quite dirty'.[96]

Bernadette's actions of penance were very mild compared with the excessive and repellent acts which were celebrated from the lives of the saints from previous eras. She did not eat lice like St Catherine of Genoa, nor kiss the sores of lepers like St Francis of Assisi. During her own time the ascetic lives of these medieval saints were recounted with veneration, but a subtle change of consciousness had taken place. It was desirable to regard such excesses as holy but not literally to imitate them. This refinement of taste had yet to penetrate the common and uneducated level of Catholic congregations, who still regarded ostentatious penances with awe, even if they rarely actually participated in them. The nineteenth-century church did not formally change its ideals of penance and asceticism but instead participated in an evolution of taste which implicitly rejected some corporeal penances in their practical, rather than ideal, existence.

This standpoint was uneasy and inconsistent, and it was in a state of flux during Bernadette's lifetime. An example of the survival of the classic penitential ideal was the beatification in 1860 of Benedict Labre, an eighteenth-century French mendicant who upheld traditional penances in the defiantly anti-modern forms of being unwashed and idle. All his life he was a wanderer, who begged for his bread and prayed. He was a difficult man to understand, even to the few people who sympathized with him. But he showed evidence of exceptional graces and after his death his fame spread. Finally, he was made a saint. The honour paid to him caused significant debate during the 1860s, which indicates the shifting tides of opinion. Yves-Marie Hilaire has written of the 1860 beatification as 'a scandal for the bourgeoisie of the Second Empire'[97] because Labre was a marginal eccentric who notably failed to live up to the nineteenth-century virtues of cleanliness and industry. For some people, Benedict Labre was an example of religious fervour, to others a proof of the retrograde and non-rational nature of the Catholic faith. The canonization of Benedict Labre has been extensively analysed by historians of French religion.[98] It illustrates the manner in which some archaic Catholic traditions were still so tenacious in the mid-nineteenth century that they required incorporation into Catholicism as an institution. But these beliefs were in conscious non-conformity to modern social standards and had to be upheld on a combative note. People who believed in Benedict Labre tended to be ultramontanes who also believed that the world had been a better place before industrialization and literacy.

The public persona extracted from Bernadette's life interacted more creatively with anti-modernism than the flouting of Benedict Labre's medieval virtues. Bernadette also was to be seen as a figure from the pre-industrial past. In her case, the role was of the ideal peasant girl from the vanishing world of traditional France. Her virtues of simplicity, innocence and miraculousness were naturally appealing to the nostalgia of the industrializing world, and these themes were also a part of secular culture. However, she could be honoured as a picturesque peasant girl only if she showed no signs of some of the real features of peasant life such as extrovert emotions and indifference to dirt.

The penitential visions of 21 to 28 February were the only occasions when Bernadette did anything which jarred the sensitivities of educated persons, and the apologetics made necessary by these brief episodes disclose the regulation of perception required in the institution of the Lourdes cult. During her lifetime, Bernadette was often confronted by people who complained that her activities during the finding of the spring were 'repugnant events; the Blessed Virgin could not have ordered them'.[99] Many, like the Procureur, thought that eating grass was acting like an animal. Bernadette tended to ask such people: 'Do you not eat salad?' This was one of her famous unanswerable replies. Others made more laboured explanations and the earliest official history of Lourdes was obliged to concede that it might seem that: 'it was not worthy of the Most Blessed Virgin, to have ordered Bernadette to drink muddy water and to wash her face in it. But does one not find a natural explanation of this difficulty, when one considers that, by these means, in a striking manner, the Blessed Virgin demonstrated the simplicity, the good faith and the obedience of the young girl?'[100]

The penitential aspect of the message of Lourdes was so unappealing to modern culture that it was downplayed and eventually forgotten. It is an irony that the statements of Our Lady of Lourdes, as reported by Bernadette, made no mention of miracles of healing, although it is for this that the shrine is now famous. The only specific injunctions offered by the apparition were the calls to perform penance, which were not to be incorporated into the eventual message of the shrine. The historian Thomas Kselman has pointed out that the substitution of a message of miraculous healing for one of penance occurred at several nineteenth-century French shrines.[101]

## A chapel and a procession

Bernadette ceased her penitential practices after 1 March. From this time forward her only activity at the Grotto was to kneel in silent adoration of her vision. On 2 March she received another message, which was to further increase the tempo of events. According to Bernadette, she was instructed to tell the priests that they should build a chapel at the site and that a procession should be held.[102] Bernadette set out for the presbytery, accompanied by her two aunts, Bernarde and Basile Castérot. Her aim was to deliver this audacious request to Curé Peyramale, a senior cleric who had held himself aloof from the events at Massabielle. Even Bernadette's redoubtable aunts were afraid to face the Curé. As Basile Castérot explained, 'to hear M. le Curé especially, that made one nervous'.[103]

Their apprehension was justified. Bernadette scarcely had time to say one sentence before Curé Peyramale exploded into an angry lecture. His reply to Bernadette encapsulated several of the points about the events in the Grotto which appeared dubious to a clerical eye – the reputation of the visionary's family, the popular uproar roused by the events, and their effective pre-emption of the powers of the priesthood:

> He walked about his room, angrily, saying: 'It is an unhappy thing to have a family like this, which creates disorder in the town of Lourdes and does nothing but make people run around! ... We could do even better: we could give you a torch of your own, you can go and make the procession; everyone would follow you, you have no need of priests!'[104]

The Curé cross-questioned Bernadette, finding her vague and unimpressive in her recital. Dominiquette Cazenave heard that 'M. le Curé had said to Bernadette, "Are you sure of this?" [i.e. that a procession should be held] "*Qu'a crédi*: I believe so," Bernadette would have said; and M. le Curé exclaimed: "Then you are not sure!" '[105] Bernadette was unable to say when the procession should be held or whom it should consist of. Her aunts left with her, feeling crushed 'like grains of millet'.[106] Despite this, Bernadette insisted that she return, later the same afternoon. In the face of the Curé's rage, she had been unable to deliver the second part of her message and only remembered it after she returned home. The *Dame* wanted a chapel as well as a procession. She was unable to convince either her parents or her aunts to return with her to the presbytery: finally she found a companion in a Lourdes woman who had recently employed her father to drive her cart. Dominiquette Cazenave had already spoken privately to the Curé and had told him that she regretted that he had never seen 'that girl in ecstasy'.[107]

When Bernadette returned on the evening of 2 March the Curé was with his two vicars. He again scolded her, although less loudly than during their first meeting. To the request for a chapel he asked her, as he had before, for the *Dame's* name. Bernadette replied that she did not know it. The vicars plied Bernadette with questions. The early rumours of a *Dame blanche* must still have been current, for one of the vicars asked: 'Have you heard talk of fairies?' and 'of witches'.[108] Bernadette replied no, which he thought must be a lie, because everyone in Lourdes had heard of witches. She had no idea what he was talking about, because he had used the French, rather than the dialect word for witch. Dominiquette Cazenave explained the word to her, but by then the conversation had taken a different turn. Curé Peyramale insisted that they must know more about the *Dame*. Bernadette left without having convinced him but was contented: 'I have done my task.'

The last two days of the fortnight were remarkable only for the unprecedented numbers at Massabielle. Some people believed that there would be a miracle on the final day of the fortnight. Visitors were arriving from all parts of the Hautes-Pyrénées and thousands were constantly assembled around the Grotto. On 3 March, the Police Commissioner wrote that all the valleys from Lourdes to Pau 'have provided their contingent of curious people. What will it be like tomorrow, market day and completion of the fortnight?'[109] Commissioner Jacomet was afraid of general forms of disorder, and he also was apprehensive of accidents that might take place because of the congestion of great numbers of people on the steeply elevated land around the Grotto.[110] He wrote that a single stone falling from above could cause grievous effects. In the event, no serious accident was to occur, but people were certainly at risk. One witness recorded that he had almost fallen into the Gave river,[111] and a spectator at a different vision was knocked off her feet when the crowd surged with excitement at the arrival of Bernadette.[112] These types of minor accidents were an indication of the serious injuries which always threaten when a crowd gathers in an unsupervised space.

Troops and Gendarmes were brought to Lourdes on special duties. They were instructed to be in full regimental dress and to 'wear their gloves at all times'.[113] They were also instructed to carry loaded weapons. On the day, the Mayor, the Police Commissioner and other officials were likewise formally dressed, even wearing their sashes of office. Such measures, designed to preserve order, would have done little to decrease the public awareness of 4 March as a climacteric day. The local authorities had been caught up in the *Dame's* timetable, and were reacting to the conclusion of the fortnight as a major event. Amid the rising tide of expectations the Lieutenant of the Gendarmerie seems to have suspected that even his own troops might be affected by the general emotions. He warned his Maréchal to 'recommend that your men have a great deal of calm, and keep near to you those who have the least of that quality'.[114] The citizens of Lourdes were likewise active in readiness for the unprecedented influx and the miraculous day. Adelaide Monlaur wrote that on 4 March those at the Grotto were 'almost all strangers, the inhabitants of Lourdes being occupied, some by the preparations for market day, and the others, fearing a catastrophe such as an earthquake or something like that'.[115]

On the morning of 4 March, Commissioner Jacomet, in the company of a senior Gendarme, awaited Bernadette in the Grotto itself. Placed as he was, he could not estimate the exact numbers but merely exclaimed: 'An immense crowd today!'[116] Antoine Clarens estimated the number at more than 10,000, gathered on both banks of the Gave. They all expected Bernadette at 7am, when she usually appeared, but she did not arrive until a quarter of an hour later. The Police Commissioner, stuck within the enormous mass of people, found 'that quarter of an hour very long, extremely long; what complaints! What murmurs! But then, at her appearance, it all ceased and a great silence reigned in the midst of that packed mass of people.' For the first time in his life, Commissioner Jacomet was glad to see Bernadette arrive at the Grotto.

Escorted by her aunts, Bernadette walked through the crowd, who made a passage for her. They appeared to be a compact sea of people, who all followed Bernadette with their eyes. Despite the expectations generated, this vision was one of the least eventful. Bernadette knelt as usual in prayer and spent about half an hour gazing at the apparition. Commissioner Jacomet recorded that at the end of the vision 'she rose up, asking to leave the area. Then she left, without saying a word.' He reported that the crowd was disappointed, after so many rumours of prodigies, 'everyone believed themselves to be duped'. However, 'a rather strange thing was that, at that hour, the crowd besieged her home'.[117]

Until late in the evening of 4 March Bernadette was visited by thousands of people, who filed past her as she sat in her family's one-room dwelling. Many kissed and embraced her, and she was also asked to touch rosary beads and give blessings. She refused to perform these two last services, but would touch other people's rosary beads against her own, for a souvenir.[118]

It seems that people were not disappointed, either by the demeanour of the visionary or by the lack of dramatic events on the day. Having arrived in Lourdes in the hope of wonderful sights, they managed to create them for themselves. Although few people were able to see her during the vision, word passed through the crowd, and as Jeanne Védère recorded, 'everyone would call out: "at present, she can see her!"'[119] The pilgrims who streamed to her home, in the hope that the sight of the visionary would assuage their longing for the marvellous, likewise devised a spectacle and a worthwhile goal for their own efforts. Adelaide Monlaur wrote on 8 March that people had told her: 'I have come so far, and I do not desire anything except to touch that child, I have succeeded, and have kissed her hand, I will go back contented.'[120]

The fourth day of March was not to be the closure of the apparitions at Lourdes, as the secular authorities had hoped. The visions had roused the entire countryside and people's expectations had become so strong as to be self-sustaining. This mood of popular belief would only develop and flourish during the next months. Although Bernadette had still not confirmed the identity of the apparition she was expected to remain in the role of the visionary. It was noticeable that:

An opinion, so strongly held as to be a certainty, reigned in Lourdes and all the countryside relative to the visions: that was that the Lady of the Grotto had not yet said her last word.[121]

97

# NOTES

1. Mme Jacomet, *Témoins*, 77.

2. The letters have not been published in their entirety. Various early edited versions of them were produced, in bowdlerized forms which eliminated their unorthodox tales from popular religion, and printed in clerical journals such as *Journal de la Grotte* 10 (1897). These distortions were corrected when Abbé Laurentin edited *LDA*. My own analysis of these letters was published in Thérèse Taylor, ' "So many extraordinary things to tell": Letters from Lourdes, 1858', *Journal of Ecclesiastical History* 46 (1995), 457–81.

3. Adelaide Monlaur to her cousin, 8 Apr. 1858, *AG*, A8.

4. Ibid., 23 Mar. 1858, *AG*, A8.

5. Quoted by Laurentin, *LDA* 1, 90.

6. Quoted by Cros, *Histoire*, 1. 198.

7. Letter and Memoire of Frère Cérase, *RdAM*, 19.

8. Lasserre, *Notre-Dame de Lourdes*, 35.

9. Procureur Impérial Dutour, Report to Procureur Général Falconnet, 1 Mar. 1858, *LDA 1*, no. 11, 176.

10. Mlle Estrade, *RdAM*, 46.

11. Adelaide Monlaur to her cousin, 20 Apr. 1858, *AG*, A8.

12. J.-B. Estrade, *RdAM*, 61.

13. Josèphe Barnigue quoted by Mlle Estrade, *RdAM*, 43.

14. Mlle Estrade quoted, J.-B. Estrade, *RdAM*, 61.

15. Ibid.

16. Both the draft and the finished versions are printed in *LDA* 1, 160–5.

17. J.-B. Estrade, *RdAM*, 62.

18. Mlle Estrade, *RdAM*, 44.

19. Ibid.

20. Statement of 21 Feb. 1858, *LDA* 1, no. 3, 161–3.

21. Commissioner Jacomet and Bernadette quoted by Mlle Estrade, *RdAM*, 45.

22. Bernadette Soubirous, 'Récit des Apparitions', 1866, *ESB*, no. 6, 85.

23. Jacomet quoted by J.-B. Estrade, *RdAM*, 67.

24. Ibid.

25. Ibid.

26. Procureur Impérial Dutour, Report to Procureur Général Falconnet, 1 Mar. 1858, *LDA* 1, no. 11, 175.

27. J.-B. Estrade, *RdAM*, 68.

28. H. Lasserre, *Sainte Bernadette* (Paris 1948, f.p. 1880), 19.

29. Italics in the original. I. Mullois, *Cours d'éloquence sacrée populaire, ou essai sur la manière de parler au peuple* (Paris 1856), 1. 47.

30. J.-B. Estrade, *RdAM*, 62.

31. This approximation of the time was provided by Bernadette, 'Visites et interrogatoires', 1866, *ESB*, no. 6, 85.

32. Ibid.

33. Ibid., 66.

34. Ibid., 68.

35. Bernadette quoted, J.-B. Estrade, *RdAM*, 65.

36. *BVP*, 2. 329.

37. This description was from her aunt, Basile Castérot, *RdAM*, 165.

38. People of the locality quoted by Adelaide Monlaur. Adelaide Monlaur to her cousin, 20 Apr. 1858, *AG*, A8.

39. Sr Anastasie quoted by Julie Garros, in religion Sr Vincent, *PON*, Sessio LXXXIV, 999.

40. An unnamed Sister quoted by Lasserre, *Notre-Dame de Lourdes*, 64. Curé Peyramale quoted by Dominique Vignes, *Témoins*, 158.

41. Ibid., 60.

42. Testimony of Mélanie Carrière, in religion Sr Anastasie, *PON*, Sessio XLV, 603. This is a different Sr Anastasie than referred to above. She was not a witness to this but is repeating a story which a Sister from Lourdes told her.

43. Marie Courrech, *Témoins*, 126.

44. Sophie Pailhasson, *PON*, Sessio LXXVIII, 931.

45. Ibid.

46. Garrison Sergeant d'Angla, *Témoins*, 68.

47. Louise Castérot quoted by Mlle Estrade, *RdAM*, 46.

48. Bernarde Castérot, *Témoins*, 161.

49. Fanny Nicalou, *Témoins*, 114.

50. Mlle Estrade, *RdAM*, 46.

51. J.-B. Estrade, *RdAM*, 69.

52. Curé Peyramale quoted, ibid., 47.

53. J.-B. Estrade, *RdAM*, 70–1.

54. Dr Dozous's memoir quoted by M.-T. Bordenave, *Sainte Bernadette. La confidente de l'Immaculée* (Nevers 1978; f.p. 1912), 33.

55. J.-B. Estrade, *RdAM*, 70.

56. Ibid., 71.

57. Dr Dozous quoted, J.-B. Estrade, *RdAM*, 73.

58. Mlle Estrade, *RdAM*, 48.

59. Abbé Pène, *Procès*, 66.

60. Dominiquette Cazenave, *RdAM*, 169.

61. The estimate of four hundred people present is given in this testimony, Fanny Nicolau, *Procès*, 66.

62. Ibid., 67.

63. Mlle Elfrida-Marie Lacrampe, *Témoins*, 101.

64. Estrade quoted, Mlle Elfrida-Marie Lacrampe, *Témoins*, 101. Estrade made the same claim to Abbé Pène, ibid., 272.

65. Mlle Elfrida-Marie Lacrampe, *Témoins*, 102.

66. Ibid., 72.

67. J.-B. Estrade, *RdAM*, 79.

68. Elfrida Lacrampe quoted, Cros, *Histoire*, 1. 259.

69. Ibid., 260.

70. J.-B. Estrade, *RdAM*, 80.

71. Bernarde Castérot, *RdAM*, 162.

72. J.-B. Estrade, *RdAM*, 80.

73. Ibid.

74. Ibid.

75. Bernadette quoted, A. Clarens, *RdAM*, 14.

76. J.-B. Estrade, *RdAM*, 81.

77. Lourdes historians usually date this event 25 February 1858. Neither Dutour's report, nor Bernadette's *récit*, recorded the date of the interview.

78. Bernadette Soubirous, 'Visites et interrogatoires', 1866, *ESB*, no. 7, 87.

79. André Sajoux, *Témoins*, 170.

80. Dutour cited, Cros, *Histoire*, 1. 195.

81. Ibid., 196.

82. Bernadette Soubirous, 'Visites et interrogatoires', 1866, *ESB*, no. 7, 87.

83. *BVP*, 1. 87.

84. Bernadette quoted, Rosalie-Antoinette Bounaix, Sr Madeleine, *PON*, Sessio XCVI, 1104.

85. André Sajoux, *Témoins*, 170.

86. Report of the Procureur Impérial to the Procureur Général, 1 Mar. 1858, *LDA* 1, no. 11, 177.

87. Ibid., 175.

88. Police Commissioner, report to the Préfet, 2 Mar. 1858, *LDA* 1, no. 13, 183.

89. Procureur Impérial, report to the Procureur Général, 1 Mar. 1858, *LDA* 1, no. 11, 178.

90. Ibid.

91. Antoine Clarens, *RdAM*, 13.

92. Ibid., 14.

93. Ibid.

94. Procureur Impérial, report to the Procureur Général, 1 Mar. 1858, *LDA* 1, no. 11, 175.

95. Madeleine Barbazat, *Témoins*, 135.

96. *BVP*, 2. 14.

97. Yves-Marie Hilaire quoted by R. Gibson, *A Social History of French Catholicism 1789–1914* (London 1989), 212.

98. See the collection of essays edited by Y.-M. Hilaire, *Benoît Labre. Errance et sainteté. Histoire d'une culte, 1783–1983* (Paris 1984).

99. Chanoine Ribes, director of the Grand Seminary at Tarbes (undated document, possibly recounting an interview of 1860) *AC*, (E) AIII (0) à (27).

100. M. l'abbé Fourcade, *L'Apparition à la Grotte de Lourdes en 1858* (Tarbes 1862), 44.

101. T. A. Kselman, *Miracles and Prophecies in Nineteenth-Century France* (New Jersey 1983), 168.

102. 'Paroles de la Sainte Vierge', 1865, written in Bigourdanian and translated into French by Chanoine Salvat, 'Vous irez dire aux prêtres de faire bâtir ici une chapelle', *ESB*, 66.

103. Basile Castérot, *RdAM*, 166.

104. Curé Peyramale quoted, Basile Castérot, *RdAM*, 166.

105. Dominiquette Cazenave, *RdAM*, 171.

106. Basile Castérot, *RdAM*, 166.

107. Dominiquette Cazenave, *RdAM*, 170.

108. M. Pomain quoted, *RdAM*, 171.

109. Police Commissioner report to Préfet, 2 Mar. 1858, *LDA* 1, no. 13, 182.

110. Ibid., 185.

111. Antoine Clarens, *RdAM*, 12.

112. Adelaide Monlaur to her cousin, 21 Mar. 1858, *AG*, A8.

113. Note written by Lieutenant Bourriot to Sergeant d'Angla, no date (2 Mar. 1858?) *LDA* 1, no. 18, 185.

114. Ibid.

115. Adelaide Monlaur to her cousin, 8 Mar. 1858, *AG*, A8.

116. Report of the Police Commissioner to the Préfet, 4 Mar. 1858, *LDA* 1, no. 25, 205.

117. Ibid.

118. Jeanne Védère, *RdAM*, 117.

119. Ibid., 116.

120. Adelaide Monlaur to her cousin, 8 Mar. 1858, *AG*, A8.

121. J.-B. Estrade, *Les Apparitions de Lourdes* (Lourdes 1920; f.p. 1899), 145.

## CHAPTER 4

# So Many Extraordinary Things
## Miracles in Lourdes, 1858

Oh how I will hurry to write you a long letter, having so many
extraordinary things to tell you concerning the affair of the Grotto.

Adelaide Monlaur, 20 April 1858

Bernadette experienced only three further visions after the dramatic fortnight,
which had ended on 4 March. For the following twenty days, she did not visit
the Grotto, nor talk of going there. The request for a chapel and processions,
which she had conveyed to the Curé, remained without any definite answer.
The Curé had told her to ask for the Lady's name, but Bernadette did not do
so immediately. During the fortnight, she passively contemplated the vision,
receiving messages but asking no questions. And after 4 March, the daily
visions stopped.

The visits to Massabielle had interrupted the daily round of Bernadette's
life, which was still centred upon attaining the right to First Communion. She
attended school every day, and hoped to achieve this step along with the rest
of the catechism class, most of whom were children younger than herself.
Children were admitted to the sacraments at the age of twelve, which was also
when they left school. In 1858 Bernadette was already fourteen, although she
only knew that she was either thirteen or fourteen, as she was ignorant of her
birthday. People in her society made no fuss about birthdays, and only knew
the year that they were born. It is important to the story of her life that during
the year of 1858 she was still very much a child, both in terms of her social
status, and in terms of how others treated her. She liked the most simple
games, and was happy to play with the very young. She had not yet reached
the stage of life when she would distance herself from childishness. But she
wanted to move on from being a schoolgirl, and to start her life as a working
member of the community. To do this, she had to make her First
Communion.

It was difficult to guess Bernadette's age, as she was a late developer. In the
nineteenth century, girls passed through puberty at around sixteen, so
Bernadette's physical immaturity could have been taken for granted. But even
among the children of Lourdes, Bernadette was short, straight-bodied and
baby-faced. Almost every witness commented that she appeared to be eleven
or twelve. This difference between her appearance and her real age would
have influenced the impression she made, especially on outside witnesses.
There is a significant difference between twelve and fourteen, and
Bernadette's insightful responses to those who questioned her are more

explicable from a teenager. To many people, such words from a little child seemed astonishing. Her conversations had an 'out of the mouths of babes' effect.

Even during the fortnight Bernadette had restricted her appearances at Massabielle to the times when she was having visions, and after 4 March she told the Police Commissioner that she did not know if she would return there again.[1] But as the days passed, it became obvious that Massabielle was attracting attention on its own. As Adelaide Monlaur wrote: 'it is surprising to see so many people go to see the Grotto ... The numbers grow still, although that child no longer goes there.'[2] On 19 March 1858 the Police Commissioner made the same observation, but with dismay: 'young Bernadette does not go any more to the Grotto since the great day (4 March) but, in revenge ... at the very moment when we thought that it was all going to end ... there have been, over the past days, a continual coming and going'.[3]

The visitors decorated the Grotto. Lighted candles, a devotional object associated with the visions from the earliest days, were deposited on the rock walls. There were also flowers, statues of the Virgin, a little altar, and numerous gifts of money and linen. The Police Commissioner regarded all of this with dismay. He gathered up the money and deposited it with the Mayor, for public charity. Mayor Lacadé received the money thoughtfully, and wrote out receipts. This was a poor area, so it would be put to good use. The Mayor of Lourdes was a model of the small town politician. He got on with everyone, was full of genial humour, always tried to smooth over problems, did favours and was re-elected every time. He did not merely restrict himself to those with means: 'He was charitable to all the poor, especially those in shameful circumstances.'[4] At first the apparitions had seemed to him to be a most ridiculous novelty. When Field Guard Callet had told him that Bernadette entranced was a wonderful sight, he exclaimed: 'Bah! – You as well, you're an imbecile.'[5] He had never had to deal with anything like this before. He was inclined to laugh, but the visitors, extra commerce and donations were a serious matter. Unlike the Police Commissioner, he saw some good in the whole thing.

André Sajoux, a friend of the Soubirous, was often asked by visitors to lead them to her dwelling. He commented dryly that if Bernadette had not told him to accept nothing, he would have been the richest man in Lourdes. 'Gentlemen from Pau visited, with handfuls of gold coins. They came to our house late at night. Bernadette was asleep. They brought a grown girl, who had been sick for a long time. They begged Bernadette to embrace her, to touch her chest. Bernadette was annoyed and said: "I am not responsible for curing people, go and wash her with the water of the Grotto." '[6] Visits by sick people put her under a particular strain, and she probably did not like being woken up by strangers with money in their hands. On 19 March, a market day, Lourdes was packed with visitors, many of whom went to the Soubirous home. The Police Commissioner noted that 'they received no-one, the door was shut to all'.[7] Unlike Bernadette, the Grotto was always available and it did not reject donations. Soon, it was the focus of every hope.

On the evening of 24 March, Bernadette told her family that she wanted to visit the Grotto again. They tried to dissuade her, because she had a cold, but Bernadette was ready to go by the following morning. This day, the 25 March, is a significant Marian holy day, it is the Feast of the Annunciation. It celebrates the day when the angel declared to Mary that she would have a child.

Bernadette returned to the Grotto, and beheld the *Dame* again. The vision lasted around half an hour, and Bernadette returned with the message that the Lady had revealed her name. Bernadette said that she had asked three times: 'Would you have the goodness to tell me your name?' The Lady replied only with a smile. She asked again, and the Lady drew herself up, raised her hands to her breast, and said 'I am the Immaculate Conception.' Later writings about Lourdes often reduce the questions – it is said that Bernadette asked three times, then was answered. According to her own words, reported in the early documents, she would have asked four times.[8] The repetition of three questions has a definite element of folklore. Fairy Queens had a habit of only answering on the third question, and the giving of their name was a special favour, which sometimes caused them to disappear for ever. The Lady of the Grotto was similar to a *Dame blanche* of the woods, but the name which she mentioned was one of the dogmas of the Blessed Virgin. Curé Peyramale had got his answer.

Bernadette walked to the presbytery, repeating the important words to herself all along the way, which would be about a twenty-minute walk. She was afraid of forgetting the words. Her Aunt Basile accompanied her. Curé Peyramale was at home, and was annoyed by the sudden visit. 'We were not well received,' said Aunt Basile.[9] He asked sarcastically: 'Well, what are you going to teach me today?'[10] Standing in his parlour, Bernadette made the announcement that the *Dame* had clasped her hands in an attitude of prayer and declared, '*Que soy era Immaculada Councepciou*'. The Curé was affronted and told her that 'A lady cannot have that name!'[11] Outwardly, Curé Peyramale maintained his dismissive attitude, but he was beginning to see that this strange affair was becoming an issue of religious importance. He wrote immediately to the Bishop of Tarbes, informing him of events.[12]

When questioned in later years, Bernadette claimed that she did not know the term Immaculate Conception before the Lady had made this announcement. Some people believed this but others have had their doubts. A scholar of religious psychology has described the 'Immaculate Conception' announcement as 'Bernadette's capitulation to the suggestion (which had been made to her often enough at that point) that Aquero was the Virgin Mary'.[13] This is a rational explanation of an issue which was to be one of the essentials of the hagiography of Lourdes. Catholic writers were to make much of Bernadette's alleged ignorance of the words 'Immaculate Conception', and it was claimed that a poor peasant girl could not have invented such a statement. In 1900 Dr Boissairie wrote: 'such an audacious pronouncement was well above Bernadette's abilities... Such a definition was outside the bounds of her intelligence. We are plainly in the realm of the supernatural.'[14]

It is not difficult to show that Bernadette should have been familiar with the Dogma of the Immaculate Conception, even if she claimed ignorance. The idea of the Immaculate Conception does not refer to Mary's miraculous conception of Jesus. Rather it hearkens back to the Virgin's own conception, and poses the notion that Mary, unique among all of the human race, had been conceived free from original sin. From the first moment when she came into existence in the womb of St Anne, her mother, she was therefore different, exempt from the stain of all Eve's children, a divine vessel for the future messiah. From the early centuries of Christianity, some theologians had maintained this idea, but others argued against it, pointing out the lack of biblical authority, and claiming that it made a mortal woman into a divine being. For centuries the idea of the Immaculate Conception, like the notion of the Assumption (the miraculous removal of the Virgin Mary's corpse into heaven), remained as a holy idea, celebrated on the Church calendar on December 8, but no more fixed than saints' days, which believers are free to accept or ignore. In the nineteenth century, a change came about, and the papacy decided to proclaim the Immaculate Conception as a sacred dogma, that is to say, an article of faith.

The odd syntax of the term 'I am the Immaculate Conception' caused some debate. In March 1858, the first witnesses tended to correct it to 'I am the Virgin of the Immaculate Conception'[15] and other more meaningful terms. After all, how can someone *be* her own conception? Several years later, while an Episcopal Commission investigated the apparitions, a theologian wrote to them that he was 'inclined to think that the expression is not theologically correct'.[16] In fact, the statement has the awkward tone of a phrase repeated without full understanding, as if Bernadette had muddled the message. The partisans of Lourdes could hardly be expected to take up such an explanation and, although people were puzzled, it eventually had to be accepted by those who believed.

The announcement of the *Dame*'s name had caused an immense *éclat* throughout the Hautes-Pyrénées, and the authorities probably assumed that the resumption of visions on 25 March would begin another fortnight, which would have taken place amid an even more heightened level of public furore. The Préfet wrote to Paris the following day, stating that he had taken action. 'I have immediately given order to have the young girl examined by a doctor, and if there are grounds, to have her interned at the Hospice.'[17]

The medical examination was carried out on a Saturday, which was a school day in Lourdes. On 27 March Bernadette was called out of the classroom by a Sister of Nevers, who brought her to Dr Balencie, who was assisted by Dr Peyrus and Dr Lacrampe. Lourdes rumour later claimed that no doctor was willing to undertake responsibility for such a decision alone, and that all had been picked because of their rationalist opinions.[18] They seem to have been men of ordinary beliefs. Dr Balencie later said that they were Catholics, but had not bothered to visit the Grotto and knew little of what had happened there. It is interesting that it was still possible to be living as a member of the Lourdes community and to be ignorant of the Grotto in late March 1858. In order to be fully informed before examining Bernadette, they asked a local journalist, Romain Capdevielle, to 'teach them what happened during the apparitions'.[19]

The doctors examined Bernadette without the permission, or even the knowledge, of her parents. It was accepted that they had the right to do so, and this was not an ethical dilemma for them. Bernadette was probably chaperoned by a Sister of Nevers, and the examination took over two hours. They looked her over physically, and asked her questions about her health. Then they asked her what had been happening at the Grotto, and she gave them her standard account of the apparitions – 'she went to gather wood with her younger sister and a friend ... she heard a sound like a rush of wind ... a form appeared to Bernadette, a white shape having the attitude of a Virgin ... the vision asked Bernadette to come to the Grotto for fourteen consecutive days ...'[20]

The doctors wrote that they found Bernadette to be of 'a delicate constitution, ... aged thirteen, but appears to be no more than eleven'. In fact, she was fourteen, but many people commented that she looked only eleven or twelve. The doctors did not note her youthful appearance in order to be descriptive. In their report, these words reflect an awareness that Bernadette is not yet at the age of puberty.

Like many observers, the doctors found her eyes striking and noted that 'her physiognomy is agreeable, her eyes are expressive' and her height petite, but not abnormal. 'She says that she is very well, has never suffered headaches, has never had nervous fits, eats, drinks and sleeps wonderfully well. However, young Bernadette is not of such good health as she believes, she is quite obviously suffering from asthma.'[21] The doctors paid particular attention to the sensational events on 19 February, when the spring had been uncovered. On this matter they stated that they had information from witnesses who had seen her 'prostrate herself against the ground, and at the height of her delirium, bite the earth'.[22] Bernadette told them that she had been totally absorbed by the vision, and she apparently did not know what had taken place. The action of collapsing and biting are redolent of epilepsy, and were probably recorded by the doctors to indicate this possibility. The doctors asked her if she had been afraid of the huge crowds pressing around her, but Bernadette said that she was unaware of them during the visions.

The behaviour of the asthmatic child did not meet nineteenth-century standards of *mens sana*, but her aberrations were restricted to the actual periods of the trances. She did not seem to them to be a religious maniac, or even a fanatic. They noted from her account that initially: 'The strange Apparition had, in effect, so little preoccupied Bernadette that if her friends had not pushed her to return to the Grotto, two days later, it is likely that she would only have conserved a slight memory of it.' The doctors explained the dynamic of the apparitions from a sceptical, yet not hostile, point of view:

> Nothing indicates that Bernadette has wanted to impose on the public: this child is of an impressionable nature, she may have been the victim of an hallucination; a reflection of light, has, without doubt, roused her attention while looking at the wall of the Grotto; her imagination, under the influence of a moral predisposition, has given her the form which impresses children, that of the statues of the Virgin which one sees above altars. She

told her friends of the vision: they led her back to the Grotto, the story went around the town; a population, growing all the time, pressed her to recount the story ... What was initially but a simple hallucination took up more power, absorbed her more and more, and was able to isolate her entirely from the exterior world at the moment of the Apparition, which is a veritable state of trance.[23]

The doctors' report explained the visions as a semi-voluntary and shared delusion. Their description of the process of hallucination, beginning with an unexpected sight such as a light or a cloud, which the viewer redefines as a figure from the extant resources of the imagination, is still current among psychologists today.[24] It is the explanation which Dominique Jacomet also agreed with. In April 1858, after one of Bernadette's final visions, the Police Commissioner meditated on the reasons for her conduct. He did not believe in the visions, but did not believe her to be lying. 'Cannot one believe that if she had had a moment of hallucination, all which acts around her could only finish by making her take this illusion for reality.'[25]

The medical report was of no use to Préfet Massy. Only in the concluding paragraph of their report did the doctors address the question posed by the official request for an examination. Their reply was evasive: 'Is there any need to treat this affliction? We have little to say on this subject.'[26] They stated that there was no real danger to Bernadette's health. In their opinion it was likely that 'when Bernadette returns to ordinary life, no longer harassed by crowds and supplications for prayers, she will stop thinking of the Grotto and the marvellous things which she recounts'. For Bernadette, that day was never to arrive.

After receiving this equivocal report, the authorities dropped the idea of confining Bernadette, and in any case her daily visions had not resumed. As the Procureur Impérial Dutour wrote:

The crowds are no longer following the steps of that young girl; the force which drives these waves does not come from her any more ... Without having read if the report justifies the placement of Bernarde [sic] in a hospital, I doubt the efficacy of that measure.[27]

Bernadette was apparently unafraid during the medical examination, although they heard her breathing become more and more laboured. She might not have realized that she was at risk of being sent to an asylum. The Tardhivail sisters, genteel spinsters of Lourdes, later invited her to their house and asked her if she had been afraid. She said no, and that: 'They wanted me to think that I am sick, but I am not so at all.'[28] When people asked her if she was afraid of prison, she said that it was not important, and when they reminded her of her father's arrest she said 'Yes, but they were obliged to let him out again.'[29]

The streets of Lourdes were noisy with controversy, as the authorities announced that the Grotto was not an authorized place of worship, and that access to it would be restricted. Visitors who wanted to know about the new shrine were disembarking from coaches, and street stalls were opened to cater for their needs. It was a hot and turbulent summer, but life went on as before at the *cachot*. Although Bernadette's visions had ceased, she was still under police surveillance, along with her whole family. Police agents were ordered to watch the house, note who ever visited, and to follow Bernadette when she went out. Many people remembered being questioned after they had visited Bernadette: ' "Have you given any money to the little one?" All replied: "no" '.[30] The experience probably put both them and the Soubirous family on their guard.

Nearly two weeks after the 'Immaculate Conception' announcement, Bernadette and her family made a visit outside Lourdes. This was on the Easter weekend of 5–6 April. Lent was over, and the holiday season offered hospitality and feasting even to the poor. Bernadette would normally have been entitled to a place at communal festivals, but her new reputation had brought an invitation from higher circles. Blaise Vergez (called Blazy) was a wine merchant and had served as Mayor of the little village of Adé, four kilometres from Lourdes. He invited the Soubirous to his residence because he wanted to meet Bernadette. This visit was the beginning of a series of invitations which would bring Bernadette into the homes of local notables. She was introduced to distinguished visitors, and being able to produce this girl, who was the object of so much talk and even newspaper stories, reflected well on her hosts. Bernadette responded with placid courtesy, and would answer their questions about the apparitions. Bernadette would quickly leave the grand houses, but she would visit the homes of friends and relatives in lower Lourdes, sometimes staying the night. It was one way of avoiding the strangers who would call at her home.

Bernadette returned from Adé at dawn on 7 April. She told the Blazy family that she wanted to visit the Grotto again. After weeks of silence, she suddenly felt the 'push' to see the apparition. They gave her a candle, and sent her home in a cart. As rural people, they must have been early risers, and it seems that they were not put out by Bernadette's request to travel at 5am. News spread that she was on her way to the Grotto, and people rushed to the site. They included Dr Dozous. This Lourdes medical practitioner had witnessed several visions, and like his friend Jean-Baptiste Estrade he had come to believe that they were genuine. During the vision of 7 April, he had an experience which convinced him. In the words of the Procureur, who wrote an exasperated report about the events: 'M. Dozous, who had previously expressed an opinion far less favourable about the visions, which he termed *farces*, and about the visionary, whom he termed a *nincompoop*, has done a sudden about-face. As far as he is concerned, there is something which human science cannot explain in the events observed at the Grotto.'[31]

On 7 April Bernadette had been given a large and impressive candle, which she stood upright on the ground. Dr Dozous had seen Bernadette gazing at the apparition, her expression transformed, and her hand cupping the flame of her candle. The flame touched her flesh, but she remained immobile, and the flame could be seen between her fingers. She finally left the candle when she moved forward to approach the apparition. Dr Dozous, who had previously taken Bernadette's pulse during a vision, claimed to have observed this carefully. The Procureur irritably dismissed it as nonsense, and thought that the Doctor must have misunderstood what he saw, or that he had gone mad, or that he was maliciously lying. After the visions, Dr Dozous examined Bernadette's hand, but found no sign of a burn. He also applied a candle flame, to see if she had normal sensations, and she quickly withdrew, exclaiming: 'You are burning me.'[32]

An anthropologist would find nothing improbable about Dr Dozous's account – but nothing supernatural either. A person in a trance can be apparently immune to either heat or cold. A slight burn, such as a candle flame, can make no impression. In Bernadette's case, an early indication of this insensibility, which went unnoticed at the time, was that she waded through the mill stream after her first vision and told her incredulous companions that the water was not cold. Marie Lamathe, a peasant woman, testified that during a vision Bernadette's godmother (Bernarde Castérot) slapped her violently, but that Bernadette did not move. People had exclaimed at this, 'there is something!'[33] Mlle Peyrard told Elfrida-Marie Lacrampe that she had driven a pin into Bernadette's shoulder during a vision and that Bernadette did not appear to feel it.[34] These and other stories greatly impressed those who were favourable to the apparitions.

## Visionaries in ecstasy

The original supernatural story which had drawn crowds to the Grotto was the report that Bernadette was physically transformed when she experienced visions. Some people claimed that her appearance was beautiful, although it could just as easily be described as morbid and ghastly. Witnesses claimed to be transfixed by 'her indescribable smile, her strange pallor, the position of her eyes of which the pupil seemed to have turned it its socket'.[35]

Bernadette's trances were met with two contemporary schools of explanation. She was 'struck with catalepsie'[36] (an epileptic subject to hallucinations) or she was 'in direct communication with God'.[37] There were some variations in these themes, as there were other proffered diagnoses of mental illness, especially hysteria. The milieu of popular culture also provided alternative and more sinister religious explanations, and some people in Lourdes said that Bernadette was 'bewitched, insane (*folle*)'.[38] Within this context the adjective *folle* encompassed supernatural, rather than medical, sources of harm. Her wits must have been stolen by whatever being it was that enchanted her in the Grotto, and, in the world of the common people of Lourdes, such cases occurred often. Some peasant observers would have found Bernadette's visions to be genuine and remarkable, while still expecting her to eventually decline to a rambling mindless freak, a person often seen among beggars and wanderers.

Whatever the explanation, Bernadette entranced was found by many people to be a remarkable sight, and this was a leading cause for the gathering of the early crowds. As Frère Cérase wrote in 1858: 'the story which spread concerning the changes in the physiognomy of the visionary when she is in communication with this being which appears to her, soon attracted prodigious crowds of people, of all ages and classes'.[39] Many people would have set out, as Adelaide Monlaur's father did on 3 March 1858, saying: 'Now then! Today I shall go and see that child entranced.'[40]

The most influential descriptions of Bernadette in ecstasy came from the pens of male witnesses who communicated educated aesthetic considerations in their writings. Jean-Baptiste Estrade was among the originators of this; as has been noted, his dramatic account of Bernadette's transformation was to be often quoted in later literature. Abbé Dézirat, the only priest who is known to have visited the Grotto during the apparitions, wrote an account essentially identical to Estrade's, although these texts were produced entirely independently from each other. Abbé Dézirat wrote that only an angel could have described her transformation:

> Her smile is beyond depiction: the most talented artist could not succeed in sketching its beauty; the most talented actor could not imitate its charm and grace ... I have observed the child when she went to the Grotto ... what a difference between that and when I saw her at the moment of the Apparition![41]

For people of Bernadette's own social milieu, and the provincial *demoiselles* who lacked education, her appearance was moving, but it inspired fear, awe and pity rather than aesthetic admiration. At the time of the first vision Toinette Soubirous was afraid of the sight of Bernadette and exclaimed that she was dead. This was not merely a quirk on the part of this girl. On 8 April 1858, Adelaide Monlaur wrote of a vision which she had witnessed and told her correspondent that 'upon seeing that child so pale that one was ready to cry and one believed that she would fall dead, for she gave three gasps like someone taking their last breath. The ecstasy lasted for a long time.'[42]

Among the uneducated, the comparison to a dying person or a corpse was repeatedly made. During one vision 'a general cry went up "My God! She is going to die." '[43] Pierre Callet thought that 'she seemed like a dead baby, resting in its cradle'.[44] The later appreciation of angelic beauty sometimes specifically mingled with memories of the corpse-like visionary. Jeanne Abadie explained that as witnesses to the second vision the group of children were 'all from poor families. Bernadette seemed like an angel, but *we* believed her to be dead, *we* looked at her and burst into tears.'[45] Some of the peasant witnesses did find her appearance beautiful, to a degree which raised apprehension as much as delight. Antoine Nicolau felt 'fear and pleasure, and for all of that day my heart was touched whenever I thought of it'.[46] Basile Castérot stated that: 'For me, in seeing my niece Bernadette in contemplation at the Grotto, I did not know what to think, but I loved her all the more.'[47]

There were a few people who witnessed Bernadette's visions, but were not overwhelmed by the sight. The Garrison Chief, Marshall d'Angla, judged the whole drama at the Grotto as being no better than a magic lantern display. 'I took Bernadette for an idiot rather than anything else. It is true that I did not know her ... she looked quite common, although I never thought her capable of deceit.'[48] He had the opportunity to witness her trances, and remained as an unbeliever, although somewhat impressed by the memory: 'I was only present during three or four of those scenes at the Grotto. Bernadette, in her ecstasy was completely immobile: there was nothing repugnant, no grimaces; on the contrary she was beautiful to see. The stillness of her gaze surprised me. I said to myself "How she believes, that little child!" '[49] Police Commissioner Jacomet had been near Bernadette throughout the whole of her lengthy vision on 4 March 1858. A woman schoolteacher from Gavarnie commented that: 'I saw with pleasure M. le Commissaire on his knees. He was only a few steps away from Bernadette and he made notes of her changes in facial expression.'[50] He did indeed do so, but his report did not record any impression which she made on him. 'Her eyes were fixed on the oval hollow between the rocks. She said her rosary twice, she did not stop except to smile and incline her head, all that lasted half an hour.'[51] Many people imagined that one could not see Bernadette in the Grotto without being converted, but in fact Commissioner Jacomet had only knelt out of respect for those around him. The Procureur Général received this and other reports from the Grotto. He cautiously said that on 4 March her eyes 'had not had that ecstatic fixity which had been observed on preceding occasions; her expression had not offered the moving spectacle of convulsions'.[52] This is in accordance with many witnesses who said that Bernadette's trances fluctuated, and that she was not constantly transformed. By describing her visions as 'convulsions', but also as 'moving spectacles', the Procureur was providing a rational response for the strange events.

Abbé Dezirat claimed that the 'most consummate actor' could not reproduce the grace which Bernadette showed during a vision.[53] The same point was spontaneously made by many others. Jean-Baptiste Estrade testified to the inquiry for Bernadette's canonization that when he had first attended the visions he had recalled the famous tragedy actress Rachel, whom he had seen at the theatre at Bordeaux. He explained that while she had been sublime, her performance was 'infinitely below that of Bernadette'.[54] He was not joking when he made this startling comparison. At the time of the visions he had told Abbé Pène that if Bernadette were an actress, she would be 'the best performer in the world'.[55] This sounds like a barbed remark, but Jean-Baptiste Estrade followed it up with the observation, which seemed so obvious to him, that any type of acting would be far beyond Bernadette's capacities. These observations must have been common currency in 1858, for they are also cited by Adelaide Monlaur, who told her correspondent that 'if she is acting a part, she knows how to act it well; and people who know better than I say ... that it is impossible to thus change one's features and expression'.[56]

In reaching for an analogy with an actress, the Lourdes witnesses were trying to affirm the miraculousness of the event. They were also giving evidence of the culture of their time, which consistently sought such spectacles, and found them in many spheres of life. The comparison between Bernadette and Rachel was natural to make in 1858. It was a time, as Elfrida Lacrampe commented, 'when everyone was talking of that actress'.[57] Rachel had been the subject of an intense public cult, which in some ways corresponded to the fame that Bernadette was to attract during the 1860s. Rachel was fascinating to many classes of society, including reactionary Catholics, the cultured Paris bourgeoisie, ordinary provincials and the unlettered masses.[58] She had died in January 1858, only eight weeks before the onset of Bernadette's visions, and her funeral had been a national preoccupation. Aside from Rachel, numerous French actresses portrayed the extremes of emotional states, the sight of which was found so fascinating. Both Sarah Bernhardt and Eve Lavallière were so skilled that they could induce physically genuine convulsions and swooning as part of their performances.

When it was convened, the Episcopal Commission of 1858-60 did not consider the miracle of the candle, nor any evidence concerning Bernadette's trances. This was because they carefully reserved their efforts simply for identifiable miracles of healing and deliberately avoided being overwhelmed by the torrent of popular tales of the supernatural. Père Cros, and other Catholic historians of Lourdes, went to the trouble of explaining that there could not be any equation of the antics of the hypnotized, or the artifice of actresses, with the visions of Bernadette.[59] The church writers also tended to contradict, or downplay, stories of burning candle flames and pins being applied to the visionary. Such unauthorized trials had an uncomfortable air of the Middle Ages, which the nineteenth-century French church wanted to forget. They needed to keep such things under wraps, because Lourdes was in the Hautes-Pyrénées, a region where superstitions were rife. Priests had often been embarrassed when French journals wrote about the extraordinary folklore believed by the peasants. Several years before the Lourdes visions a Professor at a Pyrenean seminary, M. Cousté, had been obliged to publish a refutation of a current tale that women in Pyrenean villages had been entering trances and had been possessed by devils.[60]

## Malevolent miracles and false visionaries

Until an Episcopal Inquiry was launched in late July 1858, the religious activities at the Grotto were unsupervised by the clergy, and they developed into the wildest excesses of popular religion. After May 1858, when Bernadette's visions had ceased, there was the proliferation of visionaries at the Grotto, many of whom saw evil or ambiguous spirits, and there were stories of the Virgin Mary acting against her opponents by a series of malevolent miracles. This epidemic of the supernatural, later to be termed the 'false visions', is one of the least understood aspects of Lourdes history. The activities of the other visionaries can partly be seen as a tactic of resistance to the secular powers operating in the area. In their darkest form, the other visions were a hearkening back to the fears roused by the original reputation of the Grotto as a haunted place.

The common people of Lourdes were quite willing to believe that the Virgin Mary would unleash spite and vengefulness on her opponents. In the early popular lore of the Grotto, as distinct from the later hagiography, many miracles involved the infliction of harm. People were struck dumb, paralysed or pursued by nightmares because they offended the Lady of the Grotto. One drunken scoffer, who had dared to laugh at the apparitions, was wakened at night by a supernatural apparition, who gave him several blows about the head and then seized him by the shoulder and shook him. He heard a voice saying 'Do you believe it now?' His wife said that she had come into the room a moment later and found him terrified.[61]

The idea of the Virgin Mary confronting disbelief with a crack over the head is odd enough, but other Lourdes anecdotes give her an even more direct and crude ability to fit the punishment to the crime. It was said of one local that he was a 'drunkard and a loafer; he went and emptied his bowels in the Grotto. The night afterwards: diarrhoea all night. He had to make amends. Everyone talked about it.'[62] Rather similar were the tribulations of a Gendarme, who had insulted Bernadette at the Grotto. According to a story which circulated in the village of Bartrès, he was struck with diarrhoea that night. This was the symptom of a serious illness: 'It is the cholera which has struck me! He gasped to his wife. The Virgin Mary is punishing me! ... It is done, I am lost!'[63] He recovered after his wife visited Bernadette to convey his apologies.

The threat of chastisement from heaven stopped people from co-operating with the authorities. When a barricade was constructed at the Grotto it was difficult to hire equipment. A worker at a sawmill was prevailed upon to provide the loan of a hatchet, and, as the Curé of Lourdes wrote to his Bishop in a tone of exasperation: 'By a fatal coincidence, the next day that poor man had his two feet crushed by a beam of wood. Since then he has been confined to bed. As you would think, people have not failed to cry out that this is a miracle, and that they have seen a punishment from heaven.'[64]

The idea that the Virgin Mary might appear in order to menace the faithful was a regular feature of French peasant religion. Notre Dame de Médous, who has a shrine in the Pyrenean village of Asté, appeared to a visionary in 1648. She is credited with having struck the village with plague when initially the visionary was not believed.[65] In the *Social History of French Catholicism* Ralph Gibson relates the story of Notre Dame de Redon-Espic (Périgord), who appeared to a local girl in 1814. The vision predicted the death of the visionary's parents, then of a landlord who threatened her. As it happened, they did die during a subsequent epidemic, and this established the truth of the vision among the local population.[66] Judith Devlin's *The Superstitious Mind* includes many examples of belief in the malevolent powers of the Blessed Virgin, which led to the appearance of such unexpected deities as Our Lady of Hatred. She presided over a Breton shrine where one could say three Ave Marias and bring about the ruin of one's enemies.[67]

Madonnas who threatened, or even punished, the faithful had once been a standard part of Catholic culture. But this type of miracle story lost prestige during the eighteenth and nineteenth centuries. Churchmen became embarrassed by such tales. Imagery of women, maternity and the Virgin Mary evolved together, and in the nineteenth century one can see the predominance of the merciful, intercessory Virgin. It was at this time that the norms of industrialized society led to the nuclear family and the ideal of domesticated wives and mothers. Yet the women of Lourdes still lived in a pre-industrialized world, and their legends reflected this. Infanticide was common, and peasant family life was organized around subsistence needs. It was expected that children would obey their mothers through fear rather than love. The exercise of power, whether between the members of a family, the community and the government, or the faithful and God, was likely to be harsh and arbitrary. The Lady of the Grotto would harm people if she wished – they were her children.

The activities of the 'false' visionaries of Lourdes were to be even more distasteful to later hagiographers than the malevolent miracles. From the end of April 1858, people began to report that they had seen visions, either at the Grotto or at other locations. Most were children, but they included men and women. A few of them replicated Bernadette's experiences, but most elaborated different supernatural legends. The visionaries were always granted a hearing, and were usually believed, by their fellow citizens. They enacted their community's faith, and those who experienced evil apparitions provided an expression of the fear and hostility which the official campaign against the Grotto caused many people to feel.

Despite their sobriquet as 'false visionaries', which was bestowed by Catholic historians, the other visionaries in Lourdes were frequently honoured by their own generation. The experience of being present during their ecstasies was as holy and memorable as the better known reverences paid to Bernadette. One young man present at the Grotto during the visions of a ten-year-old boy watched him:

> He made three reverences to the vision, the most gracious that it would be possible to imagine. His mouth was smiling, his features were radiant with joy; with his head resting on his hands he bowed, three times, with matchless grace. Judge our attention, our stupefaction: we were convinced that there, before us, a supernatural being was present.[68]

Françoise Junça, who watched a group of children fall into trances at the Grotto, described how 'they would cast themselves to their knees all at once, then rise up ... shriek, cry, wail, then they would promptly all kneel again: And we ourselves followed all their changes and prostrations.'[69] The eccentricity of these displays did not repulse her. She found the children too young and naive to be capable of invention, 'therefore there was a vision for them: and for us the spectators, also'.[70]

The other visionaries disquieted their own community, as well as the government authorities, when their apparitions seemed sinister. In later years one of the child visionaries recalled what he had seen: 'it was not a woman, and I could not say what it was ... I was afraid'.[71] Many reported seeing a white light, rather than any type of human figure. These lights were a relic of fairy mythology, and signalled the appearance of nature spirits. During the days of the first visions, people recalled that in previous years, woodcutters and shepherds, alone in the forest, had tried to seek shelter in the Grotto during rainstorms. They had fled after hearing ghostly voices calling from the dark interior.[72] During the 'great fortnight' people returning at night from the market at Lourdes saw lights moving in the Grotto, and they fled terrified.[73] These types of supernatural manifestations had died down as the visions were interpreted as Christian. But the original nature of Massabielle had never been forgotten, and its darker side suddenly made a return in the middle of the year.

The mythology of the Grotto is ambiguous, and even the *Dame* herself was not a sweet figure. As a priest wrote in the 1960s: 'solitary Massabielle, opening to a lair from which flowed, and still flow, the most terrifying stories'.[74] The Grotto was a gateway to the other world, and anything might come through it. As late as the 1900s, it was noted that local people were still afraid of Massabielle, and would hasten away from the area at night.[75] This writer, who conducted research in Lourdes during the 1990s, found that such attitudes still linger, and it is said that no person from Lourdes would go alone to the Grotto after dark. Immortal beings of an uncanny character haunt the mountains. Even the witnesses whose favourable impressions of the child visionaries have been quoted went away to ponder some doubts. In each case they felt that there was a genuine vision, but the question was 'if it is from heaven'.[76] Soon many visionaries were showing signs that they were in communication with either nature spirits or devils. The beings who were appearing to them were sometimes evil. There were visionaries who were lured toward precipices by the white lights,[77] or who would have cast themselves into the Gave river had they not been restrained.[78] The children at the Grotto exhibited signs that they were possessed.

The other visionaries drew no approval from the literate supporters of the Grotto, who relied upon the less colourful testimony of Bernadette. The stories recounted by the other visionaries were to remain solely as a heritage of the Occitan-speaking Pyreneans. One of the early pilgrims to Lourdes recorded the surprising fact that people in the town had told him that Bernadette was 'not the only person here to whom the Virgin Mary had deigned to manifest herself'.[79] In the following decades, people continued to remember graces and miracles which had been obtained for them by the other visionaries.[80] Some of these stories had no elements of a doubtful, Satanic or folkloric character.

The experiences reported by Marie Courrech, a servant in her early twenties, were a standard story of visions of the Virgin Mary.[81] Her recital had credibility, and it was even said that when the Bishop of Tarbes was holding an inquiry into the apparitions, the evidence of Marie Courrech was sought in order to clarify Bernadette's testimony. Henri Lasserre, who researched his book on Lourdes during the 1860s, was obliged to note that she was 'venerated by all', although he judged her visions to be unimportant.[82] Obviously, there was something about Marie Courrech, as an individual, which prevented her from obtaining the reputation of Bernadette. The sources do not state exactly what it was. Poor, unattractive, and perhaps mentally retarded (this was the opinion of Mlle Estrade), she received no recognition from the outside world.[83] Various other *femmes du peuple*, such as Marie

Cazenave and Joséphine Albario, were considered by their peers to have been in communication with the Virgin.

The visions of Joséphine Albario have been studied by Ruth Harris in *Lourdes: Body and Spirit in the Secular Age*. The history of Joséphine Albario is a sad one; she lived a hard life and saw a sombre Virgin Mary. The Albario family were not as poor as the Soubirous, but neither were they as close knit. Joséphine was rejected at home, especially by her older sister, who resented any money that was spent on her. When the visions at the Grotto began, this discontented young woman joined in, but her descriptions of a grim Virgin wearing a black helmet did not gain respectable adherents. Joséphine Albario then tried to join a religious congregation, and her problems began in earnest. Her family unwillingly paid the pension demanded by the convent for her upkeep during the novitiate. But she was unable to adjust to religious life in a distant town, and returned home in a destitute condition. Exactly why she left the convent, and what happened to her during the journey, are not stated. Even if she was dismissed for some fault, the Sisters would have arranged her passage home and given her the fare. Joséphine Albario may have been unable to handle money, or she may have left the convent under the 'protection' of someone who exploited her. Eventually, she wandered away from home and lived as a pedlar and a prostitute. She explained that she could not stay with her family, because: 'At home, no-one likes me.'[84] Ruth Harris suggests that in some ways Joséphine Albario was an opposite image of Bernadette, although both women ended up sharing the fate of having to leave Lourdes and live as exiles.

What caused a person to become a visionary? According to Catholic lore, it should be because they are exceptionally devout, and open to the influence of God. Everyone knew that there might be other motives, and thus there is the opposite figure of the visionary in theological writings – the person dominated by their ego, wishing for graces they had not received, boasting of privileges for which they were unworthy. The 'false visionary' had certain consistent traits, always described in confessors' handbooks (which considered them to be far more numerous and problematic than genuine visionaries). In our time, a sociologist would describe them as psychologically fragile, attention-seeking and often from unstable family backgrounds. One can see these patterns in the lives of some of the people who saw visions in Lourdes in 1858. Yet Pyrenean culture provided other motivations to take on this role. Not all of the visionaries were desperate to attract attention or respect otherwise lacking in their lives. Some of them seem to have been well-integrated into their community. The Pyrenean children who saw visions were often spontaneous, unself-conscious, and not dominated by the expectations of others. They were able to see visions at one time, and be ordinary selves subsequently, without regret or explanations. The supernatural world, full of divine beings and evil spirits, flickered about them – then was gone amid mundane daily life. Ruth Harris has pointed out that the visionary season coincided with St John's day, a traditional festival for youth, in which excessive behaviour and misrule were tolerated. Many of the visionaries of 1858 went on to live completely normal lives, and experienced no social stress as a result of their activities, either at the time or afterwards.

It was only those who became visionaries, rather than experienced visions, for whom 1858 was a turning point when their old lives were lost. The chief among these was Bernadette, although it was not obvious to her yet. She had no role to play when others were seeing visions at the Grotto. She was not present during their performances, and seems to have been indifferent to them, as they were to her. There was no rivalry or contest for attention. It appears that Bernadette shared the local view, which drew no sharp distinction between her own visions and the subsequent ones experienced by other people. Only once, amid all the numerous interviews recorded with her, was she ever asked the obvious question: 'Is it only you who saw the Blessed Virgin?' This question was asked by a priest who visited her at home during 1859. Bernadette replied, as if it were only a passing matter 'I am told that the Mayor's servant [i.e. Marie Courrech] saw her, on the last day that I saw her.'[85]

The 'false' visions were combated by the Police Commissioner, the Mayor and the Curé, all of whom upbraided and threatened the individuals concerned. This intimidation may have been the cause of their disappearance by September, but it seems more likely that this eccentric religious activity spontaneously ceased because by late in the year the Grotto was no longer a site of confrontation. When the Lourdes authorities stopped trying to suppress the shrine and took away the barricades, the confrontations and anger vanished, so also did the other visions.

## Miracle cures

Throughout 1858, the letters of Adelaide Monlaur reported one miracle after another, and through these documents one can appreciate how these stories were disseminated and believed. Often she recounted a tale in one letter – such as that images of doves had miraculously appeared on the Grotto walls – only to retract it in the next, when she had sought further information. Yet this had no impact on her willingness to believe. As she wrote on 18 May 1858, only one of the prodigies she had previously written about had been well founded and: 'the rest is false, except for the cures of which I have already told you about and which are more and more believed'.[86]

In the same letter in which Adelaide recorded her disappointment at the imprint of the dove she went on to write that 'that which I also told you was certain'[87] was that the miraculous cure of a blind child had been accomplished at the Grotto. She then gave another model story of the supernatural:

> Another child from Tarbes had his arms and legs paralysed: his parents took him to Bernadette Boly's home, the little one gave an apple to the child; who could not hold it and let it fall; but all of a sudden he walked and went himself to pick up the apple.[88]

This is one of the few Lourdes miracle stories of the era which can be directly compared to a statement by Bernadette. When interviewed by Commissioner Jacomet on 18 March she stated that only one invalid had been brought to her house: 'that was a young child of about six or seven years old, daughter of M. Sempolis; she was carried by the servant from the hotel'.[89] When the child saw an apple in Bernadette's pocket she reached out for it, but could not pick it up: 'the fruit fell two or three times to the floor and it was the maid who picked it up. The child left as she came.'[90] In this statement one hears the authentic, flat voice of Bernadette. From this time forward, it will provide a drab backdrop for a lifetime of miracle stories. Failures, such as the paralysed child, made no impression on the general imagination, which continued to proliferate stories of healing. Bernadette's own words counted for very little.

Miracles of healing were among the most known and esteemed of the supernatural claims which emanated from Lourdes. Innumerable stories recounted how people were cured of serious illness after washing in the waters of the spring at Massabielle. The original stories of cures proliferated in the same manner as the general ferment of the miraculous. As the Police Commissioner recorded, at the slightest rumour that an invalid had visited the spring, 'everywhere there is talk of a miracle'.[91]

One strategy to combat this was to trace some of the subjects of supposedly miraculous cures, and to investigate their claims. Several spectacular tales were debunked by this method. Yet the tales of cures multiplied, and numerous visitors to Lourdes would go to either the Curé or the Mayor in order to announce: ' "I cured myself of this or that malady, upon drinking the water of the Grotto" and, immediately, one more miracle tale circulates in the town, and adds to the public agitation.'[92]

The Police Commissioner did not find one case which he was willing to recognize as a genuine healing, whether miraculous or otherwise, but a small selection of the miracles reported during this period were to be investigated and approved by the Church. One of the earliest cures was that of Catherine Latapie (called Chouat) who had injured her hand in a fall, and was left with paralysed fingers. Her condition affected her life very badly, as she could neither cook, knit nor sew. Despite being heavily pregnant, she visited the Grotto on 1 March 1858, bathed her hand in the spring and instantly recovered the use of her fingers. She then rushed home, as her labour pains had begun, and gave birth easily after the seven-kilometre journey. Another famous cure was that of Louis Bouriette, a stonemason of Lourdes. During the 1830s, he had lost the sight of one eye in a mine explosion. Scar tissue formed in the eye, causing painful inflammation. Unable to work and suffering from his injury, he spent some months in a state of mental breakdown. Dr Dozous could improve the state of his eye, but not restore the sight to it. This continued until March 1858, when he bathed his eye in the spring and regained his full sight.

Justin Bouhohorts, an infant, received the benefits of the miraculous spring through the intervention of his mother. He had been sickly from birth, and at the age of eighteen months, in July 1858, he fell into a fever which seemed to render him unconscious. Croizine Ducoute, his mother, was advised by those near her to reconcile herself to the infant's death, and even to anticipate it: 'a neighbour wanted to put him in a shroud'.[93] They were very poor, and by her own account Croizine Ducoute frequently went hungry. In this environment a sickly child was regarded as an intolerable burden. However, she continued to hope for his life and took him that evening to the Grotto. She undressed him, pushed him into the stream, and held him there for fifteen minutes, without seeing any change in his state. The women present remonstrated with Croizine Ducoute over this prolonged immersion: 'they said to me "Take the baby from there!" One Marie Peyras, said aloud: "She wants to kill him: at least, then she will be able to rest." '[94] Justin Bouhohorts did not die at the Grotto, but neither did he recover, and his mother went sadly home. She spent the night warming him with towels and praying. At dawn the following morning, he suddenly recovered consciousness and was cured.

Isidore Pujol, a stonemason of Lourdes, entered into the historical record because he was the first person to be served with a summons when the Grotto was barricaded in July 1858. He had gone to the Grotto to wash his eye. In a grim accident suffered by many of the stoneworkers, he had a 'burst blood vessel in his eye, due to the slivers of stone which had lodged there',[95] He would have been in anguish, knowing that the loss of sight in one eye would probably be followed by the other. In July 1858, he was served with a summons at the Grotto but, perhaps out of pity, the Police Commissioner did not press charges against this afflicted man. Had not fate already dealt with him severely enough? Twenty years later, an historian noted that his interview with Isidore Pujol had been conducted on the street before the Lourdes basilica, where the former stonemason sat every day, 'a blind beggar'.[96]

An even more severe misfortune was experienced by Jean-Marie Doucet, the son of a prosperous peasant family who lived near Lourdes. He had been apparently healthy until the age of nine, when, in his own words, 'this long metamorphosis struck me'.[97] It was probably a degenerative nervous condition. He had fits and spasms and was semi-paralysed, he would remain for days with his face convulsed and his mouth hanging open, hardly able to eat or drink. Despite his infirmities, he was lovingly tended by his family and apparently received some education. He would later write a memoir, the style of which was self-taught and unsophisticated, yet poetic.

Jean-Marie Doucet was confined at home, more fortunate than many disabled children but still suffering, when the stories began to circulate about the Lady appearing at the Grotto. 'You cannot imagine the joy which I felt at hearing this marvellous news.' He desperately wanted to visit the Grotto, but his illness worsened. Perhaps, as he wrote, the cause may have been 'the chagrin which I felt in not being able to go to the Grotto, at the time when I wanted to, which brought on more fits'. His family begged the Soubirous family for a visit from Bernadette. They agreed, but as Jean-Marie Doucet himself saw, 'Bernadette would not have come to see me so soon, if my sister Joséphe had not been at the same school.'[98]

Bernadette was taken by her school friend to the Doucet farmhouse, where she had several conversations with the invalid. Their exchanges, devotedly remembered by him, were completely banal: ' "How are you? – Not too well – Are you hungry? Could you close your mouth and eat?" As soon as I could I told her that I was unable to.'[99] In later visits, she was more intimate, telling him 'at present I love you' when he would painfully manage to eat a little.[100] His accounts of her gentle teasing are similar to those given in later years by her patients, when she was Infirmarian at the Convent of St Gildard. She approached the sick with encouraging comments and humour, but could do no more for them than ordinary nursing. Jean-Marie believed that her presence improved his condition, but soon 'all the torments recommenced with the same violence'.[101] His family eventually arranged that he be carried to the Grotto, where he drank the water of the spring and returned unchanged to his home.

When visited by Curé Peyramale, Jean-Marie Doucet stated that: 'I would be cured should it please God.'[102] He also said that in this world one could not expect too many consolations. These are perfectly orthodox statements of Christian resignation, but his journal also records that after this his family took him to a different Pyrenean saint's shrine, and then to a sorceress who tried to heal him through incantations. Alongside the formal submission to authority were the heterodox traditions of popular religion, which sought indiscriminate recourse to the supernatural, according to need.

Bernadette briefly mentioned Jean-Marie Doucet, in a statement to the Police Commissioner where she acknowledged that she had visited a boy 'with his mouth always open'.[103] She denied having cured him, or having attempted any such thing. Jean-Marie Doucet adds the detail that he had wanted Bernadette to purchase a little crucifix for him, a 25 centimes one, similar to her own. She said that she would do so, but then sent word that she would be unable to, and that she was forbidden to visit again.[104] Probably she realized, as the interrogations started and her visions caused increasing controversy, that buying any object for anyone could be seen as profiteering.

She did not return to the Doucet farm, and in her personal history, he was to be only one of the thousands of distressed invalids who vainly sought her aid. In Jean-Marie Doucet's circumscribed existence, the encounter with Bernadette was the one great event of his life. He continued to venerate the Grotto, and he made a great effort to write an account of these events, illustrated with his own drawings. Imprisoned in his chair, Jean-Marie Doucet was one of the innumerable people roused to hope by the events at the Grotto, but one of the few to leave us an account of his feelings. Bernadette crossed his path, and as he went on dwelling on the fringe of life, he was one of the people who watched her from afar. The last time he saw her was late in 1858, when she was one of the children taken by a Sister from the school: 'who chose our farm as a place for a walk. I was as usual in my basket; and the children played in the meadow before me. It was thus that I saw, one last time, the holy young girl.'[105]

Jean-Marie Doucet is an example from among the faceless crowds who hoped for a miracle in Lourdes. He presented his story as one of contact with the miraculous, although he acknowledged that all the efforts 'could not give me the slightest relief ... If Bernadette could not cure me at all, at least she soothed me.'[106] He was to be paralysed until his death at the age of 50. He always believed that he had been very privileged to have met a visionary and to have visited the sacred spring. His moving account concluded with the words: 'Faithful souls see how God helps the unfortunate: even I, who am nothing but a wreck and an abortion: however my shepherd (Jesus) despite all of this, took pity on me (as you have seen).'

The miracle stories of Lourdes were received with mixtures of hope, scepticism, outrage and credulity by different audiences. Events such as the miracles at Lourdes, like the apparitions at La Salette in 1846, revealed an immense reservoir of the unsophisticated Christianity which existed behind the façade of a modern and secular French state. The latent fervour of many ordinary people had long been invisible to the intellectual classes who created textual representations.

An example of this is an article in the provincial scholarly journal *Revue d'Aquitaine*. It was published in neighbouring Gascony and had often featured articles on the Pyrenees, and even on Lourdes. In May 1858, an article was printed concerning the 'Vision of the girl at Lourdes' and informed readers of the 'odd stories which have circulated'.[107] The article listed some popular miracle stories which recounted both the marvels and the ghastly punishments suffered by unbelievers, including a peasant who had been 'devoured by his peaches, which had turned into snakes'. The bemused writer concluded that these remarkable stories proved that 'vulgar people in these regions' had persisted in the most fallacious beliefs and that 'popular superstition is still very much alive'. The tone was one of perplexity, as a provincial intellectual struggled to give an account of these close, but unexpected, events. The article concluded, with relief, that: 'Needless to say that the Church holds itself prudently, at a wise distance, and that it is completely a stranger to this mystification.'

Despite the confidence of the *Revue d'Aquitaine*, the Church could not indefinitely remain aloof from Lourdes, and would soon be obliged to intervene and regulate the situation. The article also indicates an erroneous judgement of the popular mentality, for the outbreak of miracles was treated as a surprise. Evidently the fact that the ordinary people of the area had persisted in a non-secular and anti-rationalist culture had gone unnoticed until the dramas of 1858. This is despite the fact that the writer was not an ill-informed person. The article was carefully researched and it appeared in a journal which had printed many articles on the local monuments and stories of the saints. These were presented as 'legends'. The scholars had a keen antiquarian spirit and, until 1858, they probably had known more about medieval religion than about the current beliefs of their social inferiors. The apparitions of Lourdes astonished them.

The nineteenth century was a time of such change and reaction that there was no consensus, even among contemporary observers, as to whether such a drama was typical or not. Although he prudently reserved his judgement on the miracles at Lourdes, the Bishop of Tarbes wrote that those who denied the very possibility of the miraculous had allowed themselves to 'fall into the rut of the unbelieving philosophy of the last century'.[108] In complete contrast the Garrison Sergeant at Lourdes was so affronted that he harangued the crowd at the Grotto and exclaimed that: 'It is not in the nineteenth century that one lets oneself be caught up in such beliefs.'[109]

This incident was long remembered in Lourdes, although no-one was particularly impressed. Mlle Estrade wrote in her memoir that 'one of the Gendarmes' said 'Eh! It should not be in the nineteenth century that people would come to believe in such superstitions!'[110] She went on to note that despite this the Gendarmes themselves doffed their caps during the apparition. Sergeant d'Angla could as profitably have delivered this line of argument to the men under his own command. The lower ranks of the Gendarmerie were similar to the mass of the people who flocked to the Grotto. Jacob Bigué, one of the men who served under Lieutenant Bourriot when he visited the Grotto on 21 February, recalled the sight of Bernadette entranced as extremely impressive. He returned in the company of his commanding officer and: 'on the way back, from Lourdes to Tarbes, the Chief did not scoff at all, he was a religious man'.[111]

Not all interested observers were as credulous as the populace who emerge from the letters of the government officials and of Adelaide Monlaur. In particular, the clergy took a view which balanced faith and reason. Canon Ribes, the Director of the Grand Seminary at Tarbes, heard the stories that emanated from Lourdes and later wrote a detailed recollection of his vacillating reactions throughout 1858. He visited Lourdes twice, in May and in September, and heard of many miraculous cures: 'but many of these reported cures were incomplete, or not lasting. Serious minds did not find any real evidence of divine intervention.' Finding that some cures were false had given him a 'displeasing impression ... However, I did have the disposition to believe; I looked for genuine proofs. Proofs of that sort did in fact exist, but I did not then know of them.'[112]

Throughout the entire period of the apparitions Curé Peyramale forbade any of the clergy of his parish to visit the Grotto. There is only one memoir from a cleric who witnessed Bernadette during a vision. Abbé Dézirat had just graduated from a seminary and was visiting relatives near Lourdes before being appointed to a post. Technically, he was outside of the Curé's jurisdiction, and so he cast aside his qualms: 'it seemed to me that ... I was not actively disobeying' and visited the Grotto on 27 February.[113] Seeing his clerical costume, the crowds parted for him and he gained a favoured place before the Grotto. Bernadette then approached. To his eyes she was an ordinary girl. She knelt, prayed, then he was fascinated by the change in her appearance when entranced. This favourable impression faded at the end of the vision and he began to wonder if it might be 'something other than the Immaculate Virgin'.[114] He commented on the atmosphere of devotion and respect which prevailed, yet felt himself to be 'ill at ease in the middle of that crowd, in that theatre'. When he visited the seminary at nearby Saint-Pé he told other priests of his trip to the Grotto. One was interested to hear of it, but two professors of the seminary burst into spontaneous laughter as soon as he spoke. Dézirat promised himself to say no more on the issue, and was so stung by this reaction that he only unwillingly wrote a memoir, at the request of the Lourdes historians, in later years.

As far as the clergy were concerned, the impulse to laugh at the apparitions was dying away by April 1858. During March and April 1858, while

Bernadette experienced only two further visions, the cult of the Lourdes apparitions passed through crucial developments. The apparition acquired her identity as the Immaculate Conception. The Grotto became a site of miracles and pilgrimages while the sheer volume of supernatural claims demanded clerical attention. The state authorities came to the unwelcome realization that they no longer had to confront only a visionary and her immediate followers, but an entire pilgrimage movement which focused on the Grotto as a sacred place. They embarked on a battle to stifle the unauthorized shrine. Even before the mid-year of 1858, the events at Lourdes had ceased to be a ridiculous or passing issue which could be confined to the Hautes-Pyrénées. The scene was set for a confrontation.

# NOTES

1. 'Statement from Bernadette', 18 Mar. 1858, *LDA* 1, no. 69, 260.

2. Adelaide Monlaur to her cousin, 8 Mar. 1858, *AG*, A8.

3. Report by the Police Commissioner to the Préfet, 19 Mar. 1858, *LDA* 1, no. 71, 261.

4. Antoinette Garros quoted, Cros, *Histoire*, 1. 443.

5. Callet quoted, Cros, *Histoire*, 1. 443.

6. Testimony of André Sajoux, quoted Cros, *Histoire*, 2. 50.

7. Report by Commissioner Jacomet to the Préfet, 19 Mar. 1858, *LDA* 1, no. 71, 262.

8. See references to Bernadette's récits, and the account written by Marie Dufo on 26 Mar. 1858, *LDA* 1, no. 85, 285.

9. Basile Castérot quoted, *LDA* 1, 462.

10. Curé Peyramale quoted in the testimony of Jeanne Védère, *LDA* 1, 462.

11. Peyramale quoted, *BVP*, 1. 135.

12. Unfortunately this letter is lost, and even the earliest historians of Lourdes were unable to consult it. Its existence is demonstrated by a letter to Mgr Laurence on 10 Apr. 1858, where Curé Peyramale made reference to 'my report of 25 March, which sent you that message', *LDA* 2, no. 132, 155.

13. M. P. Carroll, 'The Virgin Mary at La Salette and Lourdes: Whom did the children see?' *Journal of the Scientific Study of Religion* 24 (1985), 71.

14. Dr Boissairie, *Les Grandes Guérisons de Lourdes* (Paris 1900), 538.

15. Letter from Mlle Dufo, 25 Mar. 1858, *Procès*, 140.

16. Letter from a Professor of Theology at Notre Dame-des-Ermites, 13 Feb. 1862, quoted Cros, *Histoire*, 1. 463.

17. Préfet Massy to the Minister of Cults, 26 Mar. 1858, *LDA* 1, no. 89, 288.

18. Lasserre, *Notre-Dame de Lourdes*, 170–1.

19. Dr Balencie quoted by Cros, *Histoire*, 1. 472.

20. 'Rapport des médecins', 31 Mar. 1858, *LDA* 1, no. 104, 298–9.

21. Ibid., 298.

22. Ibid., 300.

23. Ibid.

24. M. Carroll, *The Cult of the Virgin Mary: Psychological Origins* (Princeton 1986).

25. Police Commissioner, Report to the Préfet, 7 Apr. 1858, *LDA* 2, no. 122, 146.

26. 'Rapport des médecins', 31 Mar. 1858, *LDA* 1, no. 104, 298.

27. Procureur Impérial Dutour, Report to the Procureur Général, 2 Apr. 1858, *LDA* 1, no. 112, 305–7.

28. *BVP*, 1, 139.

29. Ibid., 140.

30. Anna Dupas quoted, Cros, *Histoire*, 1. 383.

31. Procureur Impérial Dutour, 14 Apr. 1858, *LDA* 2, no. 150, 179. Emphasis in the original. Nincompoop is my translation of *drôlesse*.

32. Dr Dozous (de Lourdes), *La Grotte de Lourdes, Sa Fontaine, Ses Guérisons* (Paris 1926; f.p. 1874), 47–8.

33. Testimony of Marie Lamathe, *PON*, Sessio LXXVIII, 933.

34. Mlle Peyrard quoted by Mlle Lacrampe, *Témoins*, 101.

35. Antoine Clarens, *RdAM*, 13.

36. This term was often used by rationalist observers, 'Lavadan', *LDA* 1, no. 5, 168.

37. These opinions cited in the Report of Procurer Général Falconnet, 3 Mar. 1858, *LDA* 1, no. 22, 188.

38. Marie Courrech, *Témoins*, 126.

39. Letter of Frère Cérase, *RdAM*, 20.

40. Adelaide Monlaur to her cousin, 21 Mar. 1858, *AG*, A8.

41. 'Relation de l'abbé Dézirat, 1868', *AG*, A8. This was written before Jean-Baptiste Estrade's memoir, and, in accordance with the Abbé's wishes, it was kept in the archive and not printed during his lifetime.

42. Adelaide Monlaur to her cousin, 8 Apr. 1858, *AG*, A8.

43. Fanny Nicolau, *Témoins*, 114.

44. Pierre Callet, *Témoins*, 45.

45. Emphasis mine, Jeanne Abadie, *Témoins*, 213.

46. Antoine Nicolau, *Procès*, 33.

47. Basile Castérot, *PON*, Sessio LXII, 757.

48. Marshall d'Angla quoted by Cros, *Histoire*, 1. 214.

49. Ibid., 213.

50. Jeanne-Marie Adrian, *Procès*, 111.

51. Report from the Police Commissioner to the Préfet, 4 Mar. 1858, *LDA* 1, no. 25, 205.

52. Report of Procureur Général Falconnet, 20 Mar. 1858, *LDA* 1, no. 73, 264.

53. 'Relation de l'abbé Dézirat, 1868', *AG*, A8.

54. Jean-Baptiste Estrade, *PON*, Sessio III, 1352.

55. Jean-Baptiste Estrade quoted, Abbé Pène, *Témoins*, 272.

56. Adelaide Monlaur to her cousin, 8 Mar. 1858, *AG*, A8.

57. Elfrida Lacrampe quoted, Cros, *Histoire*, 1. 257.

58. Rachel Brownstein, 'The funeral of the tragic muse', *Yale Review* 81 (1993), 9.

59. R. D'Alger, *La Vérité sur Lourdes* (Paris 1910), 31 *passim*. Père Cros took the trouble to refute such suggestions at length. Cros, *Histoire*, 1. 232–5.

60. Lettre de M. Cousté, Prêtre, Professeur d'histore au Collége d'Aire, à M. le Rédacteur de 'l'Écho des Vallées', 26 Nov. 1854. Reprinted in Eugène Cordier, *Les Légendes des Hautes-Pyrénées. Suivies des lettres de deux abbés contre l'Auteur et de sa réplique* (Tarbes 1986; f.p. 1855), 111.

61. Adelaide Monlaur to her cousin, 8 Mar. 1858, *AG*, A8.

62. Louise Baup, testimony from the Cros archive, quoted by Laurentin, intro., *LDA* 2, 18.

63. J. Barbet, *La Dame plus belle que tout* (Paris 1957; f.p. 1909), 108. One notices in this anecdote, as in others, that it is apparently the wife who has spread the story.

64. Curé Peyramale to Mgr Laurence, 8 May 1858, *LDA* 2, no. 209, 257.

65. A. Théas, *Notre Dame de Medoux; aujourd'hui Notre-Dame d'Aste* (Tarbes 1896).

66. Gibson, *French Catholicism*, 146.

67. Devlin, *The Superstitious Mind*, 18.

68. Testimony of Abbé Glère, who was a student in 1858. He wrote a memoir for Père Cros, which is reprinted, Cros, *Histoire*, 2. 228–30.

69. Françoise Junça, testimony, *AC*, (E) AIV [o] à 15.

70. Ibid.

71. Julien Cazenave, 'Répertoire des visionnaires', *LDA* 2, no. 15, 61.

72. Ibid.

73. Adelaide Monlaur to her cousin, 8 Mar. 1858, *AG*, A8.

74. M. de Saint Pierre, *Bernadette et Lourdes* (Paris 1979), 9. Several writers have noted that the Pyrenean people continue to fear the Grotto. X. Recroix, 'Un aspect de la piété populaire dans les Pyrénées Centrales: La dévotion Mariale', *Revue de Comminges* 1 (1989), 128.

75. Père Fournou quoted by X. Recroix, 'Piété populaire', 128.

76. Testimony of Abbé Glère, Cros, *Histoire*, 2. 227.

77. Mlle Estrade, *RdAM*, 55.

78. Françoise Junça, testimony, *AC*, (E) AIV [o] à 15.

79. T.-M.-J.-T. Azun de Bernétas, *La Grotte des pyrénées ou manifestation de la sainte-vierge à la grotte de Lourdes* (Tarbes 1861), 170.

80. e.g. Marie Pailes, *Témoins*, 74.

81. Marie Courrech, *Témoins*, 126–31.

82. Lasserre, *Notre-Dame de Lourdes*, 157.

83. The opinion of Emmanuelle Estrade, *Témoins*, 99.

84. Quoted by Ruth Harris, who gives an account of her in, *Lourdes: Body and Spirit*, 92–6.

85. Interview of Bernadette by a visiting priest, 1859, Cros, *Histoire*, 3. 5.

86. Adelaide Monlaur to her cousin, 18 May 1858, AG, A8.

87. Ibid.

88. Ibid.

89. 'Procès verbal d'interrogatoire de Bernadette', 18 Mar. 1858, *LDA* 1, no. 69, 259.

90. Ibid.

91. Police Commissioner, Report to the Préfet, 14 Apr. 1858, *LDA* 2, no. 148, 170.

92. Police Commissioner, Report to the Préfet, 17 Apr. 1858, *LDA* 2, no. 158, 197.

93. Croizine Ducoute, Cros, *Histoire*, 1. 406.

94. Ibid., 405.

95. Isidore Pujol quoted, Cros, *Histoire*, 2. 172.

96. Ibid.

97. Journal of Jean-Marie Doucet, 1864, *LDA* 7, no. 1447, 212.

98. Ibid.

99. Ibid., 221, 223.

100. Ibid., 230.

101. Ibid., 222.

102. Ibid., 235.

103. 'Procès verbal d'interrogatoire de Bernadette', 18 Mar. 1858, *LDA* 1, no. 69, 258.

104. Doucet, 'Journal', *LDA* 7, 232.

105. Ibid., 236.

106. Ibid., 234.

107. J. N. 'Vision de la jeune fille de Lourdes', *Revue d'Aquitaine* 1 (1856).

108. Ordonnance de Mgr l'Évêque de Tarbes, *Procès*, 193.

109. Report of Garrison Sergeant d'Angla to Lieutenant Bourriot, 26 Feb. 1858, *LDA* 1, no. 6, 171.

110. Mlle Estrade, *RdAM*, 45.

111. Jacob Bigué, *Procès*, 43.

112. Chanoine Ribes (1879?), *AC,* (E) AIII, 0–27.

113. Abbé Dézirat quoted, Cros, *Histoire*, 1, 318.

114. 'Relation de l'Abbé Dézirat', 1868, *AG*, A8.

# CHAPTER 5

# The Spirit of Resistance
## Lourdes, May to September 1858

They take out summonses against those people who are known to have gone to the Grotto; despite the summonses, the fines of five francs, people still continue to go there. They have put barricades before the Grotto; and people have thrown them into the river. The barricades have been replaced, and some people have risked their lives, in going down by scaling the rock wall. There are fourteen or fifteen children who say that they have seen the Blessed Virgin.

Adelaide Monlaur to her cousin, 16 July 1858

When considering the outbreak of unauthorized religion at Lourdes, the government ministers in Paris, and even some of their subordinates in the Pyrenees, considered that an assertion of state authority and the suppression of the unwanted activities ought to be a simple matter. It was not without justification, as suppressions of popular religion were easily accomplished in many provincial areas. One example has been rescued from the obscurity of the French archives by Barnett Singer. In *Village Notables in Nineteenth-Century France* he relates how a disused chapel in Vienne was being used by a priest to burn candles, perform miracles and attract admiring crowds. The only unexpected feature of this story is that the miracle worker was a cleric. The result was predictable: 'the Mayor informed the Prefect, and against local wishes it (the chapel) was promptly closed'.[1] This was the type of result expected in Lourdes, but it did not happen.

Identifiable groups within the Lourdes population used different means to defend their faith in the Grotto. Always active were the *femmes du peuple*, who used their voices to decry the authorities and to spread their faith in miracles. They also insisted on depositing religious pictures and flowers at the Grotto. They regularly infringed the barricades, and their names make up the bulk of those on the lists compiled by the Police Commissioner. They can be distinguished because they are referred to as 'wife' or 'widow' rather than Mademoiselle or Madame. Women and their attendant children came to dominate the groups who went to the Grotto. Men had been present in almost equal numbers during earlier months, but from May onwards many of the labouring men of Lourdes would have been fully employed in the harvest. One group of men made their presence felt as they were situated near to the town – the stonemasons from the quarries. The stonemasons were implicated in acts of vandalism and menaces to agents of the law. Jean-Baptiste Estrade remembered that whenever they gathered they would talk about the events at the Grotto, and they believed that the Préfet was curbing their liberties: 'The word *révolte* was spoken.'[2]

Entirely different tactics were employed by Mlle Estrade, her brother, Dr Dozous, the lawyer M. Dufo and other middle-class adherents of the Grotto. They corresponded with friends in the outside world and welcomed visitors to the area, giving them their own accounts of the situation. The activities of the Estrades and their friends were very influential, particularly after August, when journalists began to visit the area. These respectable supporters of the Grotto generally ignored the folkloric miracles and the proliferation of other visionaries of Lourdes. After some promising beginnings, these other visionaries proved themselves to be part of an unrefined peasant conscious-ness of the supernatural, which could not coalesce with the religious ideals of the literate.

When reporting on the continued flood of visitors to the Grotto, and the appearance of new visionaries, a local newspaper asked if 'Bernadette, who finds herself sick, restricted to her bed, will not soon be distanced and almost forgotten?'[3] Although Bernadette was never forgotten, during mid-1858 there was a perceptible waning in the attention she attracted. This was consistent with the inactive role which she had always played amid her community's fertile creation of miracles. As this newspaper reported, Bernadette became ill during April 1858, and visitors who went to the *cachot* found her in bed. When well, she tended to be out of the house, and avoided visitors as much as possible. But her reticence eventually enhanced her reputation.

The eccentric antics of the other visionaries, and the visits to Lourdes by prestigious outsiders, combined to bring Bernadette forward into a new type of fame by late in the year. Her status as the original, and therefore the most important, visionary in Lourdes was more evident to the visitors than to her fellow citizens. The records show that Bernadette's naive story of her encounter with the beautiful *Dame* was impressive to people of status and education. Bernadette's simplicity and innocence won universal praise from sympathetic outside observers, who often had little interest in the antagonisms being enacted in the town. The national fame of a refined version of the Lourdes apparitions began in late 1858.

In April the Police Commissioner had noted that: 'Bernadette is visited by the people who come from elsewhere ... In the town, by contrast, people are far less interested in her.'[4] This comparative indifference to Bernadette was greatest at her own level of society. The people of the Rue de Petits-Fossés, and the other poor quarters of Lourdes, saw no change in Bernadette. She lived as she had always lived, sharing a hovel with her family, the daily chores with her mother, a narrow bed with her sister at night. On most school days she attended the Hospice, where she battled in the catechism class as one of the very dull pupils. Her visions at the Grotto were great dramas, and had opened a new world to her community. But the miracles remained at the Grotto and no aura of the miraculous clung to the visionary. She was not one of the holy women of popular tradition, who made prophecies and pronounced blessings or curses. Bernadette's neighbours knew her and liked her. The extravagant gestures roused by the early visions, such as mocking

Bernadette or venerating her, had faded away because there was nothing in her conduct to sustain them. By contrast, Bernadette's manner and appearance were impressive to the middle classes, who rarely involved themselves in the religious practices of poor women. Her mildness, dignity and dutiful behaviour had a special appeal which was more visible to those who did not see her every day.

The middle-class people of Lourdes often included the opportunity to speak to Bernadette as part of their hospitality to affluent visitors from the outside world. More and more of these were arriving, now that newspapers were reporting that a whole town in the Pyrenees had come to a standstill because of a girl who had been seeing visions. People such as the Estrades and the Tardhivail sisters suddenly became important because they knew Bernadette and could call her to their houses to meet these tourists. By May the Police Commissioner saw that 'they show her to visitors; and, in a word, never miss a chance to display her'.[5]

Curé Peyramale was one of the people whose opinion of Bernadette was rising. He heard favourable reports of her from the most genteel people in his parish, who were delighted by Bernadette's comportment when she was their guest. Outsiders who arrived in Lourdes seeking information often went first to the presbytery, to ask the parish priest for information. Curé Peyramale declined to become involved, and merely directed them to seek out notables in the town. However, he was being called upon, and deferred to, by people who would normally have not bothered with a Lourdes Curé. This would not have been displeasing, and in April he was host to a truly distinguished visitor.

Albert, the Comte de Rességuier, was a politician of a noble family. He was a 'Légitimiste' (a supporter of the Bourbon monarchy), and he had been a member of the Legislative Assembly until 1849. He would not return to political office until the Second Empire ended in 1871, when he was to become Deputy of Ger. He came to Lourdes on 10 April and immediately made contact with the clergy. He impressed Curé Peyramale, and presented the parish with the lovely gift of a chasuble for church. He asked to see Bernadette, and she was sent for. This would have been only a few days after the second last of her visions, when the 'miracle of the candle' occurred. Curé Peyramale informed the Bishop of Tarbes that the Comte had had a long interview with her. 'Everything about the young girl impressed him; he made her submit to a long interrogation, most detailed, most demanding, most insidious, and the child responded to all of his questions with reasoning which seems to be above her age and above her level of intelligence.'[6] One of Bernadette's clever answers was that when he challenged her that the Virgin could not have spoken to her in patois, for God and the Virgin Mary did not speak miserable dialects, she responded: 'If we know how to speak it, would not they?'[7] Bernadette was developing a reputation as someone who gave unanswerable replies. Curé Peyramale was most moved to see her indifferent to bribes: 'He offered the girl an *Imitation of Christ*, very beautiful, very tempting. She refused it. M. de Rességuier then said to her: "You will say a decade of the rosary for me at the Grotto and in return I will give you this book; you will be able to accept it then." The child answered: "I will say a decade of the rosary, but I don't want your book." '8 Curé Peyramale obviously would have liked such a volume. Perhaps he was forgetting that Bernadette herself had no use for it, and could not read. Nor could she even speak standard French. The interviews with visitors usually had to be translated by adults who accompanied Bernadette. Only visitors who were from the Hautes-Pyrénées, or other Occitan-speaking areas, could understand her fluently.

The duty of meeting strangers was irksome to Bernadette. She would call at neighbours' places like the Nicolau mill, or her Aunt Basile's home, and try to stay out of sight. Those who wanted her learnt to send to the *cachot* early in the morning. One day she was passing the house of Abbé Pène, a junior vicar of the parish. His sister and her friends, who were present, recognized Bernadette and asked him if he wanted to see her. They asked her to come up to the salon: 'Bernadette refused at first, but the ladies insisted and she came into the salon. It was there that she told us the story of her visions, since 11 February; she spoke in a natural manner, without fear or boldness, with indifference, like one who does a duty.'9

Late in April, she became ill, and there are recollections of visitors calling at her home and speaking to her while she lay in bed. Meanwhile the town of Lourdes was on the boil, and the state officials had forcibly cleared the Grotto of holy objects. Curé Peyramale became concerned for Bernadette, and also for the community, which was racked with tensions. He made a positive move by suggesting that Bernadette be sent away from Lourdes for a short while. This would give her a break, and might also lead to a calming of spirits. From 8 to 28 May 1858, she was on a visit to the town of Cauterets. The Bishop of Tarbes later revealed to the Minister of Cults that he had been consulted and was in agreement that Bernadette should be sent for a brief vacation. As the Bishop noted, it was found that her absence made no difference to events.10

It must have made a difference to Bernadette, who was taking the first vacation of her life. The visit was made with her cousin, Jean Segot, who worked in the Municipal Police at Lourdes. His wife had relatives at Cauterets and he was visiting them during his annual vacation. They had invited Bernadette to be their guest, and assured her that they would take care of expenses. (Probably, Curé Peyramale had asked them to do so, and may have reimbursed them.) The journey to Cauterets would have taken at least half a day, as it was accomplished in carriages on a winding mountain road. The route follows steep cliffs and crosses rivers, showing travellers dramatic mountain scenery. Several towns are passed on the way to Cauterets, and they are marked by medieval monuments, including Templar churches and ruined fortresses on distant crags.

Once there, Bernadette was in a new environment. Cauterets was a fashionable spa-town during the season, but very empty and inexpensive to visit in May, when she was there. Bernadette went to bathe at the mineral spa at Bruzeaud, the waters of which were reputed to have medicinal value. She probably found the baths agreeable because she returned often during her three-week stay. As she had recently been ill, but returned in perfect health, she was a good recommendation for Cauterets. It is an irony that while pilgrims were flocking to Lourdes to wash in the spring at the Grotto, hoping for a miracle, Bernadette herself went away to have recourse to the medicinal benefits of a mineral spa. Cauterets was a break from her ordinary environment, but some of the pressures of Lourdes followed her around the Pyrenees. The local police were told to watch Bernadette, and sent the following report: 'She goes regularly to bathe herself at the spa, and many people have questioned her about her claimed visions, and she maintains her original story. Several sick people have addressed themselves to her; but she confined herself to telling them that they should believe in God in order to obtain a cure. She has always refused any form of offering.'[11]

On 22 May she travelled back to Lourdes with her cousin, and the Police Commissioner was soon aware of her presence. On the Monday following Pentecost, (25 May) there was a special Mass for a confraternity of women. The Police Commissioner was exasperated that one of the women, who had the distinction of bringing the blessed bread to the altar, had given her place to Bernadette: 'who, naturally, attracted the attention of the crowd who filled the church. This was all that was needed to make her the subject, for the rest of the day, of conversations on the part of those who had almost forgotten her.'[12]

## The Grotto as a place of worship

During the last days of the fortnight the numbers of people assembled at the Grotto had been estimated as being at least ten thousand. The crowds who continued to flock to the Grotto after 4 March were less in number, but were part of a continuous stream of visitors. Public enthusiasm mounted during the festival season of Easter, and during the first week of April, more than one thousand visitors per day were pouring into the town. On Easter Monday the Grotto was visited by 3,433 strangers and 2,000 people from Lourdes and its environs.[13] The provincial newspapers had begun to feature articles on the subject. Their views dutifully echoed the views of the Préfet and sometimes were even more openly hostile. *L'Ère Impérial* described Bernadette as an 'hallucinating girl' and the Grotto as a 'swamp where she washes', but even such negative reports would have confirmed the growing fame of Lourdes.[14] The masses of visitors flocking to the town were a newsworthy event, and even the most militantly rationalist journalist did find these events a 'very interesting spectacle'.[15]

Lourdes became such an object of provincial interest that in 1858 it experienced an early tourist season. As early as March, coaches were being hired in Tarbes and Pau specifically for visits to the Grotto. The visitors included many respectable, and even prominent, citizens of the local cities, and their presence raised the status of the Grotto among the middle classes of Lourdes. Dominiquette Cazenave remembered that initially she had been 'scandalized to see what women brought her (Bernadette), protected her, lent her candles: unmarried mothers, that damaged my faith'.[16] (She was apparently referring to Bernadette's aunts.) The more socially elevated visitors who appeared from March 1858 onward gave a more reassuring impression. As Adelaide Monlaur observed with satisfaction: 'the Grotto is not only visited by the common people, but also by families of high standing [*de haut ton*]'.[17] The common people also continued to flock to the area, which they idealized as a place of equality. As Croizine Bouhohorts told a magistrate, Massabielle had always been common land where 'you are the master, and I am too'.[18] Hearkening back to its history as a pasture for swine, she reminded him that formerly 'the sucking pig of the rich and the sow of the poor went together to Massabielle: we were equal, all of us'.[19]

During March and April of 1858, the cult of the *Dame* had escaped from its lower-class origins, and a general turn in opinion brought most of the citizens of Lourdes into support for the Grotto. During the early days of the fortnight, it had been only one part of the Lourdes population who were serious about the visions, 'only the lower classes [*le bas peuple*] seemed attentive'[20] and there were numerous scoffers. In only a short while respectable people were drawn to the cult, and in the whole town 'the number of unbelievers became so small, that they were of no importance'.[21]

Cynical outsiders tended to assume that the hope of material gain had played a crucial role. It was the only motive which the state officials put forward as an explanation, and it is true that this was a factor. Mercantile interests oriented toward the tourist trade had long existed in Lourdes. After 4 March, when the town had experienced a huge influx of people with no ill-effects but only general celebrations, such business people had reason to ponder the benefits of the apparitions whether they believed in them or not. Yet obvious opportunism was rarely manifest, and factors such as the impact of social solidarity and local patriotism need to be included.

One important feature of life in Lourdes after the apparitions was that the townspeople found themselves constantly surrounded by pilgrims, and were in turn influenced by them. Elfrida Lacrampe, who offered a rare testimony of doubt in the apparitions, struggled with her own sense of unbelief while the fame of the Grotto spread:

> At the Hotel des Pyrénées, I saw people who came to pray to Our Lady at the Grotto. I was embarrassed when they would question me, I did not want to ruin the faith of others, nor affirm my own. Often those people told me of graces which they had received, that impressed me. I said to myself: 'Evidently these people did not come here for the pleasure of giving us their 100 cent coins.'[22]

Only in later years, when she met a visiting priest from Paris, did she speak her mind: 'To that good priest, I dared to confess my doubts.' Other Lourdes people might have doubted the miracles at the Grotto, but were unwilling to concede anything to authority figures. Jean-Baptiste Estrade quoted the stonemasons as saying: ' "Eh! What does it matter to the Préfet that we should believe, or not believe, in the events at the Grotto? What right does he have to forbid us to drink from this spring or any other one? Are we free men, or slaves?" '[23]

## Order and legality

Only the Mayor of Lourdes officially expressed any faith in the inherently harmless nature of the new devotion. Although always deferential to the higher authorities, the Mayor and his council were aware that prohibition could rouse stubborn local resistance, and they were also inclined to consider the benefits which a shrine and a therapeutic spring might bring. A month after the conclusion of the fortnight the Mayor optimistically suggested to the Préfet that as the 'public tranquillity reigns and order is not troubled, I think that there is nothing more to do'.[24] The Gendarmerie, also, were inclined to keep their distance. As Lieutenant Bourriot wrote when giving his instructions for 4 March 1858: 'As far as any question of miracles goes, leave that to the authorities, the Mayor, the Police Commissioner, the Procureur Impérial, the Magistrate: it is their business; ours is to maintain free movement and order, the rest does not concern us.'[25]

In other regions of France, it had been the Gendarmerie alone who were able to squash visionary episodes by their simple intervention. One example can be cited from Brittany, an area with a long tradition of peasant holy women. In the hamlet of Barillère, in the Diocese of Nantes, Jeanne Boisseau (b. 1797), an orphan who had worked as a shepherdess, then as a servant, began having visions and experiencing stigmata in 1857. As a religious pamphlet which commemorated her life simply stated: 'hundreds of people came to see her. Naturally the Gendarmerie wanted to stop these scenes.' Her surviving family bowed to this pressure and 'accepted to take her and hide her as much as possible'.[26] The word 'naturally' precludes any explanation of the motives of the authorities. Their opposition was seen as being so typical that it required no elaboration. It is also noticeable, from this brief account, that the visionary's family were persuaded to put her into a form of unofficial custody simply because the agents of the state told them to do so. In this case, the officials of the Second Empire government were able to wield an effective form of coercion which was far greater than their formal powers within the law.

From then until her death in 1871 Jeanne Boisseau enjoyed only a clandestine existence as a holy woman, confined to a room in her family's house, and never allowed to speak to outsiders. She is remembered to this day by the descendants of those who knew her. Some scraps of memory help to elucidate the attitude of the authorities. One informant, who had lived as a child in her relative's house, remembered Jeanne's prediction that one day religion would triumph and people would live in idyllic brotherhood, 'but those days will only come when the bishops have remade France'.[27]

This statement comes from the tradition of reactionary peasant beliefs, so much a part of the heritage of Brittany and the Vendée, which rejected the French Revolution. It posed a problem to the government of Napoleon III, who directly affronted the still active royalists of France. Jeanne Boisseau existed in isolation, and the authorities preferred to ensure that such people did not find a voice through the potent medium of visions. Very few French bishops had the slightest aspiration to the powers which she dreamed of. The details which have been preserved of Jeanne Boisseau's life show the perpetuation of reactionary ideals in rural Breton society, and also the toll of repression which continued to keep grievances alive. Among the misfortunes which marked her life, it was remembered that during the 1820s she had been subjected to 'the outrages of a shameless group of soldiers who left her, stripped naked and tied to the trunk of a tree'.[28] This awful incident took place before Jeanne Boisseau reached the age of twenty, and was not directly connected with the onset of her career as a visionary at the age of sixty. However, it indicates some of the risks faced by a poor woman without influence. It would have left her alienated from uniformed male authority figures, and the Gendarmes who later came to coerce her and her family may have seemed to threaten similar ill-treatments.

The comparison between Bernadette and an obscure and repressed figure such as Jeanne Boisseau indicates that the situation in Lourdes was not as bad as it might have been. Bernadette was born in 1844 and therefore missed the violence and disruption of the fall of the First Empire. She never met any looting soldiers. It was impossible for the Lourdes authorities to order her family to hide her away, and thus accomplish her sequestration simply through intimidation. As the Police Commissioner gloomily wrote: 'Bernadette knows that she cannot be prevented from going to the Grotto.'[29] In a lively and much-visited town she was not isolated or helpless, and she could not be ill-treated without the provocation of a riotous public reaction.

In fairness to the Police Commissioner and his superiors, there is no indication that they were inclined to use such tactics against Bernadette or anyone else. They wanted only to apply the law and to preserve public order, while the peculiar status and claims of a visionary made legal repression difficult. As the Procureur Impérial noted, he had tried to prevent her visits to the Grotto, but 'it would have been necessary, in order to prevent her, to use violence', which was undesirable, and would have attracted further public attention.[30]

From early in the fortnight the rumours of Bernadette's visions were met with an explanation, relevant to provincial concerns, of why she would tell such a story. In early February 1858, an article printed in the local news-sheet, *Le Lavedan*, claimed that three children had recently gone to gather wood when they were 'surprised by the owner' and ran to hide in a nearby Grotto. The 'heroine of that story' then knelt in prayer and claimed to see the Virgin Mary; in keeping with her story she was returning every day and praying in the same place.[31] The *Lavedan* article represented a common opinion in the Hautes-Pyrénées among those who did not believe in the apparitions. As Sergeant d'Angla said, 'being persuaded that the little girl had gone to steal wood, I did not believe in these visions, I said to myself: "If God wanted to make a miracle, he would not use a thief to do so." '[32] He said that he had learnt the wood-gathering story from his serving Gendarmes, 'and they had gathered their information from common talk'. When Sergeant d'Angla accused Bernadette of stealing wood he identified her as the type of troublemaker who represented both the superstitions and the disorderly tendencies of an entire population.

The apprehensions of the state officials concerned latent events. They were preoccupied with what *might* happen, and the reasoning of their reports depended upon unspoken assumptions about the disreputable Soubirous family, who must surely be engaged in fraud, and the excitable and discontented Pyrenean people, who were assembling without visible control. The people, in their turn, resented both the harassment of the authorities and the unfounded assumption that they had a natural tendency toward anarchy. In their recollections they often testified, with a note of protest, that during the popular veneration of the Grotto: 'There was no disturbance there, but much order: everyone worked to make order, without anyone commanding them.'[33] Strangely enough, the officials did recognize the peaceful and orderly nature of the events at the Grotto, and at different times various observations were made to the effect that: 'Until now, the pilgrimages are made with calm ... We do not have the slightest disorder to report.'[34] This sentence is qualified by the opening phrase – 'until now'.

The state officials of the Hautes-Pyrénées were not only alarmed by the threat of disorder from the people whom they governed. They also lived under the menace that their own careers and reputations could be blighted by criticism from their superiors. The nature of the Lourdes apparitions was unfathomable and there was an attitude that such things simply did not happen in a well-run département. The officials had been aware, during the early stages of the visions, that an over-reaction on their part would only magnify the events and, as the Préfet wrote, 'give the matter more importance than it merits'.[35] This attitude was abandoned in the face of the sustained public enthusiasm for the Grotto, and it was easy for higher officials such as the Attorney General to complain that it was regrettable 'that the authorities had not intervened earlier to prevent the beliefs from growing and propagating themselves'.[36] The minister was asking his subordinates to perform the impossible, but such a damning opinion could easily be voiced from Paris. The demand from above that 'it is necessary that nothing be neglected in order to stop demonstrations which could degenerate into scandal and compromise public tranquillity'[37] only increased the pressures on the officials responsible for Lourdes, without offering them any meaningful guidance or support.

## The voice of authority

After the fortnight, the Grotto remained open to public access, and became more and more frequented as an unauthorized shrine. On 4 May 1858 the Police Commissioner was given orders to clear the area, and the pressures of community resistance, religious fears and unwilling employees were manifest. It was difficult to hire a horse and cart, and the Police Commissioner had to personally command his unwilling subordinates to remove all the cultic objects. The Grotto was then barricaded, on the pretext that it was a mineral spa, and as such was the property of the French state.

The barricade at the Grotto had to be repeatedly rebuilt because it was destroyed on the nights of 17 June, 27 June and 10 July. The planks of wood were thrown in the Gave river, and some police agents in the town were threatened with a similar fate. Alarmed by the atmosphere, Curé Peyramale preached sermons specifically aimed at the 'common people', warning them to remain within legality.[38] Violence was more often threatened than enacted in Lourdes, and the symbolic act of destroying the barricades seems to have satisfied people's anger. Much of the campaign of 1858 closely corresponds to James Scott's well-known theory that peasants rarely openly defy the authorities, but instead resort to the 'weapons of the weak', 'foot dragging, dissimulation ... false compliance, pilfering, feigned ignorance, slander, arson, sabotage'.[39] These stealthy oppositions were utilized by the ordinary people of Lourdes, and also by the minor employees of the state, pressed into service against the Grotto.

In order to organize surveillance of the Grotto the Police Commissioner drew upon the services of the Field Guards, who were assisted in their duties by Gendarmes. The Field Guards, Pierre Callet and Jean Verges, were not ideal employees for the task. Throughout France, Field Guards were criticized as ill-educated, inefficient and very much subject to local influence rather than state control. They lacked the loyalty and organization of the Gendarmerie and, in the opinion of some French officials, they could not usually be expected to perform any useful service.[40] The Hautes-Pyrénées had the distinction of being among the three départements which paid the very lowest wages to their Field Guards, and in Lourdes their duties were badly performed. When, in the words of Pierre Callet, 'the Apparitions started to make an uproar' Commissioner Jacomet had ordered him to carry out surveillance at the Grotto and had added: "And that is serious" ' Callet sagely explained that Jacomet had said this 'because he had to give account to the Préfet'.[41]

In a letter to the Préfet, the Police Commissioner complained that 'I am sure that I cannot count on any agent in the town.'[42] The Field Guards were not only lackadaisical, they were also partisans of the offenders. They had already been posted at the Grotto to perform surveillance during Bernadette's visions, and the experience had converted them to belief. They were afraid of offending the *Dame* of the Grotto, but they were also in awe of Commissioner Jacomet, and during the barricading of the Grotto his supervision sometimes roused them to an unexpected level of efficiency.

The surveillance of the Soubirous family was also maintained. One of the police agents, Phillipe Viron, commented later that he had not lost sight of Bernadette throughout the whole period. Yet there is little information about how the family were living their daily lives. Bernadette's father accompanied her during several visions, but this duty was usually taken by the aunts. Jean-Marie Soubirous, one of her younger brothers, later recalled seeing her often questioned by strangers. He noticed that she did not like it, and would never raise the subject of the apparitions. He himself got into trouble because of visitors. One day in 1858 he came home with two francs, having been given this money by people who had asked him to guide them to the Grotto. He had earned the money in helping the tourists, but Bernadette was furious. She gave him a resounding slap, and made him go back and return it.[43] Louise Castérot appears to have been more talkative and emotionally expressive than the rest of the family. Or it may be that her position as a mother put her more into view and contact with the outside world. However, her ready tongue brought her to the attention of the authorities in May 1858, when she was terrified and intimidated all over again by the 'false news' affair.

On 20 May 1858, Lourdes was enlivened by one of the most colourful rumours to date. The local officials were annoyed when they heard that it was being said that dispatches had been received from the Emperor Napoleon III, who had decided to reverse the policies of his inferiors. He had sent a present of money (six francs!) to Bernadette, with a request for her prayers, while the second dispatch ordered the creation of a chapel at the Grotto.[44] This improbable story circulated with zest and the Procureur Impérial decided to take action.

Three women who worked as laundresses, Cyprine Gesta, Anna Dupin (*femme* Dupas) and Josèphe Ouros (*femme* Baringue) were brought before the Court on 28 May 1858, where they were charged with the deliberate transmission of *fausses nouvelles*. This was a criminal charge in Second Empire France. Poor Louise Castérot was brought into court as a witness, along with many other women, most of whom briefly deposed that they heard the story, and only repeated it because they thought it to be true. Louise Castérot, formally described as 'thirty-three years old, a housewife of Lourdes', said that 'I was told of a journal which spoke advantageously of my daughter, Bernadette.'[45] She did not say who had told her, and admitted that she had passed the story on to her friend Cyprine Gesta. The lawyer M. Dufo offered his services and made an effective case for the defence. On 23 June the Court pronounced its judgment that two of the women were not guilty, because they had repeated these tales in private homes, and not in a public place. Cyprine Gesta was found guilty, and sentenced to a fine of five francs.

The Prosecution appealed against this leniency, but the Court in Pau dismissed all charges. The magistrates who refused to convict these women, and the lawyers who represented them for free, made a statement to the effect that law-abiding Pyrenean people were refusing to join the campaign against the Grotto. When the women returned to Lourdes, whole streets of people celebrated their acquittal.

## Crossing the barricade

The Grotto was forbidden to public access, but people kept going there, and broke the law by climbing in. This gave rise to a multitude of prosecutions, but a complete documentation is not available because the *registre judiciaire* of Lourdes, which was consulted by historians during the 1860s and 1870s, has since been lost.[46] The Field Guards collected the names of people who crossed the barricade, or who were found at the site of the Grotto when they commenced their surveillance.

Both of the Guards found that the visitors did not upbraid them, although some 'grumbled against the authorities'.[47] Pierre Callet engaged in burlesque activities in order to avoid doing too effective a job. He allowed himself to be diverted into conversation with groups of local women, so that he could not see that others were climbing the barricade. When he arrived at his post he was preceded by his dog, 'Mouton' (sheep), whose appearance would give people a warning to leave the Grotto. 'It was the will of God that Mouton played that role: he saved the others, and he saved me. Everyone admired it.'[48] Although many people from Lourdes profited from the goodwill of the Guards, the Police Commissioner checked on their surveillance, and they dared not overlook too many. Jean Verges said that he told people: ' "It is forbidden, you are going to compromise me." They replied: "Oh well, write out a summons." '[49] Some people made a point of breaching the barricade, and giving their names, as a deliberate gesture of protest.

The appearances before the Police Tribunal were occasions of protest. In the first cases, the Lourdes people used ridicule and the guise of stupidity in order to create 'the most hilarious scenes'.[50] Jean-Baptiste Estrade wrote that the 'idle and curious of the town' would attend these sessions for their entertainment value.[51]

In Lourdes the accused were in their own town, before an audience of people whom they knew. The women were particularly keen to play the 'stupid peasant', a ruse which has been analysed by Peter McPhee as a standard defence manoeuvre by peasants before nineteenth-century French courts.[52] When asked their names, they affected surprise, pointing out that the Justice of the Peace knew them already. This led to rejoinders such as:

—Not so much talk! Is it true, yes or no, that you entered the Grotto by means of breaking in? (*effraction*)
—By means of *fractions*! Oh Your Honour, I am not a learned person.[53]

Such exchanges provoked general hilarity, but the mutual hostility of the authorities and accused also reverberates through the comedy:

—You are an idiot ... You think that you honour the Virgin? You disgrace her.
— But, Your Honour, when you dress up and go to make a visit to a great lady in the town, do you believe that you disgrace her?[54]

Evidently something was known of the private life of the man on the bench, and the accused took their chance to remind him of it. These *femmes du peuple* made up a distinct group and were among the most fervent devotees of the Grotto. The authorities found them to be of 'equivocal morality'[55] or even, as the Police Commissioner wrote, frightful prostitutes, addicted to drink.[56] They were among the poorest of the population and there was never much possibility that they would be paying fines. One of them, Croizine Ducout, remembered with relish how she had argued with the Justice of the Peace, telling him that Massabielle was a 'common land' not a 'private property' and that he could 'judge from on high, judge from below; I will no more pay you tomorrow morning than this afternoon'.[57] To his familiar refrain of 'not so much tongue, or I will have you taken up!' she replied that she did not fear prison, 'I do not eat bread every day; in prison, I would have some, and meat once a week.'[58]

The common women were accompanied by their betters, who were also charged with illegal entry to the Grotto. By 17 July the accused included such luminaries of local society as Marie Pailhasson, the daughter of the prosperous Lourdes pharmacist. Adelaide Monlaur witnessed this trial, where some of the 'highest and most distinguished in the town of Lourdes' sat in the audience. Alongside them seethed 'all the workers of Lourdes, quarrymen, stonemasons, etc. had risen up ... they all appeared very angry, because these workers do not want to be forbidden to go to the Grotto: one would anticipate a revolution in that audience'.[59] The small traders of Lourdes were less insolent, and afraid to go before the Court. Even being summonsed cost them a much-needed day's salary. But they appeared, and joined in the communal attitude of solidarity.

During the agitated month of July the Procureur Impérial observed, as if it were something to proud of, that the measures taken by the authorities had 'bruised numerous interests'.[60] He knew that the local notables and the Lourdes municipality were only outwardly obedient and covertly wanted the Grotto open for visitors. Virtually every social sector in the town had some reason to favour the Grotto, whether for faith, commercial gain or an obstinate inclination towards local patriotism. The Procureur had perceived from the early stages that 'passions or love of money'[61] were weighty influences and that 'the Grotto has become, for Lourdes, a dear place, for diverse reasons'.[62] The love of lucre should have been a motive which Second Empire officials could at least understand, and perhaps tolerate. Yet the officials at Lourdes remained stubbornly opposed to all the interests of the district. Napoleon III and his ministers often exhorted their Préfets to be indifferent to 'local interests', which were defined as an obstacle to the degree of power which the state claimed for its own.[63] Préfet Massy and his fellow administrators had no need of this advice for they enthusiastically erred in the other direction. Their handling of the Lourdes affair shows them to have been utterly impervious to local influences, to an extent which made consensual government a difficult task.

Bernadette was one of the few people in lower Lourdes who were willing to respect the barricade at the Grotto. When Jeanne Védère, her cousin, visited Lourdes Bernadette told her not to go to the Grotto, and suggested that later on the barriers would surely be removed. But she made no move to achieve this end. During the month of June 1858 there were other matters of importance for her. The 3 June 1858 was a great day, for which she had struggled for so long. She had her First Holy Communion, and thus was admitted to the sacraments of the Church. The ceremony took place at the chapel of the Hospice, along with the other children from her catechism class. Bernadette was dressed in ceremonial white dress and veil, which was provided by the pious ladies of Lourdes. On this one occasion, she was willing to accept charity. The making of such dresses for poor children was a traditional act of benevolence, not something specifically directed at her.

Bernadette had been thwarted many times in her wish to go to the altar rails. For at least two years, she had longed for this moment. For this, she had left Bartrès, and had persisted for a long time in the difficulties of the catechism class. The First Holy Communion was like a day of graduation. Dressed in their robes, the children came out of the chapel into a new stage of life. Most of them, including Bernadette, had completed their education. Her schooldays were over. From July 1858 onwards, she stayed at home and worked beside her mother. This was manual labour in household tasks, as well as income-producing work such as washing laundry. She was now equal to the other girls and women of her social order. On the day of Bernadette's First Holy Communion, Mlle Estrade asked her a tricky question:

—What made you more happy: the First Communion or the apparitions?
She answered:
—The two things went together, but cannot be compared. I was very happy with both.[64]

On 25 June there was the very significant Pyrenean festival *la Saint-Jean* (St John's Day). Aside from being a Christian feast day, it was also the old summer solstice. It was a festival of youth, of fertility, and of sacred fire. There were bonfires, public feasts and the opportunity for children to dress in costumes and say whatever they liked. Bernadette celebrated St John's Day by visiting Bartrès. She had often done so in previous years, but this time it was different. She had made her First Communion, she was among the young women rather than the children. She returned to the Aravant household, but this time they could not keep her, she would not be a child shepherd any more. She was asked for a recital of the apparitions, and concluded with the words:

—Godmother, do not go if you do not have the faith. One must truly believe in order to go there. (*Marreno, ne yanès pas se náouet pas pla era fé. Que la caou aoué pla la fé.*)
Jeanne Aravant, to whom this was addressed, explained:
—She called me 'Godmother' as all the others do here.
And she repeated the formula in the most clear form:
— One must have the faith or it is better not to go.[65]

It seems that Bernadette had got a word in, during the festival of free speech, and closed her accounts at Bartrès. There is no record that Jeanne Aravant ever did go to the Grotto.

On 16 July, Bernadette experienced her last vision. At dusk, she slipped away towards Massabielle, accompanied by her youngest aunt, Lucile Castérot. Almost unnoticed, she went to the opposite bank of the Gave river. It was one of the Virgin's holy days, being the feast of Our Lady of Mount Carmel. The 'great fortnight' had taken place during the dawn hours, but the last vision was at sunset. Because of the barricade, Bernadette could not approach the Grotto, but knelt instead on the high ground on the other side of the river. The hollow in the rocks was distant, but visible. Then the apparition appeared, and Bernadette said later that she saw her as clearly, and as closely, as ever. Bernadette remained for longer than usual, and recited the whole of the rosary until twilight. Then the apparition vanished, and, as Bernadette ever afterwards said, 'I never saw her again.'

Bernadette retained no messages from the two final apparitions. The most significant statements had been in earlier days, such as the request to come to the Grotto for a fortnight, the call for penance, the request for chapels and a procession, and the momentous statement, 'I am the Immaculate Conception.' In the end there were no more messages, just as there had not been on the first two occasions. At some time during the visions, Bernadette received secret statements from the *Dame*, which were not to be revealed to others. It is said that Bernadette received three secrets, and also a prayer which she recited daily.

The reception of secret messages is a standard motif of Marian apparitions in the late modern era. It began at La Salette in 1846, where the two children returned from seeing the Virgin Mary who specifically entrusted each of them with a secret message. Maximin Giraud never said anything more about this, but Mélanie Calvat published various versions in later years. Mélanie claimed that the apparition had instructed her to make public the 'secret of La Salette', a series of apocalyptic prophecies, when the time was right. The appearances of Our Lady of Fatima in 1917 also gave rise to claims about a secret message. The 'secret of Fatima' was allegedly written down by the three children, and sent to the Vatican. The Papal authorities have always refused to confirm that they have any such document, or to say if it would be released to the public. Rumours about the content of the 'secret of Fatima' have circulated for decades, and have helped to maintain an atmosphere of speculation and mystery around the shrine.

There is no tradition of a 'secret of Lourdes', because whatever it was, it died with Bernadette, and throughout her life she never wrote out any documents, or made any confidences about it. She was often asked, but simply said that she was forbidden to repeat what the Lady had told her. The secrets which Bernadette received could be seen as an imitation of La Salette, or as a different type of communication altogether. As Bernadette never made any prophecies, nor claimed to have special information about the world's fate, the apparitions at Lourdes offer no material for millenarian thought. There is another way of looking at Bernadette's secrets, which is that she was not holding them out as hidden information, but rather asserting that there were aspects of her communication with the vision which it was impossible to relate. For the rest of her life, she was to be surrounded by people who questioned her about the visions. Insisting that some things were secrets may have been her way of telling her audience that they did not, and could not, know it all.

The visitors who questioned Bernadette were sometimes polite, but they could also be condescending, demanding, frivolous or even hostile as they tried to check her credibility. Middle-class people were impressed when Bernadette endured searching interrogations with calm and simplicity. It was also often noted that she was very humble, and preferred to be with people of her own rank in society. That was probably because they did not pester her, and they did not think that others had the right to do so. In order that Bernadette be put under scrutiny, she had to be taken away from her home environment, where sympathetic locals took her part, and placed in the parlours of the middle classes. Abbé Vincent Péré visited Lourdes in May 1858, having recently been ordained. He was calling upon relatives in the Hautes-Pryénées. He knew that the Curé had forbidden clerics to be involved in the Grotto controversy, but he could not resist trying to see the visionary. Like some other ecclesiastics, he overcame his scruples and decided that since he was not of that parish, he was not bound by Peyramale's authority. Abbé Péré went to the Soubirous's home in the morning, and simply walked through the door. He found Bernadette, and claimed that he had spoken to her 'loudly and rudely' in order to test her:

—Are you that silly girl who pretends to see the Blessed Virgin at Massabielle?
—Yes, that's me.
—You lie, little cheat, it is not true.
—It is true, yes.
—I repeat, you lie, and if you continue you will be put in prison.
At the word 'prison' the mother burst into tears. The child showed no expression at all...
—Are you not ashamed to make your mother cry?
—Yes, it does bother me, but the Virgin told me to say what I say.

This conversation could have gone on indefinitely, but the Abbé was interrupted by local people, who followed him into the house. They became angry at his tone, and 'their faces were not at all reassuring'.[66] He soon left.

The tourist season in the Hautes-Pyrénées went from May until September. Therefore visitors converged on the area at the exact period when the controversy of Lourdes was at its height. These tourists included the most wealthy and influential people in Europe – Napoleon III himself was to spend September 1858 in Biarritz. For many visitors, especially in the nearby opulent spas of Cauterets and Bagnères-de-Bigorre, the stories from Lourdes were a daily topic of conversation, and soon many were willing to 'brave the edict and go to the Grotto ... out of the lively sentiment of curiosity'.[67] The notebooks of the Field Guards began to register a different type of name:

Le Comte de Galard, proprietor at Paris.
Le Comte de Chambrey of Paris
Mme la comtesse de Chambrey
Louis de Dananche proprietor at St Amour
Mlle de Maubon.[68]

The Field Guards noted with wonder that although 'the strangers could have deceived us with their names' they did not do so, and would frequently give them their cards.[69] The officials would probably have preferred that such visitors give false names. After listing a series of distinguished titles Mayor

Lacadé smoothly suggested to the Préfet: 'You will be able to decide, in your wisdom, if it is suitable to act on the summonses which could be issued.'[70] The Préfet referred the issue of distinguished visitors to the Paris authorities and was informed that when 'these things have happened without bragging and display, it is better not to prosecute'.[71] A decade later pro-*Lourdais* writings still resonated with a well-founded resentment about this: 'A deplorable thing: the law was broken with impunity by the powerful, while they prosecuted the weak.'[72] The official reasoning behind this situation was that the visitors were no risk to public order, whereas the local population was.

The ultimate example of the dilemma posed by lofty visitors occurred on 28 July 1858 when a party of distinguished ladies, accompanied by their servants, went to the Grotto. They had already called at the presbytery, where Abbé Pomain had received them, because Curé Peyramale was absent. The lady who headed this expedition was Mme l'Admiral Bruat, lady-in-waiting to the Empress and governess of the Crown Prince. Accompanied by her daughters, and a nun, Sr Saint-Antonin, she had stopped at Lourdes while visiting St Sauveur for the 'spa season'. Abbé Pomain agreed to their request for an interview with Bernadette, who was brought to the presbytery. In later years, Mme Bruat gave a brief account of her visit, and downplayed its adventurous break with the law. Her speech had the graceful tone of the true aristocrat. There was nothing of the bold interrogation, or crass offers of material rewards, in her meeting with Bernadette.

> Our pilgrimage to the Grotto, on 28 July 1858, was of no interest to anyone but ourselves. It has no doubt given my name a celebrity which I regard as an honour; but, despite my great desire to aid in the glory of the Blessed Virgin, it seems to me that my visit to Lourdes was not called to contribute to it, for nothing miraculous occurred before us... After our visit to the house of the worthy priest, where Bernadette showed herself very affectionate toward Sr Saint-Antonin, and very reserved toward our pious questions, I went with my entourage to the site of the apparition. Arriving there, I knelt before the sanctified rock, and I prayed with a profound respect.[73]

Sr Saint-Antonin brought forth an unusually enthusiastic reaction from Bernadette. Paying less attention to the great ladies, Bernadette embraced the nun as soon as she met her and stayed close to her throughout the visit. Sr Saint-Antonin asked Bernadette to accompany them to the Grotto, but Bernadette told her that it was forbidden. She agreed to walk with them as far as the bridge, and they went hand in hand.[74] The ladies knelt at the Grotto, but then were interrupted by Field Guard Callet, who had arrived hastily after a long lunch break. He pointed out the notice and told them that the Grotto was forbidden. According Sr Saint-Antonin's recollections she said: ' "As for the notice ... we have not read it." And as he persisted in wanting us to go away, I added: "Do you know who you are dealing with? It is the Governess of the Imperial Prince, take care." ' Rather than being intimidated by the officer of the law, they told Callet to fill a bottle with spring water and to gather some flowers for them.

From the point of view of the local authorities all this was bad enough. Their measures of control were being ridiculed and transgressed by both upper-class frivolity and peasant truculence. Worse still was another visitor who arrived on the same climacteric day of 28 July 1858. It was Louis Veuillot, the firebrand Catholic journalist who edited *l'Univers*. At the Grotto, he invited the Guards to take his name, and his announcement that 'I have not come here as a tourist'[75] held a certain menace.

On 28 August 1858, a lengthy account of the situation at Lourdes covered the front page of *l'Univers*. Veuillot was a thoroughly professional journalist of the popular, mass-circulated newspaper, a new phenomenon during his time. He understood the simplification, repetition and sensationalism required in such communications: 'indiscretions are inseparable from the existence of a journal'.[76] Through him, the story of the Lourdes apparitions was recounted in a lively, readable and comprehensible way.

There was the 'little girl ... called Bernadette' who in Veuillot's article lost her family name and exact antecedents in order to become a representative figure of unsophisticated rustic charm, with irreproachable morals and 'beautiful eyes'. Equally worthy were the good people of Lourdes, 'honest folk, good soldiers, good fathers of families, good taxpayers'.[77] This description would have surprised many officials in the Hautes-Pyrénées, particularly those concerned with military service, tax collection and the social problem of illegitimate births. The same officials figured in the article wearing the ever-recognizable guise of the petty, meddlesome bureaucrat. They were trying to part honest people from their quaint beliefs. Veuillot prudently attributed the blame to the lowest ranks of officialdom, rather than the Paris authorities who had the power to censor his newspaper.

Veuillot's article brought the issue to a new prominence. As the Sous-Préfet lamented, the arrival of Louis Veuillot had 'unleashed a sort of crusade'.[78] *Le Siècle, Le Journal des Débats, La Presse*, and other national newspapers took up the story of Lourdes. Most of these writings contested Veuillot's judgement of events, but every article, whether in support of him or not, was a defeat for Préfet Massy. As more and more people discussed these issues the longed-for day when 'this regrettable movement ... enters into the period of decline' receded further.[79]

During August and September of 1858, it became evident to the Paris authorities, especially the Ministers of the Interior and Cults, that the Lourdes affair was in need of peaceful resolution. During July, the Minister of Cults had asked the Bishop of Tarbes to formally condemn the Lourdes cult, but this request was rebuffed. The Bishop instead replied that he was instituting a formal inquiry into the apparitions. Moreover, Napoleon III was due to visit the Pyrenees in 1859, and an unsettled local dispute would spoil the atmosphere of goodwill which these provincial tours were designed to create.

The decision to scale down the sanctions against worship at the Grotto is not as well-documented as their establishment. The Paris officials sent contradictory orders to their subordinates, telling them to maintain surveillance of the Grotto, but not on a long-term basis. There was an unwillingness by the government to acknowledge a reversal of policy, which would have implied an admission of fault. There was a tacit request that they hear no more about the Grotto, and that any reproaches concerning this matter not be directed to them. On 5 October 1858, the mayoral *arrêté*, which forbade entry to the Grotto, was finally lifted. The people of Lourdes celebrated in the streets. Some weeks later both Préfet Massy and Commissioner Jacomet received instructions that they were to be transferred to equivalent posts in other départements. Although these removals were not demotions, they were concessions to the critics of official policy on the Grotto.

Even decades later, the devotees of Lourdes gloated over the fact that these two men had lived to see the vanity of their opposition to Notre Dame de Lourdes. In the early writings on Lourdes, the sudden death of Dominique Jacomet in 1873 is recorded with satisfaction.[80] It was found to be equally pleasing that fate sent Baron Massy as Préfet to Grenoble, the very city where the pilgrimages to Notre Dame de La Salette took place.[81] The popular mind was even more rancorous and unrestrained than these written accounts. Appropriately dreadful deaths were invented for both men, and it was said that they had been struck down by heaven for their blasphemies. Eugen Weber has cited some examples of this Lourdes folklore as an example of the unforgiving nature of the peasantry.[82] These legends also show how the resentment for the unsuccessful repression at the Grotto became concentrated on certain persons. The stories of frightful ends were totally inaccurate, both died in their beds after receiving the sacraments of the Church. The Police Commissioner died young, like Bernadette, because he had tuberculosis. The former Lourdes functionaries served in their later posts with more good fortune, and Dominique Jacomet was soon to be promoted. His widow, and the surviving relatives of Préfet Massy, had bitter memories of Lourdes, and lived on in the hope of clearing their family names. They carefully kept all the documents in their possession, which were to be precious legacies for later historians – all the more so because the French state had a way of 'losing' the records which related to the embarrassing beginning of the Lourdes shrine.

According to a persistent Lourdes legend, it was the Emperor himself who sent a telegram to his subordinates, ordering that the barriers be lifted. This apocryphal telegram is accompanied by other legends, some of which may indeed rest on fact. Stories have circulated that the Empress used Lourdes water to cure the Crown Prince of an illness, or that the affair of the *fausses nouvelles* was repeated in a conversation to the Emperor, who was touched by his people's faith in him. There was nothing in the character of either Napoleon III or Eugénie which would make such incidents impossible, and it does remain as an historical fact that the imperial governess visited the Grotto and took some water from the spring.

The campaign for the Grotto shows all the characteristics of a campaign of civil disobedience. There was an alliance of less privileged groups who felt that they had a grievance, and middle-class individuals who sympathized with them. The participation of respectable people offered the aggrieved access to literate communications and legal representation. It also helped to confine their activities to non-violent protest. Jean-Baptiste Estrade's memoir makes several references to the activities of himself and Curé Peyramale, who urged moderation at times of frustration when 'conciliation no longer seemed possible'[83] and the common people threatened violence. It is also characteristic of a civil disobedience campaign that the aggrieved people, in transgressing unjust laws, claimed a higher morality for their own. The Procureur Impérial was irritated to see that when threatened by the law, the 'clowns' of Lourdes 'do not fail to pose as martyrs for the faith'.[84] He did not see how genuine and effective a tactic it would be. However, after so much controversy, the Grotto was not to be left as the responsibility of the people of Lourdes, who had struggled so hard to gain access. As the interference of the secular authorities receded, the more sophisticated means of control favoured by the Catholic Church were to be applied.

# NOTES

1. This incident took place in Vienne in 1887. B. Singer, *Village Notables in Nineteenth-Century France* (Albany 1983), 84.

2. Workers quoted by Estrade, *Apparitions de Lourdes,* 221.

3. *Lavedan,* 6 May 1858, *LDA* 2, no. 201, 249.

4. Report by the Police Commissioner to the Préfet, 19 Apr. 1858, *LDA* 2, no. 164, 202.

5. Report by the Police Commissioner to the Préfet, 25 May 1858, *LDA* 2, no. 286, 333.

6. Curé Peyramale to the Bishop of Tarbes, 10 Apr. 1858, *LDA* 2, no. 132, 154.

7. Bernadette quoted, ibid.

8. Ibid.

9. Abbé Pène, *Témoins,* 270.

10. Mgr Laurence to the Minister of Cults, 7 Aug. 1858, *LDA* 3, no. 500, 264.

11. Police Commissioner Cazaux to Procureur Dutour, 22 May 1858, *LDA* 2, no. 272, 317–18.

12. Report by the Police Commissioner to the Préfet, 25 May 1858, *LDA* 2, no. 286, 334.

13. These figures were gathered by the Police Commissioner, who organized surveillance of the entrance to the Grotto. *LDA* 2, no. 117, 138–9.

14. *L'Ère Impérial,* a newspaper published in Tarbes, 10 Apr. 1858, *LDA* 2, no. 134, 157.

15. *L'Ère Impérial,* 6 Mar. 1858, *LDA* 1, no. 36, 217.

16. Dominiquette Cazenave, *RdAM,* 169.

17. Adelaide Monlaur to her cousin, 11 May 1858, *AG,* A8.

18. Croizine Bouhohorts, *Procès,* 130.

19. Ibid.

20. Abbé Pène, *Témoins,* 270.

21. Marie Fourcade, a middle-class woman who had been a schoolgirl at the time of the apparitions. *Témoins,* 238.

22. Elfrida-Marie Lacrampe, *Témoins*, 103.

23. Estrade, *Apparitions de Lourdes*, 221.

24. Mayor Lacadé to Préfet Massy, 1 Apr. 1858, *LDA* 1, no. 107, 303.

25. Note from Lieutenant Bourriot to Garrison Sergeant d'Angla, 3 Mar. 1858, *LDA* 1, no. 18, 186.

26. Quoted by Roberdel, *Marie-Julie Jahenny*, 21.

27. Jeanne Boisseau quoted, ibid.

28. Ibid., 20.

29. Police Commissioner, Report to the Préfet, 7 Apr. 1858, *LDA* 2, no. 122, 145.

30. Procureur Impérial at Lourdes, Report to the Procureur Général at Pau, 17 Mar. 1858, *LDA* 1, no. 68, 255.

31. *Lavedan*, 21 Feb. 1858, *LDA* 1, no. 7, 168.

32. Sergeant d'Angla, *Procès*, 59–60.

33. Josèphe Ouros, *Témoins*, 122.

34. Police Commissioner, Report to the Préfet, 19 Mar. 1858, *LDA* 1, no. 71, 262.

35. Préfet Massy, Report to the Minister of Cults, 12 Mar. 1858, *LDA* 1, no. 59, 242.

36. The Attorney General quoted by the Procureur Général at Pau to the Procureur Impérial at Lourdes, 13 Mar. 1858, *LDA* 1, no. 60, 244.

37. Ibid.

38. Ibid., 226.

39. J. C. Scott, *Weapons of the Weak: Everyday Forms of Peasant Resistance* (New Haven 1985), xvi.

40. Payne, *Police State*, 246.

41. Pierre Callet, *Témoins*, 46.

42. Police Commissioner, Report to the Préfet, 28 June 1858, *LDA* 3, no. 380, 136–7.

43. This anecdote told by him to Mère Joséphine Forestier, quoted by Trochu, *Sainte Bernadette*, 309.

44. Procureur Impérial Dutour to Procureur Général Falconnet, 20 May 1858, *LDA* 2, no. 265, 310–11.

45. Notes taken by Procureur Impérial Dutour, 19 June 1858, *LDA* 3, no. 357, 119.

46. See *LDA* 2, 100. Henri Lasserre made copies of many of the lists of names. Although useful, Lasserre's notes are not a comprehensive record and do not offer the opportunity to compare the Grotto contraventions with the other offences of the same era.

47. Pierre Callet, *Témoins*, 59.

48. Ibid., 52.

49. Jean Verges, *Témoins*, 59.

50. Estrade, *Apparitions de Lourdes*, 231.

51. Ibid.

52. McPhee, *Politics of Rural Life*, 237.

53. Estrade, *Apparitions de Lourdes*, 232.

54. Ibid.

55. Minister of Cults Rouland to Mgr Laurence, 30 July 1858, *LDA* 3, no. 464, 228.

56. Commissioner Jacomet, describing Madeleine Cazoux and Honorine Lacroix, Report to Préfet Massy, 19 Apr. 1858, *LDA* 2, no. 164, 204.

57. Her point about communal lands was legally sound. Croizine Ducout, *Procès*, 130.

58. Ibid.

59. Adelaide Monlaur to her cousin, 16 July 1858, *AG*, A8.

60. Procureur Impérial Dutour to the Procureur Général, 2 July 1858, *LDA* 3, no. 391, 144.

61. Procureur Impérial Dutour to the Procureur Général, 17 Mar. 1858, *LDA* 1, no. 68, 255.

62. Procureur Impérial Dutour to the Procureur Général, 2 Apr. 1858, *LDA* 1, no. 112, 307.

63. Bernard Le Clère and Vincent Wright, *Les Prèfets du Second Empire* (Paris 1973), 48. See also Payne, *Police State*, 108–10, concerning local interests.

64. *BVP*, 1. 158.

65. This is an extract from the interviews made by Père Cros. *BVP*, 1. 158.

66. *BVP* , 1. 156.

67. Lasserre, *Notre-Dame de Lourdes*, 229. Lasserre did concede that many were also motivated by religious faith.

68. 'Rapports du garde champêtre', 3 Sept. 1858, and 22 Aug. 1858, *AG*, A5.

69. Jean Verges, *Témoins*, 59.

70. Mayor Lacadé to the Préfet, 23 Aug. 1858, *LDA* 3, no. 562, 307.

71. Minister of Cults Rouland to Préfet Massy, 25 Aug. 1858, *LDA* 3, no. 569, 311.

72. Lasserre, *Notre-Dame de Lourdes*, 231.

73. Mme l'Amirale Bruat, *Procès*, 197.

74. Sr Saint-Antonin, *Procès*, 198.

75. Louis Veuillot quoted in the testimony of his companion, M. Jean-Marie Labeyle, Cros, *Histoire*, 2. 305.

76. Louis Veuillot quoted by M. L. Brown, *Louis Veuillot, French Ultramontane Catholic Journalist and Layman 1813–1883*, (North Carolina 1977), 97.

77. Louis Veuillot, 'La Grotte de Lourdes', 28 Aug. 1858, *Mélanges*, 2/4 (Paris 1860), 347.

78. Sous-Préfet Duboé, Report, 3 Oct. 1858, *LDA* 4, no. 773, 279.

79. Procureur Impérial Dutour to the Procureur Général, 8 May 1858, *LDA* 1, no. 211, 260.

80. M.-J. Bidal, *Bernadette Soubirous et les événements des Grottes de Lourdes de 1858 à 1873* (Vesoul 1873), 56.

81. G. Bascle de Lagrèze, *Le Château de Lourdes et la Grotte de l'Apparition* (Tarbes 1875), 233.

82. E. Weber, *Peasants into Frenchmen: The Modernization of Rural France 1870–1914* (London 1976), 354. Weber uses *LDA* as his source. The complete collection of letters which record these legends is kept in *AG*, A10.

83. Estrade, *Apparitions de Lourdes*, 225.

84. Procureur Impérial Dutour to the Procureur Général, 2 July 1858, *LDA* 3, no. 391, 145.

# CHAPTER 6

# For the Sake of Religious Enlightenment
## The Episcopal Mandate, 1858–1866

During the first six months of the events at Lourdes, while controversy raged and the actual visions took place, the Catholic Church had maintained an attitude of reserve. This could not go on indefinitely. On 22 July, the Bishop of Tarbes published an Episcopal Ordinance which instituted a commission of inquiry to investigate the alleged miracles in the Grotto. The inquiry had four topics of research. It would seek firstly to ascertain if the cures obtained by the use of the water from the spring were due to natural or supernatural causes; secondly, if the visions of Bernadette Soubirous were of a supernatural and divine character; thirdly, if 'the object appearing'[1] had made requests or communicated intentions; and fourthly if the Grotto spring had existed before the visions of Bernadette. This order of priorities was part of the reasoning which the Bishop applied to Lourdes. The cures were held to be the proof of the visions. In 1862, when the Episcopal Mandate declared a favourable judgement on the apparition at Lourdes, the miraculous was identified by the cures: 'Those cures are therefore the work of God ... there is a close relationship between the cures and the apparition; the apparition is divine, since the miraculous cures carry the mark of divinity.'[2] Mgr Laurence freely acknowledged that the impulse to investigate the issue was not only his own spiritual inspiration but the need to act 'to respond to a public need, to cure uncertainties and calm spirits'.[3]

Mgr Laurence appointed twelve priests to investigate the Lourdes matter. All the members of the commission were senior clerics of the Hautes-Pyrénées.[4] During the months of collecting evidence, the commissioners interviewed local notables, such as Jean-Baptiste Estrade and Dr Dozous. They also asked parish priests to interview the parishioners of mountain villages and to forward signed statements. They wanted verifiable documents, which 'have the desirable character of truth and authenticity'.[5] They were to call on numerous medical opinions; and to note that it was necessary 'that doctors well known for their scientific ability and strangers to the locality' be consulted.[6]

The overwhelming majority of the subjects of the cures, and the witnesses of the miracles, were an illiterate multitude. Had the commissioners been obliged to gather their evidence unfiltered by educated observers, there would have been no shortage of material, but they would have resembled the myriad of miracle stories which fill the letters of Adelaide Monlaur. Anonymous, dramatic, contradicted by subsequent reports and sometimes involving the infliction of illness or harm, the fables of popular religion were a discouraging subject for an inquiry which aimed to 'gather and classify the facts ... in order to arrive at a solution'.[7] The clergy deliberately formalized the taking of evidence, so that it did not include many of the miracles which were local favourites, such as the harm done to opponents of the shrine. This was certainly not because such stories had been forgotten, for people were still eager to recount them to Père Cros in the 1870s. It was rather because the workings of the commission determined that it could only accept a relation of events which was mannered, verifiable, and in conformity with literate values of taste and morality. Through their work, they sifted many tales of miraculous cures, and selected the most promising for further investigation.

In July 1858, during the first month of the commission's work, the Police Commissioner observed ironically that certain people wanted to 'wash away' any visions other than those of Bernadette 'in order to have only hers to put forward in evidence'.[8] His observations were well-founded, and it hardly needs to be stated that the Episcopal Inquiry did not seek information from the other people of Lourdes who saw visions. The only exception was Marie Courrech, who seems to have been interviewed by the commission, yet no record of this remains.[9] Possibly, her testimony was later suppressed. From the 1860s onward the other visionaries would be regarded as 'false visionaries' whose experiences were a fraudulent imitation of, rather than a participation in, those of Bernadette.

On 17 November 1858, members of the commission travelled to Lourdes, and Bernadette's recital was given to them in two parts. The commissioners had arranged to meet her at the Grotto and hoped that by arriving separately from her they would avoid the gathering of a curious crowd. This manoeuvre failed, as it would be apt to do in Lourdes, for 'the population began to move ... 400 people at least had arrived, in the blink of an eye' at Massabielle.[10] While awaiting Bernadette, they took the opportunity to look at the Grotto itself. They questioned several of the older men present, who were familiar with the area, about the origins of the spring in the Grotto. They received diverse opinions, but formed the impression that some water had always flowed in the area, although previously never abundantly nor from one source. They thus acquired an answer to the fourth item of article 1 of the Ordinance, which asked about the source of the spring. This occasion was the sole instance of direct communication between those making the inquiry and the community who had experienced the miracle.

The recital preserves the commissioners' view of Bernadette. They were impressed by her attitude of calm certainty and her indifference to the status of her questioners:

> she came into the midst of the commission, presenting herself with a modest respect and yet with total assurance; she found herself amid a large assembly, in the presence of high-ranking clerics whom she had never seen before, and of whom she did not know the intentions, with the same calm, the same freedom as if she had been alone.[11]

This statement is revealing of the shyness and deference which senior members of the clergy expected to encounter when meeting members of the common population. Bernadette, as a visionary, appeared to them to have a charisma in her detached attitude. It was the very opposite of the exhilarated, hysterical behaviour which they would have scorned. Nor was it the bashful submission which they would have taken for granted. To another witness to this scene, a middle-class woman of Lourdes, Bernadette's manner was too casual and lacking in devotion. Before leaving the Grotto, the members of the commission knelt in prayer, which was their usual practice at the beginning and the end of each session. Elfrida-Marie Lacrampe recorded that one of the Sisters of Nevers was scandalized to see that Bernadette did not join them but sat down on a rock, 'saying in patois: "I am pretty tired." '[12]

The document produced from the investigation, the *Récit des apparitions*, is a synopsis which shows that the commissioners were not seeking a detailed account of the actual course of the visions. The first apparition, with the now famous story of the children's journey to Massabielle, is set out in some detail and with the particulars which have made it a modern Catholic legend.[13] After that the recital became ever more concise. The description of her return visits to the Grotto, and the following events, were given little elaboration: '18 February, visit by Bernadette to the Grotto, with two older persons; same phenomena, same apparition'.[14] A series of events – the finding of the spring, the request to return every day for a fortnight, the statement by the apparition that Bernadette would not be happy in this world but the next – were telescoped as if they belonged to the one occasion. The commission defined their task as being to gather information as to the veracity of the visions, not to assemble a chronology of events. The commission also assembled a dossier of apparently miraculous cures, and referred them to medical experts. Out of the hundreds of cases reported, six were finally accepted as being beyond scientific explanation. A written account was prepared and forwarded to the Bishop of Tarbes.[15]

From 1860 to 1862, the Bishop of Tarbes had time to ponder the documents and to prepare for the issuing of his mandate in January 1862. Several important projects were undertaken in anticipation of the establishment of an official shrine in Lourdes. The two most significant moves were the purchase of the Grotto and its surrounding land, and the admission of Bernadette as a boarder at the local convent.

The acquisition of Massabielle occupied a great deal of the time and attention of Mgr Laurence from January 1860, when he first approached the Municipality of Lourdes, until August 1862 when the formalities were concluded. There was some opposition from state officials, who still resented the protest movement of 1858. The Bishop assured everyone that by acquiring the land, the Church would be able to prevent any disorder:

Crowds at the Grotto being a *fait accompli*, ... it seemed to me to be prudent and wise not to leave this religious gathering without direction, without surveillance, without spiritual help; the chapel which I am asking to build will also be an absolute guarantee of order and morality. *For these diverse motives*, I have asked your Excellency, ... to authorize me to build on the land at Massabielle.[16]

The waning of newspaper reports after 1858 did not mean a cessation of interest in Lourdes. Writing on Lourdes flourished more than ever as press accounts were succeeded by pamphlets and booklets. The Bishop of Tarbes wanted no publications to appear before his own Mandate, but this was impossible to enforce.

A notable problem was posed by the activities of an obtrusive Catholic writer with the sonorous name of Thomas-Marie-Joseph-Thérèse Azun de Bernétas. He visited Lourdes in November 1859 to gather material for a projected book. The church authorities published an open letter, expressing that they disapproved of his work, but they could not prevent him from engaging in an unauthorized investigation and publishing the results in 1861.[17] The appearance of this book may have encouraged Mgr Laurence to circulate official texts. He instructed Abbé Fourcade, the secretary of the commission, to produce 'a complete account',[18] which was printed during the same year with the title *L'Apparition à la Grotte de Lourdes, en 1858*. This work gave a description of the events at Lourdes, and it also reproduced the Ordinance. Later editions included the Mandate.

From 1868 onward, as the shrine became ever more famous, the Bishop of Tarbes tried to arrange the commission of a book-length historical work to supersede Fourcade's text. This move triggered controversy, as the successive efforts of Henri Lasserre, Père Sempé and Père Cros did not produce a satisfactory text, but only two decades of rivalry and accusations. The work of these religious historians opened one area of dispute after another as they tried to determine the exact sequence of events during the visions, and to offer descriptions of the social background at the time. What really divided them was that they were supporters of the various factions which gathered around Curé Peyramale and disputed control over the Grotto from the 1860s onwards.

## The sanctioned visionary

From 1862 onwards, with the Episcopal Mandate having been declared and published, the Church gave everyone permission to believe in the apparitions at Lourdes. It seems unlikely that this announcement, which transformed the status of the shrine, actually caused anyone to believe who had not done so already. However, it was of the greatest importance to Bernadette, changing her individual status for ever. She became one of the few women to be officially recognized as a visionary by the Catholic Church during her own lifetime. Critics abounded, and any sign of discreditable behaviour on her part would be reported across France.

From 1858 onwards, the literature of Lourdes has made frequent reference to the fact that Bernadette never accepted any offers of money. Her family were likewise circumspect, and during the period of the apparitions the vigilant police authorities never discovered them receiving the slightest material benefit. It is not well known that after the period of the apparitions, their situation was to become less pristine. Within a few years, the Soubirous family were virtual pensioners of the Bishop of Tarbes.

After making her First Communion in June 1858, Bernadette no longer attended school. This was a norm for girls of her social class. Late in 1858, around November, she made another visit to Cauterets and again stayed at her relative's house. Bernadette seems to have liked to bathe at the mineral spa, and she was a good example of its benefits, because her health improved. Otherwise she stayed at home, working with her mother, and probably also did paid work washing laundry and cleaning houses. Bernadette felt well enough to want to observe the fast of Lent in 1859, but her mother told her not to do so.

Around 1859, Bernadette had a full-time job as a nursery-maid. Her employer was Armantine Grenier, the wife of an army officer at the Lourdes citadel. She was twenty-four and gave birth to a son in March 1860. The military staff, who had secure incomes, were a source of employment in the town, and in working as their servant Bernadette was participating in a common trend. It is noteworthy that she did not seek any employment at the church, the convent or the presbytery, although they also hired servants. Bernadette liked small children, and took care of Mme Grenier's infant carefully. 'We lived half an hour from the centre of town. Bernadette pushed the little cart which carried my son.'[19] She held this job for about a year. It is likely that her sister, Toinette Soubirous, was also working in Lourdes as a servant. Curé Peyramale suggested to Bernadette that she should come and live at the boarding school of the Sisters of Nevers, but she rejected this offer, saying that she loved her family too much.[20]

Louise and François Soubirous were the same couple that they had always been. They were disorderly and irresponsible, especially in money matters, but were also loving parents, devout Catholics and kind hosts. They no longer lived at the *cachot*, as regular employment for François, and the wages of the two daughters, had improved their lifestyle. François Soubirous decided to return to his former profession as a miller and borrowed money in order to move to the Moulin Gras in late 1858.

The whole family continued to be bothered by visitors, especially during the summer holiday season. Despite the burden imposed on them, the Soubirous continued to fulfil the obligations of hospitality and courtesy which were integral to their culture.

Visitors came from as far as England. In 1859 Mr R. S. Standen wrote an account of Lourdes for the *Spiritual Magazine* – a heterodox publication which favoured paranormal topics such as seances and ghosts. Standen himself seems to have been a Protestant with a broad-minded interest in other cultures. The journal of his visit is that of a true outsider, and as such allows one to see details which French citizens did not bother with. He praised the town of Lourdes as having scenery comparable to Scotland: 'magnificent – with its noble old fort, and range of wooded hills behind'. He visited the Moulin Gras, where he found Bernadette 'a pretty-looking child, fourteen years of age [in fact she was fifteen], with large dreamy eyes, and a quiet sedate demeanour, which added some years to her appearance, and seemed altogether unnatural in so small a figure. She welcomed us with the air of one long accustomed to receive strangers.'[21] Bernadette gave him her recital of how she had visited the Grotto, had seen a lady in white, had returned every day for a fortnight, and had drunk from the water of a spring. Standen asked Bernadette about various stories which he had heard in the town, such as that she would kneel on the wet ground at the Grotto but arise with no mark on her clothes, or that she could mend her blessed candle, when broken, with a touch of her hand. 'So pleasant to the soul is mystery, that it was somewhat disappointing to hear her solemnly deny the truth of all these pretty fables.'[22]

The English tourist did not meet her parents, who were not at home, but on the way they passed François Soubirous, 'a serious-looking respectable middle-aged man. He appeared to divine what took us that way, for he saluted us very gravely as we passed, and no doubt hoped we should become converts.' In the cottage attached to the mill, 'Two bright, happy little urchins – her brothers – were playing about, and seemed in no way abashed at our entrance.' Bernadette herself 'stood by the window, and answered briefly the questions I put to her, but volunteered very few remarks of her own.' As he left, this stilted communication suddenly altered, because they passed through the mill. Bernadette saw that they were looking at the machinery with curiosity. She turned on the water to start the mill-stones:

> and explained the working of them to us very intelligently herself. We certainly left her in the conviction that we had been talking with a most amiable little girl, and one superior to her age and station both in manner and education; and whatever may be the true account of the apparition, as far as the girl herself is concerned we feel quite convinced of the sincerity of her own faith in it.[23]

Most visitors were not as polite and disinterested as Mr Standen. They were not content to leave the truth of the apparition undetermined – they wanted Bernadette to prove it to them. The Curé of Vic, who spoke to her in the presence of Abbé Pène, challenged her by saying:

> —Is it true that you saw the Blessed Virgin?
> —Yes, monsieur l'Abbé.
> —I myself do not believe that you saw her.
> Silence from Bernadette.
> —Well, do you have nothing to say?
> —What do you want me to say?
> —You must make me believe that you have really seen the Blessed Virgin.
> —Oh, she did not tell me to make it believed.[24]

She repeated different versions of this answer to many people, saying that it was her duty to tell them the story but not to make them believe it. Also, she did not speak of the apparition as the Blessed Virgin. Although she is sometimes quoted as saying so, careful witnesses who cite her exact words note that it was 'the apparition', 'the vision' or 'the Lady'. The Sisters of Nevers testified that even years later she had the habit of simply saying 'the

Lady', which her visitors translated into a more specific title when they repeated her story. In contrast to the interview cited above, she sometimes corrected her visitors. In 1863, Père Langlade, a Jesuit, spoke to her:

—Then you saw the Blessed Virgin?
—I did not say that I saw the Blessed Virgin, I saw the apparition.[25]

When interviewed by Azun de Bernétas in 1860, she still spoke about '*aquero*', which 'had the image of a lady, dressed in white'.[26] Azun de Bernétas explained that her account had been partly in Bearnais (Occitan) and partly in standard French. He wrote that:

When asked to state what happened around her and to her in the Grotto, during those visits during the fortnight, she replied: 'I could barely tell you anything, because the presence of that object, in Bearnais: *aquero*, [*sic*] usually completely absorbed me.'

Bernadette's unwillingness to give an identity to '*aquero*' persisted for a long time, but her very reticence may have been more convincing than an announcement of: 'I saw the Blessed Virgin.'

Visitors' accounts of her give no indication of how she worked and lived. Rather they indicate how she coped with visits. Although fascinated with Bernadette, the visitors did not want to know anything about her real life or environment. Explaining the workings of the mill to a visitor was a rare chance for Bernadette to speak freely, to give information and to be mistress of her own domain. The turning stones were an important part of her background; she had been born in a mill. Years later, when she was dying, she would comment: 'I am ground like a grain of wheat.'

The Soubirous parents played no role in these conversations. They are simply absent from the visitors' accounts. The account of Azun de Bernétas, who visited their mill and was charmed by the family atmosphere, is an exception. He explained that he had spoken little to François Soubirous, who was usually engaged in work outside the house, while Louise Castérot was shy. The younger children amused themselves and seem to have been oblivious to the outsiders. Azun de Bernétas interviewed Louise Castérot, and asked her to speak about Bernadette. Louise Castérot gave a brief life history of her daughter, which entirely concentrated on her health. Louise only bothered to mention the apparitions once – 'after the apparitions her health was rather weak' – and otherwise explained that at the age of six Bernadette had developed asthma, at twelve she had cholera, 'a disease which killed many people of all ages in this region',[27] and that since the apparitions Bernadette still had coughs and an occasional swelling of the stomach (probably fluid retention). Louise Castérot said that she had found it necessary to forbid her to follow the fast of Lent.

Louise Castérot's interest in Bernadette was evidently very different from that which brought visitors hundreds of miles to see her. Instead of the grand events, Louise recounted her maladies, and rather than seeing her as a saint on earth, her mother restricted her from following an ordinary religious practice. Louise Castérot was very humble, and took it for granted that her opinions would not be sought. In August 1859, when two clerics, Père Mariote and Paul de Lajudie, called at her house, Louise Castérot simply asked: 'Have you come to see Bernadette?' and conducted them upstairs. It is noticeable that François Soubirous left the house to work whenever visitors were there. They assumed that he was busy, but his peers describe him as indolent and liking to talk, drink and socialize. However, he only liked to do so with people of his own sort. The affluent educated visitors were virtually foreigners, and he seems to have been so shy of them that he was willing to absent himself from his own home.

Some visitors totally lacked in courtesy, and exhausted Bernadette. Abbé Junqua, an enthusiastic priest who wrote for Catholic magazines, arrived in Lourdes in February 1860 and interviewed her for hours.[28] He recorded her account of the apparitions, and asked her for further details on many points. After she became weary, he offered her money, and was delighted to see that she became angry and refused it.[29] He also requested her rosary.

—Will you give me that rosary? I will pay you for it immediately...
—No, monsieur. I do not want to give you, or sell you, my rosary.
—But I so much want to have a souvenir of you! I have travelled so far to see you! Truly, you owe me your rosary.
Bernadette, in effect, abandoned it to me...

She refused payment, and told him that she would buy another from her own money. The inexhaustible Abbé Junqua also asked for her medals, and a piece of her scapular (a necklace made of cloth). Bernadette told him that other people had already taken her medals, and that as for the scapular:

—Monsieur, would you divide the rosary beads which I just gave you?
—No
—Neither will I divide my scapular.

Finally she received his benediction, and before he left he asked Bernadette to be of good conduct, always to love the Virgin Mary, to pray for him, and to remember him when he next came to Lourdes. 'She promised me all this, except to remember my face, because she sees so many people, she says; and I then took leave of Bernadette.'[30]

Abbé Junqua believed that the rosary which Bernadette gave him (or ceded to him) was the rosary of the apparitions. However, she had already lost it. As she explained in later years, she one day put her hand in her pocket for her rosary and it was missing. She evidently suspected that a light-fingered visitor had taken it, because she had constantly been asked for her beads.

More than once, Bernadette had been asked by clerical visitors to exchange her rosary for theirs, and had been offered ornamented rosaries of silver in place of her wooden beads. She developed an answer which was both humble and snubbing: 'Your rosary is too fine for my poor hands, and mine is too common for yours.' In later years she testified that: 'She had never given away the rosary which she had used during the apparitions ... if anyone says that they have it, it is because they stole it.'[31] After this loss, she would give her rosaries to people who asked insistently for them. Abbé Junqua's account makes it obvious why giving away cheap sets of beads, and buying new ones, would be easier than continuing such conversations. According to Jeanne Védère, a distinguished prelate, who interviewed Bernadette in the presence of Curé Peyramale, also asked her for her rosary and her scapular. He ended by offering a donation, saying: 'My child, I know that your parents are poor; take it for them. – I thank you, but my parents can work.'[32]

In 1860 Bernadette was sixteen and Curé Peyramale was becoming increasingly concerned for her. At the Moulin Gras, the Soubirous had returned to the habits which had lost them their original inheritance. They liked the company of people of their own class, and kept an open table. Too much inclined to entertain, and to extend credit to their friends, they were falling into debt. Their household was marked by disorder, and probably heavy drinking as well. While Bernadette had been a little child, she could be seen as innocent of their disreputable ways, but at sixteen she was becoming a woman. She was pious, neat and quiet, but not conspicuously holy. Her brother Jean-Marie Soubirous remembered that: 'To me, she was a girl no different from any other; she was gay like they were, and took part in their games.'[33] A more critical view was sounded by one of the ladies of the parish, who said: 'I heard that Bernadette ran around with the other young people. I said to Curé Peyramale: – You had better bring her away from there. With the parents she has, she cannot have any good examples.'[34] Dominiquette Cazenave, who visited the mill and told Louise Castérot that she would give Bernadette dressmaking lessons, also took her criticisms to the Curé. 'You are not going to leave her in the world?'[35] He did not need to hear such statements, he knew of the problems for himself, but at first he could do nothing about it. Then, the financial problems of the Soubirous family delivered Bernadette to him.

By 1860, François Soubirous needed financial assistance. The family maintained their reluctance to accept gifts from outsiders, but they seem to have regarded the Catholic Church as a legitimate source of support and advice. When they had run out of funds, François Soubirous saw the Curé, and offered to do paid work. He was not the only one to do so, as the Church was a significant employer in Lourdes, and was about to become a major one. In reality, of course, a request from the parent of Bernadette was different from that of any other unskilled worker. He was received with generosity, and was employed as a day-labourer in building work. Unlike others, he was advanced money. The sums were not large, but were more and more significant in the impecunious household. In July 1860 Curé Peyramale renewed his request that Bernadette be transferred to the care of the Sisters of Nevers, and this time there was no refusal. She moved to their Lourdes convent as a boarder in July 1860.

During the following years, François Soubirous continued to approach the church authorities for assistance.[36] In April 1864, the Curé of Lourdes noted as an aside in a letter that 'at the moment, Soubirous is not asking for money'.[37] Despite this, the Curé considered it likely that the Bishop would eventually have to rent a mill to him.[38] Even with the financial help, the Soubirous family fell into debt at the Moulin Gras, and in 1864 they were resettled at the Moulin Lapaca, which Mgr Laurence purchased outright. Although she was then resident at the convent, Bernadette knew of Mgr Laurence's generosity to her family, which had saved them from the humiliation of another eviction. She often expressed her gratitude to him, and was now tied to the Church by bonds of obligation, as her relatives were by the firm bonds of debt.

Bernadette's family were incorrigible, but it was obviously essential to the Lourdes project that their problems not become public knowledge. By purchasing a mill specifically to be rented to them, the Bishop of Tarbes was maintaining them in a trade. He was too wise to give them the mill outright, for it soon would have disappeared in a cloud of debt. Pilgrims to Lourdes who saw the Soubirous working at their mill had a favourable impression, and knew nothing of the underhand support necessary to keep them there. Their social equals observed this contrived respectability with some humour. An old drinking friend of Louise Castérot, while denying stories that Louise had drunk herself into insensibility during her days of poverty, said that: 'she could have, however, after Monseigneur gave them that mill, for, in those days, she always had a full bottle in the pantry'.[39]

The Soubirous family had given up Bernadette unwillingly, and, according to the local historian Barbet, when they sent her to live at the Hospice they made it a condition that it would be easy for their daughter to visit her home.[40] However, after July 1860, Bernadette was permitted to see her family only rarely, and never alone. The Curé had given orders that she was not to see anyone without permission, and as Sr Damien recalled, 'that directive was rigorously observed. Whenever she visited her home, she was accompanied by a Sister.'[41] In order to see Bernadette, they had to request her presence in advance, and these visits had to be accommodated by the convent timetable.

The church authorities had every reason to be pleased that they had such power over Bernadette. An anecdote in a letter from Curé Peyramale to the Bishop of Tarbes neatly encapsulates the issue of the claims and counter-claims of religious authorities around the figure of a visionary, and their successful resolution in the case of Bernadette. He wrote that a lady had posed the question to Bernadette that if 'M. le Curé forbade you to go to the Grotto; and if the Holy Virgin told you to go there, what would you do?' The child responded without hesitation, or doubt: 'I would go to ask permission of M. le Curé.'[42] The Curé repeated this anecdote with evident satisfaction. It was proof that he maintained authority over the visionary, even in the face of hypothetical counter-claims by an apparition from heaven.

This amenable attitude was not seen during the days of the visions. In a perfect example of the type of attitude which Peyramale implicitly rebuts, Bernadette's aunt, Basile Castérot, recalled that Bernadette had defied the Curé during the course of the visions and had insisted on returning to the

Grotto: 'I prefer to disobey M. le Curé than to disobey the "Lady". I love so much to see that "Lady".'[43] As often in the memoirs of Bernadette, the question is not the accuracy of the recollection, but the claims which it enabled the witness to make about their own values, and their own relationship to the evocative figure of the visionary. Peyramale wished to assure the Bishop of Bernadette's correct attitude to authority, which was a testament to her own credibility and his control over the parish. Basile Castérot was claiming Bernadette for the people of her own community. She was 'their' Saint. 'She much preferred to talk to those of her own condition rather than grand people. ... She did not let herself be intimidated. Not by the Magistrates and the Gendarmes, nor by M. le Curé.'[44] Basile Castérot continued to maintain this view for the whole of her long life, but she was not writing the books and pamphlets about Lourdes, and Bernadette herself had vanished into the convent. After 1862, the clergy's appropriation of Bernadette was complete, and it was their view of her which prevailed.

Mgr Laurence intervened far more effectively than the civil powers when he directed his attention to the events at the Grotto. Unlike them, he accomplished his objectives – however, he set himself an easier task. Rather than trying to control Bernadette through intimidation, he allowed her family to become dependent upon church charity. After that, he was able virtually to adopt her. Instead of confronting the beliefs of the common people, he applied an investigative framework which was selective and dignified. In July 1858, in a letter which suggests that Mgr Laurence should reject the enthusiasts of the Grotto without further ado, the Minister of Cults had stated that he found 'neither in the origins, nor in the progress, nor in the results of this popular movement anything remotely serious or respectable'.[45] It was the achievement of the Episcopal Inquiry to find the serious and the respectable in the miracles of Lourdes and to write a comprehensive narrative about them. It was also an achievement that after several years of negotiations and payments, the Bishop of Tarbes owned both the Grotto and the visionary.

## The shrine at the Grotto

As soon as the ownership of the Grotto had been attained, the Bishop of Tarbes began a lavish building programme. Our Lady of Lourdes had made a request – which was a traditional feature of apparitions – that a chapel be built at the site. Dominiquette Cazenave recalled that during the apparitions Bernadette had suggested: 'any sort of chapel, even if it were quite small'.[46] Bernadette had probably envisaged the type of small oratory which proliferated throughout the French countryside. Instead, Lourdes was to have a monumental basilica. The Grotto itself was maintained in a park setting, which allowed its natural appearance of a rock cavern to be preserved.

The alterations of the area around Massabielle amounted to impressive feats of engineering. Even before 1862 masses of rock surrounding the Grotto were removed, the ground was levelled and drained and a wide granite ramp was built. Among the most major of the early excavations was the diversion of

**Plate III**    The Grotto at Lourdes, before redevelopment. © *Photo Lacaze, Lourdes*

the Gave river and the obliteration of its tributary mill stream which ran near the Grotto. The spring in the Grotto itself was traced back to its source between the rocks so that its flow was clear and unimpeded. In a letter of 1866, in which Curé Peyramale described these works, he noted that the Grotto itself had been left in its state of 'rustic and religious beauty'.[47]

The notion that a site of display can remain the same, while its entire physical and aesthetic setting is transformed in order to display it, is a consistent feature of modern tourist developments. The Grotto of Massabielle is like many natural sites and monuments which are changed in order to be made available to great numbers of people, while also still retaining the codes of authenticity.

The way in which the Grotto was transformed in order that it might be seen in its 'natural' state is analogous to the way in which Bernadette was moved to the Hospice and re-educated in order to be made available to pilgrims. Both the Grotto and Bernadette were celebrated on the one hand for their natural and folkloric identity and on the other for their cultivation. Bernadette always wore a peasant costume, but she was taught accomplishments such as the speaking of standard French and the craft of fine embroidery. The authorities responsible for her claimed that they had not 'spoilt' her, and, as Fourcade wrote, Bernadette remained in 'her primitive simplicity'.[48] Like the Grotto, she too was changed, in order that she might remain, in her 'rustic and religious' beauty.

The redevelopment of the Grotto, and the building of a church complex above it, was extremely expensive. Throughout the first decade fundraising was the major preoccupation of the clerical authorities and, despite the large

**Plate IV**  The statue of Our Lady of Lourdes in the Grotto. © *Photo Lacaze, Lourdes*

sums received, expenses were narrowly balanced against income. In 1862 7,450.41 fr. was received at the *tronc* at the Grotto, and 19,954.59 fr. was collected in other offerings. The total sum of 27,505.00 fr. was a very large amount by the standards of the time, but it fell slightly below the year's expenses of 27,754.64 fr.[49] The accounts did not move into surplus until 1864, and even in 1866 work had to be temporarily suspended for a lack of funds.

While the Grotto was redeveloped, a new and official image was produced of Our Lady of Lourdes. The marble statue commissioned from the sculptor Joseph Fabisch was typical of nineteenth-century Catholic art and, in the judgement of educated observers, was bland and lacking in originality. Bernadette, who had no knowledge of artistic standards, did not like it either. Her major objection was the positioning of the head, which turned upward to look at heaven, and the appearance of the long neck. Bernadette insisted that the head should face forward with a level gaze, and she would ever afterwards maintain that 'they gave goitre to the statues at Lourdes'.[50]

When placed in the Grotto, the statue disappointed not only the visionary, who was expected to hold unattainable ideals, but also the sculptor. Fabisch described the finished work as 'one of the greatest frustrations' of his life as an artist.[51] He had not anticipated the angle at which the statue would be placed, nor the lighting of the Grotto. He stated that the statue had a completely different appearance when seen in the niche, but accepted this disappointment with polite resignation. He generously made over all his rights for reproduction of the work to the Bishop of Tarbes.[52]

The shrine at Lourdes was professionally managed from its earliest stages. This meant that the right to produce goods associated with 'Our Lady of Lourdes' was strictly regulated. Only manufacturers licensed by the Bishop of Tarbes could do so. Before the mid-nineteenth century, such measures were unknown. The control of copyrights was a result of industrialization and developments in the legal system. Religious services at the Grotto also came under the administration of a special corps of clergy, rather than simply being part of the work of the priests of the parish.

In May 1866 three priests were appointed by the Bishop of Tarbes to take responsibility for the religious services at the Grotto. These priests, led by Père Sempé, were organized as a religious congregation and were eventually to be renamed as the Missionaries of Our Lady of Lourdes. Irritation and minor quarrels between the diocesan authorities, Curé Peyramale and the architect at the Grotto had been seen since 1863. However, the installation of Père Sempé in command of the new shrine seems to have caused a general awareness that the Grotto was no longer part of the commune of Lourdes.

Practical steps were soon taken which increased this sense of separation and dismayed many of the local people. Processions to the Grotto no longer began at the local church, and therefore the parish of Lourdes was effectively denied access to the donations of pilgrims. The Pères de la Grotte, as they were commonly known, established a religious goods store and would no longer allow people to sell merchandise at Massabielle. After Mgr Laurence's death in 1870, the conduct of the Missionaries became much more assertive. Père Sempé, who seems to have been a man of strong and authoritarian

*167 — LOURDES. La Grotte Miraculeuse. ND Phot.*

**Plate V**   The Grotto at Lourdes, 1880s. Author's collection

character, had numerous personal clashes with local notables. Relations between himself and Curé Peyramale were openly hostile from 1866 until Peyramale's death in 1877.

Such factors led to a spirit of resentment in Lourdes, and various hyperbolic anecdotes voice the grievances that were felt. It was said that a poor woman of Lourdes, Marianne Sens, had a stall selling bottles to pilgrims. She was chased out of business by the Missionaries and died of hunger.[53] The Mother Superior of a local convent complained that Père Sempé had tried to hinder her community in their reception of wealthy women pilgrims: 'the Missionaries wanted these Ladies to give their preference to the hotels and houses which they are said to own in the town'.[54] Pierre Dauzat-Dembarrère, the son of the former parliamentary deputy, believed that his family had been defrauded in a sale of land to the Missionaries. He denounced 'the hateful conduct' of this congregation, and described Père Sempé as the Torquemada of the Grotto.[55] Protests were to rage during the 1870s and did not recede until the death of Père Sempé in 1889.

In 1870, Père Sempé granted the right to make medals 'and all other forms of religious trinkets, without exception, of the image of ND de Lourdes'[56] to a Paris manufacturer. This type of agreement removed participation in the shrine from local people. The few who were able to obtain concessions from the Missionaries had to pay substantial royalties. Viron, the local photographer, agreed to pay 30 per cent of the price of each print he sold of the statue in its place in the Grotto.[57] Because of their immediate presence in making prints, photographers were the only local people to participate significantly in the manufacture of goods for the shrine. Finished articles such as statues and medals were imported from the factories of Lyon and Paris.

The only local crafts which were able to maintain themselves were the making of candles and rosary beads. The town of Lourdes grew and prospered because of its status as a place of pilgrimage, but its actual commerce was restricted to the provision of services. It is no wonder that by the 1870s the Lourdes Municipal Council was dominated by anti-clerics who firmly snubbed the Church on issues such as the running of the Lourdes primary school.

Despite the quarrels of the 1870s, the creation of the shrine at Lourdes was one of the most complete and successful institutional works of the nineteenth-century French Catholic Church. For the people of Lourdes the chain of events – from the uproar of 1858 to the professional shrine of 1868 – was unforeseeable. The specific features of the indigenous society had made the apparitions possible, but the fame of Bernadette's visions eventually relocated Lourdes into a new cultural space. The Grotto was to become a site of international Catholic culture, and the town a dependency of the flourishing trade of pilgrimage. As Michel Chadefaud writes: 'There was a decisive break, the boulevard of the Grotto marked a turning point in urban history. The period of discounts and tawdry trinkets had arrived ... the people of Lourdes would live henceforward according to the rhythm of Massabielle.'[58]

# NOTES

1. 'Ordonnance de Mgr l'Evêque de Tarbes', 28 July 1858, *Procès*, 192.

2. 'Le mandement épiscopal', *LDA* 6, no. 1044, 242.

3. 'Ordonnance de Mgr l'Evêque de Tarbes', *Procès*, 191.

4. They included Lamole, superior of the Grand Seminary at Tarbes, Lafforgue, a professor of theology, Fourcade, a vicar general who worked closely with Mgr Laurence, Nogaro, the superior priest at the Tarbes Cathedral, and Marmouget, Travès, Fouga, Tabariès, Soulé, Baradère, and Prat-Marca, all of whom were *chanoines*. Curé Peyramale of Lourdes was also appointed after the first meeting of the commission.

5. 'Procès-verbal de la quatrième séance de la commission épiscopale', 9 Aug. 1858, *LDA* 3, no. 508, 271.

6. 'Procès-verbal de la huitième séance de la commission épiscopale', 22 Nov. 1858, *LDA* 5, no. 828, 147.

7. Mgr Laurence, 'Ordonnance', 26 July 1858, *LDA* 3, no. 449, 212.

8. Police Commissioner, Report to Préfet Massy, 28 July 1858, *LDA* 3, no. 451, 216.

9. See an examination of her case by Harris, *Lourdes: Body and Spirit*, 101.

10. 'Copie du récit des apparitions fait par Bernadette devant la Commission réunie à la Grotte', 17 Nov. 1858, *AG*, A13.

11. Ibid.

12. Elfrida-Marie Lacrampe, *Témoins*, 108.

13. 'La Notice Fourcade, Récit des apparitions', 24 Jan. 1862, *LDA* 6, no. 1049, 264, passim.

14. Ibid.

15. 'Minute du rapport Fourcade', *LDA* 5, no. 934a, 127–36. This document is reproduced from the archives of the Bishop of Tarbes. Fourcade's draft copy and notes are preserved in *AG*, A13.

16. Mgr Laurence, Bishop of Tarbes to M. Dauzat-Dembarrère, 16 July 1862, Dauzat-Dembarrère, *Origines politiques*, 26. Emphasis mine.

17. M. Azun de Bernétas to the Bishop of Tarbes, 23 Jan. 1862, *AG*, A28.

18. Fourcade, *L'apparition à la Grotte de Lourdes*, v.

19. Armantine Grenier, Bernadette's employer, was born in Paris, 1834. She testified for the *procès* of Bernadette's canonization. *PON*, Sessio LXXX, 958.

20. Bernadette quoted by Laurentin, *Vie*, 115.

21. R. S. Standen, 'Notre Dame de Lourdes', *Spiritual Magazine* (1870) *LDA* 5, no. 899, 287.

22. Ibid., 286.

23. Ibid.

24. Abbé Pène, *Témoins*, 280–1.

25. Mémoire Langlade cited, *BVP*, 1. 282.

26. Enquête de Azun de Bernétas, Nov. 1859, *LDA* 5, no. 912, 327.

27. Louise Castérot quoted, *ESB*, 36.

28. Abbé Junqua, Letter, 20 Feb. 1860, *LDA* 5, no. 915, 342.

29. Laurentin, *LDA* 5, 342.

30. Abbé Junqua, Letter, 20 Feb. 1860, *LDA* 5, no. 915, 348.

31. Bernadette quoted, ibid., footnote 17.

32. Quoted by Jeanne Védère, *Témoins*, 194.

33. Jean-Marie Soubirous quoted, *LDA* 6, 83.

34. Toinette Garros quoted, *LDA* 6, 76.

35. Quoted, ibid.

36. Copy of a letter addressed to Mgr Laurence by François Soubirous, signed with an X. 9 July 1863, *AG*, A18.

37. Curé Peyramale, Apr. 1864, Cros, *Histoire*, 3. 159.

38. Ibid.

39. Madeleine Barbazat, *Témoins*, 135.

40. Barbet quoted, *Témoins*, 77.

41. Sr Damien Clamels, *RdC*, 5.

42. Curé Peyramale to the Bishop of Tarbes, 3 June 1858. This letter was felt to reflect so well on Bernadette that it was submitted to the *Procès* of her canonization. *PON*, Sessio LXIX, 827.

43. Basile Castérot, *PON*, Sessio LXII, 2. 761.

44. Ibid.

45. Minister of Cults to the Bishop of Tarbes, 30 July 1858, *LDA* 3, no. 464, 228.

46. Testimony of Dominiquette Cazenave, *RdAM*, 171.

47. Quoted by Trochu, *Sainte Bernadette*, xxx.

48. Fourcade, *L'apparition à la Grotte de Lourdes*, 34.

49. Accounts of 1862, *AG*, Serie B 1B2.

50. She made this remark to many people. Bernadette quoted by Sr Louis Lavigne, *RdC*, 49.

51. Fabisch quoted by Laurentin, *Vie*, 131.

52. Letter of M. Fabisch to Chanoine Fourcade, 21 Jan. 1864, *LDA* 7, no. 1565, 323.

53. H. Lasserre, 'Très-humbles supplique et mémoire', *AG*, A38.

54. Mère Pélagie Coustarot, Superior of the Soeurs de l'Immaculée Conception, 'Memoire Confidentiel', (E) A IV O à 15. Archives Cros, *AG*. Père Sempé was finally told by the Vatican authorities that he was to cease interference in the affairs of this convent.

55. Dauzat-Dembarrère, *Origines politiques*, 1.

56. Contract with Alfred Conin, 'fabricant de bijouterie religieuse', 27 Feb. 1870, *AG*, 11 H2.

57. M. Viron, contract, *AG*, 11 H2.

58. Chadefaud, *Origines du tourisme*, 923.

# CHAPTER 7

# 'What Will You Become?'
## The Education of Bernadette, 1860–1866

I began by saying to Bernadette:
—And now, my dear child, what will you become?
—But nothing, Bernadette answered after a moment of hesitation.
                    Mgr Forcade, *Notice sur la vie de Sr Marie-Bernard.*

While the Grotto was redeveloped and the sanctuary built, Bernadette experienced six years on public display. The move to the Hospice greatly increased the pressures upon her and her situation was ideal for the development of an aura of religious celebrity. Texts and photographs reflected people's fantasies about her, and these representations changed the path of her actual life.

Writers who publicized Lourdes liked to contrast the tranquillity of the mountain town with the hectic and corrupt cities. Likewise, they put forward an image of Bernadette as an incomparable example of a pure and untouched girl. As a booklet of the 1880s commented: 'Her soul always remained unblemished, like the summits of the Pyrenees where the virgin snow glistens, untrodden by any human foot since the Creation.'[1] Writers compared Bernadette to incorruptible substances such as a 'flawless diamond',[2] glacial snow or the clear waters of an alpine lake – 'those hidden lakes which are remote in the high mountains and where all the splendours of the heavens are reflected in silence'.[3]

The result of this type of praise was that Bernadette came to be seen as infinitely different from the other women around her. In turn, this helped to justify her segregation into an entirely unnatural lifestyle.

Many early narratives invested Lourdes and its visionary with the moral obsessions of the society which viewed them, and were quite insulting both to Bernadette and to her community. One example was the intrusion of the anti-dancing campaign into the story of the Lourdes apparitions. In the nineteenth century, particularly after 1850, the French clergy developed a vehement antipathy to dancing, an antipathy all the more surprising given that dancing was a traditionally accepted community activity (in some peasant processions, dancing youths would carry a statue of the Virgin). [4] Ralph Gibson has suggested that the clergy's hostility was part of a general reaction to changes in gender roles in the wake of the industrial revolution: 'if so, the clerical fear of dancing might then be seen as the form taken by their fear of a rising tide of eroticism clashing dangerously with traditions of soul/body dualism and the devaluation of the flesh'.[5]

Affected by this mindset, several writers about Lourdes latched onto the idea that Bernadette's companions, on her first visit to the Grotto, had behaved offensively by dancing. They crossed the stream ahead of her: 'Then they started dancing; and Bernadette scolded them because there were men working in the area who were watching them, and yet they did not cease.'[6]

None of the three witnesses present on 11 February 1858 remembered this implausible event. There were no workers in the area and, after wading through the freezing water, the two girls had not launched into a dance on the desolate riverbank. As Toinette Soubirous stated, they sat down to put on their sabots, nearly crying because of the cold.[7] The trigger for the story might have been the Police Commissioner's report of his interrogation of Bernadette, which records her as having said that, when she had recovered from the trance, 'my companions were dancing on the other side of the stream; I asked them if they had seen anything, they responded negatively'.[8] This last expression exemplifies the unnatural wording typical of such documents – 'they said no' is much more idiomatic. Being in French, the document is a translation of Bernadette's words; lost to us is the expression of hers that the document renders as 'dansaient', an expression probably referring to the girls stamping their cold feet or jumping, rather than engaging in a waltz.

**Plate VI** A popular engraving of the apparations at Lourdes. © *Bibliotheque Nationale*

Moreover, this document makes no mention of workers or of Bernadette's scolding. It is her companions not she who 'responded negatively', and they do so here merely to a neutral question. Bernadette was annoyed when her companions would not carry her across the stream, and disappointed when they told her that they saw nothing in the cavern at Massabielle.

When questioned in later times, none of the three witnesses seemed even to understand why people thought that they would dance in the Grotto. Nor is it likely that they did anything which drew sharp protests from Bernadette.

It is true that Bernadette and her companions were irritated with one another on that day, but their childish disagreements do not bear the weight of significance which nineteenth-century writers wanted to put on them.

The histories of Lourdes were written in a style which virtually conceals the fact that the apparition was an event in which the whole trio were involved, and that indeed there would have been no visions at Lourdes if Bernadette had not been prompted, accompanied and supported by the other girls during the initial visions.

The official historian of the shrine conceded that: 'Bernadette, when interrogated at various times between 1859 and 1879, has said that she could not remember any dancing, or any reprimand which she would have made to the dancers.'[9] This was despite determined questioning on his part, as he urged her to confirm this detail.[10] In the face of too many living witnesses to contradict it, the dancing story was regretfully dropped.

What would not be abandoned was the religious perception which defined Bernadette as a being at odds with fallen womanhood because she was holy. The scene of crossing the mill stream was constantly invoked in these terms; some slight basis for this was offered by Toinette's recital which recorded that Bernadette had told them to 'lower your skirt' as they crossed the water which reached to their knees.[11] Toinette remembered that they had not raised their skirts unnecessarily, and as soon as they arrived on the other side, 'we were bent over and we wrapped our feet in our skirts to warm them'.[12] The injunction to lower their skirts was to be featured in dramatic terms in the Lourdes hagiography. Later writers imagined 'the chaste Bernadette' obliging her sister to allow the hem of her skirt to be soaked in water rather than offend modesty.[13] Likewise Jeanne Abadie, who had annoyed Bernadette by rudely refusing to carry her across the mill stream with the exclamation '*Pét dé périclé*', figures in the hagiography as an impious foil to the divine visionary. Toinette explained that '*Pét dé périclé* is not a serious oath, it means blast of thunder.'[14] All the evidence indicates that Bernadette remembered Jeanne as a friend, but the religious writers were to seize on this incident to show that at these words:

> *Voilà* Bernadette astonished. At the Soubirous home one did not have such habits. She was shocked in her delicacy, in her piety. ... Bernadette felt that she (Jeanne Abadie) was the opposite of herself in all the inclinations of sweetness, politeness, and religious respect which were her most ordinary impulses.[15]

Another account listed the symbolic significance of every element in the scene of the first vision and cited 'the companions of Bernadette' as providing a warning against the folly of talking too much and lacking 'calm, meditation and prayer'.[16] The writers somehow forget that one of these companions was Bernadette's own sister, Toinette, who could not have had a greatly different upbringing and values. The literature of moral exhortation requires figures of corruption as well as heroes and heroines, and so the companions of Bernadette fell into the negative side of this illustrative function. The hagiography of Lourdes glorified a fiction of the Pyrenean identity in their legend of Bernadette, but the other women of the Pyrenees, who were her equals and first companions, can only appear as a discordant note which serves to exalt the virtues of the visionary.

The historical Bernadette seems to have resented the attempts to depict her in such terms, which might be described as either utopian or priggish. During her lifetime the *Journal de la Grotte* published accounts of the visions which offered an extraordinary picture of Bernadette as puny, self-consciously virginal, and constantly persecuted by her friends, brothers and sisters. Disregarding her status as the eldest child, the historians tried to claim that she would vainly reproach the other children for not praying. 'The younger sister had more vigour; when these admonitions irritated her, she would incite her little brother and both would fall on the poor eldest who would defend herself feebly, crying a little, but never telling their parents ... She was often beaten, but her inexhaustible goodness made her love them tenderly ...'[17]

As a child, Bernadette had indeed disputed with the younger children, but rather more effectively than these writers wanted to imagine. As the eldest, she would take over in her mother's absence, and make them do household tasks and say their prayers. Bernadette was a forceful character. According to her account: 'She (Toinette) never hit me' and 'I gave some slaps to my younger brother, but he never gave me any.'[18] Toinette herself did recall fighting with Bernadette when they were children, but Bernadette herself either forgot, or refused to remember, that her younger sister ever dared to hit her. Henri Lasserre quoted her, at the age of twenty-five, as saying that: 'As for observations which I might have made about an immodest bearing and coarse remarks of my companions, these details and these comments are absolutely without foundation, and nothing of that type happened.'[19] But few heard her words, or took them seriously.

Bernadette was not only written about but also reproduced in pictures. She became well known at the same time as the development of a new industry – photography. Bernadette was photographed for the first time in early 1862, and pictures of her were soon produced for the pilgrim trade. She was the first holy person whose appearance has become known through photographs, and it has been claimed that she was one of the most photographed people of the mid-nineteenth century.[20]

These contemporary pictures of Bernadette, although marketed as part of a religious phenomenon, were stylistically influenced by a secular genre – the use of peasants as a decorative motif in nineteenth-century France. From the late 1840s onwards, while political and religious discourse made free use of the

**Plate VII**   Bernadette Soubirous, early 1860s. © *Ed. A. Doucet*

peasants, depictions of rural life came into widespread use at all levels of French society. These images ranged from Impressionist paintings to the most mundane decorative items. The art historians Christopher Parsons and Neil McWilliam write that:

> ruralism had provided a visual counterpart to the growing mythologisation of the peasantry associated with interest in popular culture and regional customs. The genre had grown up in a climate of antiquarian research into popular usage and tradition ... In the work of such ruralists, traditional

costume was lovingly displayed and the minutiae of regional custom dwelt upon in a way which suggested that the nation's peasants had remained immune to the changes apparently affecting the rest of society with mounting speed and intensity.[21]

The photographs of Bernadette consciously depict her as a peasant from the Pyrenees. She is always dressed in the costume of her area, and her appearance became so well known that the cult of Bernadette could be described as the Catholic contribution to the peasant mythology of France during this era.

In the eyes of those who created the narratives of Lourdes, Bernadette's willingness to wear her regional costume was infused with ethical significance. In the first authorized history of the apparitions, Abbé Fourcade rejoiced that 'she had never wanted to change the simplicity, the coarseness of her costume'.[22] An incongruous aspect to the comments of Fourcade, and of all the visitors who favourably remembered this quaint and pleasing form of dress, was that Bernadette herself did want to change and to wear clothes like those of the other girls in the Hospice. She was stopped from doing so, but all her life she had a talent for *couture*. The Sister of Nevers noticed that she always liked to be well dressed, and when she finally escaped from her peasant costume into a religious habit she was skilful in arranging her veil and coif. When the superiors tested her humility by giving her an ill-made collar she was dismayed: 'To me, they only give rags.'[23] By nature, she seems to have had absolutely no inclination for any form of 'coarseness in her costume',[24] but during her years in the Hospice she was wrapped in shawls of unbleached wool, according to the expectations of her audience.

Had Bernadette not been photogenic she would not have been a suitable subject for fame and mass representation. Her unusually small size also helped to popularize her, as she could be described as like a 'child' until she was nearly twenty-five. Petite, and with finely shaped features unmarked by toil, Bernadette was a vision of beauty and youth as well as rustic charm. As Père Cros wrote:

> Bernadette is twenty-one years old, according to the civil register, but one must, in order to admit this fact, make an act of faith toward the infallibility of the records. The eyes of those who behold her affirm, in effect, that Bernadette is always the child of thirteen, of the day of the apparition ... and her youthfulness has a supernatural charm.[25]

Bernadette came to detest being photographed, referring to it as a 'trial'.[26] Possibly this was because, as an asthmatic, she became exhausted by the enforced stillness of posing. She also resented the sale of her image, which she understood to be degrading to herself. Eventually the ubiquitous photographs made it impossible for her to go out in public – even outside of Lourdes – as she could easily be recognized by people whom she herself had never seen, and she would be quickly surrounded by crowds.

The way in which she was sold and displayed through photography was oppressive because it was a process over which she had no control, and was the antithesis of her own values. In later life, when she had taken on a new identity by entering the convent at Nevers, a Sister congratulated her for showing no signs of pride. She replied, 'I do not have any basis to be proud; I have seen myself in the shop windows of Lourdes, on sale for ten centimes.'[27] This comment was not a modest disclaimer, nor even a spontaneous observation on the part of Bernadette. It was a critique of her situation which had already been voiced to her by her old companions. Mlle Lacrampe, the middle-class woman of Lourdes who was never entirely able to drop her doubts about the apparitions, had seen Bernadette go from being a poor child of a disreputable family to the subject of adoration by endless pilgrims. She was naturally inclined to address Bernadette in a rather ironic tone. She recalled that: 'When they started selling her photograph for two sous, I asked her: "Do you not find that rather dear?" She answered: "They sell me for more than I am worth." '[28] When Bernadette went on a short holiday with Jeanne Védère, Dufour suggested that he could photograph them together. Jeanne recalled that:

That pleased Bernadette ... In order to mortify her a little (always I feared that vanity would take root in her heart because of the veneration which everyone had for her), I said to her: 'Oh! no, I do not want to appear behind a shop window with you.'[29]

The sale of her photographs was a microcosm of her transition from a person into an ideal. She was made available to large numbers of people, lauded in absolutely fictional biographies, valued in terms of currency, essentialized as the exponent of the Pyrenean identity, and distanced from her own people. Photography also reflected the ever recurrent aspect of her fame that she should be situated as the unwilling recipient of the attention which she received. Once she had repulsed importunate admirers who begged her for souvenirs with the remark that she was not a shopkeeper.[30] That was in 1858, when she still lived autonomously. By the middle of the next decade she herself was being reproduced as an item for sale. Her own body was a living machine for the production of relics, as people would touch objects against her and collect pieces of her hair and clothing.

For as long as she lived in Lourdes, Bernadette had a duty to keep repeating the story of her visions of 1858. The Secretary of the Episcopal Commission of Inquiry praised Bernadette's public role as being an additional element of credibility for the whole story:

The adversaries of the events at the Grotto at Lourdes cannot object that this young girl has been surrounded, that she has been taught how to tell her story, or that she can only be questioned in the presence of masters or protectors. No, she has not been secluded from the curiosity of the public, nor even from the questions of the incredulous: she has been accessible to everyone; ... she can be seen alone, and can be questioned at length, each according to their wishes ... it is always easy to see her and talk to her.[31]

This description of Bernadette's life from 1860 onwards is quite accurate except for one point – it was not possible to see her alone. While visitors could question her freely, as Fourcade described in his text, Bernadette was always attended by a Sister of Nevers or by another responsible religious figure.

Chaperonage was partly a question of propriety, as Bernadette's life in the convent naturally imposed middle-class norms of behaviour on her. A more important motive was that despite the confident tone of the above extract, clerics did not want Bernadette giving unsupervised accounts of these officially approved miraculous events. The Sisters of Nevers recalled this apprehension as a prime motive for placing Bernadette in their care. As Sr Damien Calmels said, when Bernadette was with her family many people visited her: 'Bernadette responded very simply to whatever anyone asked her, but M. le Curé Peyramale saw a danger in this for the child ...'[32] He did not have any reservations about her being seen and questioned by many people, on the contrary he organized a form of life for her which would revolve around public interviews. As Sr Damien dryly recalled, many visitors were accompanied by 'Mgr Peyramale, always very happy to make the child talk about the Apparitions ...'[33] The danger in her life at home was that such interviews would be carried out 'indiscreetly'; from the time that she came to live at the Hospice it was specified that she was not to see anyone alone or without permission and 'that order was rigorously observed'.[34]

It was exhausting to meet the requirements of so many visitors. As Sr Damien explained, 'Sometimes the visitors succeeded each other consecutively, to the point where on certain days they allowed her not a single moment of respite ... she always went to the parlour with repugnance.'[35]

Testimonies concerning Bernadette unanimously report that she had no wish to speak about the visions and disliked being questioned about them. This attitude was consistent from 1858 onwards, as Sr Lucie Clovis said: 'That aversion to talk of the apparitions, which she kept all of her life, first showed itself in her childhood.'[36] The endless interrogations wore away her patience, as her brother saw: 'Bernadette never took the initiative to give her account of the apparitions, she only responded to questions which were posed, showing sometimes an impatience before certain importunities.'[37] Jean-Marie's recollections would refer to the time when she still lived with her family, that is before 1860. After she moved to the Hospice the growing fame of Lourdes and organized multiple visits made the demands upon her much greater.

Another exaggerated and unnatural aspect of her life was the type of personal relationships which her celebrity created. She was separated from her family and her familiar environment and made accessible to the adoration of transient strangers with whom she had nothing in common. While pilgrims irritated her by asking for blessings and even trying to kiss and touch her, the Sisters at the Hospice and Curé Peyramale, who had taken the place of her family, treated her with severity in order to maintain her humility. In so doing they were only fulfilling the moral precepts of their time, which taught that humiliations were of benefit to the soul. As someone who had been brought up in poverty, Bernadette seems to have been able to resign herself to unpleasant circumstances. Although her later way of life was bizarre and unexpected, the restrictions, the demands, the narrow horizons and lack of privacy were not impossible burdens. The most difficult and unexpected trial should have been her isolation, as she lived bereft of family and friends. Yet Bernadette did not openly complain of this, nor did she seek close relationships to replace those which she had lost. Perhaps she could not relate well to others. While visitors who met Bernadette fleetingly described her as sweet, those who lived near to her tend to give a picture of her as 'rather reserved, reticent rather than expansive', despite her witty tongue and lively nature.[38]

During the period of the visions and immediately afterward Bernadette's health improved, but after her move to the Hospice her asthma worsened. The artist Joseph Fabisch, who met her in 1863, found her appearance charming, and commented that she was 'consumptive to her fingertips [*poitrinaire jusqu'au bout des ongles*]'.[39] She was indeed ill, and noticeably thinner than when she had arrived at the Hospice (compare Plate VII and Plate VIII.)

Despite this the burden of receiving visitors continued. A description of the pious rivalry which surrounded her was given by the Abbé Montauze in 1865. He obtained permission to see Bernadette from Curé Peyramale, who suggested to him that for her sake he should 'spare her exhausted health and only make her speak a little'.[40] Abbé Montauze described how:

> the poor child was led into the salon where we awaited her. She was dressed very simply, as she is represented in photography. Her expression was of suffering, yet was calm, her countenance was of a perfect modesty without the slightest touch of pose or pretension, all inspired respect and religious confidence. Before that child, so modest and simple, the suspicion of any sort of trickery whatever cannot be entertained.[41]

Abbé Montauze interviewed Bernadette in the company of another priest and several pilgrims. He records that when asked some questions Bernadette would simply fall silent. He asked her to make the sign of the cross, but she would only do so after Curé Peyramale insisted. When leaving he met yet another priest who was hearing the unwelcome news from the Reverend Mother that Bernadette could receive no more visitors. 'The poor child is suffering so, the Superior said. Then one of the Sisters joined the conversation and said: But *ma mère* could you not make an exception for M. l'Abbé? Two of these gentlemen have seen Bernadette, and you will understand that he must be jealous.'[42] By means of these importunities this further visit was allowed and when comparing their impressions later they said to one another:

> That child is going to die ... We had the same sad impression this morning upon seeing how sick and emaciated she was. But who knows when her mission on this earth will be finished? She will live until there is no one further to convince of her simplicity, her modesty and the truth of her vision.[43]

**Plate VIII**  Bernadette Soubirous, mid-1860s. © *Photo Viron*

Memoirs such as Abbé Montauze's acknowledge the harmful consequences of Bernadette's public role, yet these observations are made with approbation because the suffering and vulnerability of the visionary add to the credibility of her story:

> Oh! How hard her task has been! And how dearly she has had to pay for the honour which she has received! There she is – for seven years raised up like a permanent and living proof for the truth of her vision before the ardent curiosity of innumerable pilgrims ... Might not her continual sufferings be a providential safeguard of her humility? It has cost this poor human being a great deal to live in constant contact with the supernatural. Never mind, Bernadette must be happy in the depths of her soul ...[44]

Another writer reassured the public firstly that Bernadette's recitals were always convincing and secondly that she was, quite properly, unhappy to give them: 'Dead to the vanities of this world, she suffers when she is visited and questioned.'[45]

Bernadette usually responded politely to the throngs of admirers. Abbé Pomain said that: 'I have seen Bernadette at the Hospice beset by visitors, exhausted, annoyed. She remained grave and calm, especially when it was a question of the apparitions.'[46] On one particularly busy day, 19 August 1864, nine hundred people visited the Hospice. There are accounts of her making caring gestures toward the sick, and of showing acceptance to those who suffered from repulsive symptoms, such as a child whom she held with special care in order not to hurt his monstrously swollen and painful head. She could relate individually to only a few such visitors, and there were always more asking for attention. She was often asked if miraculous cures had happened. 'I do not know, perhaps yes. But it is not my prayers which have obtained those favours.'[47]

Bernadette grimaced over the tasks of giving autographs and sitting for photographs, but would usually only become furious when offered money. This was the only instance in which she could legitimately show outrage at the importunities of visitors. They were captivated by her ill-temper before their bribes, because it showed her distance from the suspicion of fraud. The idea that Bernadette was uncorrupted by lucre is an important part of her legend, and it is certainly true that she took no material benefits, and appears to have never wanted them. 'I do not need anything, she would say, while returning the money.'[48] However, inevitably, the commercialism of the pilgrim trade penetrated the walls of the Hospice, where the visionary had such a limited shelter. The donations of the pilgrims were essential to the grand building programme at the Grotto. There was no possibility that she would be hidden away from them. The Superior at the Hospice said that 'Bernadette never wanted to accept money, but I would always take it for the construction of the chapel.'[49] The Sisters of Nevers said that Bernadette would hand the donations over to them, and she would do so obediently, but hastily, as if the money burned her. She was capable of saying to the visitors: 'There is a coin-box.' People tried to cut off pieces of her clothing, and she repelled them in exasperation. 'What idiots you are.'[50]

Bernadette's impatience with those around her became more marked in time, and her state of frustration was such that it would provoke asthma attacks. From this time onwards she also began to show symptoms of tuberculosis, the eventual cause of her death in 1879. During the nineteenth century asthma was less common than it is today and was not well understood as a disorder. It was often confused with tuberculosis and no effective remedies were available.[51] At the Hospice Bernadette received good medical care, and was never neglected, but the lifestyle which was imposed upon her was detrimental to her health. Bernadette's asthma was linked to emotional tension and falls within the category described by a nineteenth-century doctor as 'nervous asthma, the most rebellious type'.[52]

Bernadette's collapses with asthma were her only protest against her captive life. When angered by the restrictions, her separation from her family and the visits of pilgrims she would sometimes speak sharply. Her words were not heeded, but the Sisters of Nevers soon noticed that her anger was followed by illness. 'We observed that her worst attacks soon followed her moments of being headstrong, disobedient or at fault in any way.'[53] Upon seeing that Bernadette was angry, the Sisters would say to one another, 'she will soon become ill'[54] and indeed, 'the penance was not slow to arrive; we thought that it was the Blessed Virgin who punished her. A crisis of her illness, which would keep her several days in bed, regularly followed these sallies of ill-temper.'[55] During the days of the visions, Bernadette's moments of rage had coalesced with the defiance of her whole community, the poor of Lourdes. But now she was isolated among people of a different order, where women were never allowed to express anger. Her frustration turned inwards, and she became ill. When a companion offered sympathy to Bernadette for her illness she replied, 'I much prefer that to receiving visits.'[56] Soon it was no longer a choice between the two, as visitors would be conducted to the infirmary and interview her while she rested in bed.

Illness was a dual theme of the Lourdes pilgrimages. There was the frail health of the visionary, which became a part of her sentimental image. There were also the illnesses suffered by many pilgrims who came to Lourdes in the hope of a miraculous cure. While Bernadette lived at the Hospice they often directed their hopes of a miracle towards her and would sometimes obtain permission for her to accompany them to the Grotto. Bernadette told these petitioners that she could not cure them but she remained in the stressful position of being the focus of their hopes.[57] The doctor at the Hospice recorded that: 'Her asthma had a gravity which it does not ordinarily have at that age. The crises of constriction of her chest were on more than one occasion the result of those interrogations to which she was submitted, and those walks to the Grotto.'[58] Dr Boissarie told Émile Zola that if Bernadette had not left Lourdes in 1866 'she would have died from the pressures she was under. The visitors asked for her without ceasing'.[59] The doctor was often obliged to forbid visits in order to allow her to recover.

This invalidism increased her allure. Nineteenth-century religious literature cherished physical frailty. It was a romantic trait in youthful heroines. The conjunction of youth, beauty and an early death was a staple theme of literature, both religious and secular, popular and elite. Indeed, Bernadette's asthma was among the many contingent factors, such as her photogenic features and her peasant identity, which qualified her for the distinctive role of a female religious celebrity.

Most pilgrims enthusiastically recorded the experience of meeting the visionary of Lourdes. There was a famous observation that: 'The most striking proof of the apparitions is Bernadette herself.'[60] After his first meeting with her, the Jesuit Père Cros wrote to a contemporary that she had 'a supernatural charm which it is impossible to describe. She herself is an apparition.'[61] It is noteworthy that some people who were familiar with Bernadette were much less rhapsodic. Frère Léobard, who lived and worked in Lourdes, wrote of Bernadette that:

> Upon first seeing her, one would believe that she was full of simplicity; ... but soon those who found themselves near her would discover, on the contrary, a great deal of mischief [*beaucoup d'espièglerie*]. The last time, when at my request she came to give me again the recital of the whole story, I asked myself several times, upon looking attentively at her, if she was not an adroit actress rather than a sincere visionary; and I tell you, even though I have always believed in the reality of the apparition, I would have been reduced to a state of doubt, if the numerous cures which we have had here did not determine my conviction.[62]

Frère Léobard is plainly stating what is hinted by other witnesses, especially those from the middle classes of Lourdes. A member of his congregation explained that Frère Léobard 'had taken her [Bernadette] for a *rouée*, because she spoke with such facility'.[63] Another member of the Lourdes clergy explained that Bernadette had an intelligent manner 'and did not lack, in effect, intelligence, because she easily understood the way the mind works, and she could pass skilfully from serious things to pleasantries, and from pleasantries to the serious'.[64]

The recitals, and even the visions, of Bernadette could appear to be a performance. It has already been pointed out that Jean-Baptiste Estrade, although he did not doubt Bernadette's story, made the startling comparison of her public appearances and the acting of the great tragedian, Rachel. The Police Commissioner, who most firmly did not believe her, had seen Bernadette when for the first time, in 1858, she was respectfully received by her social superiors. His comment that 'she is very intelligent and understands the sweet rewards of the role which she plays' was made with some understanding of the girl whom he interrogated at length, and of the degraded social circumstances from which she had risen. Pilgrims only saw her as a personification of a holy young girl, too simple to deceive, but some of those near her thought her clever and adroit. Abbé Pomain, who had known her since her days in the catechism class, gave a mild and realistic appraisal:

> As far as the soul of Bernadette is concerned, and her virtues, I would express myself by saying: there was an *absence of evil*, innocence, simplicity,

and as a part of that, she lived in a very ordinary way; and after the Apparitions, she remained average, and not without some flashes of ill-temper, from time to time.[65]

Another priest recalled that when he asked Abbé Pomain about Bernadette he had been told that he had the impression that she would have liked to play cards and that she was inclined to pleasure.[66]

The chronic poor health of the visionary eventually obscured her lively nature. She was not inclined to be an ascetic, but eventually she was obliged to become one. She was without any taste for the life of enclosure and inactivity which circumstances eventually imposed upon her. As she told Henri Lasserre during her last illness, 'I was born to act, to shift about, to be always moving,' and numerous documents bear out this opinion.[67] A Sister of Nevers recalled that she had seen Bernadette, during her teenage years, actually turning cartwheels when she was playing alone in a courtyard.[68] This was remembered with affection, but when Père Sempé visited her during her early days at the Hospice he was 'slightly scandalized' to see her leave the parlour with relief, laughing, rubbing her hands, then running with the little children in the playground.[69] This liveliness vanished during her years at the Hospice, and by the age of twenty she was more profoundly asthmatic than during her deprived childhood. The later Bernadette, who could not even breathe without difficulty, was more obviously saintly than was the active working girl whom she had once been.

Not every woman visionary was willing or able to live such a life of self-suppression. During Bernadette's years at the Lourdes Hospice Mélanie Calvat was also a public figure in France. Like Bernadette, Mélanie Calvat had a vision when she was fourteen years old. She was an agricultural worker in a depressed mountain region – the hamlet of La Salette in the French Alps. She was shepherding flocks with a companion, Maximin Giraud, in 1846. They returned home with a story of having encountered a vision of the Virgin Mary, who called for prayer and penance, and predicted famine and bloodshed if her words were not heeded.

The cult of Our Lady of La Salette gained adherents partly because the crop failures and revolutions of 1848 lent credibility to the prophecy. Pilgrimages ensued, and the local bishop issued a mandate approving the vision as genuine. But neither Maximin Giraud nor Mélanie Calvat survived the pressures of public life with their reputations intact. They had been taken to live in religious houses, and their personal conduct did not match the rigorous norms of their new environment. Numerous pilgrims interviewed them, and they responded to the allure of public enthusiasm by embellishing their story with wilder claims. By 1854 the local bishop had become alarmed by their antics, and took steps to dissociate himself from the monarchist political circles that had been fostering prophetic utterances by Maximin Giraud. Mélanie Calvat was not permitted to take vows at the convent of the Sisters of Providence, because of the tales which she would tell to visitors and fellow members of the novitiate. She claimed to have received the stigmata as an infant, to have witnessed numerous miracles and to have secret revelations about the future of mankind. The Bishop of Grenoble was appalled.

Mélanie Calvat left her native region in 1854, and for the rest of her life wandered from place to place, as well as entering and leaving several convents. Although educated late, she was a fluent writer, and produced several texts of apocalyptic prophecies. These included a violent denunciation of the French priesthood, which, she claimed, had failed to heed the words of the Virgin of La Salette. She remained as a practising Catholic and still retained the loyalty of a certain number of enthusiasts when she died in Italy in 1904. Her visionary companion Maximin Giraud was a less colourful character, but also a disappointment to his early admirers. He became a heavy drinker and died as a destitute in 1875.

For the French Catholic Church the careers of the La Salette visionaries, especially that of Mélanie Calvat, were a severe embarrassment. The Bishop of Grenoble was reduced to recommending that one had to make a distinction, as he had, 'between the Mélanie of 1846, simple instrument of the apparition, and the Mélanie whom he had before him and who showed mystical pretensions'.[70] Mélanie Calvat's evolution has often been contrasted with that of Bernadette, generally by religious partisans who make the obvious point that Lourdes was far more fortunate in its visionary than La Salette.[71]

Mélanie Calvat's progress in life is an enlightening piece of social history, and it is difficult to imagine any role but a religious one which would have elevated her from her original obscurity and poverty. From an historical standpoint, her life has more significance than the problems she caused the church authorities. At the age of fifteen, when she entered the care of the Sisters of Providence, she was entirely illiterate, but she acquired the skills of literacy so thoroughly that she soon enjoyed reading. Her preference was for books about miracles, 'revelations more or less authentic' as one cleric put it.[72] Soon she would also communicate by writing, as the convent chaplain observed with disapproval: 'She has read a great deal. All which she has written since the apparition, she could have picked up during her readings.'[73] Here one can see a contrast with the celebrations of the more immutable character of Bernadette. Even after she had learnt to read, Bernadette was often praised for her apparent lack of education, which gave evidence of her simplicity and ignorance.

In the course of her life Mélanie Calvat was to show herself to be an energetic, independent, imaginative woman who travelled over Europe, spoke several languages and supported herself as a writer. All of this was unimaginable in her debased social origins. She often stated that she regretted the loss of her old life as a shepherdess. This seems to be an example of her ready response to people's fantasies, as she showed no inclination to return to her life of rural hardship. Although often derided, Mélanie Calvat fulfilled many of her ambitions in a society which generally denied women the right even to aspire to self-development.

The church authorities who were responsible for Bernadette knew of the disastrous aftermath of the career of Mélanie Calvat. It may have made them all the more protective, and restrictive, of the Lourdes visionary. However, Bernadette never showed the slightest inclination to elaborate on the original story of the visions, or launch out on her own as an independent religious authority. When confronted by visitors, her personality was calm and disinterested. Her clear eyes and still features were ideal for pictures, and her simple words were ideal for recitals. The long hours which she spent being displayed to pilgrims were always successful, at the level of publicity exercises. However, although she always looked the same, she was growing older.

## The education of Bernadette

When Bernadette first arrived at the Hospice in July 1860 she was given a place in the classroom. The entire experience of returning to school must have been strange to her. For several years, her education had been over, and she had been living in an adult world. Then, she returned to school, much older and more ignorant than the other pupils in the convent boarding school.

Although Bernadette had returned to her old school she was in a new environment. Previously, as a pupil in the charity class, she had been strictly segregated from the girls in the paying class. As a boarder at the Hospice, she was placed with this socially elevated group. The fee-paying class was itself divided into two. There was a premier group of well-off girls, and a secondary group of middling ones. By her own request, Bernadette was placed in the second category. She was not, of course, a true fee-paying student, and this was known to all. A fellow student recalled that: 'The superiors had the wisdom to try her; they said to her that she was only there for the sake of charity, and other similar things. Bernadette took all of this in good part. She said that she knew it and that she was very grateful.'[74]

**Plate IX** Bernadette with pupils at the Hospice. © *Photo Viron*

Some of her schoolbooks have been preserved, and they show that she could barely form her letters. Despite the difficulties, by December of 1860 she was able to write a New Year's greeting to her family. The short letter is ill-spelt and poorly worded, but it is a letter. Usually a Sister corrected her correspondence, and she was to need such help all her life. 'Do not be surprised if the letter is badly done, I did it without the Sister and I do not have a lot of time.'[75] Presumably, a neighbour would have read the letter to her parents, because they were not literate. Over the years, her slanted writing became elegant in style, but the standard of composition remained poor.

The effort of education left Bernadette unchanged. She did not read for pleasure, but passed her time working, talking or saying the rosary. Sometimes she would lean out the window in order to talk to her sister Toinette, who would make an irregular visit by walking up and down the street near the Hospice. During one of these conversations, Bernadette told her sister not to bother to learn how to read. Toinette had always believed that 'one had to be well educated in order to be devout' but Bernadette told her that since she could say her prayers, that ought to be enough.[76] Bernadette told Toinette that some of the young ladies at the boarding school took novels into church and read them during Mass. Then she hushed suddenly because Sr Victorine arrived and asked what they were talking about. It was many years before Bernadette saw any benefit in education.

Now that Bernadette was living at a Catholic boarding school she was expected to follow religious practices assiduously. The Sisters of Nevers found that she prayed, but that she was not exceptionally pious. 'At the chapel, she kept herself composed and prayed with fervour. But there, as everywhere else, she simply observed the Rule; if she was asked for one *Pater* more, she would have made it through obedience rather than inclination.'[77] Another Sister instructed Bernadette to make more of an effort: 'I said to her: "At your age, you ought to go sometimes to the chapel and meditate for a short while." She answered: "I do not know how to meditate." '[78] Despite her listless attitude, Bernadette maintained a level of unostentatious devotion, and after being in her company for months this Sister moderated her opinion and thought that she had 'a gift of piety'. Like many Pyrenean women, Bernadette kept her rosary always in her possession, and would recite it during any free moment of the day, or when sleepless at night.

The community at the Hospice was not large. There were about nine Sisters during the period that Bernadette lived there, and most of them were young nuns. The Sisters were very occupied with a full schedule of work and religious duties. The special care of Bernadette, and the supervision of visits to the Hospice, soon became another responsibility for the convent. The Superior of the Hospice, Mère Ursule Fardes, had the reputation of being scornful of Bernadette. In Lourdes, it was said that the Reverend Mother had never believed in the visions, and that she had only received Bernadette because the Curé asked her to. Mère Ursule left in 1861, about a year after Bernadette's arrival, and she was replaced by the 54-year-old Mère Alexandrine Roques. At the same time that Mère Alexandrine arrived, Sr Victorine Poux was sent to work at the Hospice. The 36-year-old Sr Victorine had the typical profile of a Sister of Nevers. She was hard-working and suited to an active post. Educated and dedicated, she judged the Pyrenean schoolchildren to be difficult cases, but did her best for them. She was given particular charge of Bernadette, and related her memories to Père Cros.

Sr Victorine found Bernadette to have 'a quite ordinary level of conduct'.[79] 'As for humiliations (those which I gave to her) she showed neither displeasure nor satisfaction. She never became annoyed.'[80] She seemed almost insensitive. Sr Victorine was surprised when one day Bernadette commented, after a scolding before the pilgrims, that it was 'humiliating for me'.[81] Sr Victorine nursed Bernadette through her illnesses and remembered that she had rheumatic pains as well as asthma:

> She was habitually oppressed, she had all types of pains: toothache, frequent rheumatism in one leg: one Good Friday she had pains in the shoulder which almost made her faint ... habitual coughing, vomiting and coughing up blood. Palpitations sometimes. Several times a year, violent attacks of asthma ... The long interrogations annoyed her; all of these fatigues weighed down her chest, she would then have asthma attacks; we had to carry her to bed: she never blamed the visitors.[82]

During the early 1860s, the Sisters of Nevers assumed that she was destined for an early death. A pilgrim who visited in August 1863 noticed that Bernadette left quickly after answering their questions. They could hear her coughing as she went down the corridor. 'It is always like that, the Superior said to me, as soon as she has spoken for a while. She is pious and sweet, we are very lucky to have her, but I believe that she will not live a long time, and that, when she has fulfilled her mission, God will take her.'[83] Bernadette in fact lived to be thirty-five, which was longer than expected. The rheumatic pains, especially in one leg, might be the beginning of the tumour, caused by tuberculosis, which was to tear her knee apart during the last two years of her life.

The worst periods of ill-health were early in the years 1862 and 1864. On both occasions, Bernadette was judged to be at the point of death and she received the last sacraments. The first recovery was so sudden that it seemed miraculous. In April 1862 she had been in bed for some time, then her breathing failed, and the doctor called for a priest. Then without warning Bernadette breathed normally, and there were reports that she had been cured by the Holy Eucharist, swallowed with a drop of Lourdes water. Curé Peyramale, who was rather over-enthusiastic about Lourdes miracles, spread the story that she had been cured by the spring water. But even in these letters, he was obliged to add a postscript that Bernadette herself did not believe it. Unexpectedly, she blamed her doctor for the brush with death. 'If I am sick another time, I would ask the doctor to pay attention because he mistook this illness for another one, while I could have choked from what I had.'[84] During her last illness, Bernadette was again to be truculent towards the doctor who attended her, and it may be that when ill she falsely believed that these medical experts did not take her case seriously. In fact, they did take a grave view of her health, but there was little that they could do for her.

When she was on her feet, Bernadette was as vivacious as ever. She was friendly to the other students in the Hospice. 'She had a gay character. She took part in all our games.' There are only a few anecdotes about this aspect of her life. She repulsed their queries about the visions. 'Leave me be, she would say. I have to tell it to so many others.'[85] In the classroom she sometimes played pranks, such as passing her snuff-box around, and making everybody sneeze. On another occasion, she dropped her shoe from a window into the garden, in order to give her companions an excuse to go there, and pick some strawberries.

The shoe which Bernadette threw into the garden was a sabot. Bernadette still wore peasant dress, which would have marked her out among her companions. In her early days at the Hospice she had tried to arrange more fashionable attire. Sr Victorine remembered that:

All that I could observe as a blemish in her was that, in the early days, she had an inclination toward vanity in dress. A school companion influenced her toward this, and one day I found her enlarging a skirt to give it the look of a crinoline. Another time, I found that she had put a piece of wood, as a busk, in a corset. But this enthusiasm passed quickly and left no trace. Her real fault was being headstrong, obstinate, mutinous, but to a lesser degree than many other children of her class ...[86]

Sr Victorine also noted, when speaking of Bernadette's faults, that she had found a bottle of white wine hidden in her locker.[87] This piece of information was so hot that it has rarely been reprinted.[88] When René Laurentin cited it he pointed out all the extenuating circumstances – that Père Cros had a fixation on alcohol, and always asked witnesses about it, thus eliciting replies, and also that each student had a locker where they kept provisions, so that Bernadette was not really hiding anything. Although Sr Victorine would have been prodded into producing the white wine anecdote, it would have been her truthful recollection. From Bernadette's point of view, that bottle of wine might have been nothing in particular. Among the French peasantry and working classes, even heavy drinking was normal, and moderate consumption of wine was regarded as one of the essentials of life, like bread. The Sisters of Nevers would have been alert to the possibility that Bernadette might start drinking to excess. Her life was pressured and often miserable – even they could see that. Female alcoholism was a problem all too well known, but not openly discussed, among genteel women and religious communities.

Bernadette liked wine, but was never intoxicated. Ironically, in their refinement and concern for her health, the staff at the Hospice introduced Bernadette to a different addictive substance – tobacco. As a student at the Hospice, Bernadette was prescribed snuff by Dr Balencie. Taking snuff is a way of inhaling tobacco. By Bernadette's day, it was no longer a fashionable habit, and cigars, pipes and cigarettes had taken over. But snuff was still used. It was supposed to sooth the respiration of people with allergies and asthma. The effect of the tobacco dust in the nasal passages would only have been negative. But taking snuff allowed access to nicotine, which would (like cocaine) enter the bloodstream directly through the vessels in the nose. As nicotine is a sedative, taking snuff would calm the nerves and therefore might relieve some of the symptoms. Bernadette obediently took up the habit when she was at the Hospice, and remained a snuff-taker for the rest of her life. Witnesses rarely comment on it, and there is not a single description of her making the characteristic gestures of opening the box and taking a pinch. But she must often have been seen doing so. Bernadette came to like snuff, and in later years asked her family to send her favourite mixture from Lourdes. We never think of Bernadette as a tobacco user, yet she was.

At some time during the years at the Hospice, Bernadette passed through puberty. This would probably have been when she was about seventeen years old, a usual age for the onset of menstruation in the nineteenth century. It is obvious from photographs that she lost weight during the years 1862–64. She changes from being a plump-faced young girl to having sharper, more mature features. This was partly due to illness, but at the same time her whole body adapted and changed. But her life did not change and she remained in the role of the child visionary.

## Vocations

As early as 1858, people repeating miracle stories in Lourdes said that Bernadette wanted to become a nun.[89] It seems unlikely that she said so, but people believed it because it was expected. What becomes of visionaries in the end? They enter convents and monasteries. This was an established pattern in Pyrenean Marian legends.

The famous Anglèse Sarazan had entered a Cistercian monastery where she had been treated harshly but had sustained all trials to be accepted as a nun. In this, as in so many details, Anglèse Sarazan was Bernadette's precursor. A booklet at the Garaison shrine, printed two decades before the visions at Lourdes, pointed out, under the headline *Proofs of the Apparition* that: 'The young shepherdess, enflamed with love for Mary, had left the world to enclose herself in a convent where she lived in a most edifying manner until her death. The effects of the apparition, concerning the chapel, have appeared in an infinite number of miraculous cures which it is impossible to dispute. The apparition is therefore an avowed fact.'[90] Every word of this paragraph could have been printed in a Lourdes booklet, when it, in turn, became an established shrine. The life in a convent would suit Bernadette perfectly, explained a writer in the 1870s, and 'there was, besides, a thought which was generally shared that the Immaculate Virgin would not leave in this world that child whom she had fed with the delights of heaven, and that she would compensate her for the fatigues of her apostolate by the joys of the religious life'.[91]

The ready assumption that a good visionary would make a good religious was not so universal in the religious houses themselves. The public who admired visionaries usually only had brief and inspirational encounters with them. The religious life, with its relentless and minute scrutiny, its eventless nature, and its hierarchical systems of authority, was inhospitable to ecstatic behaviour. It is true that many visionaries were found in convents, including some of the most famous saints of the Catholic Church. But it is also true that in religious establishments visionaries were treated with more rigour and less credulity than anywhere else in Catholic society.

Stories of unstable visionaries well known throughout religious congregations and the resultant prejudices were especially obvious in the case of the Sisters of Nevers. Nothing suggested, prior to the 1860s, that this select and mannered group of women would host the most famous peasant visionary of the era. There had been only a few visionaries in the history of their order, and they were of the more heady days of the seventeenth century. The most renowned was one of their founding mothers, Marcelline Pauper, an ascetic and visionary who had been approved by several contemporary clergymen. The Sisters of Nevers were so far from publicly extolling Marcelline Pauper's supernatural claims that they waited more than a century before publishing her written works. In introducing the edition, a priest from Nevers lamented that there was an assumption in the religious houses:

> passing almost for a maxim in our country ... which treats as dangerous and detrimental any books dealing with ecstasies, visions or revelations ... The pretext is the possibility of abuse ... In one community, a superior said to the young nuns: if there is anyone who claims to have visions, she will be sent away; we do not want any ecstatics in our institute.[92]

The Sisters of Nevers would have considered that they had the right to maintain such reservations. As one member of the congregation recalled: 'Perhaps what happened to Mélanie, after the apparitions at La Salette, put our superiors on guard concerning Bernadette.'[93] There were other examples, closer to home, as in at least one case from the 1840s a Sister at the St Gildard convent had suffered from mental illness and had required confinement in the convent. Word of her violent outbursts had leaked out, and a local pamphleteer described her as 'a religious in whom exaltation had degenerated into insanity'.[94] This gave an anti-clerical writer the chance to claim that: 'Such events happen only too often in convents, where many women religious, because of their intrinsic weakness, cannot control their emotions.'[95]

The Sisters of Nevers were not open to seers or enthusiasts, nor to peasant girls of little education. When the Bishop of Nevers told Mère Marie-Josephine Imbert that 'many other congregations coveted her and that he was astonished that the Sisters of Nevers had not already admitted her as a postulant,' she coolly replied that this girl had few accomplishments and poor health.[96] By the standards applied to any other candidate, she was not a desirable entrant. Mgr Forcade assured Mère Imbert that 'she can grate carrots', a comment which was to echo like a chorus across Bernadette's religious life.[97]

It is not surprising that some influential Sisters of Nevers had their reservations about Bernadette. She, in her turn, had a noticeable aversion for them. 'She was not inclined to the Sisters of Nevers,' stated her aunt, Bernarde Castérot.[98] A priest from Lourdes stated that in the town she was supposed to have said: 'If I become a sister, it will not be as a Sister of Nevers.'[99] He explained this remark as being 'quite natural in Lourdes, where people considered the congregation of the Sisters of Nevers as reserved for young ladies of a social condition much more elevated than that of the Servant of God'.[100] They were commonly known as the 'Dames de Nevers', that is as Ladies, rather than Sisters. Bernadette's other aunt, Basile Castérot, stated that Bernadette had wanted to enter an enclosed monastery, with a stricter rule, but had been advised to go to the Sisters of Nevers because of her health.[101]

Bernadette had been taken on a visit to the Carmelite nuns at Bagnères, and she sometimes was visited by Carmelite priests at the Hospice. When one of them suggested to her that she should join their order, Bernadette replied: 'If I were to become a religious, I would enter a congregation where I could follow the Rule without exemptions.'[102] A woman pilgrim had asked her if she would not like to be a nun, and her answer was brief: 'Yes, but I do not have the health.'[103] She might also have not been suited to a regime of more prayer than work, for 'she liked an active life'.[104] Bernadette herself later commented, 'No, I would not want to be a Carmelite, and stay forever indoors.'[105] Apparently she reached this conclusion during the early 1860s, and she remained at the Lourdes Hospice, tolerating the inconveniences of her life, and waiting upon the possibilities.

Bernadette thought that she would be unable to take the life of a Carmelite nun, who could never step outside the sanctuary. Yet she was, in a sense, already enclosed, and she would continue to be for the rest of her life. It was very difficult for Bernadette to take a walk beyond the walls of the Lourdes Hospice, because she would soon be recognized and hailed by people who wanted to greet her, touch her, and solicit her prayers. She may have thought that these reactions would die down with time. Instead, they increased, and the mere sight of her brought out crowds. On one occasion, they thronged before the Hospice in such numbers, and with such determination, that the Superior thought it advisable to ask some soldiers from the militia to stand in a row before the convent. In order to pacify the crowd, they were allowed a sight of the visionary, who was paraded up and down the veranda. Bernadette protested against this: 'You are showing me off like a strange beast.'[106] But the displays went on, in photography studios, in the parlour, and even in the infirmary. It was just as bad outside of Lourdes. When the Sisters of Nevers took her on a visit to the convent at Pau: 'Unfortunately, someone recognized her, wearing her capulet. In only a moment, the house was surrounded ... We were obliged to call the police ... A crowd of mothers gathered in the courtyard of the convent. The police maintained order. She went around and touched each of the children. All of this gave her a lot of bother and fatigue.'[107] The same scenes were repeated in other Pyrenean towns.

The attentions of demanding pilgrims extended to her family. Etienne-François Houzelot, a collector of religious souvenirs, came to Lourdes in February 1862. He visited Louise Castérot, and asked her if she had any of her daughter's clothes:

I believe that she told me that she had two capulets which Bernadette had worn during the apparitions. She had given the first away, and she wanted to keep the second, but after much insistence on my part, Mme Soubirous consented, not without pain, to give it to me, also the cross of the rosary of her first communion and a note from Bernadette which she wrote to send New Year's greetings to her parents, that letter is dated 31 Dec 1860.

... [He said that some have doubted the authenticity of these relics.] I have just asked the Curé to remind Mme Soubirous of me and to speak to her of the visitor to whom she gave these three things, the capulet of Bernadette, the cross and the letter, she cannot do otherwise than to recall me.[108]

Louise Castérot probably would have remembered this frightful visitor, but she was not able to reply to his request and authenticate relics for the religious goods merchants. In 1873, when he wrote this letter, she was long dead. The separation from Bernadette, the worries of her household, and the importunities of visitors, were difficulties which she endured as her health faded. She was poor and shy, and she did not know how to repulse the demands of articulate outsiders. When Louise Castérot was contending with this visitor she would have been seven months pregnant. In February 1864 she gave birth to a son, Jean Soubirous, but he died in September that same year. Bernadette had been scarcely permitted to see the baby.

Not every visitor posed such a challenge to the courtesy of Pyrenean culture. In 1864 Bernadette exchanged two letters with a young and idealistic priest, Abbé Charles Bouin. When visiting Lourdes, he contacted Bernadette's family and came to be on amicable terms with them. He also seems to have had other friends in common with her. Exactly how Abbé Bouin came to penetrate Lourdes society so quickly is not clear. Usually visitors were welcomed, but remained as strangers to the private lives of local people. He may have been a person of unusual charm, for he melted reserve wherever he went, and Bernadette wrote warmly to him that she would always unite her prayers with his.[109] Abbé Bouin corresponded with her by sending the letters to her family, rather than the Hospice, and Bernadette assured him that: 'You can be easy about your letter, no-one opened it but me: my parents sent for me to receive it, it was a good excuse for me to be able to see them.'[110]

In the whole of Bernadette's correspondence, the exchange with Abbé Bouin was unique. Bernadette asked the Abbé to send her his photograph, to pray for her brother whom she described as lazy at school, and to receive the best wishes of her family. Rather than concentrating on Bernadette as an ideal object, Abbé Bouin was friendly with her whole family. He asked Bernadette for a list of all their names, which she gave: 'I commence with my father, then all the others: François, Louise, Marie, Jean-Marie, Augustine, Pierre, Jean. I do not name the eighth one, thinking that you have not forgotten her.'[111] These letters show some development in her writing skills – she moves beyond the set phrases of the model letters which she wrote for practice, and reproduces her speech.

It was very difficult for Bernadette to find time to write: 'despite my good will, I cannot do so at present, because I am always being called downstairs;

I have just done so several times, and this is what discourages me in doing my studies, as soon as I pick up a pen I have to put it down'.[112] A month later she wrote him her second letter, which described her hectic situation and her desire to escape from it. She congratulated him for wanting to be a hermit. To Bernadette it seemed an ideal existence: 'I will pray to the Lord and the Blessed Virgin so that you may know if you should become a hermit. I would like to do the same, because I am so tired of seeing so many people; pray for me, that either God will take me from this world, or that he will soon allow me to join his brides, for that is my wish, although I am quite unworthy.'[113] In this letter, she is looking about her, and seeing all aspects of her situation. There is her family, still the strong background to her life, but becoming distant and difficult to see. She still has friends from her own class in Lourdes, and is participating in community exchanges. But the crowds of pilgrims surround her, and she cannot speak a sentence uninterrupted by their demands. Ahead are the possibilities – perhaps an early death, and she accepts being taken from this world without regret – or a religious vocation, which she estimates as an ideal existence for which she is barely qualified.

Bernadette had already discussed the possibilities of a religious vocation with Mgr Forcade, the Bishop of Nevers, who visited the Hospice on 17 September 1863. On this occasion, she seemed far from enthusiastic about the idea. In his memoir of her he wrote that:

I began by saying to Bernadette:
—And now, my dear child, what will you become?
—But nothing, Bernadette answered after a moment of hesitation.
—What do you mean nothing? One must be something in this world.
—Oh well, I am here with the Sisters.
—No doubt, but you are, and can only be here temporarily.
—I will stay always.
—That is easy to say but difficult to do.
—Why not?
—Because you are not a Sister and it is indispensable to be one in order to stay with a permanent status in a religious congregation. Here you are nothing, and on that footing you will not last long.
She seemed thoughtful and did not say anything more; after a moment of silence I began again:
—You are a child no more. Perhaps you would be happy to have a household of your own?
Her answer was sharp:
—Ah! Nothing of that sort!
—Well then why do you not become a Sister? Have you not ever thought of it?
—It is impossible, Monseigneur, you know very well that I am poor, I will never have the necessary dowry.
—My child, they accept poor girls as religious if they have a true vocation.
—But Monseigneur, the young ladies whom you take without dowries are

well-educated and skilled so they pay you back. As for me, I am nothing and I am good for nothing.

Mgr Forcade was not deterred by this frank assessment of the material contributions needed by religious houses. He assured Bernadette that:

—But see, those young ladies whom you speak of, they eat carrots but they do not like to grate them. They prefer to exercise the finesse of their fingers on paper, or in delicate handcrafts, or in playing the piano. When they become Sisters, they are naturally employed as teachers in the boarding schools, where they would soon die of hunger, if they did not have some humble companions to peel their vegetables. You can be sure that a useful role would be found for you, and also that at the novitiate they would not fail to give you a large part of the education which you now lack.[114]

By 1864 she was twenty, and therefore an adult, although so many people treated her as a child. Her life was lived in a provisional situation. She was still at boarding school, although all of her generation had long since left to begin their lives. She was directed by the Sisters as if she were a junior pupil and had no duties of her own, except for the hateful role of going to the parlour to give recitals about the visions. Occasionally she was able to earn a little money by embroidering articles for sale, but she had no ambitions to earn her living independently. Also, she showed no interest at all in the prospect of finding a partner or marrying. She never seems to have had any romantic concerns, and had little chance of developing them after she went to live in a convent. She had been distanced from her own family and community, and had little contact with men of her own class. Some upper-class men were attracted by her fame and her beautiful face. The Bishop of Tarbes did receive marriage proposals on her behalf, but they seem to have come from eccentrics who had never even met her, and were routinely refused.

Bernadette's character was usually calm, humble and reticent, but she retained her childhood attitude of defiance before orders which she found unreasonable. The Sisters of Nevers preserved a few anecdotes of her moments of ill-temper, such as when she was told to change out of her Sunday dress but declined to do so, and another time when she refused a direct order from the Superior of the Hospice, to throw potato peels into a different bucket. These trivial incidents betray the stress which resulted from her static life in the Hospice. Bernadette always apologized afterwards. When she had first arrived, she had been annoyed when she was not allowed to see her family. As the years passed, she accepted the regime of circumscribed visits, and her discontent surfaced over the obligation to go to the parlour, and the lack of any definite status in her daily life.

During the winter months of 1864 she was given a meaningful job at the Hospice. She was to help nurse a patient in the public ward. The patient was an old woman who had burnt herself. Lourdes writers described her as being 'old and in rags', and noted that she had received her injuries when drunk.[115] While the patient is denigrated in these accounts, Bernadette was much

**Plate X**  Bernadette Soubirous, mid-1860s. © *Photo Lacaze*

admired for the dedication and gentleness which she showed toward the invalid. Burns are a terribly painful injury, and ulcerated wounds are unpleasant to dress. Moreover, this woman was bedridden and would have depended on Bernadette to wash, feed and toilet her. Bernadette was the type of young woman who usually was employed in such tasks, and she made light work of it. She was quite accustomed to the ways of the poor. Also, in the *cachot* she had lived beside a cesspit, and so was used to bad odours. In future years, when she worked in infirmaries, she often encountered bedpans and putrid infections, but she never caught her breath before them. Her asthma was not roused by nursing duties. Instead, she had the satisfaction of seeing her patient return to health, and when farewelling her, Bernadette joked: 'Next time take fewer sips.'[116] This period of work could only have taken place early in the year, when the pilgrimage trade was at a low ebb. As the year 1864 wore on, Bernadette returned to the parlour and her duties to the public. Soon she was ill again, exhausted again, angry again.

The interval as a worker in the Hospice ward was a bright moment in Bernadette's life. She saw her way to a new role. During the mid-1860s, Bernadette began to consider becoming a Sister in a charitable congregation. She then decided to stay with the Sisters of Nevers and ask for admission into their novitiate. Jeanne Védère quotes her as saying: 'I know very well that it is not because of my little self that they want me to stay here, I know that very well, because I would be good for nothing: what could anyone make of me? However, I know that they would not like to see me go elsewhere … They have looked after me for a long time, I must be grateful.'[117]

These words might be interpreted as evidence that Bernadette entered the congregation almost unwillingly, and the Sisters of Nevers were not pleased when the memoir was first published in the 1920s. Yet all that Bernadette is saying is that a sense of obligation had played a role in her decision to stay with this congregation. She also appreciated the discretion of the Sisters of Nevers. In contrast with many other religious, they did not solicit her entry. In later years, it was often pointed out that the Sisters in the Hospice had been forbidden to talk on such matters to Bernadette, and that they had observed this rule. Bernadette had been attracted to their community after she had been given a responsible, if temporary, job. She had an aptitude for nursing, and a caring attitude. Abbé Pomain, who had always known her, recognized the value of her work in the hospital ward. 'She worked to care for some quite repulsive old people at the Hospice: she was devoted and worked with great charity, I saw this myself. It was this which gave her an inclination for the life of a Sister of Charity.'[118] Bernadette obviously preferred the sight of decay, senility and incontinence to visits from demanding pilgrims.

In April 1864, at the age of twenty, Bernadette formally asked to join the Sisters of Nevers. She spoke to Mère Alexandrine Roques, who communicated this to the Mother House. They made no immediate move to take her at Nevers, and she was twenty-two years old by the time that she finally arrived. She lived on at the Lourdes Hospice, but when asked about her future, she would tell people that she intended to stay with the Sisters of

Nevers. Her health remained very poor, and she collapsed again in February. For a while it appeared that she might die. Instead, it was her younger brother, Justin Soubirous, only ten years old, who died on 1 February 1865. This must have saddened Bernadette. They had a special bond because she had been his substitute mother during the years of poverty. He had been the baby whom she had cared for, and carried out to nurse while Louise Castérot worked in the fields.

Louise Castérot gave birth again, in 1866, but the baby died as soon as it was born. When the previous baby was born, Bernadette had not been able to visit, and the Sisters of Nevers remembered that it made her angry. This time, she was allowed leave from the Hospice, and she wrote a letter to the Duvroux family, who were employing her sister as a servant. 'Marie [that is Toinette, in family letters she is given her more formal name] would have been a Godmother, but God disposed otherwise; we had a little girl but did not have much time to rejoice in her, the Lord had not created her for this world. We were able to give her holy water, and she left for heaven, poor little angel! As you can imagine, that has been a heavy sorrow for my poor mother ... '[119] Bernadette also was sad, but her letter passed on quickly to other subjects, and recounted how lively and amusing Toinette was being. Infant mortality was taken for granted. They might have been more worried if they had noticed that their mother's health was seriously failing, yet there is no mention of this. Louise Castérot, who was forty-one years old, had less than a year to live.

For the whole of 1865, Bernadette followed the usual routine at the Hospice. She was not pressured to join the Sisters of Nevers. In fact, they gave her a chance to reflect and to show commitment before the move to Nevers. In later years, a Nevers Mother Superior claimed that: 'According to the notes of our Sisters, it was not only the state of health which delayed her admission to the postulancy, it was also because she asked for time to consider.'[120] By 1866, the Superiors judged that it was time to receive her, but her departure was again delayed, this time by the building programme in the Grotto. The crypt was scheduled to open, and the Bishop of Tarbes wanted her to be present at the inauguration.

It was not until July 1866 that the Soubirous family gathered to farewell Bernadette. She had prepared for her departure by giving away most of her few possessions, and paying visits to her friends and family. The photographer Phillipe Viron took special photographs of her with her family, and delivered the prints to her in person. She considered herself a customer, and paid for them. He offered to give them to her, but right to the end, she would not take gifts. Her refusal was a dry comment on the whole photography business which had made her image the property of others. 'No, I wish to pay, for if you give them to me, they will not truly be mine.'[121]

On the night before her departure, the Sisters took Bernadette to the Grotto for the last time. Presumably, she was there after dark in order to avoid crowds. She prayed for a while, then kissed the ground in tears. 'The Grotto, that was my heaven.' On the following day, 4 July, she had dried her tears. Basile Castérot explained:

**Plate XI**   Jeanne Abadie of Lourdes. © *Author's collection*

We all went there, all her close family, her mother, her Godmother, and I along with the others, all saw Bernadette on the day of her departure at the Hospice. She was very glad to leave. We cried, but she did not. It is too good of you to cry, she told us, but I could not stay here for ever – for she did not want to stay in Lourdes.[122]

They accompanied her to the station and waved her away on the train, calling out 'adichàt' [adieu in Occitan].

In 1866 Bernadette left Lourdes for ever. She made a break with her past, and stepped into a new environment. It was a daunting step, but she had the courage to make it and not to look back. In later years, she made no attempt to keep up friendships which she had made at the Hospice. She knew that it was her duty, once she became a Sister of Nevers, to commit herself entirely to the congregation. This would have been one reason for her choices. Another would have been that the life she lived in Lourdes after the visions had been intolerable for her. In later years, she stated that she did not want even her dead body to be returned there.[123] 'It is finished. Never again in my life will I see Lourdes.'[124]

# NOTES

1. P. M. (professeur) *La Bergère de Lourdes, Bernadette Soubirous* (Toulouse 1880), 36.

2. Bishop Lelong in Bernadette's funeral oration, quoted by Trochu, *Sainte Bernadette*, 324.

3. Lasserre, *Notre-Dame de Lourdes*, 14.

4. Berenson, *Populist Religion*, 64.

5. Gibson, *Social History*, 93.

6. Account of a visit to Bernadette by a lawyer of Dijon, July 1858, *AG*, A9.

7. Deposition of Toinette Soubirous, *RdAM*, 156.

8. 'Procès verbal', 21 Feb. 1858, *LDA* 1, no. 3, 162.

9. Cros, *Histoire*, 1. 93.

10. Question 17, Questionnaire 1st series, *AG*, A20.

11. Deposition of Toinette Soubirous, *RdAM*, 156.

12. Ibid.

13. Chanoine J. Belleney, *Sainte Bernadette, Bergère en Chrétienté* (Paris 1936), 58.

14. Deposition of Toinette Soubirous, *RdAM*, 156.

15. Yver, *L'Humble Sainte Bernadette*, 80.

16. Boyer, *Notre Dame de Lourdes*, 111.

17. *Journal de la Grotte*, quoted *BVP*, 2. 82.

18. Bernadette quoted, ibid.

19. Bernadette's declaration of 13 Oct. 1869, reproduced in *PON*, vol. 3, 1290.

20.  B. Corrado Pope, 'Immaculate and powerful: The Marian revival in the nineteenth century', Atkinson et al., *Immaculate and Powerful*, 179.

21.  C. Parson and N. McWilliam, ' "Le paysan de Paris": Alfred Sensier and the myth of rural France', *Oxford Art Journal* 6/2 (1983), 38.

22.  Fourcade, *L'Apparition à la Grotte de Lourdes,* 33.

23.  *BVP*, 2. 63.

24.  Fourcade, *L'Apparition à la Grotte de Lourdes*, 33.

25.  Père Cros, *RdAM*, 216.

26.  Laurentin, *Vie*, 120.

27.  Sr Justine Pelat, *PON*, Sessio XXIV, 295.

28.  Mlle Lacrampe, *Procès*, 223.

29.  Jeanne Védère, *Témoins*, 197.

30.  Bernadette quoted by Azun de Bernétas, *Procès*, 223.

31.  Fourcade, *L'Apparition à la Grotte de Lourdes*, 34.

32.  Sr Damien Calmels, *RdC*, 5.

33.  Ibid.

34.  Ibid.

35.  Ibid.

36.  Sr Lucie Clovis, *RdC*, 30.

37.  Jean-Marie Soubirous, *PON*, Sessio LVII, 709.

38.  Ravier, *ESB*, 213.

39.  Letter from M. Fabisch to his wife, *LDA* 7, no. 1500, 280.

40.  Memoire de l'abbé Montauze, *AG*, A21.

41.  Ibid.

42.  Ibid.

43.  Ibid.

44.  Ibid.

45.  Bidal, *Bernadette Soubirous*, 56.

46.  Abbé Pomain quoted, *LDA* 7, 111, footnote 617.

47.  Bernadette quoted, *LDA* 7, 117.

48.  Bernadette quoted, *LDA* 7, 96.

49.  Sr Ursule Court, *PON*, Sessio CIII, 1173.

50.  Bernadette quoted, Harris, *Lourdes: Body and Spirit*, 143.

51.  For a description of asthma in France at this time see F. B. Michel, 'L'asthme tardif de Prosper Mérimée: de l'asthme et des lettres', *Bulletin de L'Académie des sciences et lettres de Montpellier* 14 (1983), 145–58. Mérimée was prescribed 'le soufre, l'arsenic, la codéine, le sirop d'éther, les cigarettes de stramonium' and other medications, ibid., 152.

52.  Professeur Trousseau, quoted, ibid. Harris etc.

53.  Sr Victorine Poux cited, Cros, *Histoire*, 3. 182.

54. Ibid.

55. Sr Aurelie Gouteyron, *PON*, Sessio LXXV, 895.

56. Quoted by Laurentin, *Vie*, 121.

57. Bernadette quoted, Sr Damien Calmels, *RdC*, 7.

58. Dr Balencie's written testimony from the Cros archive, quoted in Laurentin, intro., *LDA* 7, 112.

59. Quoted by Dr Prosper Boissarie, *PON*, Sessio LV, 695.

60. Cros, *Témoins*, 301.

61. Ibid.

62. Memoire, Frère Léobard, *RdAM*, 31.

63. Frère Cérase, *RdAM*, 26.

64. Abbé Pène, *Témoins*, 268.

65. Emphasis in the original, Abbé Pomain, *Témoins*, 265.

66. André Labayle, *PON*, Sessio LVIII, 722.

67. Lasserre, *Sainte Bernadette*, 215.

68. 'La vocation de Bernadette', *Recherches sur Lourdes* 72 (Oct. 1980), 229.

69. Quoted by M. de Saint Pierre, *Bernadette et Lourdes*, 117.

70. Stern, intro., *La Salette. Documents authentiques*, 23.

71. Charles Payrard, SM, *PON*, Sessio LXXXVIII, 1028.

72. Le Hidec, *Les Secrets de la Salette*, 90.

73. Quoted, ibid.

74. Marie Fourcade, a student at the Hospice quoted, intro., *LDA* 6, 85.

75. To her parents, 31 Dec. 1860, *ESB*, no. 14, 145.

76. Toinette Soubirous, *AG*, A21.

77. Sr Géraud quoted, *LDA* 6, 83.

78. Sr Victorine Poux, *Procès*, 215.

79. Sr Victorine Poux quoted, *LDA* 6, 85, footnote 223.

80. Ibid., footnote 231.

81. Ibid., 85.

82. Sr Victorine Poux quoted, *BVP*, 1. 249–50.

83. Mme H. de la V., 7 Aug. 1863, *LDA* 7, no. 1484, 264.

84. Bernadette quoted by Curé Peyramale. Letter to Chanoine Fourcade, 30 Apr. 1862, *LDA* 7, no. 1300, 361.

85. Bernadette quoted by Adèle Moura, *LDA* 7, 92.

86. Sr Victorine, *Procès*, 214.

87. Sr Victorine Poux, quoted, *LDA* 6, 84, footnote 223.

88. For example, it was omitted from the documentary collection *Procès*, which includes all the rest of Sr Victorine's statement.

89. Quoted by Adelaide Monlaur, 8 Apr. 1858, *LDA* 2, no. 126, 149.

90. M. Suberville, *Histoire de la chapelle de Garaison* (Toulouse 1836), 28.

91. P. M., *La Bergère de Lourdes*, 107.

92. Abbé Dominique Bouix, Introduction, *Vie de Marcelline Pauper de congrégation des Soeurs de la Charité de Nevers. Écrite par elle-même* (Nevers 1871), x.

93. Sr Henri Fabre, *PON*, Sessio XXI, 272.

94. L. de M., *Réflexions sur le depart de Nevers de la soeur Dorothée* (Nevers 1842), 10.

95. Ibid.

96. Quoted by Sr Marie-Valentine Gleyrose, *PON*, Sessio XX, 258.

97. Ibid.

98. Bernarde Castérot quoted, *LDA* 7, 105.

99. André Labayle, *PON*, Sessio LVIII, 723.

100. Ibid.

101. Basile Castérot, *PON*, Sessio LXIII, 777.

102. Ibid.

103. Bernadette quoted by Mme H. de la V., 7 Aug. 1863, *LDA* 7, no. 1484, 263.

104. Sr Victorine's description of Bernadette quoted, *BVP*, 1. 322.

105. Ibid.

106. Sr Henri Fabre, *PON*, Sessio XXIV, 301.

107. Sr Victorine Poux quoted, *BVP*, 1. 387.

108. Lettre Houzelat (?), 12 May 1873, AG, A20.

109. To Abbé Charles Bouin, 9 July 1864, *ESB*, no. 29, 160.

110. Ibid., 161.

111. To Abbé Charles Bouin, 22 Aug. 1864, *ESB*, no. 30, 163.

112. To Abbé Charles Bouin, 9 July 1864, *ESB*, no. 29.

113. To Abbé Charles Bouin, 22 Aug. 1864, *ESB*, no. 31, 162.

114. A. Forcade, *Notice sur la vie de Soeur Marie-Bernard* (Aix 1879).

115. Barbet quoted, *LDA* 6, ft 220, 83.

116. Ibid.

117. Bernadette quoted, Jeanne Védère, *Témoins*, 193.

118. Abbé Pomain quoted, *LDA* 7, ft 595, 107.

119. To Mme Duvroux, 1866, *ESB*, no. 46, 179.

120. Sr Marie Josephine Forestier, *PON*, Sessio XVII, 220.

121. Bernadette quoted, Laurentin, *Vie*, 145.

122. Basile Castérot quoted, *LDA* 7, ft 703, 127.

123. Soubirous family letters, June 1880, *AG*, A20.

124. Bernadette quoted, *LDA* 7, ft 695, 126.

**PART II**

# Nevers
## The Afterlife of a Visionary

## CHAPTER 8

# 'I Have Come Here to Hide Myself'
## Life in the Novitiate, 1866–1867

Marcelle Auclair, who published a life of Saint Bernadette in 1957, has commented that 'only with difficulty, could we imagine in these days, what the entry of a little Soubirous to the *Soeurs de Charité* – they who were then called '*Dames de Charité*' – could represent in the environs of 1866'.[1] The egalitarianism of our own age makes the class barriers of previous times unimaginable. It is also difficult for readers of the post-1960s world to conceive of the self-discipline which was voluntarily undertaken by individuals who lived previous to our consumer society. They put up with ways of life now considered intolerable, and maintained fixed attitudes which we cannot appreciate in any positive way at all. This is part of the difficulty in imagining what Bernadette, and her peers, encountered in religious life.

Aside from the effort in putting our own expectations aside, and imagining theirs instead, we are faced with a contradictory historical record. Religious life lent itself to representations built solely from ideology. These texts make up the majority of our sources. More mundane details of human life, when they can be gathered, intrude upon this picture as jarring notes. Yet both the ideal and the tangible are part of the historical reality. The lives of the women religious of nineteenth-century France were ordered according to a tableau of perfectionism and sanctification. These women, and their convents, also present a study in snobbery, authoritarianism, affectation and neurotic behaviour.

Bernadette's journey from Lourdes to Nevers took four days. After taking the train from Lourdes, she went to Bordeaux. She was with a small party of one other postulant and two Sisters of Nevers who were visiting the Mother House. They stayed three days in Bordeaux, and the experience was described by Bernadette in a letter to the Lourdes Hospice. Rather tactlessly, she commented on the opulent appearance of a large house of the congregation.

> I must ask you to believe that we profited well from our time and went about a great deal, in carriages if you please! They took us around all the houses. I have the honour of telling you that it was not a question of convents such as that of Lourdes, instead it was like the Institution Impériale; one would have thought it a palace rather than a religious house.[2]

The building in Bordeaux which she described was an important institution. It was both a convent and a school for deaf mutes. Henceforward, she herself would dwell in one of these impressive buildings, as the Mother House, in Nevers, was built according to the grand proportions of the nineteenth-century religious houses. To the naive eyes of a provincial, they seemed veritable palaces, at least from the outside.

Bernadette saw a number of new sights in Bordeaux. Apart from the thrill of being taken about in a carriage, she visited a Carmelite church, and then was taken to the Garonne river to see ships – an unknown sight in the shallow mountain rivers around Lourdes. Yet the spectacle which impressed her most was a minor one. In the Botanical Gardens, there was a display of goldfish. 'Fish: red, black, white, grey; what I found most wonderful to see was how these little creatures swam about in the presence of a crowd of children who were watching them.' For a long time, Bernadette had been an animal on display, but as a tourist in Bordeaux she had a few days of freedom. Wearing a secular blue dress, she was unrecognized by the public, and she circulated freely. For once in her adult life, she joined the onlookers. Then, the journey resumed. 'On Friday, we slept at Périgueux. The next day, we began travelling at seven in the morning and we arrived at Nevers toward ten thirty in the evening.'[3] They arrived late at Nevers railway station and were admitted to the Mother House in profound darkness. They were greeted with only a few words, and shown immediately to their beds.

For Bernadette, the journey from Lourdes to Nevers was an enormous one. An entire change of society, of status and of identity was covered along with the physical distance. Her new home, which she would have first seen indistinctly in the darkness, was a huge convent complex covering several acres. The grey buildings with shuttered windows were three storeys high. It was an austere but graceful environment, walled off from the surrounding town, and populated by veiled women dressed in black.

The congregation which Bernadette had joined was an eminent one. Among the teaching and nursing orders, they were relatively long-established, as they had been founded in 1680. They had been founded in the town of Nevers by a Benedictine priest, Jean-Baptiste de Laveyne. He had begun a small house, with Sisters who visited the poor and ministered to them in their homes. Soon the congregation flourished, and during the nineteenth century it had become more oriented to the middle classes than to the poor. During the 1860s the Sisters of Nevers were an extremely large organization, and had 260 convents throughout France. They attracted between sixty and one hundred entrants per year, approximately two-thirds of whom would take final vows after three years of training. The works of the congregation ranged from charity hospitals for the poor, to refined boarding schools for the daughters of the wealthy. All of these institutions were professionally managed, according to the hierarchical norms of the nineteenth century. The Sisters of Nevers only accepted entrants of a good family background, and each girl was asked to bring a dowry and a trousseau. They were also required to pay board during the novitiate. In order to train their novices, and to have a central administration, the Sisters of Nevers had built their Mother House, the St Gildard Convent, in Nevers during the 1850s. It was here that Bernadette arrived in 1866, and where she was to spend the rest of her life.

Bernadette spent one year as a novice, although she was professed early as a result of ill-health. For every religious, the passage through the novitiate was a trial and a transformation. The novitiate has often been described to candidates as the most important period of the religious life, and it was commonly said that if a religious lost her fervour then, she would never regain it. Bernadette's novitiate was outwardly uneventful, except for an episode of illness. Despite this calm, it was a time marked by emotional intensities, questions which went unasked and therefore unanswered, and minor incidents which were charged with the significance of hidden transformations. In all of this, it was a typical story of convent life.

From this point in her life onward, the historical source materials are solely religious, and indeed, devotional in tone. Once she had arrived at St Gildard, Bernadette was no longer under observation by any secular figures at all, and only rarely did she meet anyone who was not either a priest or a nun. There were no longer any sceptics, mockers or acid remembrances from her former companions in the slums of Lourdes. She ceased to see her family, but this time by her own consent, and she no longer quarrelled about it. There were critical views of her during the Nevers period, but they came from people who were committed to the cult of Lourdes, and their disapproval of her was concealed in clerical language.

Long before she went to Nevers, Bernadette was the property of the Catholic Church, but it was only once she was within St Gildard that she became purely absorbed into religious culture. She is not only an object of display, as in Lourdes, but a participant in rituals and devotions. When living in the convent, she also began communicating in new ways. She was assessing herself according to spiritual maxims, and actively attempting to conform to the patterns set by the Rule of the congregation.

This work of personal transformation led to a degree of scrutiny of her own nature, and some of her conversations have a tone which was entirely different from the unself-conscious personal attitude shown in the testimonies about herself in her younger years. In Bernadette's convent life the written word became more important, her correspondence increased, and for the first time in her life she was reading and writing by inclination. Religious books were available to her in the convent library, and she not only read them but copied out extracts. She also began her *Carnet* (Personal Notebook), a collection of quotations, individual observations and notes to herself.

The written records from this period appear to offer an interior view of her consciousness which was never expressed in her previous life. Although the letters and notes do give indications of her state of mind, there are several obstacles in providing an historical reading of them. Despite the advances of her literacy, Bernadette never became a fluent writer. Her response was to rely upon the words of others; she copied out extracts from written works, and sometimes asked others to write out texts for her. These Sisters, of a much better level of education, helped her with written tasks, just as she helped these cultivated ladies with their sewing. Her letters show distinct signs of repeating standard formulas, and this was an ordinary part of elementary letter-writing during this period. Many documents, ostensibly from Bernadette's pen, were not really her own work. One does not have to be an historian to recognize this. Her old acquaintance from Lourdes, Jean-Baptiste Estrade, noted that: 'I left Lourdes in 1860. When Bernadette was at Nevers, I wrote to her, but her replies were made up of beautiful phrases which did not come from herself.'[4]

Aside from direct interpolations from other sources, her letters were circumscribed by convent life. Sisters were restricted in the matters which they could discuss, especially anything pertaining to their lives within the community. Also, all letters could be read by the superiors. Considering these factors, one might expect to find that Bernadette's letters were banal and repressed. It is not entirely so, and particularly in later years the letters became more expressive and assured. Even in her earlier writings, there were expressive sentences between the trite phrases of greeting, pious aspirations, and then the laboured signing-off favoured in the French language. An exact delineation between what Bernadette was meaning to say and managing to say is impossible to arrive at now, and of course the texts most meaningful to a twentieth-century historian are not necessarily those which the writer herself esteemed. The most artificial missives were possibly those which she regarded as most worthy. One easy means for editors of her works to detect if a sentence came straight from Bernadette's pen has been to look at the spelling of the words. When copying, she could form the words correctly, but when writing on her own the words are frequently ill-spelt and divided wrongly (*de puis* for *depuis*). A linguistic scholar could possibly study her unedited written works and determine whether her irregular spelling reflects phonetic patterns, and thus records some shades of her nineteenth-century Pyrenean accent. As it is, the written works have been carefully presented and annotated in the *Écrits* edited by André Ravier. The correspondence, like many other documents of her life, conceals a great deal, but it is still there to be read.

## The novitiate

From the time of her arrival at St Gildard, until the profession ceremony in October 1867, Bernadette was under the care of the Mistress of Novices, Mère Marie-Thérèse Vauzou. A Novice Mistress was responsible for the formation of her subjects, for their instruction in the ways of the community, and for the recommendations as to whether they should be admitted to vows. The novitiate was a deliberately secluded area in which the young Sisters were sequestered for a period of instruction. The Novice Mistress was expected to be stern, and to constantly point out faults. The manner in which the novices bore humiliating penances was an important part of the assessment of their suitability. Despite the harsh nature of her supervision, the Novice Mistress was not a purely forbidding figure. The novices were expected to have an attitude of love, as well as respect and obedience, towards her. This was all the more easy to cultivate because most novices were between the ages of sixteen and eighteen, and had only recently been separated from their mothers. The domestic culture of the time accustomed girls to the presence of matriarchal authority figures who were the source of both reproofs and caresses. The type

**Plate XII**  Mère Marie-Thérèse Vauzou, Mistress of Novices. © *Archives St Gilard*

of young woman who presented to religious congregations was likely to be loyal and submissive to such a person.

The novitiate had an atmosphere all of its own, and the relationships of the novices to each other and the Mistress were genuine psychological dramas. Some people left the novitiate with lasting emotional trauma, memories of trust betrayed and devastation of their self-esteem. Others, who were more fortunate in either their Novice Mistress or the relationship which they had with her, found it to be a true foundation of their religious life, and usually a transition to maturity as well. The commitment, self-scrutiny and communal loyalty required of a group of young people who were gathered initially as strangers to one another is difficult for the modern reader to appreciate. The only comparable scenario in our world is found in the training of military recruits, which often gives the intense bonding of a new life and a shared ordeal, but which also often leads to cases of isolation and bullying by either peers or authority figures.

Within nineteenth-century French Catholicism, religious vocations abounded, and the active congregations had particularly large novitiates. Standards of behaviour were high, and the process of selection was rigorous. A large number of postulants and novices either left or were rejected before taking vows. Even in the outside world, tales circulated about the tribulations of novices. This was incorporated into the general 'black legend' which anti-clerical opinion held about convents.[5] In a *memoire* from a Marseilles convent one religious stated that before entering 'she had been given a most ridiculous and untrue impression of the life of a Visitation nun. Among other calumnies she was told that by way of trial, the novices were ill-treated ... A feeling of revulsion at such treatment rose within her, but, still, loving her vocation, she braced herself for the conflict, saying to herself "It is all right, if others can bear it I will bear it." '[6] This text reassuringly concluded that such fears were unfounded. Not every case could be so satisfactory. One of the paragons of French Catholicism, St Thérèse of Lisieux, was a fearless practitioner of the doctrine of self-sacrifice, and an advocate of rigorous training for novices. Yet even she, after witnessing the humiliation of a novice at the hands of an irresponsible superior, exclaimed that 'there are some ways in which people should not be tested, and this is one of them'.[7]

The exact issue which St Thérèse had protested against is tactfully omitted from the testimony. One of the strongest values of convent culture was that they did not make details of community life public. However, it is indisputable that such 'ways' were often practised. René Laurentin, himself a priest, has written that during Bernadette's lifetime religious training was excessive and unwise, while some Novice Mistresses led their charges through 'orgies of initiation'.[8] The atmosphere at St Gildard, he added, was sane by comparison. However, the atmosphere at St Gildard was to come under general criticism because of an impression, which has been discussed in every life of St Bernadette, that the visionary was ill-treated by her Novice Mistress, Mère Marie-Thérèse.

It is possible that the image of Bernadette as an oppressed novice was only partly a reflection of actual details from her biography. A contributing factor in this memorializing might have been that the persecution of novices was an emotive issue which could not usually be openly complained of in convents. Because of her exceptional status, Bernadette could be remembered as a figure of blamelessness and innocence, who endured unjustified suffering. Many others went through similar, or far worse, ordeals, without their experiences ever being judged worthy of comment. The duty of testifying to Bernadette's sanctity meant that certain issues, which were otherwise confined to gossip and private thoughts, could be legitimately be put forward for scrutiny.

On her first day at St Gildard Bernadette was summoned before an assembly of all the Sisters, in order to give a narration of the visions at Lourdes. She was dressed again in her Pyrenean costume, and spoke in a stilted way, prompted by questions from the Reverend Mothers. After this there was a formal announcement that the subject was closed, and that Bernadette would not speak of it again without permission from the superiors. She put on the black dress and bonnet of a postulant, and began to learn the rules of the house. Like most new arrivals, Bernadette and her companion Léontine Mouret passed through an initial period of homesickness and tearfulness. On 20 July 1866 she wrote a letter to her previous residence, the Hospice at Lourdes, saying that she and Léontine had cried throughout the whole of Sunday: 'The Sisters encouraged us, telling us that this was the mark of a good vocation.'[9] However, she assured them that this had passed, and that she had already come to love the novitiate, which was like the 'house of God'.[10]

As was the custom, for the first week she was in the care of two other Sisters from the novitiate, termed 'guardian angels'. Their duty was to show her over the convent – a lengthy task in so vast a building – and to instruct her in the daily routine. These fellow neophytes also cushioned the loneliness and disorientation of the first week, and were often selected in order to be compatible with the postulant. In Bernadette's case, her Guardian Angels were both fellow Pyreneans, Sr Emilienne Duboé and Sr Philomène Tourré. Sr Emilienne was an unusually mature novice, even older than Bernadette at twenty-seven years. Sr Philomène was nineteen, and had only been in the Mother House for three months.

Sr Emilienne Duboé helped Bernadette to unpack her luggage, which had been arranged for her by the Sisters at Lourdes. It included many gifts for the Mother House, such as chocolates and delicacies, and Bernadette commented that it would make her look like a glutton when she presented it to the Mistress.[11] The Sisters at Lourdes had also provided Bernadette with the items of underwear which each postulant was required to present. This generous trousseau was too much for Bernadette, who thought that they had 'put too much linen, saying that she could never live long enough to use it all'.[12] This is a typical comment of a poor girl, who has never seen a new wardrobe of clothing assembled for her. In her childhood she had only the clothes in which she stood up, and the servant at Bartrès remembered that Bernadette would borrow linen from other women when she washed her clothes. At St Gildard, everything would be provided for her, but both she and the superiors remembered this background of poverty. Most Sisters brought a dowry. Bernadette brought the prestige of the miracles of Lourdes, but little else. An item in the Book of Entries meticulously notes these debts and obligations: 'Mlle Bernadette Soubirous, postulant from Lourdes, aged 22, entered the 8th of July 1866. Gratis admission. The Superior spent 60 francs for her habits. We gave her 135 francs worth of linen and objects for the trousseau to the value of 22.50 francs. We are happy that the Virgin Mary has deigned to send her to us.'[13]

The Guardian Angels took their duty of instruction seriously, and found an apt pupil. Bernadette was anxious to learn her duties from them, and showed a punctilious attitude about being on time. The food in the refectory was wholesome, but Bernadette suffered from the too-abundant servings, which she was obliged to eat. She already knew enough of religious mores to know not to complain: 'she preferred to suffer than to appear fussy',[14] Sr Philomena said. Bernadette was to be disconcerted by her next view of convent relationships. She was thirsty in the July heat and Sr Emilienne went to obtain some drinking water. However, the novice was so intimidated by the Sister in charge of the kitchen that she did not dare ask for the key to the refectory; instead she climbed in through a window. Bernadette was scandalized by the means by which her drink had been obtained – 'That is acting like thieves' – and did not ask again for water.[15]

The novices were restricted to contact with their Mistress and each other. The Rule specifically stated that the novices and the professed Sisters should live side by side, but not mix except during the relaxed regime of certain authorized feast days. The vowed Sisters were above the novices, they had the right to give them orders, and the duty to reprove them whenever they were, or might be, at fault. The novices were not permitted to complain, give excuses, or even to reply to a Sister without permission. The novices usually did not have any contact with them unless they were doing domestic tasks under their direction.

The novitiate of the Mother House had its own chapel for minor devotions, its own recreation room and separate sleeping quarters. Here the novices learnt to follow the routines of their Rule, without disrupting others by their mistakes. They were enjoined to practise silence, detachment and charity in their dealings with each other and were expected to relate to one another as members of a religious community. This meant refraining from unnecessary speech, not expressing irritation, affection or other individual reactions to their fellows, and maintaining a serene demeanour. These attitudes are not easy to maintain, and the constant reproofs of the Mistress were designed to impose convent norms as a second nature on the novices.

Many of the faults of the novices were not transgressions in ordinary life. They were simply expressions of their inherent personalities. The word 'natural' was used with disapproval in any convent. Natural affections and natural impulses were denounced as contrary to the Rule of the community. Another pejorative term was 'singularization', which meant marking oneself out in any way, expressing one's character, or performing tasks differently, worse, or even better than one's sisters. If the young women were to learn how to live in obedience and harmony, they had to abandon their own judgements and proclivities.

Bernadette spent very little time as a postulant. Her period at the Lourdes convent, in preparation to leave for Nevers, was considered to have been a period of admission into the congregation. On 29 July 1866, only three weeks after her arrival at St Gildard, she pronounced her vows as a novice and received the habit and a religious name – Soeur Marie-Bernard. On her 'clothing day' she commented to a companion: 'I have come here to hide myself.'[16]

At the chapel at St Gildard, ranks of novices and postulants were formed, with the appropriate dress, to take vows. The postulants were dressed in the habit before their appearance in the chapel, the only ornamentation being a white gauze veil, which was replaced by the black one as they pronounced their vows and were given their names in religion. They approached the altar in rows of two abreast, and ordered according to their height. There was always great excitement at St Gildard on these days, which were prepared for by a special retreat, and marked by great bustle in the dormitories where the postulants experienced wearing the coif and veil for the first time.

Among the Sisters of Nevers, the ceremonies of taking the habit and profession of vows were combined, with postulants and then novices offering their different pledges. The novices of the Sisters of Nevers were dressed in a habit exactly similar to that of the professed. The only difference was that the professed were given a cross to wear, and the veil of the novices was of silk rather than wool.

Throughout the 1860s, the Sisters of Nevers held three ceremonies per year for the taking of the habit and the profession of vows. These were usually held in July, October and November/December. Bernadette thus joined the first intake of 1866, and was with 44 postulants who took the habit and 19 novices who pronounced their vows of profession. A further 46 novices would take vows on 30 October 1866 and 21 more postulants became novices on 13 December 1866. Sr Marie-Bernard was one of a total of 65 postulants received into the novitiate that year. Not all of these 65 would have been continuously resident at St Gildard for the following twelve months. The periodization of religious vows of the Sisters of Nevers was surprisingly variable. They spent anything from one year to three as novices, and their perpetual vows were usually, but not always, taken ten years after the first profession. It was only after 1875, when a revision of the constitutions of the Sisters of Nevers brought them papal recognition, that they came under the full requirements of canon law concerning admission to religious institutes. From 1875, they were obliged to seclude their novices in the Mother House for the entire period of their training, and a formal schedule for admission to vows was universally followed.

During the 1860s novices were sent for periods of residence and work in other houses of the order, then returned to the novitiate for more instruction. The majority of the novices began their religious life as postulants for several months in one of the houses of the Sisters of Nevers. They were then transferred to the Mother House, and lived there as postulants for a further three months, before taking vows as novices. Soon afterwards, they would be sent out to a community to participate in the works of the congregation. This period was known as the 'Novitiate in the Houses' and went on for about twelve months. Their training was therefore in the lived experience, rather than the theory, of religious life. After this, they returned to St Gildard for a more formal period in the real novitiate, which might last a year before they were admitted to the vows of profession. This structure changed during the years of Bernadette's religious life. The status of the congregational Sisters was reviewed, and the formalities of monastic life were introduced – among them the requirement that all members of the community must initially spend at least one continuous year cloistered in a novitiate.

The custom of the 'Novitiate in the Houses' did not apply to Bernadette, and in fact her religious life anticipated the changes of 1875. She spent all of her time as a novice in the Mother House, and was professed after one year. This was a more simple and intense training than the meandering course followed by her companions who came and went over two or three years. Unlike them, Sr Marie-Bernard was circumscribed in the tasks which she could learn, as she could not appear in the hospital wards and classrooms of the order. Her training was also limited by her level of education, which was still very low, despite all her years at the Lourdes boarding school. She could not do even basic grammar exercises. During angry sessions of correction, the Novice Mistress and the Superior General termed her an 'idiot'.[17]

Another handicap was her uncertain health. The stresses of a new environment seemed to undermine her equilibrium, because although she was healthy when she arrived at Nevers, by mid-August she was ill enough to be sent to the infirmary. This was only three weeks after she had taken her vows to become a novice. The illness first manifested itself as 'fatigue', then totally incapacitated her. She must have wondered if she would not be dismissed as being too weak for religious life. In reality, the Sisters of Nevers were prepared to make special concession for her state of health, and had accepted her with full knowledge of her disabilities. This was not communicated to Sr Marie-Bernard herself, as it was important that she regard her novitiate as being as much of a testing period as that of anyone else. As if to underline her anxieties, the novice in the next bed had tearfully received the blow of hearing the doctor's opinion that she should be sent home. Sr Marie-Bernard tried to encourage her, pointing out that she could try again later in another congregation.[18] This proved to be the case, as this Sister subsequently refuted the judgement of poor health by joining the Sisters of St Joseph de Cluny and serving for sixty years. She was grateful for the memory of Sr Marie-Bernard's words, and regarded them as prophetic. In fact, Sr Marie-Bernard might have been wondering if she would soon face such a dilemma herself.

Initially, Sr Marie-Bernard was well enough to help with tasks in the infirmary, but soon she was in bed every day. After two weeks, she wrote a letter of thanks to Mère Augustine Ceyrac who had sent some pills. She wrote of her: 'fervent thanks for all the favours which you have given me. I believe that the good Lord has not yet finished trying me, for, ever since I came to Nevers, I suffer every day from pains in the stomach and head, but this does not prevent me from being happy in the Novitiate, where everyone is too kind to me.'[19]

The illness mounted and two months passed. Sr Marie-Bernard apologized to her companions for coughing at night and began to spit blood. By the third week of October she was vomiting blood and seemed totally exhausted. She had reached such an extremity that the question of whether she was healthy enough for religious life was decided to be no longer relevant. A novice who showed poor health would be sent home, but one who was actually dying would be admitted to final vows. Receiving a profession *in articulo mortis* is an old custom within the Catholic Church, and was a frequent event during this era. Canon law states that should the novice recover they are to return to their normal instruction and duly pass through the later profession ceremony, but the death-bed vows remain valid.

The Sisters of Nevers acted with their usual circumspection before the crisis of Sr Marie-Bernard's illness. The Novice Mistress visited her daily, and all the novices were urged to pray for her recovery. The superiors waited, and it was not until the afternoon of 25 October, when the doctor had stated that it was unlikely that she would survive the night, that they asked the Bishop to accept her death-bed profession. Mgr Forcade was away from his residence, and hurried to the convent as soon as he received the message, not wishing 'to cede to anyone the honour of receiving that profession'.[20] He found Sr Marie-Bernard apparently in her last hours, her gasping breaths sounded to him to be the death rattle, and she had vomited a dish of blood.[21] She had received the last sacraments some hours earlier. She could not speak in order to pronounce the formula of vows, but assented to his reading of it. Such ceremonies took place at sick beds, but every effort was made to give full significance to the ritual, and the veil and cross, which she would now have the right to wear, were blessed and placed on her bed.

According to Mgr Forcade's account, at this moment of pious conclusion the atmosphere was unexpectedly reversed. He had stepped out of the room, assuming that he would never see her alive again, while Mère Joséphine Imbert remained at the foot of the bed 'with the holy intention of closing her eyes'.[22] Abruptly, the dying woman recovered her voice and announced: 'You have professed me because you thought that I would die tonight, oh well [*eh bien*] I will not die tonight.'[23] The Bishop was stupefied, the Mother General enraged. She angrily reproached Sr Marie-Bernard, asking her why she had not told them, if she knew that she would not die that night, and declaring, not for the last time, that she was a 'little idiot'.[24] Mère Josephine threatened to make her begin the novitiate again, and Sr Marie-Bernard replied tranquilly: 'As you wish, *ma chère mère*.'[25] Mgr Forcade was so struck by their exchange that he was uncharacteristically silent. In his memoir he censured Mère Josephine's reaction – 'it seemed to me to be excessive' – but remained apparently bemused by Sr Marie-Bernard's audacious declaration. Other contemporary commentators disputed whether 'a person so delicate and well-bred' as Mère Josephine would really have replied in such a manner;[26] but although he obviously reconstructed dialogue from memory, there is no reason to believe that Mgr Forcade would have falsified his account.

If the people around Sr Marie-Bernard in October 1866 had known more of her medical history, with its desperate collapses and instantaneous, apparently miraculous recoveries, they might have been more hesitant to believe that she was on her death-bed. However, they had watched her condition deteriorate over eight weeks, and the haemorrhage was a most serious symptom. It is conceivable that the symptoms lifted because after the profession ceremony she was suddenly free of the anxiety which must have increasingly weighed on her in the infirmary. During the next few weeks, she celebrated her new security and kept the symbols of her profession on her bed, while her fellow novices shared her gaiety: 'I saw her profession veil and crucifix on her bed and said smilingly to her: 'Thief!' She replied: 'I may be a thief! But in the meantime they are mine and I will keep them, I belong to the congregation now and they cannot send me away.'[27] She remained for some days more in the infirmary, then resumed the habit of a novice and returned to convent life.

Sr Marie-Bernard's health remained fragile, and she was in a state of convalescence for some months. The loss of significant amounts of blood would have greatly weakened her, although the mild regime at St Gildard meant that she had adequate nourishment. The upsets to her health during the first year at St Gildard recall the bad period of the early 1860s, when she first went to live at the Lourdes Hospice. The strain of new surroundings was no doubt a contributing factor to these collapses, although her asthma, her poor digestive system and possible tuberculosis in the lungs were physical realities which meant that the haemorrhages would have begun at some time. Had she been at home with her family, it is quite likely that she might have already been dead by 1867; although it is also possible that a more active and open-air life would have preserved her strength, and that with more love, more privacy and more natural surroundings Bernadette could have more successfully contended with the lesions in her lungs. The careful nursing, suitable food and professional medical attention which was offered in the Catholic institutions was always given along with moral scrutiny and the demands of public life. Whatever the benefits of her role, by this time Sr Marie-Bernard had obviously left her original life irrevocably behind her, and along with the taking of vows, a vital link to her home and family was broken at the end of 1866.

On 8 December 1866 her mother, Louise Castérot, died at the age of forty-one. She had been ill for some months, but only took to her bed in the last two weeks. According to Sr Victorine Poux, Bernadette's former teacher: 'Before going to Vespers, on the Feast of the Immaculate Conception, I passed by Bernadette's mother, whom I knew to be very ill. I spoke to her of her dear child, and before leaving, as the bell for Vespers was ringing, I told her that I would write to Bernadette, in her name. The poor dying woman made signs to me, expressing her agreement and her thanks. Upon leaving Vespers, I returned to the Soubirous house: Louise was no longer in this world.'[28] So that letter was never written. Instead a formal missive from the superior at the Lourdes Hospice informed the authorities at Nevers of her death. Despite everything, Louise Castérot was always loved by her women relatives, who

214

romantically attributed her death to Bernadette's departure: 'Louise could not live any more, after her daughter left.'[29] This statement, whether truly attributed or not, became part of the Lourdes local legend. It was an improbable notion, for had not Bernadette left Louise Castérot many years before? Even when she lived in Lourdes, they were not allowed to see each other. Of course, there were other people in Louise Castérot's milieu who gave different explanations for her demise. Her brother-in-law flatly said that 'she died of drink'.[30] The more refined circles around Sr Marie-Bernard did not enter into either the scandals, sentimentality or excuses roused by her mother's blighted life. The clerics had always known of her alcoholism, along with the whole family situation, and had kept these problems in the category of matters not spoken of. The only comment which they made was the comforting observation that Louise Castérot died on a holy day, the Feast of the Immaculate Conception.

Sr Marie-Bernard was ill again, and shocked by the news. She wrote to Abbé Pomain to ask for prayers for the repose of her mother's soul, and this letter has a rare tone of spontaneous expression. 'I cannot tell you of the pain which I felt in learning so suddenly of the death of my mother, I learnt of her death before I even knew that she was sick. I understand that this was done in order to spare me pain, but alas! the blow was no less cruel, for in the letter which our Reverend Mother wrote me, I was not deceived, I knew immediately that my Mother had left this world.'[31] She did not enter into the issue of the cause of her mother's death, and may have felt that no explanation was needed.

## The Mistress of Novices

In formal terms, Sr Marie-Bernard had a substitute mother in her religious superior, the Mistress of Novices. The relationship between them eventually became as fraught as any family drama. At the time of Bernadette's arrival at St Gildard, Mère Marie-Thérèse had informed the novices of the importance of this entrant, 'a privileged child of Mary', and she went so far as to state that for herself 'it would be one of the great joys of my life to see the eyes which had seen the Blessed Virgin'.[32] This eulogy was followed by the more moderate advice that Bernadette was to be treated as any one of them, and that they were forbidden to discuss the visions with her. The subsequent relationship between Bernadette and Mère Marie-Thérèse did not fulfil these original expectations, and after the Novice Mistress had seen the eyes of the visionary, she showed signs of disillusionment. Specifically, she became cold toward Sr Marie-Bernard after she returned to the novitiate from the infirmary.

Mère Marie-Thérèse Vauzou was a 41-year-old woman, who had been in religious life for twenty-two years. She was born on 10 August 1825, at the Châtelet-de-Beauregard in Corrèze, and named Laure-Guillaumette Vauzou. Her family was well placed, and her father and grandfather had been lawyers. She was educated by the Sisters of Nevers, in their boarding school of Saint-Alexis de Brive. Her obituary notice, prepared by the Sisters of Nevers, included some details of her early life, and claimed that with her 'lively and ardent nature', even as a schoolchild, she had dominated other girls:

> it would be rash to say that Laure was one of those children who abide easily by the rules, and indeed she even threw them aside at times: the intelligence and the wilfulness of her character gave her, even before her First Communion, a certain power over her companions, and willingly, even at that age, she would put them through various ordeals, to see if she could count on their submission.[33]

There is another anecdote which stated that a doctor, who was a friend of her family, entrusted his young daughter to her care when she first went to the same boarding school. Laure Vauzou took the child aside and instructed her, presumably as a test of loyalty, to speak aloud in the dormitory at night. This would have been a breach of the rules, but as the Obituary Notice put it: 'You must obey me, she intimated to the little innocent, if you want me to protect you.'[34] That evening, her young companion timidly began to recite a poem aloud after the curfew. But the next day, when the story came out, it was Laure Vauzou who was blamed.

These anecdotes are remarkable. Laure Vauzou is revealed as one of those people who, very early in life, show a taste for domination. It is also interesting that such stories are repeated even in her convent obituary. They are not the usual accounts of the childhood of a future religious, and have unwholesome overtones. The Sisters of Nevers wrote this with a tone of tolerant humour, but perhaps with a subtext of revealing the psychology of their honoured superior's contentious character. The significance of these stories is not only in their content, but in the fact that they were remembered and repeated so long after the event. They must have come from the Sisters who were acquainted with Mère Marie-Thérèse as a girl, and were no doubt advanced in explanation of why she was the person whom she was.

Laure Vauzou did not enter the convent directly from school, as many girls did. She left the boarding school of the Sisters of Nevers, apparently because of an illness. After spending some time in convalescence at the house of her grandmother, she was sent to a private boarding school of high repute, 'that of Mlle de Brètes'. In later years, 'she said that she had learnt there how easily the hearts and minds of young girls are influenced by general opinions'.[35] Perhaps she was referring to the atmosphere of snobbery, and the almost desperate desire to achieve status within a group, which flourishes in such institutions. Laure Vauzou herself, even when dedicated to religion, and outwardly obliged to regard everyone as her equal, was extremely class-conscious.

Her education concluded at the age of seventeen and she returned home, where she spent two years. She was therefore a comparatively mature young lady of nineteen when she presented herself as a postulant for the Sisters of Nevers in 1844. Having received the name Sr Marie-Thérèse, she spent two years as a novice, and must have impressed her superiors as a dedicated religious of correct behaviour. Her profession took place in 1846, and soon she was given an important post as a mistress in a teacher's college at Montpellier. At the age of twenty-eight, she was moved to a new post, and was responsible for the foundation of a new school. She succeeded in this undertaking, and returned to Montpellier, this time as director of the teaching college. After founding another school in 1860, she was recalled to the Mother House to take up the post of Mistress of Novices, and was to hold it from 1861 to 1881. This was followed by her election to the peak position of Superior General of the whole congregation, which she held for eighteen years before retiring at the age of seventy-four.

Mère Marie-Thérèse Vauzou was, therefore, a woman in the prime of life, and in the midst of a rising career, when she met Bernadette in 1866. Her life appears to have been an unbroken series of successes. Yet she was not a perfect religious, and while many Sisters regarded her with love and respect, a minority opinion had criticisms of her imperious temperament. Even when she passed to a higher office, she had difficulty in resigning the special privileges of a Novice Mistress, and as one Sister coolly stated: 'Mère Henri Fabre, who had replaced Mère Marie-Thérèse as Mistress of Novices, was the former Assistant General, a holy nun, calm-natured, judicious, extremely charitable. She confided to me that she had suffered a great deal, and especially for the first three years, from the cold attitude of our Mère, who imagined all sorts of things which were not true at all.'[36] The favourable adjectives which describe the next Novice Mistress – calm, judicious, charitable – seem to draw an unspoken comparison.

The first recorded conversation between Mère Marie-Thérèse and her celebrated novice took place during Bernadette's recital to the convent assembly. When Bernadette described the famous scene where she had discarded the muddy water three times before being able to obey the apparition's instruction to drink it, Mère Marie-Thérèse interjected, 'You were not much mortified!'[37] Her criticism was based on one of the standard aspects of monastic self-discipline, the ability to eat or drink whatever was put before one. Awesome anecdotes were told of religious figures who had calmly consumed such delicacies as salty water and decomposing fruit, rather than rejecting their assigned portion. Bernadette replied on a cheerful and still secular note: 'That water was really quite dirty.'[38] This exchange did not bode well for the future. The Superior already appears critical, the novice pert and independent. Bernadette's way of debunking the pious pretensions of others had served her well during her audiences with the public. It would not be so in the convent. However, the more introverted side of her nature gave more promise. Even during this recital at St Gildard witnesses noticed that Bernadette appeared to want to speak as little as possible, which was a becoming sign of modesty.[39]

Mère Marie-Thérèse had the power to direct Sr Marie-Bernard's activities, to pass judgement on her behaviour and to order her to perform penances. In all of these aspects, she soon showed herself to be remarkably harsh. The testimonies from Bernadette's contemporaries depict a relationship of tension. Less explicitly, these recollections also indicate that this behaviour of the Novice Mistress was the subject of conversation and conjecture among the Sisters for many years afterwards.

Biographers of Saint Bernadette have accounted for this conflict by weighing the evidence against Mère Marie-Thérèse and either condemning or exonerating her. Francis Trochu points out all the indications that she was a proud and emotionally demanding woman, who was quite possibly jealous of the visionary, and later repented of her conduct. Père Petitot gives the darkest portrait of Bernadette's treatment from her superiors, and sees her suffering in the religious life as part of her spiritual martyrdom. André Ravier has put more emphasis on Mère Marie-Thérèse's qualified acts of generosity to Sr Marie-Bernard, and suggests that her apparent hostility was not real. All writers, from the 1870s onwards, have relied upon the idea that Bernadette's suffering was in any case a gift from divine providence which made her humility genuine and manifest, and even might have kept her from becoming like the visionaries of La Salette. A saying of Pope Pius XI is often quoted: 'If they had treated Mélanie like Bernadette, many problems would have been avoided.'[40] This odd notion even appears in biographies of Mélanie Calvat herself, although the most sketchy knowledge of her character shows that an encounter between herself and a Mère Marie-Thérèse would have been a public disaster rather than a retreat into saintly behaviour. Mélanie Calvat was a figure of co-relation for all of Bernadette's life, perhaps even before the visions, when the Curé of Bartrès had said that the children of La Salette must be like her. By 1866, that would not have been a compliment. As a Sister from St Gildard said: 'At that time, people talked a lot about the children of La Salette; it was said that it would have been better to have kept Mélanie from public display; perhaps this gave Mère Marie-Thérèse a motive for fear concerning Bernadette.'[41] If so, she did not mention it. Mère Marie-Thérèse made no recorded references to the controversial careers of France's other visionaries. When speaking of Bernadette she did not compare her to anyone, but disparaged her supposed virtues and constantly claimed that she was 'good for nothing' and 'conceited'. At best, in later years, she would concede that Sr Marie-Bernard was an ordinary religious. More often, she commented disparagingly 'Oh, she was a little peasant!'[42]

One possible line of defence and explanation for Mère Marie-Thérèse's severe attitude is that it was not a display of personal aversion but an adherence to a policy set by her own religious superior. Mère Joséphine Imbert, the Superior General of the entire order, resided at St Gildard at the pinnacle of the community. Having doubtfully received Bernadette she wished to test her commitment to religious life, and to emphasize that her status in the outside world counted for nothing at St Gildard. This policy extended well beyond the novitiate. Her attitude toward Sr Marie-Bernard, even as a professed Sister, was noticeably cold, and she inflicted several public slights upon her. A characteristic instance was when she returned from Rome in 1870 and was greeted by the Sisters in the cloister. She affectionately embraced and spoke to each of them, except for Sr Marie-Bernard, whom she passed with a glance. The Superior General's snubs may have intimidated Bernadette even more than those of the Novice Mistress, for she was on record as saying 'Mère Joséphine, oh! How I fear her,'[43] whereas she referred to Mère Marie-Thérèse 'our good and worthy Mistress' with a correct attitude of respect and affection.

Several of Sr Marie-Bernard's companions asked her if she was offended by the Novice Mistress's harshness, but she always repulsed their sympathy and curiosity, stating that she was very grateful to Mère Marie-Thérèse for the good which she did to her soul. Some of Sr Marie-Bernard's amiable concession to her superior's strictures have a slightly ironic ring: 'the Mistress of Novices is very right, I have a great deal of pride'.[44] Too much, perhaps, to complain? On one occasion, Sr Marie-Bernard was asked to take the office of *zélatrice* at the novitiate, and to give a talk for that day. She spoke very briefly, commenting: 'Sisters, today is Friday, the day of the Sacred Heart, let us love Him well. Who will love him if we do not, we who must be his brides? But you know that better than me, I who am so proud.'[45] By Sr Marie-Bernard's standards this was a long speech. She usually refused to give any addresses, 'I don't know what to say ... you may as well try to squeeze words out of a stone.'[46]

Almost all of the Sisters at St Gildard commented on Sr Marie-Bernard's reserved character. She was lively, and would engage in repartee, but gave away little of herself. This was more integral to her than the detachment taught as a part of religious behaviour. As one Sister, who had known her at Lourdes, said: 'that self-effacement, which, later on, became a virtue, seemed to have been in her childhood, a trait of character'.[47] This was a nature which offended the Novice Mistress, 'Mère Marie-Thérèse was a Mistress who expected reliance and expansiveness on the part of her novices. Sr Marie-Bernard was of a markedly reserved nature, and there was some element in this of Basque pride.'[48] This Sister has made an error about the visionary's ethnic status (as she was Bigourdanian, not Basque) but she was probably astute in her assessment of the element of pride in Sr Marie-Bernard's modest reserve. It seems likely that this independence was an irritation to Mère Marie-Thérèse. There were even hints that Sr Marie-Bernard could have made herself a favourite of the Novice Mistress, if only she had been willing to relate to her at an emotional level. As one Sister rather dryly commented of Mère Marie-Thérèse: 'she gave a lot of affection to her novices, but she needed to be paid in return. I believe that if the relationship between Bernadette and Mère Marie-Thérèse was so cold, perhaps it was because she did not make such a show of affection as others did toward the Mistress of Novices.'[49] This almost sounds as it if were Mère Marie-Thérèse who received the initial rebuff, but others judged that she had an inherent dislike of her novice. Sr Joseph Garnier said that it seemed to her that the Novice Mistress had taken up an attitude: 'on the one hand through duty, on the other by inclination'.[50] Sr Henri Fabre commented that Sr Marie-Bernard had an ardent heart and could easily have become too attached to her Mistress, 'who knew how to make herself well-loved by her novices'.[51] There is little in Bernadette's lifestory to give credence to this fear. It will be seen that throughout Sr Marie-Bernard's religious life she maintained a distance from other people, although she was affable in manner. Sr Henri Fabre's comments were perhaps based upon other cases, when novices had fallen into Mère Marie-Thérèse's psychological toils. Sr Henri Fabre also shows the inclination, found all throughout the convent documents, to discern providential influences in every outcome. This tendency ordered their recollections, but sometimes memory itself insisted upon other factors: 'I know very well that the Superior General and the Mistress of Novices believed that they were fulfilling conscience in their role as instruments of providence *vis-à-vis* the Servant of God; but I also believe that there was in Mère Marie-Thérèse a sort of natural antipathy for Sr Marie-Bernard.'[52]

But how was this antipathy demonstrated? There are many mentions of unjust reproofs, angry scolding and cold demeanours in the documents, but very few witnesses give specific examples of how Mère Marie-Thérèse expressed her antagonism toward her harassed novice. Most of the Sisters simply recalled that Mère Marie-Thérèse always spoke to Sr Marie-Bernard in a harsh manner. It was the unvarying nature of this criticism which made it noteworthy. Other novices were subjects of reproofs often enough, but it was not usually unceasing. It was only Sr Marie-Bernard for whom there was 'never any encouragement'.[53] Mère Marie-Thérèse 'never let slip a chance to impose a humiliation on her',[54] and in degree and harshness this was conspicuous. 'She liked to correct Sr Marie-Bernard more than the others,' said Sr Joseph Caldariou, 'sometimes I heard our Mistress say to her: "Sr Marie-Bernard, you have done such or such a thing which you should not do." And we were all surprised at that reproach, for we knew that it was not deserved.'[55] According to a statement which became oft-repeated at St Gildard, one of Sr Marie-Bernard's contemporaries had exclaimed: 'As a young novice, seeing Bernadette submit to a humiliation, I often said to myself in my lack of fervour: How lucky not to be Bernadette!'[56]

A striking thing about this recollection is that the visionary was still referred to by her original name, rather than her title in religion. This shows that her original identity persisted, and is one of the reasons why the superiors were determined to quell her with severity. The famous phrase from the novitiate 'How lucky not to be Bernadette' also shows that the original project of treating her just as any other novice had also failed. Exceptional reproofs were judged to be necessary, because the novices, in their immaturity, were ever ready to recreate Bernadette's worldly celebrity in the convent. After giving a lesson in the novitiate, when Bernadette was placed near her, Mère Marie-Thérèse sharply asked one novice 'Why were you staring at Sr Marie-Bernard?' She received the reply, 'I was thinking that you must have been so happy to have Sr Marie-Bernard sitting next to you.'[57] This was wonderfully tactless. It should have been an honour for Sr Marie-Bernard to sit near the Mistress, not the other way around. With pardonable asperity, Mère Marie-Thérèse said that 'I would have been equally pleased to have any of you by me. Sr Marie-Bernard is living an ordinary life here.'[58] Such incidents would have made the Novice Mistress wary of relaxing her guard for a moment.

Aside from Sr Marie-Bernard, there were others who were unfortunate enough to be treated especially harshly by Mère Marie-Thérèse, just as there were those whom she appeared to favour. The Sisters from both of these categories tended to state that they had 'noticed nothing' particularly severe in Mère Marie-Thérèse's attitude toward Sr Marie-Bernard. 'When she spoke to Sr Marie-Bernard she kept the manner which was normal to her,' said Sr

Julienne Capmartin, 'and I believe that she always treated her as she did the others, without favours, certainly, but without injustice.'[59]

The experiences of Sr Julienne, who along with Sr Marie-Bernard encountered Mère Marie-Thérèse's severity, are very descriptive of the novitiate. Sr Julienne admiringly described the Novice Mistress as a woman 'with a firm hand, who knew how to master the most difficult natures'.[60] One morning Sr Julienne did not feel hungry at breakfast, and therefore decided not to eat anything. This is typical of a novice's fault; she did not think it necessary to ask permission to miss a meal.

> But I had not counted on the vigilance of our Mistress. I was called to her terrible office and had to confess my fault: 'Little one, she said to me, you will eat your breakfast on your knees before the whole community for the following week. This will make you remember to ask for permissions.'
> And I did as she said.
> For me, I found this entirely natural. I made my confession because I knew that the Mistress wanted what was best for me; and even on my knees, during my penance, I did not cease to love her as a mother.[61]

Sr Julienne's submission was the correct attitude, and the penance prescribed by the Novice Mistress was to be expected in the circumstances. However, her second example of Mère Marie-Thérèse's punishments is more chilling, 'it was a harsher trial'.[62] When the novices were assembled to be called for profession, the Mistress read through the list and all were named, except Sr Julienne. She was left, before the others, without explanation, and supposed that she had not been accepted. She retired in tears, but then was surprised when a Sister later approached her and told her that she was expected with the others in the office of the Superior General. Mère Marie-Thérèse greeted her with a smile. Sr Julienne maintained her loyalty throughout this severe test, but the demonstration of the Novice Mistress's power, in this case, seems manipulative.

Most novices bore their trials without resentment, and were grateful for the rigours which stood them in good stead in attaining maturity, detachment and self-discipline. The attitude of a Novice Mistress became more punitive and less helpful if it seemed to be an exercise in personal denigration, and the few sources which give any details of Mère Marie-Thérèse's taunting of Sr Marie-Bernard indicate that the Novice Mistress was fond of pointing out Bernadette's lowly social origins. The romance of pastoral imagery cut no ice with Mère Marie-Thérèse, who made sarcastic gibes, addressing Sr Marie-Bernard as 'a shepherdess'.[63] The issue of class-consciousness was nominated by some observers as the reason for the entire rift. 'I saw in all this only a difference in education between her and her novice,' suggested a priest who worked at St Gildard. 'In my opinion, Mère attached too much importance to questions of style. In my mind, I compare Bernadette to Jeanne d'Arc. I think that Mère Marie-Thérèse Vauzou would have found Jeanne d'Arc rather ill-bred.'[64]

Some of Mère Marie-Thérèse's comments sound as if she could not imagine why Bernadette would be a visionary at all. The Canon of the Nevers cathedral actually quoted Mère Marie-Thérèse as saying: 'If the Blessed Virgin wanted to appear on earth, why would she choose a coarse and uneducated peasant, rather than a learned and virtuous religious?'[65] He was so astonished by this outburst that he later raised it with three senior Sisters of the order, who assured him: 'Did you not know that our Révérende Mère is not at all an enthusiast for the events at Lourdes? She has spoken the same way to us.'[66] 'She scarcely believed it,' one Sister commented, but most of the community at St Gildard were silent of the issue of Mère Marie-Thérèse's scepticism. This was a much more sensitive issue than excessive penalties for a novice. However, it is unlikely that the Novice Mistress seriously believed that Sr Marie-Bernard was a charlatan. She permitted her presence in the congregation, and in later years allowed her to converse with the novices, which she could not have tolerated if she had serious doubts about Sr Marie-Bernard's morality. Rather, Mère Marie-Thérèse probably found the story of Lourdes cloying, and almost unbelievable when one was obliged to confront the visionary, a plain and laconic provincial woman.

Some of the Sisters of Nevers blamed Mère Marie-Thérèse for her excessive severity, and others excused her for acting as an instrument of Providence for Bernadette's benefit, but all agreed that the Novice Mistress was no minor figure in the congregation. 'Her prestige was immense at the Mother House, and in the Congregation her influence prevailed.'[67] Sr Marie-Bernard's attainment of the status of a figure of admiration was one of the few hiccups of her career. Mère Marie-Thérèse's strong personality dominated the affections of those around her: 'Beneath an appearance of coldness, she had need to give and receive a great deal of affection; she exercised a sort of attraction over us, we loved her a great deal.'[68] Mère Bordenave also described this powerful charisma and authority: 'she was one of those people about whom one could not remain indifferent. One had to fear or love her a great deal, and rather often one felt both at the same time. Her manner was such that she could always rouse either suffering or pleasure.'[69] These observations hold a veiled criticism, for such a reign of temperament is contrary to the self-effacement and disinterested charity recommended to all religious. In this departure from the ideal pattern, Mère Marie-Thérèse is an important historical example, for there were many such dynamic figures in the women's congregations of this era. When they had the chance to apply their energies and talents, they wielded great organizational power. When confined or frustrated, they tended to oppress others with their emotional intrigues. Mère Marie-Thérèse probably played both of these roles at different times in her life.

Those who divined Mère Marie-Thérèse's wishes negotiated with her unpredictable reactions. As one Sister explained: 'I loved our Mère; but also had to suffer a great deal from her temperament, especially in the early years. Later, when I knew her better, I always made the first approach to her, and then I would hug her and see her coldness vanish; although this did not always succeed. I wonder did Bernadette realize that one had to act this way.'[70] Sr Marie-Bernard's companions noted with admiration that she never sought consolation in human relationships, not even by seeking sympathy among her companions, much less by being drawn into the arduous game of seeking Mère Marie-Thérèse's uncertain affections. Considering the empire which the Novice Mistress held over the majority of those around her, the experience of encountering Sr Marie-Bernard's 'closed character'[71] must have been an unpleasant surprise.

Sr Marie-Bernard relied upon the formal rules of behaviour, and received her public corrections and penances without 'the slightest change of expression, she received humiliations with calm, I would say even with piety'.[72] Others saw her blush or turn pale, but never a word of protest or complaint. With reason, a novice complimented her for 'letting nothing appear on the exterior; you are impassive'.[73] This calm was a religious virtue, but it pointed out the limits of the Novice Mistress's power, and it would have been recognized by the government officials at Lourdes. The Rule of the Sisters of Nevers commanded that all the novices 'will submit to the Mistress, respecting and honouring her as their Mother; not only will they obey her in all that she commands them … but they will make it a duty to consult her in all their sorrows and problems; and in all of their conduct interior and exterior.'[74] Mère Marie-Thérèse reinforced this, saying often to them: 'Have no secrets from me, unless it is a matter for the sacrament of Confession.'[75] Despite her obedience, one wonders if Sr Marie-Bernard fulfilled the letter and the spirit of this part of the Rule. Even if she did, she appears not to have satisfied Mère Marie-Thérèse's thirst for demonstrated personal loyalty. And after September 1866, when Sr Marie-Bernard had made her early profession, there was nothing Mère Marie-Thérèse could do about it.

From her days as a young girl being interrogated by the Police Commissioner, Bernadette had always shown a calm appraisal of the real power of authority figures, and she had never been easily intimidated. She could be humble and obedient, but with an air of equanimity rather than servility. This was a standing affront to Mère Marie-Thérèse's controlling nature, and also 'she appreciated souls according to the access which they gave her to their interior lives'.[76] As Mère Bordenave pointed out, after the illness when Bernadette made her final vows, she had no such access. Mère Marie-Thérèse was inclined to make a capricious display of her power to refuse to admit novices to vows, as a means of keeping them in suspense. After the illness of Sr Marie-Bernard, the Mistress was in the unusual position of having a professed novice. Sr Marie-Bernard could be upbraided, isolated and publicly humbled. But the trial of the novitiate was only a formality now, and both she and Mère Marie-Thérèse knew it. In any case, the prostrations, the kissing of the floor and the listening to admonitions were not necessarily as awesome to Sr Marie-Bernard as they would have been to a woman from the better ranks of society. Mère Marie-Thérèse could not lash out with her fists, whack a novice with a cane, or shriek out drunken tirades. She had less forceful means of chastisement than Bernadette's mother, aunts and wet-nurse had once had.

It is conceivable that Sr Marie-Bernard held more power in her relationship with Mère Marie-Thérèse than is usually recognized. Rather than merely being a passive victim of the older woman's dislike, she may have drawn her own limits of intimacy, and refused to respond to someone with demanding and invasive affections. As time went on, Sr Marie-Bernard came to be on friendly terms with another of the leading figures of the house, Mère Eleónore Cassagnes, the Secretary General of the congregation. When deputizing for the Mother General, Mère Eleónore had reason to be in contact with the novices. Her work was administrative rather than personalized, and she may have had a manner more attractive to Sr Marie-Bernard, who was said to hold her in great respect. Mère Eleónore was a much less colourful character than Mère Marie-Thérèse, but was a sensitive and refined woman, esteemed by some to be 'a perfect religious'.[77] As one of Mère Eleónore's later protégées said: 'Sr Marie-Bernard, who did not much reveal herself, spoke to [Mère Eleónore] more easily than to others.'[78] Predictably, this caused 'some stormy feelings from Mère Marie-Thérèse'.[79] Sr Marie-Bernard's friendship with the Secretary General was a significant move on the chessboard of convent politics.

Mère Marie-Thérèse was to outlive her former novice by twenty-eight years, and saw her posthumous reputation flourish. She spoke of Sr Marie-Bernard, usually with reservations, and recalled that the Lourdes visionary had been 'inclined to self-love'.[80] She could not supply any anecdotes to support this view, although, as one Sister said, 'if there was any grounds at all to say so, she certainly would have'. [81] Occasionally, as she mused over the past, there were acknowledgements that she had been harsh to Sr Marie-Bernard. Sr Léontine Villaret remembered her saying that: 'Every time that I had something to tell Bernadette, I was inclined to say it sharply.'[82] A famous scene, handed down in the oral history of the order, seemed to indicate repentance. Sr Joséphine Forestier claimed that Mère Marie-Thérèse felt compelled to consult a famous Cistercian priest, who had the gift of discernment. She left his confessional reassured, and told her companion on the pilgrimage that 'God permitted that Mère Josephine Imbert and I acted severely toward Sr Marie-Bernard, in order to maintain her in humility.'[83] Mère Marie-Thérèse had need of a quiet conscience, because during her last years of retirement she was sent – of all the houses in the order – to Lourdes. This is so singular that one wonders if the reigning superiors included women who had their own grudges against Mère Marie-Thérèse, and sent her to the famous shrine as a means of retaliation. The convent overlooks the Grotto, and sometimes, 'before the sight of crowds she would seem irritated and brusquely close the shutters'.[84] However, on her deathbed she was heard praying to Our Lady of Lourdes. Despite the wavering of her later years, the old hostilities never completely vanished, and when the subject of Bernadette's possible canonization was raised with her she could not bear to hear of it: 'Wait until I am dead.'[85] They did so, and the first formal testimonies of Bernadette's sanctity were gathered in 1907, the year that Mère Marie-Thérèse died.

Readers of the Lourdes literature are always informed of how much Bernadette had to endure as a novice, and the calm way she bore this is judged to have been one of the proofs of her sanctity. Whether they blame or exonerate Mère Marie-Thérèse, such commentators do not assess her feelings.

She may have been more unhappy than Bernadette. The figure of Mère Marie-Thérèse could benefit from historical revision, for it seems probable that this 'instrument of God' was the victim of an inability to live up to her own standards. Jealousy, curiosity, avidity and other signs of a lack of emotional self-control are evident in her story. These flaws bore their inevitable result in frustration and a degree of resentment which finally was inexplicable to Mère Marie-Thérèse herself. Mère Marie-Thérèse did not conform to the almost inhuman degree of detachment and psychological segregation preached in the nineteenth-century convents. Manipulative and inconstant, she 'seemed to wish to attract hearts and absorb them into her own'.[86] This is not a means to attain tranquillity or self-conquest.

## Final vows

The postulants and novices admitted to St Gildard were sifted by the training in the novitiate. The numbers of postulants who left is not recorded, as they never became formal members of the community. Accounts of community life give the impression that the departure of unsatisfactory postulants was common. Having taken temporary vows, novices showed dedication, but at St Gildard during the 1860s, almost one in five novices was not admitted to profession. From 1859 to 1866 the *Calendrier* shows that 627 Sisters took vows as novices, but only 515 passed through the ceremony of profession. A significant number of candidates either would find the religious life was not for them, or would be rejected by the superiors as unsuitable.

The final vows were a lasting commitment, but the Church did not require that sisters be absolutely bound by them. An official release from the vows could be obtained without trouble, although usually with an attitude of official disapproval. Also, for the Sisters of Nevers, the first profession was binding only for three years, after which time it would be renewed. A lifelong vow was taken ten years after this. Many Sisters left the religious life in later years, and these departures were seen as a defection. An even worse problem was some of those that stayed. After vows were taken it was very difficult for the congregation to expel an unsuitable member. Most Sisters lived lives of dedication, but a few degenerated into difficult, idle, depressed and even mentally ill women. The convent became permanently responsible for them.

At the time of the taking of final vows, a list of candidates would be submitted to a Chapter of Superiors. The Chapter was a meeting of the senior Sisters who voted for or against the admission of each candidate. In order even to be considered by the Chapter, a novice had to show satisfactory conduct to the Novice Mistress who proffered the names for review. Acceptance was far from guaranteed. In the intake of 30 October 1867, out of 60 names presented, only 44 were accepted by the Chapter for profession. Although Sr Marie-Bernard was among this intake, the Chapter did not have to consider her name, because she had already been accepted in the course of the vows which she made *in extremis*.

Despite the degree of stress which they were under, the novices still managed to find outlets for the playfulness natural to their age. They sometimes made jokes, and arranged games, usually with a theme of enacting religious roles and mocking their own failures. Memoirs of the life of Bernadette have recorded some of these ephemeral diversions. On one occasion she and Sr Louise Brusson put a notice on the mirror in the linen room: 'Rather, look at your soul.'[87] This was a reproach to postulants who still had the tendency of unreligious behaviour and were inclined to regard themselves in the mirror. Although merely a jest, this was not permitted to the novices, and Mère Marie-Thérèse soon asked who were the guilty parties who had put up the notice. Sr Marie-Bernard owned up. Although she was reproved, her pious jests were not seen as a serious fault.

The most serious flaw in Sr Marie-Bernard's character, which had been observed long before she became a novice, was her quick temper. Her flashes of ill-humour occasionally appeared, although in exactly what circumstances is not recorded. She never seems to have shown disrespect for her superiors, for if she had done so it would have caused repercussions. Sr Marie-Bernard seems to have retained a habit of snapping at people who annoyed her. In the convent, these would have been her contemporaries among the novices. Sr Henri Fabre, and others, recalled in non-specific terms 'some sharp retorts for which she would soon humbly apologize'.[88] Mère Marie-Thérèse noted this fault. A priest who asked her about her recollections of Bernadette said that she had told him of 'some answers of Sr Marie-Bernard where she did not find the perfectly measured tone which it seemed that a saint would have kept. She told me what these were but I do not remember them exactly ... But I do remember that I observed to the Reverend Mother that, at that time, these replies seemed to me to have nothing reprehensible about them, and I saw in them only a difference in education between her and her novice.'[89]

When making her final notes about each novice, the Mistress gave a moderate but fair assessment of Sr Marie-Bernard. She wrote of a 'stiff character, very irritable; modest, pious, devout, she is very orderly'.[90] When submitting these notes for examination by the ecclesiastical authorities, Mère Marie-Thérèse's successor defensively noted that a stiff appearance was merely due to Bernadette's ethnic origins, 'a Pyrenean temperament', while she should be esteemed as 'sensitive' rather than 'irritable'.[91] These excuses were offered in later years, during the process of Bernadette's canonization. At the time, most people would probably have agreed with the Novice Mistress, who was among the many who saw Bernadette's unyielding nature and sharp tongue. In noting this, Mère Marie-Thérèse also recognized her novice's qualities, and devotion, modesty and orderly ways were extremely important in convent life. The Novice Mistress gave a just account in this formal summary. She did not comment on the issue of Sr Marie-Bernard's poor health. It was an established problem, and there was no useful comment to make.

During the last week of October 1867 the novices at St Gildard went into a retreat of seven days. This special period of prayer, silence and daily sermons was in preparation for their vows of profession. The retreat was led by a Jesuit, Père Pauley, and Sr Marie-Bernard made brief notes of the messages which he gave them. His topics for preaching were the Last Days, holy indifference, sin, Saint Joseph as a model of obedience, Jesus of Nazareth as a model of the interior life, the crucifix, and the Eucharist. The stress on the Holy Family and Nazareth suggests that the Jesuit was preparing the Sisters for their role as working religious. Consistently, the message which the Sisters received was a stern admonition to remember the Last Judgement, avoiding sin, distractions and their own inclinations, in favour of the standard devotions of Catholic spirituality. The teaching was simple, there was no attempt to enter into the fields of mysticism or theology, while the central idea of dutiful responsibility was clear. Sr Marie-Bernard copied out the main points of the preaching, and reminded herself to seek God alone, everywhere. 'The means to see God in everything are self-restraint, abnegation and mortification.'[92] For her, mortification was to follow swiftly upon the ceremony of profession.

The ceremony was held on the morning of 30 October 1867. It was a solemn occasion, for which all the novices had been extensively prepared. Their period of trial, which for some of them would have been extended to three years, was completed, and they had just spent a week of silence in the sanctuary of the Mother House. Each Sister had written out a *billet*, according to the formula of vows, and would recite her intention to live in poverty, chastity, obedience and charity, for as long as she remained in the congregation. The Bishop read out a series of set questions, to which the novices replied together. He asked what they wanted, 'Monseigneur, we ask you to receive us to profession,' and he then reminded them, 'Do you know what it is that you ask for? Are you convinced, as much as possible, of the excellence of that profession, of the eminent holiness which one must have in order to conduct oneself in a manner worthy of the state which you aspire to? ... You will be regarded as servants of Christian charity, which makes Martyrs as easily as the Faith does. Do you know then, that all your care, all your attention must be to cultivate charity, humility, obedience, poverty, purity of body and soul, peace, unity and the practice of good works?' They answered in unison that they did understand this, and that they hoped that 'the mercy of God, which has inspired us with the desire to commit ourselves, will give us the graces necessary to accomplish our vocation'.[93] After this the Bishop blessed their habits, 'this attire which is a symbol of humility and scorn of worldliness, which will be an exterior confirmation for your servants of their holy resolution'.[94] The second blessing was of 'the veil which will cover the head of your servant; that this garment may be blessed, consecrated, rendered pure and holy'. Each Sister kissed her veil and received it, then left the chapel to be clothed in her new habit. They then returned and, as the choir sang, each knelt before the altar, made a short declaration, and received communion.

Sr Marie-Bernard passed through like the others, but, because of her fame, was noticed more. Sr Bernard Dalias testified later that: 'I well remember the voice of Sr Marie-Bernard at the moment when she pronounced the formula of vows. Her tone was firm and sweet, with absolutely no affectation. At the tribune, the singers held their breath to hear better.'[95] After this, each Sister was given a blessed candle, 'a physical light, as a sign of the spiritual light which must guide your way to eternity'.[96]

In the afternoon of the profession ceremony, an assembly was always held in the hall of the novitiate. There the Bishop and the Mother General gave each of the new Sisters a crucifix, a copy of the Rule of the Congregation, and a 'letter of obedience', which directed them to the convent where they would work. These 'letters' were anxiously awaited by the Sisters, as they had no idea where they would go, or whether they would receive an appealing or a difficult post. They might be sent to a large and prestigious convent, or to a remote and tiny community. Likewise their duties ranged from instructing music pupils, to nursing the insane. Each was called in turn, but Sr Marie-Bernard was left sitting in her place, still waiting to hear. She whispered to a companion: 'They have given them to everyone. I would so much like to be able to have one like everyone else.'[97]

Mgr Forcade and Mère Joséphine Imbert had already arranged this scene, because they had discussed the question of Bernadette's future. Because of her poor health, and the public curiosity which would always pursue her, it was impossible to place her in any of the congregation's establishments. She could only be sufficiently guarded and sustained in the Mother House. However, it was rare for a newly professed Sister to have the honour of a posting to St Gildard, and they did not want to appear to favour her unduly. Therefore when the Bishop turned to Mère Joséphine and said: 'And Sr Marie-Bernard?' the superior replied: 'She is good for nothing.' Sr Marie-Bernard approached and knelt at the Bishop's feet, but there was still no letter of obedience for her. Bishop Forcade recorded the following conversation, and his reactions to it, in his memoir:

—Is it true, Sr Marie-Bernard, that you are good for nothing?
—The Mère Générale is not mistaken. It is true.
—But then, my poor child, what are we going to do with you, and what is the good of your entry to the Congregation?
—That is just what I said to you at Lourdes, and you told me that it would make no difference.
I had not expected this answer, which was not provided for when we planned this little drama, and frankly I did not know what to say. Happily, the excellent Mère Joséphine, who was never caught short, came to the rescue. She leant forward again: 'If you wish, Monseigneur, we could keep her for charity's sake in the Mother House and employ her in some way in the infirmary. Since she is always sick, that would be exactly the right place for her. She could do some cleaning, and learn to make tisanes, if there is ever any way to teach her.'[98]

The blistering words of the Mother General impressed the novices, who were no doubt glad, all over again, that they were not Bernadette. Sr Marie-Bernard took the reproof calmly, and afterwards joined the celebrations with a serene air. It seems that this censure made a mark on her, because in later years she was to refer to herself as good for nothing, and as being unfit for a post in the convent. Her lack of education, accomplishments and health would always be a burden on her, and even make her see herself as a burden on others. The novitiate ended on a sour note of unwilling acceptance, but Sr Marie-Bernard had been accepted. For her, 30 October was a holy day, the anniversary of her profession.

# NOTES

1.   M. Auclair, *Bernadette* (Paris 1957), 202.

2.   To the Sisters at the Hospice in Lourdes, 20 July 1866, *ESB*, no. 81, 241.

3.   Ibid.

4.   Jean-Baptiste Estrade, *PON*, Sessio I, 1333.

5.   For a description of the 'mythical nun' who inhabited the French rationalist mind see Olwen Hufton, *Women and the Limits of Citizenship in the French Revolution* (Toronto 1992).

6.   Anne Cecile Olivier, quoted Visitation, *Anne Madeleine Remuzat* 59.

7.   Quoted in the testimony of Sr Aimée of Jesus, *St Thérèse of Lisieux by Those who Knew Her* (Dublin 1975), 280.

8.   Laurentin, *Vie*, 218.

9.   To the Sisters at the Lourdes Hospice, 20 July 1866, *ESB*, no. 81, 241.

10.   Ibid.

11.   Sr Emilienne quoted, *BVP*, 2. 24.

12.   Ibid., 16.

13.   Livre des Entrées, *ESB*, 239.

14.   Sr Philomena quoted, *BVP*, 2. 24.

15.   Sr Emilienne quoted, ibid.

16.   Quoted, *ESB*, 256.

17.   Mère Marie-Thérèse quoted, *BVP*, 2. 349. Forcade, *Notice sur la vie*, 26

18.   Annette Basset quoted, *BVP*, 2. 33-4.

19.   Letter to Mère Augustine Ceyrac, 3 Sept. 1866, *ESB*, no. 84, 248.

20.   Forcade, *Notice sur la vie*, 25.

21.   Ibid.

22.   Ibid.

23.   Ibid.

24.   Mère Josephine Imbert quoted, ibid.

25.   Sr Marie-Bernard quoted, *BVP*, 2. 40.

26.   Letter from Chanoine Guynot, July 1934, *RdC*, 183.

27.   Quoted by Trochu, *Sainte Bernadette*, 386.

28. Sr Victorine quoted, Cros, *Histoire*, 3. 211.

29. These words are repeated in several Lourdes sources, as if they are a commonplace. This quotation is from Bernarde Castérot; 'It is her Aunt Bernarde who said it' is given in Bordenave, *La Confidente*, 103-4. It somewhat contrasts with a better-sourced statement from Bernarde Castérot in *Témoins*, 163, which states that Louise Castérot was already ill when Bernadette left Lourdes.

30. Dominique Vignes, *Témoins*, 157.

31. Capitalization as in the original. To Abbé Pomain, 2 Jan. 1867, *ESB*, no. 87, 250.

32. Mère Marie-Thérèse quoted, *BVP*, 2. 10.

33. 'Notice sur notre vénérée Mère Marie-Thérèse Vauzou', quoted by Trochu, *Sainte Bernadette*, 373.

34. Ibid.

35. Ibid.

36. Mère Joséphine Forestier quoted, Trochu, *Sainte Bernadette*, 375.

37. Mère Marie-Thérèse quoted, *BVP*, 2. 14.

38. Bernadette quoted, *BVP*, 2. 14.

39. Sr Emilienne Duboé, *PON*, Sessio LII, 668.

40. Pope Pius XI quoted, *Revue Bernadette* 4 (April 1939), 122.

41. Sr Marie-Valentine Gleyrose, *PON*, Sessio XX, 258.

42. Quoted by Trochu, *Sainte Bernadette*, 397.

43. Bernadette quoted, Laurentin, *BVP*, 2. 26.

44. Ibid.

45. Sr Marie-Josephine, *PON*, Sessio IX, 150.

46. Sr Marie-Bernard quoted, Sr Stephanie Vareillaud, *RdC*, 120.

47. Sr Joseph Garnier, *PON*, Sessio C, 1143.

48. Ibid.

49. Sr Marie-Josephine Constance, *PON*, Sessio VII, 133.

50. Quoted by Père Le Cerf, *PON*, 987.

51. Sr Henri Fabre, *PON*, Sessio XXI, 276.

52. Ibid.

53. *BVP*, 2. 351.

54. Sr Lucie Cloris quoted, *BVP*, 2. 349.

55. The Procés Apostolique de Nevers quoted, Trochu, *Sainte Bernadette*, 403.

56. Mère Stephanie Vareillaud, *PON*, Sessio VIII, 137.

57. Sr Bernard Dalias quoted, Trochu, *Sainte Bernadette*, 395.

58. Ibid.

59. Mère Julienne Capmartin, Guynot, *Contemporains*, 59.

60. Ibid., 57.

61. Ibid., 58.

62. Ibid.

63. *BVP*, 2. 357.

64. Charles Payrard, SM, *PON*, Sessio LXXXVIII, 1030.

65. Claude Boillot, *PON*, Sessio CII, 1160.

66. Sisters quoted, *BVP*, 2. 357.

67. Mère Josephine Forestier, *BVP*, 2. 365.

68. Ibid.

69. Mère Bordenave quoted, *BVP*, 2. 366.

70. Sr Forestier quoted, *BVP*, 2. 367.

71. Sr Jospeh Garnier, *PON*, Sessio C, 1143.

72. Sr Casimir Gallery quoted, Mère Bordenave, *PON*, Sessio XXIX, 344.

73. *BVP*, 2. 368.

74. *Explication*, 35.

75. Mère Marie-Thérèse quoted, Mère Julienne Capmartin, Guynot, *Contemporains*, 57.

76. Mère Bordenave, *PON*, Sessio XXVII, 326.

77. Sr Marie-Alphonse, *PON*, Sessio XXXIII, 482.

78. Ibid.

79. Mère Bordenave, *PON*, Sessio XXVII, 325.

80. Recollections of Mère Henri Fabre, Trochu, *Sainte Bernadette*, 398.

81. Ibid.

82. Quoted, Trochu, *Sainte Bernadette*, 402.

83. Mère Marie-Thérèse quoted, Sr Josephine Forestier, *PON*, Sessio VII, 134.

84. Jean Le Cerf quoted, *BVP*, 2. 356.

85. Sr Marie-Josephine Forestier, *PON*, Sessio VII, 133.

86. Sr Justine Pelat quoted, *BVP*, 2. 365.

87. Quoted, Laurentin, *Vie*, 165.

88. Quoted, Trochu, *Sainte Bernadette*, 397.

89. Père Charles Payrard quoted, ibid.

90. 'Déposition de Mère Bordenave concernant les "Notes" de Mère Vauzou sur Sr Marie-Bernard novice', *ESB*, no. 90, 253.

91. Ibid.

92. Quoted, Trochu, *Sainte Bernadette*, 419.

93. 'Cérémonial de la Profession', *Trésor*, 299.

94. Ibid., 301.

95. Quoted, Trochu, *Sainte Bernadette*, 419.

96. *Trésor*, 305.

97. Sr Marie-Bernard quoted, *BVP*, 2. 69.

98. Forcade, *Notice sur la vie*, 32–3.

# CHAPTER 9

# 'Watching Over the Sentiments
of My Heart'
## Religious Life at St Gildard

Detachment from people and things, watching over the sentiments of
my heart.
The communal life is a holy life.

St Bernadette, Notebook, 1873

In 1867 Sr Marie-Bernard commenced her active life as a professed Sister of
Nevers. Despite the rules of behaviour impressed upon the Sisters, human
affections, likes, dislikes, rivalries and irritations simmered beneath the
surface. There were also the irreducible barriers of class difference. Sr Marie-
Bernard had ostensibly been accepted as an equal member of the community,
as much a Sister and lady as any of the others who were called *Dames de
Nevers*. In reality, of course, her origins were not forgotten. Her appearance
was refined (although she had the darker complexion of a southerner) and her
personal habits were fastidious. This was just as well, for she was among
women who were ready to see her as a representative of the lower orders. This
is shown by their very words of praise for her. When Mère Philomena Roques
commented upon her simple speech and dignified manner one almost winces
at the compliment, for she said that if Sr Marie-Bernard: 'did not have the
culture and the accomplishments, I would even dare to say the polish, of the
upper classes, she was no worse off for it, still less was *she the vulgar little
peasant that one might think her to be*'.[1]

Once out of the novitiate, the Sisters entered fully into the life of their
community. They were in a position to judge others, to become enervated by
the routine of their lives, and to realize the imperfections of those whom they
were called upon to respect. The novitiate was a time of subordination, but
also of idealism and companionship. Moments of tension were more likely to
arise between the professed Sisters, because their lives were not an endless
cycle of work and prayer. There were times of recreation, conversation and
relaxation. Amid the times of amusement, there were also moments of
mockery, opposition and misunderstanding. There were also the ever-present
rules to follow, and the duty of reporting oneself, or being reported, to the
superiors for any fault committed.

Sr Marie-Bernard maintained evenness in religious life because she was
willing to work, did not become indolent when confronted with unpleasant
tasks and was realistic in the face of correction. She was also capable of
showing a playful nature, and this balance of humility and cheerfulness suited

the pattern of work, formality and recreation among the Sisters. The currents of snobbery must have affected her, but even amid the refinement of St Gildard, her very lack of middle-class inhibition provided the Sisters with some fun. Sr Eudoxie Chatelain remembered seeing a group of professed Sisters in the garden during recreation. The presence of Sr Marie-Bernard among them made her stop and look, 'for I never missed a chance to see her or listen to her'. One of the Sisters picked up a newly laid egg from a barrow, and 'happily asked her companions "Who would like to drink an egg?" ' This raised some repartee:

> The question had hardly been asked when a voice answered: 'Me.' It was Sister Marie-Bernard. You know that she was very spontaneous.
>
> — It is quite warm, replied the first Sister.
> —That is just how I like them, replied Bernadette.
>
> Sr Joseph exclaimed against this, saying that a raw egg would be frightful...
>
> —No, she said, it is not bad.
> —In that case, it must be difficult to do, I would not attempt it myself.
> —You will see, replied Sr Marie-Bernard, that there is nothing more easy.
>
> She took the egg, tapped the shell, and drank it in one gulp. The egg had hardly disappeared when Bernadette flapped her hands, half laughing half crying, and as much astonished as if she had just awaked from a dream.
>
> —What have I just done, she said. I have to go immediately and find the Soeur Assistante and confess my fault. Everyone laughed, and I did the same in my watching place.[2]

Sr Marie-Bernard could evidently relate to the other Sisters in an easy manner, and even after years of convent life she still had some peasant ways, such as the ability to drink eggs. One can also see that despite the joviality of this anecdote, Sr Marie-Bernard was always being watched. She was noticed, in an admiring way, by the novice, and in a friendly way, by the other Sisters. But she was not in a position to commit the slightest fault unnoticed: 'they always had an eye on her and I believe that they were more severe in noticing, in her, things which would have been let pass in another'.[3]

## The three vows

Sr Marie-Bernard had respect for the externals of convent life, which were an important part of a religious identity. She especially valued the habit of the Sisters of Nevers, and her attention and fidelity to this form of dress was quite different from her indifference to the Pyrenean costume which her admirers had liked to see her in. During the whole of her life, she dressed very neatly, but it was at St Gildard that she seems to have enjoyed her clothes rather than merely worn them. Sr Marie-Bernard never omitted the slightest item of the religious dress which it was her privilege to put on. During her bouts of ill-health, she would continue to be fully dressed as a patient in the infirmary, for as long as possible. She also liked to help other Sisters to dress, and would arrange their coifs and veils for them. On the day when novices took their vows, she was one of the Sisters who would go to the dormitory to help the novices be 'clothed' for the first time. When she arranged their cornettes, she would say: 'Those that I put are secure.' She arranged her own veil carefully, and was conspicuous for always wearing it forward over her shoulders.

Along with the wearing of the habit, came the practice of the Rule and the observance of the three vows. Sr Marie-Bernard's observation of the vow of poverty was universally praised, and she is depicted as a person who never failed to observe the Rule when in possession of material objects. Religious poverty was a constant effort, as it required each member of the community to refrain from considering any material goods which they use as being their own. Therefore Sisters had to consider breakages and accidents as serious offences against the community, and be constantly prepared to exchange even such convenient items as pens and embroidery instruments for different ones. They could not give anything away without permission, and could not keep any items in their possession if they did not need them. This meant that, in theory, even humble and useful items, such as a few pins, should not be kept in reserve. On the other hand, if a Sister found herself unable to present herself in chapel, because she lacked a pin for her veil, she was judged to have committed a fault and would be obliged to perform penance. These petty restrictions made up the rigours of community life.

Bernadette had always been poor, but religious poverty did not replicate her previous experiences. The abundant presence of the necessities of life impressed Sr Marie-Bernard, especially when she was ill, which was usually a crisis of destitution for people of her class. When being nursed in the infirmary, she said that 'here, everyone spoils me' and also commented that 'the poor are not treated this way'.[4] A background of poverty was not necessarily the best preparation for religious poverty, because often members of the lower classes had more, not less, desire for their own goods. They also might be more feckless and pleasure-loving when in a position to indulge themselves. The whole story of the Soubirous family was one of a failure in poverty; they squandered their material goods and suffered the indignity of relying on others. Bernadette was different from the rest of her family, and her detachment from both poverty and materialism marked her out. Despite being orderly and particular in her ways, she shared the common possessions at St Gildard without complaint. One of the few personal items permitted to a Sister was a notebook, for the recording of spiritual advice. Sr Marie-Bernard kept several, but they were frail pieces of scrap paper, which she had sewed together herself. She expressed no preferences in her tastes for food, and repaired her habit so that she could get the longest possible wear from it. 'She was exquisitely neat,' said Mère Joséphine Forestier, 'she took the greatest care of the things given for her use. She did not set her heart on them ...'[5]

Sr Marie-Bernard's observation of the vow of poverty was unqualified, but in doing this she did no more than many other Sisters. The same point could be made even more forcefully in regard to the vow of chastity. During

Bernadette's lifetime, it was not acknowledged that chastity was anything but easy and natural for religious women. Therefore, they received little information about sexuality, even in the form of exhortations to virtue, and were not given credit for purity of life, as this was seen as an expression of their natures, rather than as an achievement. During the early-modern era, chastity had been defined in more robust terms, and even consecrated virgins were understood to have contended with the demons of lust. Sixteenth-century texts had illustrated the themes of the assaults of temptation, alongside such remedies as self-flagellation and violent acts of penitence. By the nineteenth century, these extremes were banished by notions of taste, and the sexuality of the respectable middle-classes was to remain unrepresented until the outburst of Freudian discourse in the 1890s.

The Sisters of Nevers avoided sexual impurity for the highest of motives – it was the duty of their vocation. In the Lourdes of Bernadette's childhood, sexuality had been shunned for more utilitarian reasons; it was a means by which women were burdened by men. This would have been one of the first messages that Bernadette had learnt on this subject, as she had worked in her aunt's tavern, and had mixed with her cousins who had been born out of wedlock. In one of Sr Marie-Bernard's rare statements about modest behaviour, she still shows some signs of regarding the opposite sex as a crude menace. When giving advice to a young Sister, who was about to take up work in one of the community's hospitals, she reminded her that 'if you go into a room where a man is, make sure that you always leave the door open'.[6] A more mannered observation was brought forth by the sight of a doll, which Sr Claire Bordes had dressed as a present for the housekeeper's daughter. The costumed doll evidently amused Sr Marie-Bernard. 'She took it in her hands, making it dance, and said: – Oh my poor little doll! You look like those unhappy girls who frequent the park. How unhappy they are who do not understand the beauty of chastity.'[7] The park in question would have been the large public garden facing the Convent of St Gildard. It is a favourite meeting place for people in the town. To judge from this anecdote, Sr Marie-Bernard had looked over the park from the windows of the upper floor of the convent. She may have seen gaily dressed girls meeting their lovers, or prostitutes making assignations. Either way, she drew her own conclusions, which were recalled by playing with the doll.

Many male clerics who wrote about Bernadette praised her as an example of virginity. Often this was linked to the glorification of her poor health. A priest who published a text about Lourdes, during her lifetime, wrote that: 'The lily of virginity never grows better, and is never better protected, than when surrounded by the thorns of suffering. This is why these thorns were Bernadette's burden, from her earliest years.'[8] There is a difference in gender, and perhaps status, on this issue, for the Sisters who knew her in the convent did not find Sr Marie-Bernard's physical decline to be a symptom of her moral purity. They cherished her heroism when facing pain, but this was an example of rising above physical weakness, rather than of being as far removed as possible from carnality. Women were more likely to suggest that physical pain had given Sr Marie-Bernard the chance to develop patience and self-control. 'Sr Marie-Bernard, with her nature of a mountain-dweller, had a task in subduing her own will; I believe that she had worked at that for all of her life, and that she was aided in this by the suffering and the sicknesses which she was almost always burdened with.'[9]

For the women in the convent, Bernadette in pain was an example of dedication and asceticism. For men preaching in the pulpit, Bernadette ailing was the ultimate example of the virginal female state, incapable of desiring and rousing desire. This difference may have been founded upon the fact that the women had actually seen and personally tended her, rather than imagining a meaning for her illness. 'On the subject of chastity, I can only say that I noticed that the Servant of God was extremely modest.'[10] This does not mean that the Sisters did not provide very stylized interpretations of her purity, which reflected their ideological preoccupations rather than her experiences. Sr Joséphine Forestier said that 'according to my personal impression – and I am not the only person to think so – Sr Marie-Bernard kept for all of her life her baptismal innocence.'[11] This claim is made repeatedly. Sr Casimir Callery had 'often heard that the Servant of God had kept her baptismal innocence ... because I myself saw her and knew her, I am persuaded of this. Everyone who saw her was impressed by the expression in the eyes, which had something of the celestial in it.'[12] Baptismal innocence is a symbol of absolute purity, a soul untouched by even the knowledge of sin, much less its enactment. In terms of our contemporary understanding, they are claiming that she never experienced an orgasm. It is not an impossible claim, as some women do live in indifference to, or ignorance of, sexual pleasure, and in Bernadette's lifetime, this was expected of respectable women. 'Therefore, in all that regards Chastity, there is only one unanimous opinion that Sr Marie-Bernard was angelic.'[13]

It is noticeable that the very idealizations of Bernadette's purity posit her as rather more innocent than those who admired her. When they looked into her eyes, and decided that she retained her baptismal innocence, they were assessing her in terms by which she herself was supposedly entirely untainted. Sr Marie-Bernard was not necessarily unaware of the element of passion which she roused in her admirers. There was a factor of distaste in her withdrawal from them. Sr Joséphine Forestier noticed that: 'She was extremely afraid of the regards which she attracted, and she herself had a modest gaze. She tried to avoid even the visits of women, and for much more reason any contact at all with men.'[14]

Women were active agents in the glorification of Bernadette, and were appreciative of her beauty. The many descriptions of her lovely dark eyes, her clear gaze and her pretty features are given as readily by women as by men. This was of particular significance when she was living in the female world of the convent. Sr Marie-Bernard liked the novices, and with these junior members of the community she had a rare chance to act as an authority figure. The only drawback to her friendly and supportive manner was that she became a subject of admiration for some novices, and sometimes their ways of reacting to her sound like a gentle and feminine form of sexual harassment. Sr Dominique Brunet said that she had restrained herself, out of respect for obedience, 'which had forbidden that I should enjoy her person and her presence. But I knew one postulant who knew how to make more use of her within the given limits. Having noticed that Bernadette passed regularly down the stairs at a particular hour every day, she arranged to wait for her there, then seized her with an ardent embrace!'[15] There are other anecdotes about postulants discomforting her by staring at her, kissing her hands, and 'to her chagrin, seizing her veil to kiss it' as she passed.[16] She never seems to have sought physical contact with others, and so would not have had much understanding of others' claims on her. The novices were probably trying to get attention and affection from her. Their overtures seem to have been innocent of anything but childish affection; or they may reflect a way of relating to Bernadette as if she herself was a pretty child, to be seized and kissed at will.

The significance of demonstrations of affection between women has changed so much, in the course of the twentieth century, that we are unable to empathize with the women in the 1870s. But it is fair to point out that these irregular gestures were a breach of convent decorum, and regardless of the motives of the young women concerned, it is unlikely that they would have wanted to touch or kiss an aged or unattractive woman. The glamour that Bernadette brought to the role of the visionary was always closely related to her appearance. This was one factor in her ideal image, and it continued to be, even in the chaste precincts of St Gildard.

All spiritual directors are agreed that obedience is the most difficult of the three vows. Any person who has lived under obedience can confirm this, and the truism is well illustrated by reading any memoir of St Bernadette. At St Gildard, Sr Marie-Bernard was unfailingly neat, hard-working, simple, humble and pure. It was more difficult to put aside her own will, and to obey commands which might at times be senseless or conflicting. Her obedience was literal, rather than perfect. Even as Sr Marie-Bernard, there were still some signs of the old Bernadette. Sr Joseph Garnier, who had been in the infirmary during an illness, saw that Sr Marie-Bernard would sometimes lie fully dressed on her bed. This was, presumably, when Sr Marie-Bernard was well enough to be sitting up, but ill enough to be confined to the sickroom. The sight of a Sister in her black habit, reclining on the bed, struck the other people in the infirmary: 'because it is in that position and in that costume that our Sisters are exposed on their deathbed'.[17] In order to give this impression Sr Marie-Bernard must have been lying on her back, propped against the pillows. Her unconscious imitation of a holy corpse was not appreciated by a superior, who told her to get up, which she did. However, Sr Joseph added, 'she resumed again the following Sunday. She had a certain tenacity in her ideas.'[18] At another time, also in the sickroom, Sr Marie-Bernard and the other Sisters were visited by Mère Marie-Thérèse Vauzou. The Novice Mistress was annoyed to find that Sr Marie-Bernard had opened a window. 'That is just like you. Do you wish to chill yourself further?' she exclaimed. After Mère Marie-Thérèse left, Sr Julie Durand went to shut the window, but Sr Marie-Bernard said to her: '*Chut! Chut!* Mother did not say to shut it, she only scolded me for having opened it.'[19]

237

Despite the flashes of humour, and even ill-humour, Sr Marie-Bernard was conquered by the regime of the convent, and in turn made a conquest of her own nature. She disappeared into the regulated life, and made the sacrifices necessary in order to follow this way. A final anecdote which is melancholy, yet exact and true, exemplifies this process. Sr Victorine Poux, who had known Bernadette during her time in the Lourdes hospice, found her changed at Nevers. One day, probably during 1874, she visited St Gildard to make a retreat. She took the opportunity to converse with Sr Marie-Bernard, and reminded her of how in the past she would become indignant at any unfairness suffered by her schoolfellows. Sr Marie-Bernard agreed that she had once taken such an attitude, but said that she held it no more. As Sr Victorine stated: 'She was sensitive (before her departure for Nevers) to little injustices, imputations which were not true. She had triumphed over many of them ... But she said at Nevers: Now, I am indifferent.'[20] She suffered injustices, and saw them inflicted on others, but retained the proper serenity of a religious.

## Receiving visitors

As a nun, Sr Marie-Bernard was often advised to 'live the hidden life with Jesus'.[21] This advice was given to everyone, but more frequently to her, as she was seen as being at risk of being tempted by pride. The recommendation by superiors to 'remain hidden' seems somewhat ridiculous, considering that one of Sr Marie-Bernard's greatest penances was that she was constantly called to the parlour in order to be interviewed.

At Bernadette's funeral, Bishop Lelong was to say with assurance that: 'You are witnesses, my Sisters, that she was not hidden, she hid herself, and never as much as she would have wished.'[22] He added that she 'could barely dissimulate her impatience with visitors ... she had a manifest repugnance to receive them'.[23] When she was told that visitors were expected she would exclaim – 'Oh it is so annoying!' – and then would make herself scarce. 'One had to go around the whole convent in order to find her. She would flee like a mouse.' And she would remind the superiors, 'But I was promised ...'[24] Sometimes the Sisters pointed out that this was no way to behave, but her particular friend Mère Eleónore Cassagnes was more coaxing: 'when she was unwilling to meet visitors in the parlour, Mère Eleónore Cassagnes said to her: "Come now, put on a good face and be gracious, it is a question of a benefactor of the Congregation." '[25] For a woman who had been admitted by charity, without the necessary dowry, this was a strong line. It showed how Bernadette had finally been caught in the web of gifts and gain, which she had resisted for so long. Whatever the arguments, they did not always work. She was sometimes reproached by her superiors: 'I heard our Superior General tell her during recreation: "Sr Marie-Bernard, you were not nice enough in the parlour." '[26] 'She was apprehensive of visits. Then she would be more gracious when she was in their presence.'[27]

The visitors to Sr Marie-Bernard were no longer pilgrims from the ordinary level of society, as at Lourdes. They were senior clerics, who might occasionally be accompanied by influential members of the laity. Among those who were presented to her were the Papal Delegate, Mgr Chigi, Mgr Landriot, Archbishop of Reims, Mgr Dupanlou, Bishop of Orléans, thirty other French bishops and at least fourteen bishops from the overseas missions, including those from Japan, Guadeloupe, Canton, and New Caledonia. Mgr Forcade wrote that 'I had the satisfaction of presenting her to many cardinals and bishops. She made a favourable impression on all of them, and I never saw any sign that the welcoming attention which she received had the slightest effect on her humility.'[28]

This condescension missed its mark, because Sr Marie-Bernard, far from being tempted by the favour of bishops' visits, regarded them as a particular bore. When summoned to the parlour she told Sr Joseph Caldairou, 'I must go there again. God only knows what it costs me to appear before bishops.'[29] 'Especially bishops!' she would exclaim, when complaining about the burden of visitors.

Their arrivals were often ill-timed. One day she and the other young professed Sisters were sent for a day-long excursion to the *pensionnat* of Notre-Dame-des-Anges. Such recreational days were rare and served as vacations when ordinary restrictions such as the rule of silence were lifted. Sr Marie-Bernard would indulge in the simple pleasures of walking under the trees, sitting on the very edge of the riverbank, and singing songs in Bigourdanian. She laughed to see that the other Sisters could not understand the words in dialect. However, her presence among them was a disadvantage, because early in the afternoon, in the midst of the enjoyment of their day, an urgent message summoned them back to St Gildard because some bishops had arrived. Although only Sr Marie-Bernard was wanted in the parlour, it was decided that the whole party should be recalled, in order not to singularize her situation. It was the type of sacrifice required often of Sr Marie-Bernard, but she made it rather crossly. ' "Those good bishops, they would have done better to have stayed in their dioceses than to ask for us, we were going on so well here!" ' She said this, recalled the witness, 'with her rebellious look'.[30]

She knew very well that when the Bishop of Nevers came he would bring a string of dignitaries with him. It was no more than a more pompous version of the displays in Lourdes when she said that she was being shown off like a strange beast. The Sisters saw how recalcitrant she was:

One day she saw the Bishop of Nevers, accompanied by another ecclesiastic, arriving at the Convent. They were heading for the infirmary. All of a sudden Sr Marie-Bernard disappeared and hid herself, I do not know where ... Eventually they found her.
—Quick, quick, Sr Marie-Bernard, the Reverend Mother is asking for you. Monseigneur has come to see you. She answered:
—Monseigneur did not come to see me, he came to have me seen.[31]

Aside from receiving the bishops, Sr Marie-Bernard sometimes was sent on short visits to neighbouring convents. The Sisters of Nevers maintained a school at Coulanges, which was three kilometres from the Mother House. Sr

Marie-Bernard had been sent there when some of the Sisters would walk over. She also travelled, almost every year, to the Home of the Good Shepherd at Varennes, which the Sisters ran as an orphanage and a home for aged nuns. She was taken by the Mother General, and made the seven-kilometre journey in a carriage. The Mother General's visits were occasions of some pomp. She would be received by the entire community, and Sr Marie-Bernard would give almonds to the youngest children. She would also embrace each of them in turn. Sr Marie-Bernard liked children, and made these visits happily, although they may have been some effort. On her last visit, she was so ill that she had to be moved about in a wheelchair, as her diseased leg would no longer carry her.

The promise of being hidden at St Gildard was never fulfilled. This was despite the fact that the superiors were anxious to restrict visits for their own reasons. They wanted to maintain her humility, and also to prevent her from having a status noticeably different from that of the other Sisters. Visitors who came without the recommendation of the Bishop of Nevers were usually turned away, and refused any information about her. Mère Marie-Thérèse Bordenave remembered that: 'In order to avoid indiscreet questions, we would often say to people, "She is a religious like the others." This was a sort of *mot d'ordre*.'[32] The superiors sometimes arranged means by which she could be seen, without officially drawing attention to her. A bishop was brought to the community hall to meet the Sisters. 'Shortly before arriving in front of Sr Marie-Bernard, the superior began announcing "Monseigneur, this Sister is from the diocese of Rodez, this one from Paris, this other from Beauvais, etc." But our astute little Pyrenean had seen the strategy: a door was near her and she quickly left by it.'[33] A priest who was preaching a retreat at the convent asked to have her pointed out to him. The Mother Superior made a pretext to bring her forward by using her and one other Sister as examples to show the difference between the silk veil of the novices and the wool veil of the professed. Sr Marie-Bernard co-operated with the display by pulling her veil forward over her face. 'I realized what they wanted, but he wasn't able to see much.'[34]

These incidents are almost breaches of the rule of obedience, because Sr Marie-Bernard was avoiding what she knew her superiors wanted. But she was never formally censured for her recalcitrance, presumably because the instructions were not overtly expressed, and also because Sr Marie-Bernard was being faithful to other, prior, instructions which had insisted that she avoid drawing attention to herself. The issue of obedience related only to circumstances where she was directed by her superiors; she owed no duty to visitors who came to the convent but were not formally introduced to her. St Gildard was not an 'enclosed' convent. It was relatively easy for approved visitors, such as parents of Sisters or schoolgirls making a retreat, to enter the living quarters and try to seek out Bernadette. Sr Marie-Bernard had an amusing strategy to deal with these requests. When asked about Bernadette she would 'bow graciously and go off as if in search of her'.[35] One woman who asked her if she might see Bernadette was told, 'Certainly Madame. Watch that door, she will be going through it.' Sr Marie-Bernard then escaped through the door, leaving the visitor waiting and watching it.[36]

The game of finding and chasing Bernadette, that former individual who lived on through Sr Marie-Bernard, distorted her religious vocation. There is no indication that any of the Sisters felt envy of her special status, although one anecdote expresses why they could have. Sr Victoire Seurre had permission for a visit from her mother. Such family visits were rare privileges, but this one dissolved into a search for the coveted introduction.

I brought her [my mother] to St Gildard to satisfy her ardent desire to see Bernadette. Having glimpsed her on the terrace, I went towards her but as soon as she saw a stranger with me she hastened away. I finally caught up with her and said 'If your mother were here, I would receive her in a more friendly fashion.' Seeing that she had hurt me, she went immediately to my mother, greeting her affectionately and was very charming to her. So much so that my mother told me: 'I am very happy to have spent some time with you (she had not seen me in several long years) but I am even more happy to have kissed Bernadette.'[37]

Sr Victoire recalled this unbalanced statement with pride rather than rancour, but her mother's attitude is disquieting. Natural affections were set aside in favour of the false intimacy of a greeting from a celebrity, who was only induced to meet her by the dignified reproof of Sr Victoire, who pointed out that she would have done as much for Bernadette's mother. Except, of course, that Bernadette's mother would not have had any wish to meet a strange nun. On other occasions, Sr Marie-Bernard did not bother to be polite about people's relatives. Sr Raphael Laffaille told Sr Marie-Bernard that her brother, a priest, had seen her when she had been at Lourdes. Sr Marie-Bernard commented that 'He would have done better to stay at home.'[38]

When praying in the chapel, Sr Marie-Bernard had a habit of pulling her veil forward around her face. She said that it was 'a little chapel of my own'. People often slowed down when passing her in the chapel, in order to look at her face. One Sister followed her so closely that she even overheard Sr Marie-Bernard in the confessional. Aside from watching and listening, people sought her prayers. Sr Marie-Bernard refused to answer letters from the outside world, except those from her family. She was told that the pupils at the Hospice wanted her to answer their letters, but she declined to do so. 'Let them leave me in my solitude.'[39] Some people in the outside world could beseech her by asking Sisters to forward their requests. Sr Joseph Vidal, a young nun who was making a retreat at St Gildard in 1873, informed her correspondent of a veritable campaign to get prayers from Bernadette. Her description is vivid and unintentionally funny:

I have been happy to be able to go to Nevers in order to recommend your intentions, with still more insistence, if that is possible, to our dear Bernadette, whom my importunities did not leave alone for a moment. I have been repeating them to her even in church, and have made her pray especially for all the intentions of your well-loved family. I promise you that I have virtually broken the rules because they do not want us to address this angelic Sister directly, so many precautions are taken to preserve her virtue.[40]

Sisters who taught in the schools had a large number of prayers to ask. 'They would soon go to the group where Sr Marie-Bernard was during recreation, and it was there by preference that they would make their demands. The more daring would insist on a word from her: "Sr Marie-Bernard, did you hear what I have said?" – Yes, yes, I heard.'[41] Sometimes she would cut off such requests. On days of retreat Sisters would come after her, saying: 'This Monsieur, that Madame has asked for prayers from you.' Sr Marie-Bernard replied briskly 'They want prayers do they? Good, let them pray for me.'[42] As she had no hope of following up every request, Sr Marie-Bernard simply said a rosary every day for the benefit of those who had asked her to pray for them.

## Protests, historians and Lourdes

Until 1869, the negative consequences of so many visits was borne by Sr Marie-Bernard, rather than the community at St Gildard. Then, without warning, the quarrels which were dividing the town of Lourdes followed Sr Marie-Bernard to Nevers, and the St Gildard superiors were drawn into events.

Under the leadership of Père Sempé, the Missionaries of the Immaculate Conception had taken over the management of the Grotto. The community of Lourdes, even including its clergy, had no involvement with the shrine. This was a great blow to Curé Peyramale. He had begun to build a new, large parish church. As Curé of the parish, he had personally guaranteed the loans for the church, and donations from pilgrims were needed for its ambitious budget. The Lourdes faction of opinion supported Curé Peyramale, and they grew ever more bitter as the debts mounted and the Missionaries monopolized the Grotto. The most public of Curé Peyramale's supporters was the writer Henri Lasserre, who published the best seller, *Notre Dame de Lourdes*, in June 1868.

Henri Lasserre was known throughout France as a leading champion of the shrine at Lourdes. He visited the shrine in October 1862, and had been cured of having very weak eyesight by application of the water from the spring. He was a lawyer by profession, but had moved into the field of Catholic writing and journalism. He proposed to write an authoritative account of the apparitions at Lourdes, in order to replace the short volume written by Abbé Fourcade at the time of the Episcopal Inquiry. Henri Lasserre was authorized by the Bishop of Tarbes to write this history, but to the dismay of the Bishop, he became a friend, and then a vocal partisan, of Curé Peyramale. While awaiting the publication of Lasserre's book, the Bishop of Tarbes allowed a different text to appear. This was the *Petite histoire de Notre-Dame de Lourdes*, written by the two senior clerics at the Grotto, Père Duboé and Père Sempé. It was published in a serial form in the magazine *Annales de Notre-Dame de Lourdes*, in April 1868. Henri Lasserre was furious that the Bishop had allowed this publication. No writer likes to see a different book, on the same subject, appear shortly before their own publication. It also infringed on his personal status because, until then, Lasserre had been the sole official historian of the shrine.

In 1869 Henri Lasserre came to Nevers and visited St Gildard. He was well received by both the Bishop of Nevers and the convent authorities, none of whom were aware of the brewing quarrels in Lourdes. Henri Lasserre brought a copy of Père Duboé's *Petite Histoire* with him, and under the pretext of wanting to check its accuracy, arranged to read certain passages to Sr Marie-Bernard. Henri Lasserre found Père Duboé's text to be a most inferior work of history. According to Lasserre, it was based on gossip and hearsay, it embellished events in extravagant prose, and it presented a caricature of Bernadette. Lasserre was a biased critic, but it is true that Duboé's *Petite Histoire* was extremely over-drawn and inaccurate. Just as the Grotto was cut off from the Lourdes parish by the Pères de la Grotte, so also Bernadette was alienated from her neighbours and family in the texts which they produced. Henri Lasserre claimed that: 'In that account ... they have drawn a picture not of the simple and naive Bernadette whom everyone knew, but a puritan and bossy Bernadette, confirmed in bigotry, a Bernadette of fantasy, drawn by a gross form of art, and whom no-one can recognize.'[43]

In the parlour of the convent of St Gildard, Henri Lasserre read out the accounts of the apparitions. It included scenes of Bernadette appalled by her sister's immodesty as she crossed the millstream, and calling upon her to lower her skirt until it be soaked in water. In another improbable scenario, Bernadette had the effrontery to call her family to prayers, and led the saying of them. Sr Marie-Bernard stated that these, and several other anecdotes, were not true. This was music to the ears of Henri Lasserre, who planned to use her testimony to discredit the Pères de la Grotte. He wrote out a series of points on which she disagreed with the published version of events, and asked her to sign it. However, Sr Marie-Bernard, and the superiors, declined this, saying that she could sign nothing without the permission of the Bishop.

Henri Lasserre spent an afternoon at the convent, then dined with the Bishop of Nevers. Mgr Forcade was impressed by his erudite and charming guest. After some hours of general conversation, Henri Lasserre asked the Bishop for permission to visit St Gildard again before leaving Nevers. He said that as part of his work as an authorized historian of the shrine, he needed to obtain a signed declaration from Bernadette about certain important facts. As it was now late at night, the Bishop suggested that these matters could wait until the morning. Henri Lasserre told Mgr Forcade that he was obliged to leave that evening by the late train, in order to return to his wife who was about to give birth. At a later date, Mgr Forcade wrote irritably that he had wondered why, therefore, Henri Lasserre had left his wife at such a moment.[44] However, it was an assertion which the Bishop found difficult to contradict that evening. He allowed Henri Lasserre to 'clarify' points about the history of the apparitions, and to return to St Gildard and see Sr Marie-Bernard. The only limitation which the Bishop put on Henri Lasserre was that this declaration signed by Bernadette was not for publication.

Henri Lasserre returned to St Gildard, and showed the superiors that he had obtained the Bishop of Nevers's permission to sign his document. Sr Marie-Bernard duly affixed her signature. The Bishop of Nevers later claimed that he had misunderstood the nature of Henri Lasserre's document, and that Bernadette had misunderstood the 'permission' as being an order from him that she should sign it. In fact the document was a 'Protestation' against the published *Petite Histoire*. When Henri Lasserre forwarded a copy to the Bishop of Tarbes, he pointed out that Bernadette herself objected to his rival's work. He demanded that it be withdrawn. The existence of a declaration, signed by Bernadette, disputing with historians about the history of the apparitions, was a bombshell. The Bishop of Tarbes immediately wrote to the Bishop of Nevers and asked how such a thing could have been allowed. The Bishop of Nevers, in turn, descended upon the convent at St Gildard and informed the dismayed superiors that they had been caught up in a public scandal.

In itself the 'Protestation' was not a sensational document. Henri Lasserre claimed that he had written down exactly what Bernadette had told him. Many of the statements do indeed reflect the tone of her other declarations. She dismissed stories of improper conduct by her companions on the day of the first visions, and made points such as that: 'I knew only my rosary, and when we prayed together, it was always my mother who said the prayers.'[45] Henri Lasserre obviously added a final section which stated that she objected 'to the ensemble and physiognomy of the whole work'. These words are not likely to have been used by Sr Marie-Bernard, and she had not even read the book in question. In later copies of the Protestation, Henri Lasserre removed this sentence.

Père Sempé went immediately to Nevers to confront Sr Marie-Bernard. She was badly affected by the stress and became ill. Père Sempé emerges from the historical record as one of those people who eventually quarrels with everyone who crosses his path. While Henri Lasserre and Curé Peyramale were difficult people, there were innumerable others such as the Lourdes Parliamentary Deputy, Pyrenean clergy, and the Sisters of the Assumption, who all denounced Père Sempé in the strongest terms. On one occasion, the Vatican authorities had to intervene and inform him that he was not entitled to any power over convents of women religious at Lourdes. The superiors at St Gildard soon joined the large number of people who found Père Sempé overbearing. The tone of the documents in which he discusses his visit are revealing of his demanding nature. He arrived with the intention of getting Sr Marie-Bernard to sign a 'Counter-Protestation'.

I was convinced of the delicacy of that mission. To find Bernadette in contradiction with herself, seemed to me to be a great misfortune; to contribute to making her contradict herself, that would be in my eyes a great crime; to interrogate her with extreme simplicity and with the sole desire to arrive at the truth, was for me the most elementary and rigorous duty.[46]

Père Sempé found that: 'Like a child who has committed a fault, she feared to see me. She arrived in tears ...' At the end of their conversation she knelt to ask his blessing. 'It seemed to me that this was a reparation for the involuntary wrongs which M. Lasserre made her do toward the Missionaries of Notre Dame de Lourdes.'[47] Perhaps, but the truth was that he left without managing to make her sign a Counter-Protestation. Nor was he able to shift her on the actual matters in her statement. He questioned her and pointed out contradictions between her current and earlier accounts of details such as crossing the millstream on 11 February 1858. Did she or did she not say that the water was warm? Sr Marie-Bernard agreed that she might have compared it to 'dish water', as the witnesses agreed, but she could not remember having said so and she certainly could not remember having found the water hot. In the *Petite Histoire*, they had written that she exclaimed at the high temperature and had emerged with her feet conspicuously heated. Bernadette denied this, and Henri Lasserre, in the Protestation, commented that they were trying to make a miracle where there was none. Sr Marie-Bernard reaffirmed to Père Sempé that: 'I said only that I did not find the water cold, because the others had said it was icy.'[48]

Both Père Sempé and Henri Lasserre misunderstood Bernadette's appreciation of this scene. She was insensible of heat and cold immediately after the trance, and she was probably unable to feel any temperature in the water at all. The same issue of her unaware state made accounts of the second vision, when she was carried back to the Nicolau mill, a great matter of contention. In their history, the Missionaries stated that Bernadette had remained in a trance for the whole of the journey, and that she had continued to see the apparition which followed her to the mill. She had told Henri Lasserre, 'I do not remember any of that.'[49] Statements by other witnesses indicate that she was simply immobile and unaware of her surroundings. The idea that the Lady followed her is an obvious embroidery of the original story, but when confronted by Père Sempé, Sr Marie-Bernard had no means to deny it, because she could not remember any of these events. All that she could tell Père Sempé was that she: 'could not recall what happened that day, on the path from the grotto to the mill, nor at the mill'.[50] Père Sempé wrote these words down, then crossed them out and questioned her further. He then wrote: 'She does not deny having been carried to the mill, and having seen the Blessed Virgin there.'[51] Other points of contention were whether or not she saw a light before the apparition appeared, or if the light glowed after it vanished.

While the details were trivial, the questioners were motivated by weighty considerations. Curé Peyramale, Henri Lasserre, and the other members of the Lourdes faction were to suffer great financial losses because of their disadvantage before Père Sempé's power. The best weapon, for each side, was the word of Bernadette, her credibility and her allegiance. Bernadette's enraptured experiences in the Grotto had begun the whole thing, but the very nature of these experiences made her a poor witness. Dazzled by the beautiful Lady, she entered a different state of being. Upon her return to the ordinary world, she paid little attention to what she said or what others said to her. All of this had become completely distant in the intervening years, Sr Marie-Bernard had little in common with the fourteen-year-old girl who had run through the streets of Lourdes and pulled her stockings off to wade through a millstream.

Père Sempé found that by 1869: 'She did not want to say anything, and she kept repeating that she had forgotten, and that her account had been written down at the time, and that people should keep to what had been recorded then.'[52] Père Sempé was unable to make her side with him. His account glided around these difficulties. He claimed that she was willing to sign his document, but that he himself had decided not to ask her to, because it would have been 'a useless cruelty to impose a signature, as others have done, which would trouble her nervous conscience'.[53] He 'interrogated her for long periods' without getting anything better than 'it is proved that ... just as M. Lasserre has said himself: Bernadette has forgotten a great deal.'[54] Père Sempé passed into absolute falsehood in claiming that Henri Lasserre had long conversations alone with Bernadette, and that she cried and was ill after his visits. No visitors were ever alone with Sr Marie-Bernard at St Gildard, for the superiors chaperoned all her meetings. The Sisters of Nevers must have been outraged by some statements from Père Sempé. For example, he wondered aloud: 'What happened during those long conversations, and by what artfulness that insinuating and opinionated mind entered into Bernadette's confiding, naive soul and her always rather limited intelligence ...'[55]

One can see that possession of Bernadette, and possession of her story, has become a matter of rivalry, and even passionate jealousy. Père Sempé made the improbable claim that: 'The visits of M. Lasserre had left Bernadette in remorse and tears; mine left her joyful.'[56] The Sisters of Nevers flatly contradicted him on that point. Père Sempé seems to have made such a negative impression that Henri Lasserre rose in their estimation and remained as a friend of the community. Surprisingly, he was allowed to visit St Gildard again, although they reproached him over the affair of the Protestation. Mère Josephine Imbert reminded Lasserre that Sr Marie-Bernard did not protest against the 'ensemble and physiognomy' of the other history 'but only against the ensemble of facts which you cited to her. She had not read the *Annales de Lourdes*, any more than your book, you know it Monsieur!'[57] But she also stated in writing that Père Sempé's allegations were untrue. 'Sr Marie-Bernard was not troubled after your visit, but she was a great deal upset in the presence of Père Sempé; she wept and she contradicted herself by faults of memory on certain points of little importance.'[58]

Père Sempé returned to Lourdes with no signed document from Bernadette, and the Missionaries did not dare to reprint the *Petite Histoire* until decades later. Henri Lasserre continued his public battle with the Grotto authorities, and his various articles in the newspapers are judged to have caused the shrine 'great damage' during the 1870s.[59] Henri Lasserre's own book, *Notre Dame de Lourdes*, was almost as flowery and inaccurate as that of his rivals, but it succeeded in attracting many readers. The superiors at St Gildard decided that Lasserre still had credibility, and they declined to be drawn into Père Sempé's antagonisms. As women religious, they owed obedience to the clerical hierarchy, but there were so many factions in Lourdes that they were justified in keeping their distance from some of them. They felt profoundly sympathetic to Sr Marie-Bernard. The Journal of the Community recorded that:

> Sr Marie-Bernard is constantly suffering, and due to her state of health we are secluding her from the numerous visitors who ask to see her. Our good little Sister, always simple and modest, fears nothing more than visitors and questions. She has, however, been obliged to reply to questions asked of her by the authors who write about the apparitions at Lourdes. Our Sister always replies to them with the directness and simplicity which is natural to her. One of these writers, M. Henri Lasserre, has been generally applauded for his book entitled *Notre-Dame de Lourdes*, approved by Pius IX.[60]

Faced with all the controversies arising from Henri Lasserre's history book, the Bishop of Tarbes tried to mend matters by commissioning a new historian. This was Père Cros, a learned Jesuit who began working in a serious way by collecting documents and oral testimonies. He was rapidly drawn into the atmosphere of rivalry among the Lourdes writers, and he became convinced that his own work would be monumental, and based solely on the truth with every fact verified. He also aimed to show that every other history and memoir, whether authorized by the Bishop or not, was a pathetic failure. Cros's work was to raise a host of new controversies, and eventually the Bishop of Tarbes was to regret ever having heard of him. He did not regret these histories as much as Sr Marie-Bernard did. She suffered a great deal of stress in 1867. She had never been willing to talk about the apparitions, but during her Nevers years, as she was interrogated by obsessive historians, she became afraid to do so.

# NOTES

1. Mère Philomena Roques, 'Un portrait de Soeur Marie-Bernard', Guynot, *Contemporains*, 87.

2. Sr Eudoxie Chatelain, Guynot, *Contemporains*, 37–8.

3. Sr Dominique Larretchard, *PON*, Sessio XV, 205.

4. Quoted, Trochu, *Sainte Bernadette*, 496–7

5. Ibid., 496.

6. Advice to Sr Julie Garros, Laurentin, *Vie*, 245.

7. Sr Clair Bordes quoted, *Logia*, no. 488, 170.

8. Marcel Bouix, *Apparitions de Notre Dame de Lourdes et particularités de la vie de Bernadette et du pèlerinage* (Paris 1878), 246.

9.  Sr Marie Joséphine Forestier, *PON*, Sessio XIV, 195.

10. Sr Marguerite Marcillac, *PON*, Sessio XXXVII, 524.

11. Sr Marie Joséphine Forestier, *PON*, Sessio XIV, 200.

12. Sr Casimir Callery, *PON*, Sessio XXXIX, 549.

13. Sr Marie Joséphine Forestier, *PON*, Sessio XIV, 204.

14. Ibid., 200.

15. Sr Dominique Brunet, Guynot, *Contemporains*, 168.

16. Sr Victoire Cabanié, ibid., 170.

17. Marie Jeanne Garnier, in religion Sr Joseph, *PON*, Sessio C, 1151.

18. Ibid.

19. Sr Julie Durand, *RdC*, 41.

20. *Logia*, 2. 52.

21. Abbé Peyramale to Sr Marie-Bernard, 9 Nov. 1868, *ESB*, no. 100, 275.

22. Mgr Lelong, *Allocution prononcée par Mgr l'évêque de Nevers dans la chapelle de la maison-mère des Soeurs de Nevers, aux obsèques de Bernadette Soubirous, en religion Sr Marie-Bernard, le 19 avril 1879* (Nevers n.d.).

23. Ibid.

24. Mère Générale and Mère Secrétaire, Interview with Père Cros, 1878, *ESB*, 517.

25. Joséphine Marie Constance Forestier, in religion Sr Marie Joséphine, *PON*, Sessio VII, 130.

26. Marie Jeanne Garnier, in religion Sr Joseph, *PON*, Sessio C, 3. 1145.

27. Mère Générale and Mère Secrétaire, Interview with Père Cros, 1878, *ESB*, 517.

28. Cited by Bordenave, *La Confidente*, 115.

29. Sr Joseph Caldairou, *PON*, Sessio XXIV, 296.

30. Bordenave, *La Confidente*, 116.

31. Quoted, *BVP*, 2. 339.

32. Bordenave, *La Confidente*, 118.

33. Ibid., 116.

34. Ibid., 117.

35. Ibid., 118.

36. Guynot, *Contemporains*, 208.

37. Bordenave, *La Confidente*, 119.

38. Jeanne Crillon, in religion Sr Veronique, *PON*, Sessio XLVII, 622.

39. Témoignage de Sr Aurélie Gouteyron, Sept. 1873, *ESB*, 324.

40. Témoignage de Soeur Joseph Vidal, 29 Sept. 1873, *ESB*, no. 140, 324–5.

41. Mère Julienne Capmartin, Guynot, *Contemporains*, 51.

42. Bordenave, *La Confidente*, 123.

43. Henri Lasserre, 'Très humble supplique et mémoire', 3 Nov. 1869, *AG*, A38.

44. Forcade, Postscript to *Notice sur la vie*, 52–62.

45. Protestation, 3 Nov. 1869, *AG*, A38.

46. Letter from Père Sempé to the Bishop of Tarbes, *AG*, A39, 11.

47. Ibid., 18.

48. *BVP*, 2. 86.

49. *BVP*, 2. 90.

50. Père Sempé's notes are quoted with an explanation by Laurentin, *BVP*, 2. 101.

51. Ibid.

52. Ibid., 106.

53. Ibid., 103.

54. Letter from Père Sempé to the Bishop of Tarbes, *AG*, A39.

55. Letter from Père Sempé to the Bishop of Tarbes, *AG*, A39, 18.

56. Ibid., 15.

57. Mère Imbert's letter, 10 Dec. 1869, *BVP*, 2. 100.

58. Mère Josephine Imbert, *PON*, Sessio CXII, 1283.

59. Harris, *Lourdes: Body and Spirit*, 192.

60. Journal of the Community, 16 Nov. 1869, *ESB*, 261.

# CHAPTER 10

# Silence of the Self
## Bernadette as a Sister of Nevers

*... humility consists of the 'silence of the self'. With Bernadette, that was it. In her, there was no 'me'.*

Recollections of Sr Saint-Michel Duhème

The everlasting position of being the visionary went on and on, but at St Gildard Sr Marie-Bernard at least had other roles to play at different times. There were more satisfactions, and even a degree of personal autonomy, in her working life. As a novice, she had been assigned the duty of writing letters for the Secretary's office at St Gildard, but it was said that this work did not suit her. Sr Marie-Bernard's post there is scarcely mentioned in memoirs of her life. Sr Valentine Gleyrose explained that 'she showed little inclination for the work, it rather bored her'.[1] As her spelling was very poor, and her literacy only recently acquired, she may have been given this task in order to practice writing. After the scalding interview at the time of her profession it was suggested that she work in the infirmary, and she took up this duty at the end of 1867. She had the title of aide-infirmarian. The title of infirmarian was still held by Sr Marthe Forest, who was too ill to actively manage her post any longer, and had in fact become a patient. As aide-infirmarian, Sr Marie-Bernard soon had full responsibility for the nursing rooms and their patients. It was to be the most demanding and authoritative job in her short working life.

Sr Marie-Bernard's work in the infirmary ranged from the most menial tasks, such as serving food and emptying bedpans, to the most responsible, in particular making up the medicines in the pharmacy. The infirmary was scattered over several rooms. There were rows of ten or twelve beds in each room, which were known by saints' names – 'St Martha's Room', 'La Sainte Croix', etc. The pharmacy, which also functioned as Sr Marie-Bernard's office, was a small adjoining area, furnished with shelves and a desk. To judge from photographs, it had the appearance of a nineteenth-century laboratory. It was partly antique, with surfaces of polished wood and brass, but also ornamented with the mysteries of science – bubbles of glass, miniature scales, and walls covered in jars of coloured powders.

The patient records from the infirmary of the 1870s have not been preserved, and indeed, comprehensive medical notes of the modern type were probably never made. Sr Marie-Bernard's notes were only kept as souvenirs of herself, and their actual content is so far from being seen as important that they are not reproduced in full in her *Complete Works*.[2] The notes were

**Plate XIII**   Sr Marie-Bernard. © *Convent of St Gildard*

utilitarian. Some were instructions about medicine and treatments, jotted down according to the doctor's words. She made a lengthy table converting the weights and measures of Old Regime France to the decimal system. This was necessary as many medicines were made according to pre-1780s prescriptions. There were instructions on how to make medicines by mixing, by solution, by distillation and by evaporation. There were also lists of medicines for haemorrhaging, dysentery, scrofula and fever. It is impossible to say what illnesses Sr Marie-Bernard encountered in her patients. Only a few cases have been preserved through the memoirs of witnesses, and these included conjunctivitis, influenza, breast cancer and at least one case of the dangerous typhoid fever. It is also likely that the infirmary had patients with tuberculosis.

Sr Marie-Bernard's work in the pharmacy was, in theory, not in accord with the regulations of the French state. This was because she was not a member of an accredited pharmacists' association. Nor could she ever have joined such an institute, because they did not admit women. The practice of pharmacy at St Gildard had been a matter of controversy in the decade before Bernadette's arrival. French doctors maintained a constant battle against nuns, whom they accused of the illegal and unqualified practice of medicine. In the town of Nevers, this medical demarcation dispute was also maintained by chemists, who felt that their exclusive right to practise pharmacy was being intruded upon, sometimes by doctors, but more often by religious sisters. In 1859 the Société des Pharmaciens de la Nièvre had been formed. They challenged the right of doctors to provide medicines, although doctors also complained that pharmacists in their turn often illegally practised medicine. The pharmacists also complained about:

> the constantly growing abuse, and illegal procedures of the Soeurs de la Charité de Nevers in the question of pharmacy. At Nevers this competition is ever more open: we are in the presence of a central laboratory, furnished with a small pharmacy school, which has Sisters for its teacher and pupils. With the aid of a token pharmacist, who lends them his name, the Dames de la Charité have gained a considerable understanding of commercial operations, they deliver medicaments to all and provision the religious pharmacies of the département. It is noted that they make a true form of commerce from these illegal practices, it is profitable to their interests, and it deprives both the rich and the poor of the medicines which the pharmacist has the sole right to prepare and sell.[3]

The outraged tones of these complaints eventually reached the Minister of Agriculture and Commerce, who in turn approached Mgr Forcade, the Bishop of Nevers. In 1861, before Sr Marie-Bernard arrived at St Gildard, the Sisters of Charity closed their pharmacy and no longer dispensed medicines. The superiors of St Gildard evidently tried to mend the rift, and even offered to sell their equipment and materials to the Société des Pharmaciens. The pharmacists also wanted to close any repository of medicines within convents. The career of Sr Marie-Bernard shows that this had not been achieved.

By the time that Sr Marie-Bernard worked in the infirmary, she had left the secular world far behind her. The only lay person who could freely visit a convent was the doctor – at St Gildard this was Robert Saint-Cyr, a senior physician who was Président de la Société des Médecins de la Nièvre. He was an almost daily visitor, as the large community constantly had Sisters in the infirmary. The superiors sought his opinion when considering the health of novices who might be too weak for religious life. Unmoved by the pleas of sickly novices – 'his severity was proverbial'[4] – he was inclined to send many girls home. The superiors adhered to his judgements, and he had a level of influence which even the convent chaplain rarely attained. He saw the Sisters in every stage of their lives, decided their fate at the outset, and was privy to the distressing scenes of physical degeneration and mental breakdown which were sometimes found in the convent infirmary.

Robert Saint-Cyr had a generally high opinion of the Sisters of Nevers. Sr Marie-Bernard was his patient from her early days as a novice, and went on to work under his direction in the infirmary. True to his discretion as a physician, he did not mention her in the outside world, but he was given the duty of speaking out when her name was besmirched by the medical profession. Bernadette's disappearance from the outside world generally went without comment, but those who were hostile to the Lourdes miracles assumed that she was being hidden for disreputable reasons. Doctor Voisin, a physician at the famous Paris mental asylum the Salpêtrière, alleged in 1872 that: 'The miracle at Lourdes was based on the faith of an hallucinating girl, who is now shut away in a convent of the Ursulines at Nevers.'[5]

The church authorities evidently thought that they could not afford to allow such a statement to stand, and Mgr Forcade published a denial in the newspaper *Univers*. The Bishop began by pointing out the unanswerable but not very important point that Bernadette had never set foot in an Ursuline convent in her life, but rather was in the congregation of the Sisters of Nevers, where she entered and stayed as freely as any other Sister. He went on to say that 'far from being insane', she was a person of unusual wisdom and tranquillity, and moreover, that Dr Voisin, or any other professor from the Salpêtrière, was free to examine her:

> If he has the goodness to let me know the date of his arrival, I shall arrange to put him in contact with Sr Marie-Bernard and, in order that he could have no doubt about her identity, I will ask M. Le Procureur of the Republic to present her. It will then be allowed that he can examine her, and question her, for as long as he pleases.[6]

Sr Marie-Bernard would not have thanked the Bishop for making this offer, but the confident tone of Mgr Forcade's pronouncement had its effect. Neither Dr Voisin, nor any of his colleagues, ever took it up. The allegation that Bernadette eventually deteriorated into insanity continued to be made in rationalist literature, and was a required outcome according to the psychiatric theories of the time. As one doctor wrote in 1910:

What became of Bernadette after the Apparitions? It is probable that the hysterical sickness continued to develop under various forms ... which happens in the case of these neurotics. If Bernadette, at a later time, was taken from her family in order to be placed firstly in a convent in Lourdes then, not long after, in a monastery of the Sisters of Nevers, it is likely that this was because other symptoms developed, very unsuitable for a person sanctified by contact with the Immaculate Conception.[7]

This statement indicates a preoccupation with female sexuality, which was marked in the psychiatry of the era. If Bernadette had been examined by such medical experts, it would have been an unpleasant experience for her.

Dr Voisin's allegations were picked up in medical circles, and Dr Saint-Cyr took the trouble to write in detail to a colleague who made enquiries of him. In September 1872 he addressed Dr Damouseau, who was president of the medical society of Orne.

My Dear Colleague,

You could not do better than to ask me for the details which you wish to have about the girl from Lourdes, who is today Sr Marie-Bernard. As the doctor to this Convent, I have given attention for some time to this young Sister, the poor health of whom was an issue of some concern. She is now much better, and from being a patient has become a nurse, and perfectly fulfils her new role.

Small, and of a delicate appearance, she is twenty-seven years old. She has a calm and sweet nature, she cares for her patients with much intelligence, and never fails in the details of any instructions given. She has great authority in her work, and I have complete confidence in her.

You can see, my dear colleague, that this young Sister is far from being insane. I would say more: her calm nature, simple and sweet, gives not the slightest cause for any apprehensions of that sort.[8]

Unused to writing descriptions, Dr Saint-Cyr repeats the words calm and sweet twice, it seems that this was the only way that he could describe her. She had vanquished any prejudices which he may have had about her as an ill-educated peasant, and one notes that his admiring words include a description of her refined appearance. Sr Marthe du Rais stated that he 'greatly esteemed her; he almost had a veneration for her, because she cared for the sick so expertly ...'[9]

We do not have any words from Sr Marie-Bernard, as nobody asked her what she thought of her physician and senior colleague. When entertaining the other Sisters during recreation, she often recounted amusing scenes from the infirmary, and one former novice stated that Sr Marie-Bernard could do very comic imitations of the doctor: 'she would relate funny stories, and we would laugh as one only laughs at that age ... she never spoke of her home or childhood; it was generally the little scenes in the infirmary, where Dr Robert sometimes played a role. This good man had his little ways, which we all knew well; and Bernadette diverted us to the point of tears in imitating him, with a lively spirit and even a touch of malice. But the bounds of charity were always respected.'[10] Sr Marie-Bernard's skills as an actress and mimic were unimpaired by convent life. The scenes in recreation do not necessarily indicate a straightforward mockery of the doctor, for both the actress and her audience are indicating a fondness in their observation of him. He was the only man whom they could comment upon, such levity about a priest would have been unthinkable, and his special role within the convent, as a liminal figure between themselves and the outside world, was reaffirmed by their keen awareness of his presence. Dr Saint-Cyr and Sr Marie-Bernard were on good terms during most of her life at St Gildard, although there was to be an unexpected decline in their relationship before her death.

During the 1870s there were radical changes of government in France, but the day-to-day controversies did not penetrate the convent parlours. Ordinary women usually did not read newspapers. Nuns certainly did not. But the changes which shook France during the 1870s were so enormous that they reverberated even in the cloisters, and had even the Sisters at St Gildard exchanging the latest rumours of events.

In 1870 war broke out between France and the newly unified states of Germany. The French government was overconfident, and took on the Germans without considering the advances in organization and technology which Bismarck had introduced. The French army was ill-equipped and old-fashioned; once on the field of battle their tactics, and even their uniforms, were revealed as no more than a nostalgia for the days of the Napoleonic wars. Dressed in field grey and armed with weapons such as the rapid-fire machine gun, the Germans advanced quickly across France.

The Emperor Napoleon III had ruled France since 1851, when Bernadette was seven years old. His regime, the Second Empire, dominated France for the whole of her lifetime, but now this old order was passing away. She saw it go without any regret or perturbation. More remarkably, she seems to have felt no interest in the violent events which were sweeping the land.

The German army occupied much of France and stormed Paris. Nevers was hard hit by the war, it is a city just south of the capital, strategically placed on the major routes. It was a focus for the Prussian advance in 1870, just as it was to be flooded with refugees after the fall of France in 1940. In December 1870 ordinary activities were suspended, the superiors of the community were assembled daily to be informed of events. A field hospital with twenty beds was set up inside St Gildard. Wounded troops were nursed, and emergency assistance was also given to the injured and homeless who called at the door. Although Sr Marie-Bernard was the acting infirmarian, she did not participate in these activities, but stayed in the convent infirmary, where there were still many sick Sisters in her care.

The war went badly for France, but hope died slowly and rumours swept the distressed nation. On 2 December 1870 the Sisters recorded that: 'We have just learnt, at 10 in the evening, of a victory over the enemy forces at Paris. That news revived everyone's courage, and the Bishop ordered that a Te Deum be sung.' By 9 December they had a picture of the true position. 'It has been announced that the Prussians are at the borders of the département. All of the town of Nevers is in uproar. Our wounded officers (from the field hospital) fear to be taken prisoner, and have fled south, but, in parting, they expressed their gratitude for the care which they had received.'[11]

The Prussians took control of the city. They entered in an orderly manner, but as conquerors. They lodged their troops in the Bishop's residence, and the Sisters were obliged to have some of their horses in the convent stables. They were fortunate that they merely had to take horses, rather than having a large number of Prussian troops billeted with them. This happened in many of the larger French convents and monasteries. St Gildard was still dominated by the field hospital, which was filled with defeated troops too ill to flee. Thus the whole of December dragged on amid crisis. On Christmas Day, the chapel was not open to the public for midnight Mass, and the choir service during the day was cancelled.

Sr Marie-Bernard seems to have taken it for granted that the war would not touch her personally. She regarded the Prussians with indifference. In theory, the Sisters were supposed to be above nationalistic politics, but their country was at war, and of course many shared the emotions of panic at defeat and hatred of the enemy. Sr Marie-Bernard failed to join in, and instead set an example of non-patriotism and indifference before fate. In November 1870 she wrote to her father, who had planned to visit Nevers until the outbreak of war had paralysed the whole country. Only one fragment of her letter survives, and it represents one of her rare comments on the war:

> It is said that the enemy is approaching Nevers. I could do without seeing the Prussians, but I do not fear them: God is everywhere, even in the midst of the Prussians. I can remember that when I was little, after a sermon by M. le Curé, I would hear people say: 'Bah! He is just doing his job.' I think that the Prussians are also doing their job ...[12]

In October 1870, with the other Sisters, she stood on a terrace at St Gildard to see a spectacular atmospheric event which turned the whole of the evening sky scarlet. They remembered that she sighed and commented, 'still, people are not converted', which indicates that at this moment she saw nature as a portent of the divine.[13] The evening sky may have made some watchers fearful: 'one would have said that it was a sea of blood'.[14]

It was easier for Sr Marie-Bernard to be tranquil during wartime as, unlike many other Sisters at St Gildard, she did not have a member of her family in the armed forces. She sympathized with several Sisters who worried about their brothers, but she did not believe that Sisters should concern themselves with dramatic items of news.

If the French public had known that Bernadette of Lourdes had nothing to say about the war, they would have been aghast, or disbelieving. She was an icon of Catholic France, a fervent, patriotic group who were horrified by events and were searching for omens about the proper direction of their country. French Catholics awaited news with the greatest anxiety, they shared this fate with everyone. Particular to themselves was an inclination to listen to clerical advice, a scrutiny of the disasters as a punishment for the sins of the secular government, and a longing for signs and portents. At St Gildard the superiors were aware that the name of Bernadette of Lourdes was being invoked by agitated fellow-citizens. 'A rumour circulated in several towns that Sister Marie-Bernard has had new visions and that she has an important mission to fulfil in respect of the government. Our Reverend Mother has had numerous letters about this, and has replied that the story is false.'[15] The Bishop of Nevers inserted a notice in the Catholic newspaper, *La semaine religieuse*, to the same effect. If Sr Marie-Bernard knew of these rumours, an attitude of sullen indifference might have been her reaction to such extravagant hopes. It could also have further influenced whatever image she had of French society.

Sr Marie-Bernard almost never passed beyond the walled gardens of St Gildard. On the sole occasion when she went with the other Sisters for the procession of the feast of the Assumption at the cathedral of Nevers, she had been suddenly recognized and surrounded by a crowd of people crying 'Bernadette! Bernadette!'[16] In her view, the world outside the gates was filled with an hysterical acclamation which prevented her from leaving the convent or having a career as a working Sister. Because of such crowds, she could not go outside, she could not visit Lourdes or ever see her home and family again. In 1871, they even expected her to predict the outcome of the war. People who were in the midst of a national crisis, like people who were very ill, were inclined to fasten their hopes upon Bernadette. Since 1866, she had spent her life avoiding them.

If Bernadette of Lourdes was unable to supply any revelations for suffering France, others filled this natural need in popular consciousness. At the town of Pontmain, on 17 January 1871, a group of children saw an image of the Virgin Mary reflected in the night sky. A message in writing then unfurled around her, promising hope to those who prayed. Crowds gathered at the site, and it was said that none of the men of Pontmain who were serving in the war were killed. One is able to relate, with relief, that this charming vision did not destroy the lives of those who received it. The children of Pontmain were not appropriated by public desire, they never became celebrities. This may have been because they were a group, so that the event was not focused upon a powerful individual figure. Another factor was that the Pontmain vision was particular to the war of 1871, and although the shrine remained and was respected, its message quickly faded in later years. It is one of the innumerable little shrines in France. Each of the children of Pontmain went on to live an ordinary life. They simply joined their fellow parishioners as honoured members of the community, not as seers.

The Franco-Prussian war culminated in the tragic drama of the Paris Commune of 1871. The people of besieged Paris were so dissatisfied with the conduct of the war by Louis Napoleon and his generals that they threw off the authority of the French state. A revolutionary, socialist government was formed. The Paris Commune drew inspiration from the revolution of 1848, but its tone was harsher and less utopian. The events of the Paris Commune echoed across the nation, and were as mythic and resonant as anything that had ever come from Lourdes. The revolutionaries took on the role required by their national history, rising up from the lowest depths, speaking the name of liberty, and flying their secular icon – the tricoloured flag. They were opposed by the middle classes, the conservatives and the fearful. Opponents of the revolution drew a picture of frightful mobs desecrating the national capital, destroying France at a time of war, and threatening the whole nation with anarchy.

During the revolution of 1848 the Catholic Church had been sympathetic to the people's will, and Curés in parishes across the nation had blessed liberty trees in order to commemorate the event. By 1871, such liberal sentiments were long gone. The socialists and the Catholics hated each other to the point of extremism. Clerical opinion was hostile to the Commune from its first days. These sentiments were confirmed on 24 May 1871 when the communades who held the Archbishop of Paris, Georges Darboy, as a prisoner, suddenly put him to death. His secretarial staff, and other priests, were also subject to summary execution. The French Army was sent to subdue the capital, and fought with the people of Paris between 21 and 28 May. It was known as the 'bloody week'. At least 30,000 people were killed during these events, and some estimates of the casualties go as high as 100,000. The Commune fell on 28 May 1871, but the killings continued, with both unofficial reprisals and legalized executions of communades.

We do not have one word from Sr Marie-Bernard about the Paris Commune, a conspicuous silence. These were issues talked about everywhere, and people tended to memorialize anything that Bernadette said, especially about events of importance. It may be that she said absolutely nothing, and was silent out of consternation, passivity, or because of her awareness of her own ignorance of politics. News circulated of the scandals, such as when the communades burnt the Tuileries, a spectacular palace in Paris. Sr Madeleine Bounaix rushed to tell her of this, but Sr Marie-Bernard checked her enthusiastic informant with the remark: 'Don't worry about it. They would have been in need of cleaning, the Good Lord has swept them out.'[17] She said nothing more, and Sr Madeleine found that 'it disconcerted me a little'.[18] We have only one remark from her, several years later. In 1875 she wrote to her family, at a time when she was concerned about floods which had devastated the south of France and caused many casualties. She interpreted these events as divine punishment, and linked this to the events of the Commune:

> We are punished by God ... The streets of Paris have run with blood of a great number of victims, and this has not sufficed to touch hearts which are hardened by sin; it seems now that the streets of the south must also be washed and that they also have their victims. My God! How blind people are if they do not open their eyes to the light of faith! After such dreadful misfortunes, would we not ask ourselves what could have provoked such chastisements? Listen well, and from our own hearts comes a voice which tells us: it is sin, yes sin, because the greatest sins provoke the greatest punishments. The harm which we have done through malice rebounds on us; see the happiness and advantages which we get through the work of sin.[19]

This is a pious and emotional reaction to the misfortunes of the 1870s, yet it is also quite detached. The streets of Paris have run with blood, but with whose blood? That of the insurrectionaries or their opponents? She does not say, and discusses it as if it was a natural disaster, which was inevitably followed by others.

The year of 1871 also brought sad news to her at a personal level. In February 1871 the four-year-old daughter of Toinette Soubirous, who was named Bernadette, died. Then in March 1871 her brothers wrote to inform her that their father, François Soubirous, had died after a short illness, at the age of sixty-four. This was a sudden event; only a few months earlier, in December 1870, he had been well enough to propose a visit to Nevers. The visit had been postponed because of the war. Sr Marie-Bernard wrote to her sister Toinette, saying 'I have just cried with you, but let us be resigned and submissive, although quite afflicted ... My dear sister, I have shared some of the pain which your maternal heart must have felt on losing your little Bernadette, but console yourself, she is an angel in heaven now, praying for us who have so much need for it. It also seems that our Aunt Lucile is very ill, perhaps she is now dead. I am expecting news, please write to me, and do not hide any news from me.'[20] Lucile Castérot, in her turn, died on 16 March.

When writing a condolence letter to her brother Pierre Soubirous, Sr Marie-Bernard asked him to pray for the souls of their parents and their aunt, also 'do not forget our sister Marie (Toinette) in your prayers, she has need of support and health to take care of her little son. Her maternal heart has greatly suffered because of the loss of little Bernadette.'[21] Toinette's son, Bernard Sabathé, was only one year old. He had been born with a club foot and had poor health. On 30 August he also died. Toinette Soubirous had six children, but only one survived until adulthood. He was Jean-Alexis Sabathé, who in turn was to be one of the countless French soldiers who died in 1915 on the battlefields of the First World War. He was not born until 1880, several years after the death of his famous aunt. The Soubirous family never seemed to escape their heritage of poverty and early death.

## Infirmarian

In an optimistic moment, Sr Marie-Bernard began her personal notebook of 1873 with the words: 'That which concerned me no longer concerns me, from now on I belong entirely to God.'[22] Most of her writings are attempts to reach this goal. In her own notebooks, there are no mentions of Lourdes, or of the past. Rather, she was concerned with religious life, with the rules of the convent, and ways to improve her own spirituality.

There is no indication that Sr Marie-Bernard was restless in the enclosed world of St Gildard. Although she longed for work and responsibility in the active houses of the order, she does not seem to have chafed against the confines of the Mother House. It was a huge convent, with large grounds, and she sometimes walked the whole length of the gardens to visit the shrine of Notre Dame des Eaux. This was a pretty white statue of the Virgin Mary, which stood in the furthest corner of the St Gildard garden. It marked the site of the convent's original well. Although she rarely liked statues, Sr Marie-Bernard seems to have enjoyed this modest outdoor shrine. As a novice, she asked Mère Marie-Thérèse for permission to visit it every day. The request was granted, and indeed, such visits may have been common for the whole community. In order to reach it, Sr Marie-Bernard walked down long paths through greenery. The chance to be outside may have been one of the attractions of the shrine. St Gildard had a courtyard, and extensive decorative gardens around three sides of the convent. These were in the formal French style, with lawns, clipped cypresses and lavender beds. Like most convents, St Gildard also devoted a large piece of land to vegetables and fruit. It was this kitchen garden which Sr Marie-Bernard walked through to reach the shrine.

Within the convent, Sr Marie-Bernard worked in spacious rooms with bare white walls and uneven polished wooden floors. St Gildard had the austerity of a religious house. There was no individualism in decoration, nor any comforts such as plush furniture. But like many of the larger convents, it was extensive and impressive, and the neediness of poverty was far removed from its grand structures. The only form of decoration at St Gildard was in the form of religious art, especially statues. The Sisters were responsible for keeping these simple works of art clean and dusted, and sometimes ornamented with flowers. The statue in the garden was the only one which Sr Marie-Bernard liked. She often made disparaging remarks about the art in the convent, and asked other Sisters if they really did find the statues attractive. Once, when cleaning a statue, Sr Marie-Bernard climbed all the way up and stood in the niche on the wall. She commented: 'I am putting myself in a niche while I live, for fear of not being there after my death.'[23]

This enigmatic remark seems to have been a joke about the general expectation that the visionary of Lourdes would eventually become a saint. A companion once exclaimed: 'Sr Marie-Bernard you will not be canonized because you take snuff. St Vincent de Paul almost missed being made a saint because of his snuff box.' Sr Marie-Bernard commented dryly: 'And you, Sr Casimir, you who do not take snuff, you will undoubtedly be canonized.'[24]

Despite the light repartee, most people took this subject seriously, and would often try to get 'relics' by getting her to touch rosary beads, holy cards or other items. She would not do so willingly. One redoubtable attempt to get an object which had been touched by Saint Bernadette was made by a bishop who visited St Gildard in 1873. She was ill and confined to the infirmary. As Sr Eléonore Bonnet said: 'The Sisters in the parlour had told the visitor, in vain, that Sr Marie-Bernard was ill. He declared himself willing to go up, if the Sister could not come down.' Mère Louise Ferrand, a high-ranking superior, went to conduct him to the infirmary. At the end of his conversation with Sr Marie-Bernard, he dropped his cap onto her bed and did not pick it up, leaving her to return it to him. But Sr Marie-Bernard merely looked at it and did nothing. Finally the Bishop was obliged to say to her: 'Would you return my cap to me?' But she refused, saying: 'Monseigneur, I did not ask you for your cap; you dropped it, now you can pick it up.'[25] Mère Louise intervened at this point, and told Sr Marie-Bernard to do as the Bishop asked. Many of the Sisters at St Gildard wanted to obtain 'some sort of souvenir of

Sr Marie-Bernard; but she was on her guard, and it was not easy to outdo her in finesse'.[26] Sr Claire Bordes wanted her to touch a rosary, but knew if she asked directly she would be refused. So she asked her to look at the chain, saying that she thought it was rusty. Sr Marie-Bernard replied that it must be because she wasn't using them often enough.[27]

These attentions were objectionable enough within the convent, but Sr Marie-Bernard was angry when it appeared that her family at Lourdes was involved. During the 1870s, her sister and brothers were involved in trade through religious goods stalls. Sr Marie-Bernard would have preferred that they stay at the mill, and that their children go to school. Rumours reached her from Lourdes, and Sr Casimir heard her speaking of her 'discontent that some of her relatives used her name as an advertisement for their commerce'. These ventures went badly, and Sr Marie-Bernard was not at all surprised: 'God could not bless that.'[28] She also heard that her letters were being passed around as souvenirs for pilgrims, and she threatened to stop writing if this continued.

Sr Marie-Bernard was very different from the girl who had once lived in Lourdes. As a sixteen-year-old she had leaned out a window of the school to tell her sister that she should not bother to learn how to write. In the intervening years, she had come to see the value of education, and even seems to have hoped that her family would improve their situation. During the 1860s Toinette Soubirous had in fact improved her literacy and was able to exchange letters to Nevers. In her own correspondence, Sr Marie-Bernard constantly reminded them to send the younger generation to school, and to extend their education as long as possible. Sr Marie-Bernard was very worried by news that her younger brother Pierre Soubirous might be leaving the college at Garaison, where he was receiving a good education, and be set to work in a religious goods store which her family was planning to open. She refused to consent to this move. 'You must not impede the child's studies.'[29]

The concern that her younger relatives be educated remained as a preoccupation for the rest of her life. The last letter she was to write, only a few months before she died, was addressed to her cousin Bernadette Nicolau. She had just left school at the age of fifteen, which was a late age by the standards of her time. But Sr Marie-Bernard found it a pity: 'I regret to see you leave classes so young; it is the moment when you would profit most, at present when you have more years and reason.'[30] The only move that she ever made to have a material benefit from the Church was when she wrote to Curé Peyramale and Père Sempé during the 1870s, in order to press the claims of her young relatives who needed free places at Catholic schools.

While Sr Marie-Bernard was very interested in her family, she maintained as much distance as possible from the Lourdes shrine. She was sent a booklet of songs, made for use in the Grotto, but took the first chance she had to give it away. She said to Sr Bernard Dalias: 'Here, take it, it is more your affair than mine. I have permission to give it away.'[31] When Sr Irène Ganier showed her a picture of the Grotto, Sr Marie-Bernard was polite but not expansive. She commented that she could hardly recognize it, but then agreed to point out the location where she had knelt and where the water had flowed.[32] Sr

Irène found that on another occasion showing Sr Marie-Bernard pictures was not worth it. When confronted with a banner of Notre Dame de Lourdes 'she turned away with a shrug, her expression seemed to say, "What is that?"'[33]

Sr Marie-Bernard feared that she would be left in purgatory, with no one praying for her soul. 'They will come after my death, she said, to touch rosaries against me, and at the same time, I will be burning in purgatory.'[34] She frequently told other Sisters that she was afraid of purgatory, and asked for their prayers. Usually she was cheerful, but there were periods in her religious life when she was overwhelmed by a sense of sin, of having received many graces in life but having responded to them poorly.

When Sr Marie-Bernard spoke of having been unworthy of graces in her life, she never specified what they were. The most obvious reading of this statement would be that she felt that she had inadequately received the honour of the visions. But this is not necessarily the case. 'Graces' were a theological term for a person's general circumstances. People who were sullen, indifferent or recalcitrant could be reproached for the 'abuse of grace' – a serious sin.

The *Trésor spirituel des Soeurs de la Charité*, a spiritual guide written especially for the Sisters of Nevers, had a section entitled 'Sur l'abus des Grâces'. The Sisters were warned that: 'It is essential not to abuse grace ... These graces are not only the inspiration of the Holy Spirit, but also all that happens to one – both sad and joyful – i.e. the severities of a superior, the wisdom of a confessor.' A life lived with outward compliance, and no real conscience, was an example of the abuse of grace. It was one of those interior sins which could only be perceived by the person themselves. The consequence, they were warned, was: 'She who is accustomed to talk without circumspection, live without meditation, confess without sorrow, take communion without love, and multiply without scruple the faults which are termed light.'[35]

As a professed Sister of more than five years' standing, Sr Marie-Bernard had this book in her possession, and had no doubt pondered its meanings. Her whole life, as a Sister of Nevers, was one of unexpected circumstances which had been imposed by providence. She knew very well that she was not the type of person who would normally be living at St Gildard. 'She believed that she should have a particular gratitude toward our congregation, saying that they had received her out of charity, and that she was a charge on the Maison-Mère.'[36] The only reason why they had was because she was a celebrity within the Catholic world. But that was another role, another 'grace', which she was inclined to reject. In her notebook she wrote a resolution to go to the parlour with joy, and ask God to release a soul from purgatory each time she made the effort to meet a visitor.[37] But these good intentions broke down all too often, as the visits continued and she remembered that she had been promised that she would be hidden at St Gildard.

Sr Marie-Bernard had more contact with novices and postulants than did most of the professed Sisters. 'She liked the silence of her infirmary and had little taste for visits, but the postulants were always welcome. She herself sometimes said to them: "If you are feeling unhappy come and see me." '[38] Many of the 'little bonnets' remembered her words of encouragement. 'You will see how happy you will be in religious life. The Good Lord has given you much grace.'[39] Rather surprisingly, Mère Marie-Thérèse Vauzou encouraged Sr Marie-Bernard in this role. The Novice Mistress was prepared to make use of Sr Marie-Bernard's charisma, and a meeting with the visionary of Lourdes was often a reward for a favoured girl, and a consolation for a struggling one. Mère Marie-Thérèse also sometimes told Sr Marie-Bernard to take her recreation with the novices, where her company was enjoyed.

All of the entrants arrived at St Gildard knowing that Bernadette was a member of the community, but it was often some time before they had the opportunity to meet her. Usually they were warned by the superiors not to speak to her about the visions. This prohibition was often breached, but not in an open or consistent manner. One novice, Sr Bernard Dalias, waited some days after arriving at St Gildard before telling a Sister that she had not yet had the chance to see Bernadette. The Sister turned to a small religious standing nearby, whom Sr Bernard had already seen several times, and said 'but there she is'. Sr Bernard described how she had 'probably made an ideal somewhat more complicated of the wonderful visionary, and a tactless, almost an impertinent word escaped me: "That!" Sr Marie-Bernard laughed and offered her hand saying "Yes, mademoiselle, only that." '[40]

After this awkward beginning, Sr Bernard became a friend, and despite her initial disappointment at the ordinary appearance of Bernadette she proceeded to glamorize her as much as any pilgrim from Lourdes. As if she had forgotten her own assessment, Sr Bernard saw reflections of the divine in Sr Marie-Bernard's features. 'The angels, when they conducted her to Paradise, must have seen that resemblance to the Blessed Virgin, our Mother.'[41] This pattern of initially finding Sr Marie-Bernard quite average, but then discerning the myths which were expected, is found in several accounts which show that people will find what they expect to see. Another novice was Sr Irène Ganier, 'to see her was my great desire ... and on the first occasion possible, I greeted her and spoke to her without finding anything extraordinary in her person: little in height, regular features, but her dark shining eyes struck me and I said to myself: "They are brilliant, it is a reflection of the divine grace of Marie-Immaculate." '[42]

If the subject of Lourdes was raised, Sr Marie-Bernard sometimes told the novices that the Blessed Virgin had used her like an ox to plough a field, or like a broom to sweep the floor, and when one is finished with a broom, one puts it away. In comparing herself with bovine, vulgar and even dirty articles Sr Marie-Bernard was reasserting her common nature, and explaining why someone like her had come to play such a role. She was also explaining that it was all over, and that she had now been put away. There were other occasions when she was exasperated by questions, and some Sisters found that 'it sufficed to speak to her of that subject (Lourdes) to provoke some replies on her part which we found quite sharp'.[43]

Sr Marie-Bernard may have been kind to the novices because she herself had been treated harshly. Her welcoming manner and consoling words might have been a silent comment on the trials that she herself had endured. Another motive for her interest might have been her consistent fondness for children. The teenage postulants were only girls, and when at school Bernadette had always liked the company of the little ones. With them, she resumed her familial role of the eldest sister, admonishing, directing and encouraging. When in the company of the novices, Sr Marie-Bernard had a degree of power that was missing elsewhere in her life. The professed Sisters were almost all her superiors; only with the newcomers was her lack of accomplishments overlooked. Although much of her influence over them was due to the famous visions, she was also in a position to control their communications. Theirs were the only questions that she could snub.

Sr Angèle Lompech remembered when she had received news from home that her mother was very sick, and had stood in the corridor in tears. She was approached by Sr Marie-Bernard, who 'must have read my feelings from my face, and she judged no doubt that it was one of those cases when charity must replace the Rule. Her kind heart gave her permission to break the silence.'[44] Sr Marie-Bernard assured the postulant that she would pray for her mother, who later recovered. Sr Angèle was surprised that a religious had stopped to speak to her in the corridor. It was not permitted, and in any case, 'a postulant in tears, that is not unusual'.[45] Rather than hurrying past these woebegone faces, Sr Marie-Bernard found it rewarding to speak to them. Sr Adélaide Martin attracted her attention by crying as she swept the stairs. She had suppressed her homesickness for days, 'I imagined that they would have sent me away if they saw me crying.'[46] But when she did break down during her work a Sister spoke to her mildly, asking why she was upset and offering her encouragement. As soon as this conversation was over, another religious approached and said 'Do you know who you have been speaking to? That is Sr Marie-Bernard – She who saw the Blessed Virgin eighteen times at Lourdes.'[47] The Novice Mistress did not indulge in such indiscretions. Her introductions were direct and polite. In 1873, when a new postulant was wretched with homesickness, Mère Marie-Thérèse asked her: 'Would you be happy to see Bernadette?' She then took her to Sr Marie-Bernard, saying, 'My Sister, here is a girl who has only just arrived and is already upset.'[48] The postulant, Louise Poujade, said that she found that a welcoming kiss from Bernadette was better than a sermon.

In 1871, Sr Marie-Bernard was officially designated as a companion (a Guardian Angel) for a new postulant. It was Julie Garros, who had been at school with her at the Hospice. Although she was younger than Bernadette, Julie Garros had helped her with her lessons when she had first returned to the classroom. During the first days, the two were allowed to speak freely, and they recalled the people whom they had known at the Lourdes Hospice. Julie Garros told Sr Marie-Bernard of a Mlle Claire, a member of the Children of Mary who was exceptionally pious and who was prone to illness. Mlle Claire actually prayed for more pain: 'If it is not yet enough, may the Good Lord add to it.' Sr Marie-Bernard reflected on this and said: 'She is very generous; me, I would not do as much. I content myself with what has been sent to me.'[49] Like Sr Victoire, who had also known Bernadette at the Hospice, Julie

Garros found Sr Marie-Bernard more resigned to life, no longer inclined to speak up against what she thought was unjust. Julie Garros reminded her of a Sister at the Hospice who accepted unjust reproofs with joy. 'Do you remember that Sister? You would not have done as much, you never let yourself be blamed if you had done nothing.' Sr Marie-Bernard remembered her old self and answered, 'Perhaps not.'[50] There would be plenty of time for Julie Garros to learn about the realities of convent life at St Gildard. Soon she became a novice with the name Sr Vincent.

Although she was a sympathetic figure, Sr Marie-Bernard gave the novices direct examples of how to bear unjust censure. 'I found myself with her,' recounted one Sister, 'when returning from the novitiate to the infirmary, when we met our Mother General who, wanting no doubt to try us, upbraided us as "useless persons". As I was not very strong in the face of anything which wounded my self-love, I immediately began to cry. "You cry for so little, said my companion. Oh! console yourself: you will get plenty of that!" ' The same Sister confirmed that she often saw Sr Marie-Bernard corrected and scolded 'and often without deserving it. I never saw the slightest change in her expression.'[51] Sr Angèle Lompech, who came to St Gildard as a novice in the early 1870s, witnessed Mère Josephine Imbert upbraiding her in the cloister. Mère Josephine was 'loud and forceful' while Sr Marie-Bernard was humble and apologetic. 'It was a scene which edified me a great deal.'[52] She gave reproofs as well as receiving them. One former novice remembered quite proudly that she had been corrected by Sr Marie-Bernard, who told her not to laugh aloud in the refectory. When Sr Vincent Garros made the sign of the cross quite imperfectly, Sr Marie-Bernard asked her if there was something wrong with her arm. 'She gave me several reproofs, which were certainly merited, but she tempered them with a smile.'[53]

Novices were often in the infirmary, either as patients or as assistants. Many of their memories of Sr Marie-Bernard come from this environment of work, illness, pain and nursing. The infirmary could be a confrontation for girls who were encountering the reality of charitable work for the first time. Sr Vincent Garros was told to take the aged Sr Anne-Marie Lescure, who was blind and suffering from cancer, for a walk. Sr Marie-Bernard told her to take care of her as if she was the blessed Lord himself, but Sr Julie could not resist replying 'Oh! There is a great difference.' That evening, Sr Vincent was appalled when she saw Sr Marie-Bernard dressing the putrefied wound on the patient's breast. 'I could not bear the sight of it ... Bernadette dressed it very delicately.' Sr Anne-Marie was in her last days, and after she died, Sr Vincent refused to help to lay out the corpse 'through repugnance'. Sr Marie-Bernard reproached her with telling words 'A Sister of Charity who cannot touch a corpse, what does that amount to?'[54] Sr Marie-Bernard went through the same experiences with other girls in the infirmary. She instructed them in nursing, and did not force them forward, but lightly told them that they were 'poltroons' if they could not bear the unpleasant tasks. Usually, like Sr Vincent, they needed time, to develop their confidence before they could approach the sick.

Other novices were in the infirmary as patients. When Sr Eudoxie Chatelain was in the infirmary, she got up without permission because she felt better. A companion warned Sr Eudoxie against this rash move, but the buoyant novice was ignorant of the need for authorization. 'I replied that when a person is well they don't need permission to get up, or, if there is a permission, it is nature which gives it.'[55] Sr Eudoxie attended Mass, but found when she returned that the infirmarian was angry with her. Sr Marie-Bernard told her 'You prepare yourself very badly for the religious life if you don't know how to obey ... You will only ever be happy in obedience.'[56] She told Sr Eudoxie that she had to return to bed, and made her stay there all day. 'She only had the charity to bring me some books to lift my boredom ... My religious life has been founded on that sermon of Bernadette's. It has followed me always. I have been tempted from time to time to indulge myself or take my ease; but the words come back into my memory: "You will only ever be happy in obedience." '[57]

Sr Marie-Bernard often told sick novices that they would have to get used to pain, and quoted the maxim: 'A religious must learn to love suffering.' It was a useful hint for those who were facing injections, incisions and the dreaded dentist's drill. Sr Marie-Bernard herself often collapsed with illness such as abscesses, toothaches and vomiting blood. So she was obliged to take her own advice, and to accept medical care from her own assistants. She seemed to have become accustomed to the brutal medical treatments of the era, and urged the novices, when they were gingerly changing the bloody bandages on her leg, to merely pull them straight off. 'Pull, pull. I am like an old cat, I won't die.' In 1872 they had applied a 'silicate bandage' to a wound on her knee, which was beginning to cause anxiety. In fact, the opening in her flesh was the arrival of a tumour caused by tuberculosis. Beneath the skin, the joint would have been diseased, as the infection ate away at the marrow of her bones. The wound closed for a while, as her body's defences fought back against the infection. But it would return, and she walked with a limp. She tended to accept pain rather than to welcome it, but she had come to recognize that it played a role in life. 'Why is it necessary to suffer?' she wrote in her notebook 'Because, here on this earth, pure Love cannot live without pain.'[58] This is a theological interpretation, which she would have drawn from her readings. She followed it up with a note to herself: 'Be more charitable in future toward my neighbour, and toward their physical and spiritual pains.'[59]

Sr Marie-Bernard's guidance was realistic. When Sr Vincent Garros had completed her novitiate Sr Marie-Bernard gave her parting advice: 'Accept illness as a caress from the hand of God; dedicate yourself to the service of the poor, but with prudence; do not let yourself become exhausted.'[60] She commented to novices that the more that a poor person is repellent, the more one must care for them.

The novices were transient at St Gildard. Almost none would remain in the convent after their vows were made, and many were sent out to different houses during their second year. Sr Marie-Bernard, therefore, was farewelling them as often as greeting them. They often left the Mother House with some trepidation, but Sr Marie-Bernard envied them their new lives. As she said, they would have work, and posts to fill, while she was left 'only good to grate carrots'.[61] Some of them tried to keep objects associated with her, but she asked to be remembered in their thoughts. When Sr Vincent Garros departed, Sr Marie-Bernard suggested that they exchange only a kiss: 'When people love each other, there is no need for souvenirs.'[62]

In the opinion of some Sisters, she was a saint. They observed her with adoring eyes, and were not disillusioned by her. Her observance of the Rule, her practice of silence, and her transcendence of ordinary personal relationships were often described as faultless. 'For three years I saw perfection with my own eyes.'[63] Many of the novices stated that they had tried to imitate her, but had never succeeded. She lived, said one: 'in obedience, humility, prudence and an astonishing self-possession'.[64] Her simplicity was noted, and as one Sister recalled, for 'a long time she gave me the impression that holiness is an easy thing'.[65] Another postulant, who had been sixteen years old when she knew Sr Marie-Bernard, remembered her as merely 'so little and so unimportant' and looked back in wonder. 'It is true that then I could not discern in her all the holiness which is celebrated now. I was too young. But since then, upon reflection, and with the knowledge which I have acquired of the human heart, I distinguish more clearly what escaped me ... I have learnt that humility consists of the "silence of the self". With Bernadette, that was it. In her, there was no *moi*.'[66]

These adulatory opinions are not the full story. Her life could be seen as undistinguished, and her religious duties no more than faithfully performed. Her quick temper also repelled some Sisters. Sr Marie-Bernard's sharp tongue came out on such occasions as when she was in the chapel, and she saw that senior Sisters were taking each other's places in the queue to the confessional, thus leaving novices, who dared not protest, to wait their turn indefinitely. Sr Marie-Bernard crossly pointed out to the Mère Assistante what was happening. Later that same evening, she realized that she should not have spoken sharply, and apologized.[67] She also reproached a Sister who returned her clothes so badly laundered that they were all torn up. One of her companions justified Sr Marie-Bernard's behaviour, saying that she believed 'that as for some acts for which she was reproached as impatient or sharp, it was rather the sentiment of justice which motivated her'.[68]

The Sisters who found Sr Marie-Bernard to be a model religious were almost all women who had first known her as novices. The professed Sisters at St Gildard, and Sr Marie-Bernard's superiors, took a cooler view. Sr Joseph Garnier was quoted as saying: 'For all her visions, she is like anyone else.'[69] The people who found fault with Sr Marie-Bernard were those who had more power over her, whereas she attracted adulation from her subordinates. The critical opinions are rather muted, and offered without details. Sr Léontine Villaret testified at the *Procès* of Bernadette's canonization that she had been shocked by her impatience when being reproved by Mère Marie-Thérèse Vauzou:

> While I was making my novitiate I came to the Mother House with several professed. We were going to greet the Mères in the community room ... Sr Marie-Bernard arrived ... very tired and in pain, walking with difficulty because of a tumour on her knee.

When Mère Marie-Thérèse said a sharp word addressed to Bernadette. Sr Marie-Bernard who suffered a lot at that time said:
—'Oh! Our Mistress!'
As one who means: 'She is always after me.'
That at least was what I understood. Then Mère Marie-Thérèse replied:
—Ah! We have pricked that self-love.
I thought that Bernadette being so sick could have done without this compliment. However, I was astonished by Bernadette's reaction ... We had such a cult of our Mistress that I could not tolerate anyone responding to her like that.[70]

This anecdote was scrutinized closely by the Vatican authorities, and it was judged not to be too important a diminution of Bernadette's virtues, because Mère Marie-Thérèse did not at that time have authority over her. Sr Marie-Bernard had ceased to be a novice for more than five years, and therefore owed Mère Marie-Thérèse no particular obedience.

The convent chaplain, Père Douce, did not live long enough to testify at her canonization. He was said to have regarded Sr Marie-Bernard with disfavour and to have shared the opinion of Mère Marie-Thérèse Vauzou. When asked about Bernadette, he told Père Payrard that she was 'a good religious, nothing extraordinary about her'. His informant had the impression that Père Douce did not want to be questioned any further. As chaplain, Père Douce had 'gained an impression from certain Béarnaise responses of Sr Marie-Bernard, which did not seem to him to correspond with the idea of sanctity'.[71] Sr Marie-Bernard must have been aware that Père Douce disliked her. He heard her confessions, advised her on spiritual matters and frequently visited the infirmary when she was both patient and nurse. She faithfully wrote his recommendations in her notebook.

The 'Counsels given by P. D. (Père Douce)' are of a standard type. They have an austere tone but are not excessively harsh. Unexpectedly, he seems to have spoken to her about her role in the Lourdes visions: 'Remind yourself of the words spoken to you by the Blessed Virgin: Penitence! Penitence! You must be the first in putting this into practice.'[72] Most of the recommendations were drawn from general religious examples, which would have applied equally to all the Sisters. 'Regard our Master, he suffered a great deal and said nothing ... Following his example, carry the cross hidden in your heart with courage and generosity, for the love of Jesus.'[73] Sr Marie-Bernard added 'I have sinned, it is just that I suffer.' She recorded his admonition to 'Make an examination of conscience every month. Have I been faithful in following all of the counsels which have been given to me by my confessor for such circumstances, and all of the prohibitions which have been made?'[74] No-one remarked on her attitude to Père Douce. He may have been critical of her, but she would have been correct and submissive towards him. Yet despite the serious notebook, she also included his name when playing a game of acrostics. This was a pious amusement, followed when Sr Marie-Bernard was ill in bed. Holy names were used to make lists of inspiring words. The acrostics were a 'manner of inscribing the names in my heart'.[75] For instance

Jesus was written *joie* (joy) *espérance* (hope) *souffrances* (sufferings) *union* (union) *soumission* (submission). Inspiring words such as glory, light, devotion and goodness were used to make up acrostics for Gabriel, Martha and Mary. But a slightly different list made up Douce. *Douleur* (pain), *oubli* (darkness), *union*, *confiance* (confidence), and for the last letter, E, Sr Marie-Bernard hesitated. At first she wrote *éprouvant* (annoying) but then crossed it out and put *exigeant* (trying). As the editor of her writings put it, 'this choice says a great deal'.[76]

Mère Eléónore Cassagnes and Sr Nathalie Portat, the two Sisters whom Sr Marie-Bernard was inclined to speak to, spoke little about her, and this may have been the foundation of their friendship. They would have been obliged to testify if they had been summoned before the *Procès*, but by then they had died. By contrast, three Sisters from St Gildard who did testify at length for her canonization, Sr Gabrielle de Vigouroux, Sr Marthe du Rais and Sr Joseph Garnier, had not always been on good terms with her during her life. These three were identified by Mère Bordenave, a historian of the community at Nevers, as being 'the companions' which Sr Marie-Bernard wrote of in her notebook. Sr Marie-Bernard's notebooks during 1874 and 1875 were peppered with mentions of the need to mind her temper, and to accept harsh words from others. 'I must work to become indifferent to all that is said to me, or thought about me, on the part of my superiors or companions. Practise detachment in order to attach myself uniquely to God and save my soul. I must often remind myself of the saying that: "God alone is good, and from Him alone must I expect a reward." '[77]

The brushes which caused these reflections are not described by others, and indeed Sr Marthe and Sr Joseph, in their testimonies about Sr Marie-Bernard, actually claimed to have been particularly united with her. This would not surprise any historian who has worked in the field of biography, or any person who has had experience of friendships and rivalries around a person who has become famous. In retrospect, some of the most antagonistic of relationships are converted into claims of close understanding and particular confidences. As far as Sr Joseph Garnier was concerned, the tactful memoirists of Nevers suggested that: 'her tongue, if not her heart, had kept even in religious life some asperity: she was a Parisienne whose sharp mind and abrupt manner could disconcert Sr Marie-Bernard'.[78] It is quite possible that Sr Marie-Bernard also did some disconcerting in her own right. In her notebook, she reminded herself to 'unreservedly combat my dominant fault, irritability. Go before the person who has mortified me, and be good to her.'[79] At times, she apologized for her sharp words. In a note to Sr Joséphine Daynac, an assistant of the Novice Mistress, Sr Marie-Bernard 'begged pardon for the bad example which I have given before you, as well as all the others who have been displeased. Please forgive me and pray for me, you can see how poor I am in virtue.'[80]

We do not know exactly what Sr Marie-Bernard said during the unguarded moments when her temper got the better of her. As a girl she had never been short of a piquant, or even an insolent, reply. In Lourdes, this had not been a fault. Quite the opposite – it was a way of contending with the world. In the convent, it was a serious, although common, breach of decorum. A rare anecdote which does record exactly how Sr Marie-Bernard irked others and then provided rejoinders, belongs to one of her periods of illness. As Sr Marie-Bernard was sick, the Sister in the infirmary sent a message to the kitchen asking for 'an appetizing dish' for her. This was not well received, and the Sister in charge of the kitchen asked: 'Did her mother feed her chicken every day?' This was repeated to Sr Marie-Bernard, who exclaimed: 'That is true, but what my mother gave me, she gave with a good heart.'[81]

It is significant that this exchange took place at her sickbed. During the 1870s, Sr Marie-Bernard's health failed. By 1874 she had entered the last stage of tuberculosis, and her bones were decaying from within. She was always in pain, and probably became more difficult to deal with. Her notebooks, during the mid-1870s, are more copious, with many jottings, reflections and copies of prayers. This indicates that she had more leisure, as she was becoming incapable of work. She also seems to have been in a more reflective frame of mind. In 1874 she had reached the age of thirty, and had lived at St Gildard for eight years. It was up to her to make a success of religious life, to reform her nature, confront her sins, and be worthy of the deathbed which awaited her in the near future.

Some writers have suggested that Sr Marie-Bernard underwent a period of depression, or even a 'dark night of the soul' during the mid-1870s, because her notebooks make frequent mentions of penance and suffering, while there are reports from other Sisters that they sometimes found her dejected and even tearful. Sr Marie-Bernard declined to say why she was upset. Her written words, in themselves, do not justify an account of this period of her life as particularly dark. All religious writings of this time plainly stated the difficulty of virtue and the cost in suffering. Sr Marie-Bernard was writing what any other Sister at St Gildard would have put on paper, indeed, most of the statements are quotations from retreat notes and spiritual guides consulted by everyone at St Gildard. Considering that she was in the grip of a painful and terminal malady, Sr Marie-Bernard seems to have been relatively cheerful. In 1873 she wrote:

> The Christian life has not only its combats and its trials, but also its consolations. If we are obliged to leave Tabor and go to Calvary, from Calvary, we return to Tabor with Jesus. There, we have a foretaste of heaven. The soul can only make one journey, from Golgotha to Tabor. It leaves Golgotha to look for strength and courage at Tabor. The whole of life is this ascent.[82]

She immediately followed it, on the next line, with the statement: 'I must work energetically to destroy my self-love and self-indulgence.' She knew how difficult that was, although it was no harder for her than for anyone else. 'It is said of Père Villefort that he craved for opportunities to be charitable. How I would like to be such a person.' It was a physical as well as an emotional effort. Her confessor suggested that eating whatever she was given, and rising immediately upon being woken in the winter mornings, were excellent means of cultivating asceticism. She noted these suggestions, and told herself to be more attentive in chapel.

> Preparation for Holy Communion.
> Preparation requires meditation. I do it so badly!
> Renew and fortify the resolution which I took on this subject.
> But I am so tired in the mornings. I should recall the temptation of Père Avila, who hesitated one day on his way to Mass, because he was so tired. Our Lord appeared to him and showed him the wound on his heart, recalling to him that fatigue had not prevented him from going to the summit of Calvary. Courage! And I too must learn how to force myself.[83]

In 1876 Sr Marie-Bernard wrote to her brother, 'such is life: full of pain and sacrifice, we must recognize that happiness is not found in this world'.[84] She was resigned to hardships, and had managed to live her life with integrity. It was evidently a lonely existence. A priest who visited St Gildard in 1871 in order to research the history of the congregation commented on her anomalous situation. The community was large and distinguished, she was a small figure in a spotlight.

> She has before her an imposing group, where she sees nothing but examples of virtue: on the one side, the retired Superiors and senior Sisters; on the other the novices, and at the head the Mother General and those who have responsible administrative posts. In the midst of these Servants of God, Marie-Bernard is lost in humility. She sees the others so capable with their education, their talents, their aptitudes, ready to serve God and their neighbour. As for her, frail of health and always suffering, from time to time collapsing with serious illness, she sees herself powerless to do much for others.[85]

As he concluded: 'It is there she has been placed for the moment, and where she will stay, it appears, until the end of her days.' By the mid-1870s, this last stage of her life was looming.

# NOTES

1.  Sr Marie-Valentine Gleyrose, *PON*, Sessio XX, 257.

2.  Notes d'Infirmière, ibid., gives a facsimile of a few paragraphs, which are quoted from above. Otherwise the contents of the Notes are merely paraphrased by the editor. This is apparently because they are treated as copies of documents, rather than as her own writings.

3.  Cited by Guy Thuillier, *Pour une histoire du quotidien au XIXe siècle en Nivernais* (Nevers 1977), 105.

4.  Guynot, *Contemporains*, 161.

5. Dr Voisin's statement was made during a public lecture. Quoted, *ESB*, 309.

6. Mgr Forcade's letter to *Univers*, 3 Oct. 1872, cited in Bordenave, *La Confidente* 109.

7. Dr Rouby, *La Vérité sur Lourdes* (Paris 1910), 55.

8. Dr Robert Saint-Cyr to Dr Damoiseau, 3 Sept. 1872, *ESB*, no. 126, 309.

9. Note Cr., ibid.

10. Mère Elisabeth Meyrignac, Guynot, *Contemporains*, 83.

11. Journal of the Community, 2 and 9 Dec. 1870, quoted by Trochu, *Sainte Bernadette*, 428.

12. To her father, Nov. 1870, *ESB*, no. 104, 279.

13. Bordenave, *La Confidente*, 141.

14. Ibid.

15. Community Journal, 7 Nov. 1870, *ESB*, 261.

16. Sr Marie Josephine, *PON*, Sessio VII, 131.

17. Sr Madeleine Bounaix, *PON*, Sessio XCVI, 3. 1103.

18. Ibid.

19. To Marie Soubirous, 4 July 1875, *ESB*, no. 155, 395.

20. To Marie Soubirous, 9 Mar. 1871, *ESB*, no. 105 bis, 282–3.

21. To Pierre Soubirous, after Mar. 1871, *ESB*, no. 107, 285.

22. Carnet 1873, *ESB*, no. 145, 343.

23. Sr Louise Lavigne, *RdC*, 48.

24. Quoted by Trochu, *Sainte Bernadette*, 452.

25. Sr Eléonore Bonnet, Guynot, *Contemporains*, 118.

26. Ibid.

27. Madeleine Bordes, in religion Sr Claire, *PON*, Sessio XLI, 558.

28. Sr Casimir Callery, *PON*, Sessio XXXIX, 549.

29. To Marie Soubirous, 29 May 1872, *ESB*, no. 122, 305.

30. To Bernadette Nicolau, 11 Jan. 1879, *ESB*, no. 227, 509.

31. Marie-Antoinette Dalias, in religion Sr Bernard, *PON*, Sessio XLVIII, 634.

32. Marie Ganier, in religion Sr Irène, *PON*, Sessio LI, 660.

33. Ibid.

34. From the notes of Abbé Febvre, *PON*, Sessio XLII, 581.

35. *Le trésor spirituel des Soeurs de la Charité et Instruction Chrétienne de Nevers* (Nevers 1860).

36. Sr Marthe du Rais, *BVP*, 2. 310.

37. Carnet 1873, *ESB*, 366.

38. Guynot, *Contemporains*, 157.

39. Ibid., 156.

40. Sr Bernard Dalias, *RdC*, 24.

41. Ibid.

42. Sr Irène Ganier, *RdC*, 56.

43. Sr Joseph Garnier, *RdC*, 67.

44. Guynot, *Contemporains*, 106–7.

45. Ibid.

46. Ibid., 163.

47. Ibid., 164.

48. Ibid., 159.

49. Laurentin, *BVP*, 2. 141.

50. Ibid.

51. Bordenave, *La Confidente*, 121.

52. Sr Angèle Lompeche, *PON*, Sessio LXXXI, 959.

53. Guynot, *Contemporains*, 18.

54. Laurentin, *Vie*, 244.

55. Guynot, *Contemporains*, 32.

56. Ibid., 33.

57. Ibid., 34.

58. Sr Marie-Bernard, Carnet 1873, *PON*, 345.

59. Ibid., 359.

60. Jules Marie Le Cerf, *PON*, Sessio XLII, 573.

61. Mère Joseph Ducourt, Guynot, *Contemporains*, 135.

62. Laurentin, *BVP*, 2. 387.

63. Guynot, *Contemporains*, 28.

64. Mère Julienne Capmartin, ibid., 47.

65. Sr Eudoxie Chatelain, ibid., 24.

66. Sr Saint-Michel Duhème, ibid., 67.

67. Trochu, *Sainte Bernadette*, 449–50.

68. Sr Marie-Josephine Forestier, *PON*, Sessio XII, 183.

69. Sr Joseph Garnier, quoted by Sr Philippine, *PON*, Sessio CVI, 1203.

70. Quoted by Laurentin, *BVP*, 2. 223.

71. Charles Payrard, SM, *PON*, Sessio LXXXVIII, 1028.

72. 'C.P.D.' 1874 Carnet, *ESB*, 376.

73. 'Conseils donnés' 1874, *ESB*, 375.

74. 'C.P.D.' 1874, *ESB*, 376.

75. Jeux d'Acrostiches, probably 1873–4, *ESB*, no. 147, 384.

76. André Ravier, *ESB*, 384.

77. Notes from the Retreat of July 1875, *ESB*, no. 157, 400.

78. André Ravier, 'Interprétation des Documents', *ESB*, 411.

79. Carnet 1874, *ESB*, no. 145, 375.

80. Billet d'Excuses, Sept. 1874, *ESB*, no. 148, 384.

81. Mère Joséphine Forestier quoted, Trochu, *Sainte Bernadette*, 50.

82. Carnet 1873, *ESB*, no. 145, 357.

83. Ibid., 361.

84. To her brother Jean-Marie Soubirous, Nov. 1876, *ESB*, no. 181, 443.

85. P. Marcel Bouix, *Une héroine de la charité au XIXe siècle. Élisabeth de Brugelles, perle du midi de la France* (Paris 1875).

# CHAPTER 11

# Atrocious Sufferings
## The Deathbed, 1875–1879

> On her knee, there was an abscess for the whole of winter (she was
> suffering all that it is possible to suffer) ... the winter afterward, a tumor
> which ankylosed the knee: atrocious sufferings; one didn't know how to
> move her ...
>
> Mère Éléonore Cassagnes

'It is not enough to begin well. One must continue well and finish well.' This
was one of the maxims recommended to the Sisters of Nevers. The saying
dryly criticizes a common human tendency, which religious life magnifies into
a disastrous fault, of starting with enthusiasm and faltering before difficulties.
The saying applied equally to the idealistic novice who could decline into a
peevish religious, or to the enthusiastic Sister who began work without
finishing it, or more grandly, to the whole course of life, which begins amid
physical vigour and ends in testing affliction. One must finish well. The
sanctity of Bernadette, the perfection of her life, is based upon this. She not
only departed for Nevers, and endured a difficult admission, but she finished
the course. She ended her life as she had lived it.

This final chapter set the seal not only on the sanctity of Bernadette, but
also on her romantic image. Bernadette died from a lingering and painful
illness, in an attitude of calm and resignation. She also died as a virgin, in a
religious habit, and at the age of thirty-five, that is, while she could still be
considered young. All of these factors had a sentimental allure. Her last illness
can be evoked through simple and powerful images – the white curtained bed
which she termed 'my white chapel', the seclusion of the infirmary, the dying
nun faithful to her vows. Yet her death was extremely long, for she was an
invalid for over two years, and the last period of her life was turbulent. All the
principal actors of the Lourdes story sprang up around her, more full of life
than ever. The Soubirous family bickered about debts and money, the convent
authorities considered her status as scrupulously as they had ever done, and
the historians returned to question her about every last detail of the
apparitions. On her deathbed, Sr Marie-Bernard had nightmares about the
Grotto, endured inquisitions by scholars and hid her hands under the blankets
in order to avoid importunate Sisters who wanted to kiss them.

Despite the frequent mentions of Bernadette's health in the primary
documents, it is not possible to make an accurate reconstruction of her
medical history. The constant typification of her as a sickly person actually
obscured the details of her bodily condition, which was generalized into

**Plate XIV** The 'white chapel'. *Archives, St Gildard*

adjectives such as 'frail', 'delicate', and, on one occasion, a word with a more specific warning 'consumptive'. The narratives of Bernadette's life so consistently describe her as ailing, that her decline and death at an early age pass almost without explanation. It seems to have been regarded as a pre-ordained fate. Naturally, this story was always going to end on a youthful deathbed, and very few witnesses are concerned to give exact details of the illnesses. What they observed was not really illness, but a recognizable type, the delicate young person who was too good for this world, and would shortly leave it. Many aspects of Bernadette's biography are clarified by considering that people expected an early end to her existence. When she had lived at the Hospice of Lourdes as a teenager, during her days as an object of display, no prospects were arranged for her, and this was no doubt due to the fact that her health was so bad. The supposition that Bernadette had no long-term future was realistic enough, but again and again it was proved wrong.

## The malady

According to her family, Bernadette had always been feeble. She was a child who needed special food and stockings in winter. 'Her malady', asthma, set her apart from her siblings, and then the cholera had left her digestion impaired. Yet, amid the poverty and the Soubirous's downward spiral, Bernadette survived several rigorous passages that left many thousands of contemporary children dead. Despite a catalogue of physical collapses, she clawed her way back, and went on to live and work. From the time of the cholera epidemic in 1855, through her situations in Bartrès, Lourdes and Nevers, Bernadette recovers against all odds. Despite her merited reputation as sickly, there is an underlying narrative showing the persistence of a sturdy body, which over time succumbed slowly to illnesses that could not be arrested once they had taken hold. Indeed, if she had not been physically strong, she would have died quickly in her early thirties, and been spared the inching progress of her last illness.

The most general symptoms, which were to overtake her all her life, were the breathlessness of her asthma, and vomiting from her weak stomach. This last symptom was mentioned less often than her wispy breath, being a far more repugnant condition of the body. Her delicate appetite and inability to consume a large meal invited admiring descriptions, but the consequences of her inability to digest were usually left without comment. Sr Marie-Bernard herself did describe her chronic nausea, especially after 1876, when it was becoming worse. 'I am always in the infirmary: I do not suffer a lot, but I am as weak as anything, and my stomach rejects all food.'[1] Her companions in the infirmary gave an account of one of her jokes. After being given a quail for lunch, which was a delicacy, Sr Marie-Bernard exclaimed: 'Quick, quick a basin. My little bird is going to escape, he is flying away.' Which he did, commented one Sister, 'he flew away, but not towards the sky'.[2] This quip was criticized by nineteenth-century Catholic journalists, who claimed that it could not possibly be true. Even in 1973, the editor of a study of Bernadette's words stated regretfully that it seemed to be 'sordid and without meaning' and that he 'would have left it to one side' if he did not have the duty to record everything which she said.[3] Biographies of St Bernadette do not include this story. By contrast with such fussy reactions, one could see this as a light anecdote, which showed Sr Marie-Bernard's sense of humour and lack of self-pity. Clerical writers have relished descriptions of her serious agonies, but they have been reluctant to regard her own, more prosaic, approach to illness.

The asthma came and went. She seems to have improved after childhood, as people who met her after the age of sixteen no longer comment on her constant rasping. But there were occasional collapses, closely related, as has already been shown, to psychological stress. At times she was very active, and there are descriptions of her, between the ages of sixteen and twenty, hopping, skipping, and even turning somersaults. As a woman over thirty, when engaged in banter with two other Sisters, 'she performed a pirouette with the vivacity of a young girl'.[4] 'As a Sister, when she was well, she would play in the garden, skipping with the youngest – as lively as a little child.'[5] But at other times she was wheezing with asthma. Claire de Mevolhon, the little niece of the Superior General, was allowed to play in the gardens at St Gildard, and was put in the care of Sr Marie-Bernard. 'We avoided running, in order not to tire her, for she was soon made breathless. I can still hear her puffing, when she had to hurry after us.'[6] The artist Joseph Fabisch, who described her as consumptive at the age of eighteen, seems to have been ahead of the facts. He probably saw the laboured breathing of an asthmatic and confounded this with advanced tuberculosis of the lungs.

Bernadette had anticipated that her state of health would make it impossible to follow a religious rule, and this was one of the factors which had caused her to hesitate before entering any religious order. The moderate way of life practised by the Sisters of Nevers was the best compromise that could be offered, but she was the type of person usually rejected on the grounds of health. Her novitiate had been partly spent in the infirmary, and this was an indication of the state of things to come. Periodically, from the age of twenty-two to thirty, she would have spells of retching, asthma, spitting and even vomiting blood. She also stated that she felt pains in her head and stomach almost every day, probably a sign that her body was stressed. Her immune system must have been weakened, and in her thirties she suffered from several abscesses, including an excruciatingly painful one in her ear. As early as 1866, Dr Saint-Cyr had warned the superior that she could die during one of the episodes of vomiting blood, yet she lived for more than another ten years. This bleeding is something of a mystery symptom. If this was a haemorrhage from the lungs, one would have expected her to have been at the final stage of terminal illness. The blood may have been coming from her stomach – as the term 'vomiting' suggests – and would have been the symptom of a profound digestive disorder, perhaps ulceration of the stomach wall, with perforation and scarring. If the blood was coming from her lungs, it indicates that the tuberculosis was destroying her lungs, but then was repeatedly being confined by the walls of calcium which the body builds as its defence.

The Bishop of Nevers, awed by her invalidism, wrote of that 'incredible complication of incurable illnesses, of which one would have sufficed, according to the common laws of the frail human body, to take her quickly to her grave. It must have been a veritable miracle that her life persisted during more than twelve years; but also, during that long period, what a weighty burden of continual and frightful sufferings.'[7] Among many witnesses, only the infirmarian at St Gildard gave an unusually specific account of the reasons for her death: 'The Servant of God was asthmatic for many years, she had recurrent vomitings of blood, but she died from decay of the bones.'[8] Bernadette died of tuberculosis, the great disease of the era. She developed a rare form of this common complaint; and rather than the tissue of her lungs, it was her bone marrow which was the major site of infection. The contemporary French sources did not mention the word *tuberculeuse* but relied upon nineteenth-century medical terms to describe her malady: *tumeur au genou* (tumour on the knee), *tumeur blanche* (a white tumour, as distinct from a visible infection) and *carie des os* (decay of the bones). This illness was slow and extremely painful. It was known that these lesions on the bones produced a violent agony, which sufferers compared to the raging ache of a decaying tooth.

The decay of her bones was to give Bernadette the opportunity to decline patiently amid physical agonies, and to prove an intensity of sanctity not demonstrated by the glamour of her visionary career. Her death was not markedly different from that of some other Sisters of Nevers. With their self-effacement and their hidden heroism, such women faced agonies without complaining or seeking rest. But the status of Sr Marie-Bernard meant that her ordeal was recorded for posterity. It is also a factor that Sr Marie-Bernard's suffering, while not unprecedented, was especially prolonged. When young Sister Vincent d'Eauga died of a tuberculous tumour on the knee in 1861, her sufferings were terrible. It began with rheumatic fever. 'Soon after a more serious illness appeared, more painful still, it fixed onto her knee with all the characteristics of an ankylose, and immobilized her, at the same time that a feverish cough tore at her chest. It is impossible to express what her sufferings then were ... ' said the obituary notice sadly.[9] This was bad enough, but unlike Sr Marie-Bernard, she declined over only a few months, rather than several years. As the Bishop of Nevers wrote, Bernadette's survival was a wonder, and was unexpected given the gravity of her complaints.

On the day Sr Marie-Bernard took her first vows, and failed to receive a post in the congregation, the Mother General had commented to Mgr Laurence that she might as well be employed for light tasks in the infirmary. 'She is always ill, it would be precisely her affair.'[10] This was a harsh joke by Mère Imbert, and perhaps a mark of resentment that their congregation had been obliged to accept a sickly low-class woman. Despite the imperative to humiliate Sr Marie-Bernard, one has to wonder if Mère Imbert truly realized what she was saying. There was debate about whether consumption was a disease which could be communicated, or whether it was an innate condition brought out by certain circumstances, but it was recognized that there was a 'consumptive type', of which Sr Marie-Bernard was a good example. Consumptive types were weak people with poor appetites and lung trouble.

In fact, this recognizable sort of person was probably actually in the early stages of the disease, rather than open to it. Consumptive types were not usually thought of as being suitable to work around medicines and sick people, rather there was an uninformed, but perceptive, reasoning that in unhealthy circumstances they were a danger to themselves and others.

In Sr Marie-Bernard's case, the requirements of holiness always seemed to be in opposition to the care of her health. She went willingly to work in the infirmary, and her superiors saw nothing wrong in this. One wonders how many patients she infected with tuberculosis while she was there. Or is it possible that despite all her gasping and bleeding she was still free from the disease in 1867, and indeed that she, in her turn, may have been infected by one of them? No-one in the 1860s had the slightest notion of the spread of bacteria. When nineteenth-century people discussed the spread of disease, they often attributed it to the miasma of bad smells, as foul air often seemed to presage disease. This was another common-sense notion borne out by experience, as well-drained and ventilated places saw less illness. The convent of St Gildard was a very clean environment, unusually so by the standards of the era, but in the infirmary there was no escaping the sight and smell of illness. Once away from her post, Sr Marie-Bernard was regarded as being as hygienic as anyone else, and one reads of the enthusiastic postulants and novices who would try to kiss her hands and her veil as she walked with them in the gardens. Sr Marie-Bernard would draw away from them, saying, 'you know very well that is not allowed'.[11] One hopes that she deterred them in time, before they picked up her disease. For at least several years, and possibly as long as five years, she worked with the sick, while carrying an epidemic illness. Although she enjoyed her work, and performed it well, it involved risks.

Sr Marie-Bernard's own letters are not a good source of information about her terminal illness. In earlier times, such as during a health crisis of 1873, she had frankly informed her family that: 'I have just been seriously ill.' But between 1875 and 1879 there are fewer mentions of her physical state, and she actually often wrote that she felt well, and that she would soon be up again. Like many chronically ill people, she had developed ironic terms for her state of health. These were often used when writing to her fellow Sisters of Nevers. 'What can I say on my account? That I am always a prop for the infirmary.'[12] 'I am always seedy [*toujours patraque*].'[13] 'I am still in the infirmary: I do not suffer a lot but I am extremely weak ... Adieu, dear friend, I am obliged to end this letter because my hand shakes like that of an old woman.'[14] 'I am always in my white chapel.'[15]

During the last two years, she usually wrote only to her family, and she avoided telling them how bad her state was. She told her sister that there was nothing wrong with her chest, and claimed in 1876, when she entered a downward spiral, that 'I get a little more strength each day. Do not worry about me, I will not die this time.'[16] In a letter of October 1878 she told her brother Pierre: 'I am still rather rickety, but for the last three months I have abandoned my canes. Do not be worried, it is nothing serious, merely a sciatic pain in the knee which has made me suffer a little, but that is passed.' All this was very far from the truth. She had abandoned the canes because she could not stand up at all, and had to be carried out of the bed when she was moved. And the tumour, having eaten her knee, was spreading up through the bones of her leg. The letter to Pierre, while giving false reassurance, is full of mixed messages. She told him that she had cried when reading his most recent letter, and that she sympathized with all his feelings: 'I know what your good heart felt. Come, dear friend, a little generosity is needed from both of us: and if God asks of us that we will never see each other again in this world, let us make the sacrifice with joy.'[17]

## The final employment

In October 1873 Sr Marie-Bernard was removed from her post as assistant infirmarian and was given the less physically active role of assistant sacristan. She continued to be available to work in the infirmary when needed. The Bishop of Nevers, remote from the daily life of the convent, considered such a change as a welcome one. In his memoir, he wrote with admiration that Sr Marie-Bernard stated no preference, and did not voice any relief at being given new duties.[18] Her admirable self-control was, in reality, exercised in the other direction. The Sisters in the convent thought it virtuous of Sr Marie-Bernard to obediently give up her post in the infirmary without grumbling: 'I know that it cost Bernadette a great deal to leave the infirmary, where she had many friends, and her patients missed her so much.'[19]

The last period of Sr Marie-Bernard's work in the infirmary had been marked by some stress, as she had been under the direction of Sr Gabrielle de Vigouroux. Although Sr Marie-Bernard had always had the title of assistant, she had taken all the practical responsibilities, as the infirmarian, Sr Marthe Forest, had herself been ailing. In November 1872, with the death of Sr Marthe, Sr Marie-Bernard became 'infirmarian in charge', but this was a temporary measure. Sr Marie-Bernard's failing health, her lack of education, and her equivocal position as a religious being held 'in humility', prevented her from officially rising above the level of assistant. When the post of infirmarian became vacant, Sr Gabrielle de Vigouroux was appointed. She took up her duties energetically, and Sr Marie-Bernard learnt the difficulties of being subservient in the very post which she had once directed. Suggestions about the means to perform tasks were not well received, and the new infirmarian accused Sr Marie-Bernard of being *orgueilleuse* (proud, conceited), the very same term used by Mère Marie-Thérèse Vauzou in the novitiate. Sr Gabrielle was a model Sister of Nevers. She was well educated, came from a good social background, and was a punctilious religious. She had authority over Sr Marie-Bernard, although she was younger in both age and religious life, and she shared the severe attitude of the convent authorities. 'Sister Marie-Bernard, she once said, was not indulged, neither by me nor by the superiors.'[20] It was Sr Gabrielle who was to be in charge of the infirmary during Sr Marie-Bernard's lengthy stay as a terminally ill patient. The two women did not have to work together for long. Sr Marie-Bernard's post as assistant was soon terminated, as she was becoming too ill to carry out the duties.

Sr Marie-Bernard may have been heartened, during this period of illness and demanding relationships, that there was a sudden thawing in the attitudes of those above her. Père Douce had already gone. Having served as the chaplain at St Gildard, he announced in August 1876 that he would be departing, and that his superiors had decided not to appoint any more Marist priests to this post. In September 1876 Abbé Febvre, the former Curé of a parish, took up the position. Abbé Febvre's style of preaching was in contrast with that of his predecessor. He put a greater emphasis on divine love and mercy, and minimized the theology of fear. This may have been due to his character, or because of his different background. He had toiled in the ordinary atmosphere of a parish, away from the perfectionist scrutiny of the religious orders. While Père Douce had been cool toward Sr Marie-Bernard, Abbé Febvre took a milder view. He found her lively, somewhat temperamental. She had: 'moments of ill-humour, especially when she was well – when seized by illness, she became more genial. The vagaries disappeared, a sign of the action of God.' In his view, 'the passive virtues abounded in her'.[21]

Even more significant to Sr Marie-Bernard's life was a change in the government of the convent. In January 1878 Mère Joséphine Imbert, who had been in poor health for some years, entered her final illness. She died in March 1878. On 28 January 1878 Mère Adélaïde Dons was elected to the post of Superior General. She was sixty-six years old, and had previously directed the hospice at Nevers. She was a woman of an expansive and affectionate nature, 'robust ... with broad masculine features'.[22] The more feline style of convent refinement was not her style, and nor did she test the strength of others through rigour and malice. She did not judge it necessary to put Sr Marie-Bernard on trial any longer. All the sources state that the advent of the new superior caused a new attitude toward Sr Marie-Bernard. No longer would she be treated with 'a cold reserve' and 'be maintained in humility'.[23] The discretion of the convent forbade that any of the witnesses comment on a detail which would have been equally obvious; that Sr Marie-Bernard was extremely fortunate that Mère Marie-Thérèse Vauzou was not elected Superior General at this time. She would have been a natural person to fill this post, and was to be elected in later years, after Sr Marie-Bernard's death.

Mère Adélaïde Dons was a friend of Sr Marie-Bernard's highly placed confidante, the Secretary, Mère Eleónore Cassagnes. From this time onwards, Sr Marie-Bernard was allowed certain marks of favour and recognition from the superior, such as having her opinion sought in conversation before others. These details seem insignificant in themselves, but were of decisive importance to life in such a hierarchical institution. She was no longer being treated like a novice, as someone whose loyalty and commitment were always under review. At the very last stage of her life Sr Marie-Bernard could be regarded as an equal of the other professed Sisters.

The recollections of Mère Adélaïde Dons were affectionate, although not uncritical, toward Sr Marie-Bernard. Like most members of the community, she found her neat, orderly, and, despite her temper, more refined in manner than her social origins would suggest.[24] She stated that Sr Marie-Bernard 'was not demonstrative in affection', and, true to the standards of her culture, regarded this as a grace.[25]

After leaving the infirmary in 1874, Sr Marie-Bernard was given duties in the sacristy. The sacristy is a series of rooms which served as the antechamber of a chapel. It is where the vestments worn by the priest, and the bread, wine and vessels of the altar, are cleaned and prepared. The atmosphere of a sacristy partakes of the holiness and silence of a chapel. The rooms are usually dark and panelled, the air scented with wood, polish, camphor and incense. The sacristan works in an atmosphere that might be considered a heightened version of the entire convent experience. She is surrounded by the sacred, and her own life passes in a purified space where human vitality is swept away. Food, activity and conversation never appear there. The sacristy is like a chapel, a library or a cell. It is a place of silence and serenity, or possibly of boredom and unease. Convents have stories of sacristans who attained the heights of contemplation, and lived through their duties as a spiritual exercise rather than work. There have also been tales of the opposite fate, of sacristans who became blasé about the chapel, annoyed by the priest who disarranged their realm, or who even reacted to their solitary post by becoming addicted to the wine which is stored there. Such extremities were more likely to occur in the enclosed contemplative orders. At St Gildard being the sacristan was an important post, and more busy than in most convents because of the size of the Mother House. The presence of the novitiate added to the numbers of religious services, although the novices also had access to a small chapel of their own for their daily prayers. The chapel at St Gildard also served people from the town, who were free to visit it during services.

When Sr Marie-Bernard left her nursing post, she entered a very different area of responsibility, but these duties were well suited to her capabilities, being the simple arrangement of the altars and candles, and needlework for the vestments. Her lack of physical strength counted for less, amid the delicate tasks of the sacristy, while her innate talent for needlework and decoration was an advantage. The quiet of the sacristy was a great change from the bustle of the infirmary, and for the first time in her religious life, Sr Marie-Bernard often worked alone. As novices were sometimes sent to act as her assistants for major religious ceremonies, this solitude was far from absolute, and she continued the relationships of affection and teaching that she had always had with them. There was also an unwelcome aspect of working near the chapel, for this area, although the most quiet and sacred of the convent, was also most open to the public. Many people who came to St Gildard on errands would visit the chapel before leaving, and once it became known that Bernadette worked in the sacristy, some would try to see her there. Sr Marie-Bernard dodged them as best she could. The anecdotes about her telling people to wait and see Bernadette pass the doorway, or to wait while she went to look for Bernadette, belong to this era.

Sr Marie-Bernard had not been appointed sacristan, but was made *aide-sacristine*, just as she had been *aide-infirmière*. It seems, however, that she directed herself in the post, as the real sacristan had been unofficially retired. Anyone but Sr Marie-Bernard would have been given the official title. The need to prove her humility, her lack of education, and the poor health which made her merely a provisional occupant of the position, would all have been reasons why she was always an 'aide'.

It was said that 'working in the sacristy could cause one to become careless, through familiarity with the sacred objects'.[26] but Sr Marie-Bernard showed no sign of such a failing, nor did she transfer the brisk gestures of the infirmary to the sacristy. Her painstaking style in approaching a task made her a fastidious sacristan. Her habits of scrupulous counting, as seen in the pharmacy, were manifest in her careful measuring, decorating and provisioning of the altar; and she was conspicuous for her reverent handling of the sacred vessels used for the Eucharist. Even when granted assistance, she reserved such tasks for herself.

She began a major lacework project, the making of an alb for Bishop Forcade. This was a long, flowing white garment, most of which was formed from netted lace in a floral motif. It was not finished until 1878, for Sr Marie-Bernard had little choice but to work slowly. Soon she felt useless, because of the lengthening periods when she could barely accomplish even simple tasks. There were days when she could not rise from bed, and fainting spells when she did attend work. After some religious ceremonies the Sisters would be obliged to revive their sacristan, who was often found unconscious on the chapel floor. A kindly symbolic meaning for these collapses was provided with the statement that, 'like the candles of the Mass, she seemed to consume herself in the service of the altars'.[27] Sr Marie-Bernard knew that this was no way for a sacristan to behave: 'My God! she would exclaim, How my Sisters must be scandalized by my lack of courage.'[28]

By October 1875, only eighteen months after she had become sacristan, Sr Marie-Bernard was relieved of her duties. She was becoming a complete invalid, a fate which had long threatened. The Bishop of Nevers's observations on this point were shared by many. He suggested that it could truly be said that in all of her religious life she had but one real employment: 'It was the work of being a victim for the expiation of our sins, and consequently for the triumph of the Church and the salvation of France.'[29] Particularly in retrospect, these large and glorious meanings were easily attached to the sufferings of a simple woman. Like much of the Lourdes literature, these panegyric claims could only validly be made by those around Bernadette; if she had voiced such sentiments herself, she would have appeared egotistical. However, from 1875 onwards, as she found herself more often bedridden, she began to refer ironically to her new post *l'emploi de malade* (the occupation of being ill). The beds in the infirmary were draped with white curtains. Sr Marie-Bernard called her bed, on which she was confined for endless days, her 'white chapel'. This narrow space became her dwelling, and she assembled her few belongings there. Visitors noted how tidy her bed always was, as she carefully arranged her needlework or craft objects near her hands. Pride of place, on the bed, went to her veil, which was carefully folded and ready to be worn when she received communion. Except for the days when she was able to walk to the chapel, Sr Marie-Bernard would no longer have been wearing her habit. She would have had a modified costume, with a night-gown or a dress, and a white cap rather than a coif.

Sr Marie-Bernard did not fit well or naturally into the role of the invalid. Like many people who have worked as nurses, she disliked the helplessness and inactivity of the sickbed. 'She could not bear being idle' commented one Sister, and the same observation is made by many others.[30] In a letter to her sister Toinette she described her illness of early 1873, when she had been confined to bed for three months. It had begun with an asthma attack, followed by 'an abundant vomiting of blood, which did not allow me to make the slightest movement without renewing it; you will believe without difficulty that to be nailed down like this did not suit my lively nature'.[31] The Sisters who cared for her stated that her illness was a martyrdom: 'she who liked to come and go, to be active, to speed through the house as she had once run on the hills of the Pyrenees ... instead bedridden, reduced to a few insignificant tasks'.[32]

By 1875, she was entirely confined to bed for long periods, and lamed by pains in the bones. Although she was not totally immobilized by the illness until the very end, henceforward she would move cautiously and often with the aid of sticks and other people. Considering her inclination for movement, it was a particular trial that she should lose the use of her legs. Sr Marie-Bernard, and her community, did not see ill-fortune or the workings of fate in this, but the will of God. She gave a melancholy acknowledgement that the divine will had required that she sacrifice part of her own nature in this illness. As she told Henri Lasserre: 'It is a good thing that God does not let us choose our destiny, because I would never have chosen this. I was born to move, to be active, not to be nailed to a bed.'[33] She believed that it was good because she assumed that the particular forms of self-sacrifice involved in meeting such trials were of the greatest benefit. It is part of our human nature that we would not have the resolution to choose such misfortunes.

The task of being ill was no doubt the most onerous of her life, but it had to be done. From October 1875, she no longer had any post at all. She was without that essential part of a Sister's prestige and identity in the convent. She would still perform small tasks, such as decorating eggs, painting holy cards, and continuing, with minute stitches, the profuse lace of the Bishop's alb. She had returned to the infirmary as a patient, to fall totally under the power of the astringent Sr Gabrielle de Vigouroux. In the eyes of the infirmarian, Sr Marie-Bernard was 'sometimes impatient, and there were also some little demands. I attribute this to her suffering, and also her lack of early education.'[34] To the very end, Sr Marie-Bernard was still judged by her poor background. Another of the patients, Sr Philippine Molinéry, said that: 'The servant of God was on very good terms with her companions, who esteemed and loved her. However, I believe that I saw some ill-feeling between her and the infirmarian, Sr Gabrielle de Vigouroux.'[35] Sr Philippine followed up this comment with an anecdote which was a mixture of the amusing and the acerbic. 'One day she (Sr Gabrielle de Vigouroux) was worn out and was confined to bed. An old Sister, Sr Elisabeth Auvray, who is dead now, came into the infirmary and said to those who were there: – You have made your nurse sick. – If she is sick, Sr Marie-Bernard replied, we are even more so, and if she is tired because of us, it is her duty to be so.'[36]

It is unlikely that Sr Marie-Bernard was an ideal patient, and no doubt the struggle to remain indifferent, and to conceal the interior warfare, continued to the very end. Her heroism during so prolonged and appalling an illness was much admired, but she judged herself according to high standards, and often apologized for complaining or showing impatience. She also found the company of others a trial, and may have over-compensated, in her attempts to cultivate detachment, and have begun to appear aloof. This is indicated by her gentle witticisms over the decorating of the Easter eggs. Several witnesses recalled her saying, 'If anyone says that I have no heart, tell them that I make them all day long.'[37]

## The return of the historians

The government of Mère Adélaïde allowed a supportive atmosphere of mutual respect during Sr Marie-Bernard's last months, and Sr Marie-Bernard had need of her superior's understanding because of a resurgence of historians' enquiries during 1878. The character of the historians of Lourdes remained as obsessive and competitive as ever. In 1878, the antagonisms at the shrine were intensified by a new entrant into the contest of producing a history, and he was to be a worthy opponent of all other writers. Léonard-Marie Cros, a 47-year-old Jesuit priest from Toulouse, was drawn to the idea of writing a history of the events at Lourdes. He had visited Lourdes and had met Bernadette in 1865. Although not an easy person to impress, he had been charmed by her manner, which he described as one of innocence and simplicity. Then he thought about writing on Lourdes, and in 1876 he was willing to put aside his considerable historical research into the Jesuit order in France, in order to take up the project. Père Cros was a friend of Père Sempé, and in broad terms a member of the clerical faction in Lourdes. The Missionaries at the Grotto had not been able to write a lengthy or scholarly work on Lourdes, and Père Cros offered his services. Although he was in sympathy with Père Sempé, and was scornful of Henri Lasserre and Curé Peyramale, Père Cros had different motives from all other contenders in the field.

Père Cros had a more academic approach than any of the previous historians. He also had an acerbic intellectual style, and an inclination for subtlety and detail, which is characteristic of the Jesuit tradition. His own approach to the subject of Lourdes was to uncover the 'pure truth'. All subsequent historians are obliged to be grateful to Père Cros, as a large amount of the primary source material of this topic was produced or collected through his efforts. He belonged to the empiricist school of research which dominated the late nineteenth-century academies. Although profoundly opposed to modernism, he was inherently affected by it, and his whole approach to his work is infused by the positivist philosophy. In this view, the accumulation of knowledge was a progress toward certainty, and the assessment of all forms of data was an objective process. A greater difference from the relativist view of our own time could not be found. Today, historians tend to regard the historical narrative as a creative effort, and source materials as having no inherent meanings, but only those which are contrived from their use. Père Cros belonged to a different age. The truth was there, he had only to arrive at it. In pursuit of his goal, he employed many path-breaking methods of research, especially the oral testimonies which he collected in Lourdes during 1878–80. This wealth of data was transcribed by Père Cros, and he also pursued every avenue to collect letters and documents contemporary to the apparitions.

Père Cros's personality was not irrelevant to his enquiry and its effects. He was not an easy-going or tolerant man. One of his Jesuit superiors wrote resignedly to another that: 'I am not surprised that Your Reverence has had difficulties with the good Father Cros. This is a misfortune which I believe that no-one can avoid, as soon as one disagrees with him.' In working on the history of Lourdes he was indefatigable, zealous, and scornful of other people. They merely served his purpose. In his crusade for absolute authenticity, he was not willing to leave out details or gloss over unpleasant facts. He discovered that the Soubirous parents had a drinking problem and made a point of asking people about it. He recorded the sleazy nature of Bernadette's early life, and decided that as it had suited God to raise her from this level, scholars should faithfully record the divine work. Worse still, he discovered minor discrepancies in stories of the apparitions and miracles, and wanted to strip away all unfounded stories as mere popular myths.

Père Cros was so sure of the apparitions at Lourdes that he held them up as proof against studied enquiry. He never doubted that the Virgin Mary had appeared in the Grotto, and he ascribed a large theological significance to this event, as he claimed that it was the proof of two recently proclaimed dogmas, the Immaculate Conception and Papal Infallibility. To modern eyes, it would seem that Père Cros had plenty of superstitions of his own, but they were of a literate and educated type. He was profoundly opposed to the popular superstitions of the people of Lourdes, and he made a point of exposing the inconsistencies in well-loved tales such as the 'miracle of the candle'. He also was not afraid to point out the way in which people's memories of events tended to become elaborated over time. In writing his history, Père Cros wanted to rely upon original documents and to distil a pure and inspiring original from under the layers of vulgar babble. In time, as René Laurentin observes, 'his critical sense sharpened into a sort of phobia for hagiographic conventions and received ideas'.[38]

It is hardly necessary to state that the nineteenth-century authorities at Lourdes were ultimately dismayed by Père Cros's work. When he delivered his manuscript in 1879 it was thoughtfully read by the priests at the shrine, who respected its learning and meticulous research. However, they did not wish to see it in print. It was passed over to his Jesuit superiors, with the suggestion that some of Père Cros's uncharitable criticisms of previous writers be edited out. Père Cros also prepared a short history of the shrine, with much less detail and analysis, which was published in 1892. But he refused to make any changes to his extensive history. In his last years, he stated that 'what I have written, I will entirely maintain, towards and against anyone, until my death and, in the next life, I will defend it again against all alteration ... My death will be useful to Our Lady in two ways, because I will offer it to her and also because my death will give people the freedom to arrange the manuscripts in any way that they wish. Until then, I thank God for having made me invincible against all human will.'[39] Possibly Père Cros's clerical colleagues did not relish the prospect of meeting him in the next life and resuming these arguments. His death in 1913 did not lead to the revision of his *Histoire de Notre Dame de Lourdes*. It remained, unprinted, in the archives of the Jesuits at Toulouse. In 1925–6 a three-volume edition was published which was entirely faithful to the original, under the editorial care of another Jesuit, Père Cavallera. Thus Père Cros's work eventually came to the public gaze. It was no best seller, but has been respected by all scholars of Lourdes.

In 1878, while Sr Marie-Bernard languished on her deathbed at St Gildard, all of these events were still to happen; but the obsessions and conflicts which were to echo over several decades were already in play. The Sisters of Nevers had been put on their guard by the painful incident of the 'Protestation' of Henri Lasserre, and were not disposed to grant free access to any more historians. Moreover, Sr Marie-Bernard was in a different position. Mère Adélaïde Dons was willing to listen to her demand that 'people not make her available, as formerly', and even Père Cros's status as a priest was not enough to move the Mother General. In August 1878, Père Cros visited St Gildard and found her implacable: she would not allow him to question Bernadette. As superior of the convent, she was accustomed to command, and did not mince words: 'I do not wish it, it is useless, you will get nothing ... All your efforts will be in vain.'[40] Père Cros was affronted by these words, and also by her manner. He found that Mère Adélaïde was rigid, was cold, and had showed 'a type of rudeness'.[41] Naturally, he was appalled. Mère Adélaïde's lack of femininity had been noted even by friendly eyes. In her unyielding attitudes she was rather similar to Père Cros himself. But she was subject to obedience to the church hierarchy, and Père Cros, aided by the authorities at the Grotto, was able to obtain a written mandate from the Vatican in December 1877. This obliged all the faithful to co-operate in his endeavour and to offer any assistance for which he asked. His battle to gain access to Sr Marie-Bernard was thus eventually won.

Required to co-operate with the historical enquiry, Mère Adélaïde did not do so in an unconditional manner. In view of Sr Marie-Bernard's failing health, neither Père Cros, nor any other historian, was to interview her directly. Instead, they were to send written lists of questions, and the authorities and St Gildard would arrange that replies be recorded.

In view of the previous encounters, it was decided that Père Cros would not return to St Gildard. Instead Père Sempé, well known to the superiors, arrived with a questionnaire and diplomatically made arrangements for it to be filled. On 12 December an assembly of impressive size and prestige gathered in the infirmary around Sr Marie-Bernard's bed. Père Sempé was accompanied by Vicaire Général Dubarbier, and Mère Adélaïde Dons was flanked by her two assistants and the secretary Mère Eléonare. Both Père Sempé and the Mother

General had copies of the list of thirty-three questions, and each would make their own records of the replies. The questions involved such issues as whether Bernadette knew what route had been taken when she was carried to the Nicolau mill on 14 February 1858, or what was said there, and how many companions she had with her that day. Had she previously been to any of the grottos at Massabielle, to the shrine at Bétharram, to the catechism class at Bartrès? Could she remember the lamb who was her favourite in the flock at Bartrès? At the time of the third apparition, did she speak to anyone on the way to the Grotto? Had she been to Mass that day? To catechism? To school? To Confession? When beholding the Lady did she see her hair, could she estimate her age, and how did the Lady place her hands?[42] A typical example of Père Cros's minute detailing of question was his enquiry as to whether, at the time of the first apparition, Bernadette had both her shoes off, or both on, or one on and the other off. To this, as to the majority of the questions, Sr Marie-Bernard replied that she could not remember.

Most of Bernadette's interlocutors had only ever wanted a recital of the visions. Père Cros wanted confirmation of specific points, by reference to the accounts of other participants. The attempts to gather a picture of the vision were natural to a Catholic historian. Some of his enquiries show that he was also seeking to establish her prior acquaintance with religion and folklore. It remains a pity that no-one recorded any reminiscences from Bernadette on this topic. Although Père Cros wanted information, he did not have the knack of extracting it. He was not allowed to speak to Bernadette personally, and confronted her through lists of droning questions. The formula of the questionnaire was not one to inspire expansive replies. Even if Père Cros had been able to interview her freely and in person, it is doubtful that he could have obtained a lively and revealing account of 1858, such as that offered to him by other people from Lourdes. Sr Marie-Bernard was too wary, and too distant from these events which had uprooted her life. She was also fatigued and ill. Père Sempé wrote that she had answered each question with 'naivety, joy and simplicity' but that she was evidently very sick. He visited her again the next day. It was a much less formal occasion and he found her somewhat better. The interrogation, unwillingly undergone, was now over, and she was cheerful and communicative. They talked about the past, and she unexpectedly related some anecdotes of her childhood. Perhaps the mention of Bétharram had roused her memory, for it was on this occasion that she told the story of her uncle returning from the shrine with gifts for the children, including a ring which became stuck on her finger.

Père Sempé was able to write to Père Cros that: 'Thanks be to the Blessed Virgin. My mission has been accomplished. Bernadette has forgotten most of the details, but she does not deny them, she only says, which is true, that she does not remember.'[43] It did not end there, as all the participants hoped, for Père Cros was to return with more queries. He was in the midst of his work, and wanted Bernadette to confirm the chronology of events, and the words heard during each vision. He obtained a written version of the Lady's declaration on 18 December 1878, then sent two new lists of question on 31 December. The questions went into infinitesimal searches for each feature of the vision, such as the fastening of the blue girdle. There were hundreds of questions, and even reading them now, as a researcher in the archive, is tedious and fatiguing. The overwhelming impression is of legalistic interrogation and disputation. Sr Marie-Bernard continued to reply in brief and negative terms. The only exception was when she made a series of comments on Antoine Claren's memoire of her recitals, which she thought could not be literally accurate, as she was quoted as using elaborate formulas of speech which she did not understand even years later. Otherwise her responses were minimal, and irritable when Père Cros challenged her own version of events. He wanted dates, but she explained repeatedly that she did not know them. When she nominated days of the week, he claimed that she must have been mistaken, and she then asserted points such as that 'it was a Monday *and a Friday* that the apparitions did not appear' with ever more emphasis.

Père Cros's inquisitorial instincts were roused still further, and he wrote to Mère Adélaïde that there was 'a multitude of particular details which she has lost sight of, and which we must recall to her mind'. The Reverend Mother did not agree, and even supervising the interrogations of Sr Marie-Bernard was fatiguing for the Sisters. She suggested that if he had any more difficulties, 'you should address yourself to Mgr the Bishop of Nevers. We do not have the courage, without an express order on his part, to torment still more our Sister, who is already suffering so much at the moment.'[44] This permission must have been granted, because the questionnaires went on, and became longer. There were 155 questions sent on 11 February, 98 questions on 14 February, 65 on 18 February, and a further 100 on 21 February. He considered his enquiries as a means of reviving her consciousness of these all-important events, while Sr Marie-Bernard, who had the sympathy of the Sisters of Nevers, saw it as a torturous review of unimportant details. 'I want a total description of the veil,' he wrote, 'position, length, width, folds, material, etc.' The Superior General recorded her dismissive response: 'Sr Marie-Bernard made an expressive gesture and said: How am I to remember all that? If he wants to know, he should make her come back ... '[45] This is rather reminiscent of the old Bernadette during the confrontations of 1858, a flash of the humour and the replies which rebutted all criticism. She was usually much more subdued, and the historians had weapons like no others. In their recasting of a multitude of memories and contemporary documents, their production of knowledge is made visible, and the power which operated through this process put the former visionary in a subordinate position. Père Cros really knew far more about her visions than she did herself, and she could not respond to his authoritative discourse. It was at this time that she made her famous recommendation to historians. She suggested that they ought not to write too much: 'out of the wish to embellish events, people distort them'.[46]

Père Cros dismissed the notion that he would ever be inclined to embellish anything. 'It is very much to the contrary, there is much to be de-embellished.'[47] He continued to send more lists of questions. Mère Adélaïde Dons transmitted Sr Marie-Bernard's replies, but said that she could not question her very well, because the former visionary was 'very exhausted'.[48] Moreover, she 'does not understand why people are returning thus to the charge, after all that the Episcopal Commission had written, according to her statement, at the time of the event'.[49] The picture of the historians tormenting Bernadette on her deathbed is not a pleasant one, and it left a lasting impression at the convent of St Gildard, where the community has rather an antipathetic attitude towards historians, to this day. Mère Dons informed Père Cros that 'I must tell you, Reverend Father, that it cost me a great deal to torment her further' and asked that Sr Marie-Bernard's state of health be taken into account.[50] He must have been aware of their reproaches, and took the unusual step (for him) of making excuses. He claimed that he 'had not been aware of how near to the end of her strength Sr Marie-Bernard had been'.[51] He was merely the last of a long line of clerics who saw Bernadette wearied by recitals, but who pressed on regardless. The historian's questionnaires completed the theme which had dominated her existence since 1858, and maintained the consistent note of scrutiny until her last period of life. Despite the protests of the superiors at her convent, the questions went on, and the final interrogation about the apparitions took place in early March 1879, only six weeks before she died.

The fact that Sr Marie-Bernard had obviously come to the end of her life made it more, not less, imperative to get the complete story of Lourdes from her. Père Sempé, after he had seen Sr Marie-Bernard in December 1878, obviously began thinking about the posthumous biography. He wrote to Mère Adélaïde Dons, making a suggestion which may have been taken up at St Gildard. 'Permit me again, Reverend Mother, to remind you of an idea which you may make use of in the future, if you think it right. It seems to me that there would no longer be, as there was in the past, anything wrong in a religious who has the confidence of Sr Marie-Bernard conversing with her about the apparitions, and all of the past, then immediately to write down the memory of that conversation ... etc.'[52] It is not known if this suggestion was put into effect, but attempts may have been made. It is noticeable that in the last year of Sr Marie-Bernard's life several Sisters conversed with her about the apparitions, as if the ban on such conversations no longer existed. Notably, Sr Gabrielle de Vigouroux testified that she had received a complete recital of the apparitions from Sr Marie-Bernard, one night in the infirmary, and that she had made a written record of Bernadette's words the following day. Given Bernadette's lifelong habit of never raising the subject of the apparitions herself, it is likely that Sr Gabrielle must have asked her about it. Sr Gabrielle was no giddy novice. If she broke the silence and questioned her about Lourdes, it would have been because she had permission, or even instructions, to do so. And as Sr Gabrielle was in the position of a superior over Sr Marie-Bernard at that time, if she asked for such an account it would have to be given. In September 1878, at the time of the final profession, one of Sr Marie-Bernard's companions had asked her about Lourdes. Sr Stanislas Tourriol was merely her equal, and therefore could not require her to communicate. 'I tried to get her onto the subject of Lourdes; I would have liked to know if she believed in the miracles which had taken place there ... I could not obtain the slightest allusion, one would have said that she knew nothing at all about it.' Sr Marie-Bernard had other things on her mind. 'When she was leaving us, I asked her for her prayers: "Yes, yes, I will pray," she said, "but not in this world. I have not long to live, I am so sick." '[53] These questions may have irritated her, especially as they intruded on the holy day of Perpetual Vows, when her life as a Sister of Nevers ought to have been confirmed. Sr Joseph Caldairou met her at the same time:

> On the day, or the day after, our Perpetual Vows, I met Sr Marie-Bernard, who seemed agitated, like one who is annoyed. I squeezed her arm and said:
> —Ah Sr Marie-Bernard, what is wrong?
> —Leave me alone, pray for me.[54]

## The family in Lourdes

While the historians from Lourdes pursued Sr Marie-Bernard, she herself turned her eyes towards home, because she was concerned about her family. During her last two years of life, Bernadette was involved in family arguments, and was often worried by news of relatives in Lourdes. Her correspondence with her relatives took on a note of censure, and she believed that she had the responsibility to admonish them, because their parents were dead. She, therefore, had the traditional Pyrenean role of the 'heiress', the head of the family. Evidently, Sr Marie-Bernard did not share the view of some cloistered religious that the vows of profession severed one's links with one's family. Nor did her family feel that religious life made Bernadette less of a Soubirous. They meekly took the advice of their elder sister, as it was proper for them to do. They also sought her good opinion, sometimes by running each other down in their letters to her. The family rivalries reached a high pitch during the late 1870s. This was partly because of circumstances – at their age a final division of assets had to be made. Another factor may have been the failing health of Sr Marie-Bernard. She was their link to power, wealth and authority. When her family knew she would soon be gone, they were motivated to get as much as possible in the short period left.

In 1876, only four siblings were left from the Soubirous family of nine. Both Jean-Marie and Pierre had considered entering religious life. Jean-Marie Soubirous had actually entered the novitiate of the Frères de l'Instruction Chrétienne, while Pierre became a junior scholar at the seminary of the Garaison priests. As a student, Pierre Soubirous had made no commitment, but if he had completed his studies, he would have been eligible for ordination. Jean-Marie Soubirous left the Frères in order to do his compulsory military service, which concluded in November 1876, and did not return to the novitiate. In the same year, Pierre Soubirous abandoned his studies at Garaison. All of this caused some concern to Sr Marie-Bernard, although she recognized that neither of her brothers had made a binding pledge to his vocations, and they were free to leave. The question raised by their departures was the vexed one of where they would live, and what they would do. If they had continued in religious life, as she had done, it would have been a benefit to the sibling who remained in the world – Toinette Soubirous. By taking vows, Bernadette had relieved her family from the duty of supporting her and giving her an inheritance. If her brothers had done likewise, Toinette Soubirous and her husband could have inherited absolute rights to the Lacade mill, without partition. Such a benefit, in a family of few resources, was one of the reasons why vocations to the accessible active congregations were so encouraged during this era. However, with the exception of Bernadette, none of the Soubirous was the type of person to live in institutions. By 1876, with their parents dead, they were all under the one roof again, as the 25-year-old Jean-Marie and the seventeen-year-old Pierre Soubirous had moved back to the mill where Marie Soubirous and Joseph Sabathé were living. It was not a happy arrangement, as it was obvious that their sister and brother-in-law had assumed that they would not return.

Shortly before Jean-Marie Soubirous had finished his military service, Sr Marie-Bernard wrote to him. Her letter had a tone of concern, because he was vague about his plans for the future:

Tell me what you plan to do, you must be aware that I take an interest, whether I am near or far. If I ask you this question, it is not through curiosity; no, dear friend, it is because we no longer have our parents, it seems to me that this is my duty, as your eldest, to watch over you; needless to say I feel a strong interest towards all of you. I tell you that at this moment I am preoccupied about your future and that of Pierre, I pray every day to Our Lord and the Virgin Mary to enlighten you.[55]

As soon as he returned to the family house, a rather meagre inheritance which was now to be shared, tensions were felt. These went as far as Nevers. 'I read your last letter with dismay,' Sr Marie-Bernard wrote in November 1876, 'because of the discontent which you suffer in regard to my brother-in-law and sister; I fear that you are making too much of yourself; it is not during a moment of irritation that one should speak or write.'[56] She advised him to think before acting, and assured him that Marie had said nothing to her about the future of the mill, and in any case: 'You can arrange nothing until Pierre is of age. I advise you to be patient and to keep peace in the household, for the good of the whole family.'[57]

This advice sounded hopeful rather than realistic, and soon Pierre, too, was at home. Sr Marie-Bernard heard that he intended to leave the seminary, and was apparently offended that she received this important news from a third party. But it is understandable that both brothers felt uncomfortable in sending word of their setbacks to the paragon at Nevers. Their communications with her had never been close, and became brief and irregular as they contended with life. In the same month of November 1876, while she was reproaching Jean-Marie, she wrote to Pierre that she had been told that perhaps you will not return to Garaison in the coming year. If you really believe that the Lord has not called you to the religious life, I strongly advise you to learn a trade. I urge you, dear brother, to think well before God; I would not want, for all the world, that you make yourself a priest for the sake of a good position, I would rather that you were a rag-picker. I hope that you realize that it is out of concern for you that I speak of this.[58]

Her concern, impotently displayed in letters of advice, was to continue over the following year. It was clear that her brothers did not heed her words and avoided her judgements. In February 1877, only three months after his return home, Sr Marie-Bernard was startled to hear that Jean-Marie Soubirous had married. She complained that she had found his letter cold in tone: 'It is not that I am annoyed that you should get married, no; but it seems to me that it would be better if I were to learn this a few days at least before the wedding; it would have been a great happiness for me to have been able to unite my prayers with yours that day.'[59] She also asked if his wife was from Lourdes, and from a Christian family. The household at the mill was growing rapidly, and in a way which recalled the quarrels and rivalries of Bernadette's childhood. At least the younger generation did not face the outright destitution which had faced François and Louise Soubirous, but they were still poor. The family disputes reached a height when Pierre was said to have publicly insulted Marie and her husband, and then left the house. Sr Marie-Bernard reproached Jean-Marie Soubirous: 'It seems that it is because of you and your wife that Pierre has left the house ... Tell me what effect this will have on the strangers who are obliged to take care of our brother ... I am ashamed of you others: what must be the thoughts of the people of the town to see you in dispute as you are, you who ought to be giving a good example?'[60]

The notion that the Soubirous should be an example before others was a new one within their own family. Sr Marie-Bernard's letters show that by the age of thirty-five, and after ten years of religious life, she had thoroughly internalized clerical standards. Once she had not cared what visitors to Lourdes thought, and had been uncritically loyal to her low-class family. It was the years in Nevers which had given her a certain distance and judgement. Unavailingly, she tried to impose higher standards on her relatives, and to remind them that it was important that they be of good repute. During the month of November 1876, the same month in which she had been rather shrilly addressing her brothers, she also snapped at her cousin, Lucile Pène, the daughter of Aunt Basile. She stated that she had heard with dismay that Lucile Pène's husband had to be urged to go to Mass, and that they were operating a religious goods store which traded on Sunday. Sr Marie-Bernard stated that: 'You must be an example, not only to the people of the town, but also to visitors who come to Lourdes.'[61] The Soubirous brothers replied to her in deferential letters. Each defended his own behaviour, and explained the reasons why they were at odds with their brother-in-law Joseph Sabathé. Pierre Soubirous described how he was addressed with teasing and name-calling; these petty insults made life in the family home impossible for him. Jean-Marie Soubirous was concerned with the weighty matter of dividing the family inheritance. He warned his sister not to believe all that she heard: 'because financial interests make many things said which are not true'.[62]

The full story of these quarrels is not known to us, because some passages of the letters relating to family disputes have been suppressed by the clerical authorities, and do not appear in the collected writings of St Bernadette.[63] The surviving letters of November 1876 are so acrimonious that most scholars who have read them have felt obliged to apologize for her. The editor of her letters noted that part of her sanctity was that she struggled with her own nature.[64] It has also been pointed out that she was very ill in 1876, which aggravated her feelings, and that she was far from events, and therefore received exaggerated impressions. All of this is true, but it need not be the reason why Sr Marie-Bernard took such a tone. To a certain extent, she was simply penning letters in an irate mood. She was probably in need of her own advice: as she wrote to Jean-Marie, one should not write or speak when angry. But also, she was speaking to them as she thought she had the right to speak. She had inherited only one thing from her parents, which was their authority as the eldest in the family. To a Pyrenean, gender was not important; she was the heiress and had the duty to order the others around. Considering that some eldest daughters treated their siblings as 'slaves', Sr Marie-Bernard's letters were comparatively conciliating.

The basis of Sr Marie-Bernard's advice was that if her brothers were not to be clerics, they had better provide for their own futures. Also, the whole family had to remember their status, and observe decorum. She never exactly states why they are an example in the eyes of the world, but it is obviously because of her visions and the establishment of the shrine. There was another reason, which may not have been part of Sr Marie-Bernard's reasoning, but which the Soubirous would have done well to consider. Their very limited resources were a gift from the Church, and it was only because of the generosity of Mgr Laurence that they had the right to lease a mill on concessional terms. Now that the parents were dead, the younger Soubirous could be shrugged off if they became an embarrassment, and their position without a home would have been very marginal.

After the flurry of angry letters in 1877, the disputes were smoothed over by Père Sempé, who took Pierre Soubirous to live at his own residence and employed him to work in the house and garden. Eventually, he was given a place with the Bishop of Tarbes. Sr Marie-Bernard wrote to Père Sempé expressing her gratitude for the 'great interest which you have deigned to show towards my younger brother, who, for some time, has caused me grave disquiet, I tremble when I think of the responsibility which I will have to show to God for that soul'.[65] Père Sempé responded with reassuring messages. Pierre Soubirous recovered his morale and wrote again to Sr Marie-Bernard, this time asking her to intervene in a quarrel with his brother-in-law, who had borrowed his watch and had not returned it.[66]

During her earlier years at Nevers, Sr Marie-Bernard had been disturbed to think of her relatives profiting from her fame. During the years 1875 to 1879

Toinette Soubirous, her husband and Pierre had worked at religious goods stalls. They had taken up what was, to Bernadette, a repulsive identity, but her protests were disproportionate to their actions. After all, while their parents were working the mill, the grown children needed to provide for themselves, and in Lourdes during the 1860s there were not many chances of making a living outside of the field of religious souvenirs. She cautioned them 'not to enrich themselves', a rather ludicrous warning which suggests that in her annoyance she had forgotten what they were actually like. There was, of course, not much chance of any of the Soubirous children becoming rich. It was far more likely that they would get into debt and have to be rescued again by the Bishop. However, they muddled through, and meekly accepted her advice that they should not trade on a Sunday, which was often the most profitable day of the week. 'She cared about all of us and was most affectionate, she was most concerned, I should say uniquely concerned, with the interests of our souls' explained her brother Jean-Marie Soubirous.[67] He added that she had assured him that 'God and the Blessed Virgin would know how to recompense me during the week for whatever I might lose on Sunday.'

After Bernadette left Lourdes, there were several projected visits between the Soubirous family, but each time it came to nothing. Both Sr Marie-Bernard and the superiors at St Gildard wanted her to stay at the Mother House. A postulant who made the beds in the infirmary had one day 'dared to say to her that no doubt she would be happy to return to her home and see her own family again. She answered me: "I love my brothers and sister a great deal; however, there would be no greater sacrifice for me than to return to Lourdes." '[68] The family at Lourdes contemplated visiting Nevers, but had been deterred by the cost of the journey and their own pressing concerns. It was not easy for people of limited means to cease their endless toiling and start travelling. As Sr Marie-Bernard wrote to her sister in 1873, when a family visit to a niece at Saint-Pé was contemplated: 'it seems that Joseph has been to see her. I would suggest that you do so as well, but it is too far.'[69] The town of Saint-Pé is close to Lourdes, and this statement shows that even short journeys were prohibitive for the poor. However, in late 1878 the Soubirous family realized that if they did not go to Nevers they would not see Bernadette again.

Jean-Marie Soubirous benefited from the generosity of a pilgrim, M. Legentil, who paid for his visit to Nevers in December 1878. The arrival of Bernadette's brother was unexpected. Mère Dons commented that Sr Marie-Bernard had been brought down to the parlour in an armchair, and 'their interview was not without emotion on both sides. That good young man, after a stay of two days at Nevers, left altogether satisfied with his visit, but quite sad to leave his sister bed-ridden.'[70] This is a tactful recollection. Jean-Marie himself had a rather more resentful account of events. In 1892 he told Émile Zola that at first they wanted to refuse him admission to the convent. He refused to accept this. 'He threatened to make such a scandal, that they let him in. He found his sister worn out, but resigned.'[71] Jean-Marie took the opportunity to press his case for better employment. He claimed that his sister believed that he had been given an 'easy, well-paid position lighting candles at the grotto, whereas he was only a labourer, earning 45 sous per day. She promised to write to Père Sempé.'[72] There is no record of her having written such a letter, and it is unlikely that she would have promised much to Jean-Marie. All accounts of the visit emphasize her exhaustion. She was no longer able to stand, and barely able to move at all. She and her brother were never alone together, but the Sisters who accompanied Sr Marie-Bernard, who were struck by the emotion of the brother and sister, could not understand a word of the conversation, because the two spoke in Bigourdanian. It must have been the first time in many years that Bernadette had used her own language. 'With her brother, she was tender, and concerned for her family.'[73] These concerns had been considerable for several years.

The visit of Jean-Marie Soubirous shows the isolation and obligations which surrounded Bernadette until the very end of her life. It seems outrageous that, while she was ruthlessly being made available to clerical historians, an attempt was made to prevent her own brother from seeing her. The reason was that a male member of the laity should not be admitted to the convent infirmary. Exceptions could be made, but it seems that initially the Mother Superior was inclined to be dismissive. But Bernadette was still a public figure, and such rigidity would not look good in the eyes of the outside world. In threatening to publicize their refusal, Jean-Marie Soubirous was making a powerful threat. A compromise was soon arranged, by putting Bernadette on an armchair and carrying her to the parlour. There is no doubt that she loved her family, and would have been pleased to see him. But Jean-Marie himself was no disinterested visitor, and seems to have been quick to use the visit for his own advantage. Like so many of her relatives, he assumed that Bernadette's special position in the Church ought to be of benefit for himself, and his desire for a cushy job seems to have been uppermost in his mind. Émile Zola, who took his account from Jean-Marie, claimed that: 'Nothing has been done for the two brothers. The younger one is at the moment working as a servant for the Bishop of Tarbes.'[74] The Bishop of Tarbes would have disputed the idea that nothing had been done for them. Aside from buying the family a mill, employment for the younger brothers had always been offered, although only at the minimal level which their unskilled status allowed.

After Jean-Marie, Toinette Soubirous arrived in Nevers on 18 March 1879. She came with her husband, but could not bring even one of her children. Each one of them had died, which was a family tragedy. In contrast to the earlier visit, there was no difficulty in allowing them to see Sr Marie-Bernard. They visited her bedside in the infirmary. She was so ill that conversation was impossible. Toinette would have known how gravely ill her sister was when she set out, and would not have been surprised, although she may have been upset, to see her wasted and immobilized. Sr Marie-Bernard looked at them and nodded, but could barely whisper a reply to their remarks. Little could be said, but the visit was made, and the family achieved their aim, seeing one another for the last time. When Toinette left the infirmary, it closed the chapter on their relationship, which had been distant, but constant, for the whole of Bernadette's life. The two sisters had set out together on that momentous walk to Massabielle in 1858, twenty-one years earlier. Toinette Soubirous returned to Lourdes knowing that she would not hear from Bernadette again, and that soon there would be nothing left of her but memories.

Sr Marie-Bernard received other news from Lourdes, because the situation of Curé Peyramale had become ever more difficult. In December 1876 she wrote to him, sending best wishes for the new year. 'I have heard with much joy, Monseigneur, that the building of your new church is advanced.' She assured him of her prayers and expressed 'once more the gratitude which I feel for all the generosity which you have show towards me and my family'.[75] This letter may have heartened Mgr Peyramale, but he was in a most difficult situation. Père Sempé and the authorities at the Grotto continued steadfastly to refuse to include the parish organizations in any pilgrim events. The parish church was being built, and the Curé maintained an optimistic front, but he was crushed by debt and the works were proceeding too slowly. On 9 December 1876 he was summoned for an interview by the Bishop of Tarbes. Mgr Peyramale blustered when asked about the parish church in Lourdes. He said that the project was going well and that he 'had no debts except for a few bagatelles which I could pay off at any time'.[76] This was not true, and the Bishop knew it. Mgr Peyramale, trapped and unhappy, could not bear the stress. According to the Episcopal authorities: 'On 8 September 1877, death removed the Curé of Lourdes from a situation which was full of risk on every side.'[77] Sr Marie-Bernard was very saddened, and wrote to Abbé Pomain: 'It seems that the chagrin which he felt on the subject of the new church would have contributed a great deal to his death.' She commented that one must respect the designs of God, 'otherwise, I believe that I would feel resentment toward my dear Lourdais for having given such trouble to the good father who cared so much for them'.[78] In the event, the church planned by Curé Peyramale remained unfinished for decades. As late as the 1890s, Lourdes, of all the towns in France, was without a parish church of its own.

## Dying

While the family letters, and the academic questionnaires, were exchanged, Sr Marie-Bernard was in the last stages of her illness. She lay helpless in the hands of others. There was nothing unusual in what was happening to her. A comparison can be given by relating the story of Sr Reine Basset, who died in the infirmary of the Mother House on 23 May 1866. Her obituary stated that when not in bed she would try to perform small services for the infirmarian. 'Her illness, however, made rapid progress; frequent vomitings of blood and continual suffocation made it obvious that her end was near. Three weeks before her death her sufferings were intense and she spent her nights on an armchair – she never spoke a word of complaint ... She had certain faults of character, expressions of a personality which was opposed to constraint.'[79] Although Sr Reine sometimes expressed her frustration, she always regretted it later, and died at the age of twenty-nine in a holy manner. Every word of this account could also be applied to Sr Marie-Bernard, who died in the same location, and was probably supported by the same armchair, in 1879. Sr Marie-Bernard died at the age of thirty-five; like Sr Reine, she did not live to see the middle years of life. Wishing to be useful, but confined to bed, never complaining, but sometimes giving way to rage, vomiting, bleeding and suffocating, the victims of consumption gasped their way out of life. Many Sisters of Nevers, not to mention other people across France, died from tuberculosis. In Sr Marie-Bernard's own congregation during the 1860s, amid numerous cases of tuberculosis in the lungs, there had been several cases of the rare variety of infection in the bones, which befell her. There was no cure available, but the few treatments which medicine could offer were available in the infirmary at St Gildard.

Although Sr Marie-Bernard was well cared for, she did not relate well to the medical professionals who were close to her. The long-standing lack of sympathy between herself and the infirmarian has already been noted. Then, during the last stage of her illness, there was a rift with the doctor. Dr St Cyr had apparently been on the most friendly terms with Sr Marie-Bernard during her earlier years at St Gildard. He had spoken of her warmly, worked with her harmoniously, and must have been the medical consultant during her previous illnesses. There was no hint of tension between them then, unless in the seemingly innocent anecdote of Sr Marie-Bernard giving comic imitations of his manner. Yet, somehow, their relationship frayed during the long ordeal of her final illness.

It is not easy for a doctor to tend a patient with whom they are personally acquainted. This may have been a source of friction. Sr Marie-Bernard had related to him on a more social or professional level, but then, when she became bedridden, had to reassume the passivity of the female patient. If she disliked this she may have made it difficult for Dr Saint-Cyr to give her directions. Or the impatience may have been on the side of the medical practitioner, who, along with his patient, was faced by an irreversible, agonizing disease. In the nineteenth century, members of his profession were accustomed to facing such horrors, but it cannot have been easy, especially when the patient whom he could not cure, or even assuage, was a trusted friend.

By December 1876, when she had entered the last stage of her illness, Sr Marie-Bernard seems to have had difficulty in getting a response from Dr Saint-Cyr. The sources are limited, but in a letter written that month she told Abbé Pomain that 'my stomach is not co-operative; I suffer constantly when digesting; however, I have been able to keep down some food for the last month. I was telling the Doctor that this was a long time, but he turned away, saying that I have a terrible enemy. I am beginning to think that he is losing his grip. [*Je commence à croire qu'il perd son latin.*]'[80] The description of her illness as a 'terrible enemy' does sound very odd, when coming from a medical practitioner. Dr Saint-Cyr sounds either dismissive, or appalled, much like a person from Bernadette's own level of society. He may have merely been preoccupied at that moment, considering whether she would die soon, or whether she was suffering from a further new disease. Some of Sr Marie-Bernard's symptoms during her agonized last months were not consistent with tuberculosis. This is particularly evident when considering her stomach pains and vomiting. One of the priests at St Gildard claimed that Sr Marie-Bernard eventually was angry with the doctor and said, 'I do not want him; he should not come back.'[81] She would not have been in a position to refuse his services entirely, but it is noticeable that he is not mentioned in the accounts of her last weeks, and was not present at her deathbed. Abbé Febvre claimed that Sr Marie-Bernard was given to 'childish outbursts of rage, caused especially by the Doctor. He treated her as an imaginary invalid [*malade fantastique*].'[82] The doctor may have rejected her own interpretations of her illness, and reserved for himself the right to make diagnoses. He may also have given her false reassurances about her state of health, and told her that she was not about to die. This type of confabulation was common in medicine at the time. Many doctors believed that it was their duty to calm the sick and hide the knowledge of their mortality from them. It might have sounded patronizing to Sr Marie-Bernard, which would explain her ill-temper toward him.

It was not very polite of Sr Marie-Bernard to say that she wanted Dr Saint-Cyr to go away. But if she did not want his services, this was the logical response. It was more difficult to repel the Sisters who had claims on her as fellow members of the community. They continued to make visits, even during her last weeks. This was a convent custom. It was part of the trials and consolations of the community life that the sick and dying were surrounded by well-wishers who supported them in their ordeals. Because of Sr Marie-Bernard's special status, she had far more visitors than normal, and rather than offering prayers for her, they were inclined to ask *her* to pray. One Sister, who was visiting from another convent, had brought a very long and specific list of intentions which she wanted Sr Marie-Bernard to address. There were, according to Sr Victoire Cassou, thirty-six recommendations, 'prayers of all sorts'. When she finally left the infirmary, Sr Marie-Bernard exclaimed: ' "There she goes. I would rather see her heels than the tip of her nose. When one is in pain, one needs to be alone." "You'll say the same thing about me when I'm gone," said Sr Victoire. "Oh no, my dear friend, it is not the same thing at all." '[83]

Sr Marcella Poujade also worked in the infirmary, but did not converse with Sr Marie-Bernard on such equal terms, being only a novice. However, even she noticed how annoyed Sr Marie-Bernard was when she was unable to make a thanksgiving after communion, because Sisters who had just finished their breakfast passed the infirmary, and dropped in to see her. The lively Sr Marcella, known to be of 'hot blood and prompt decision', sympathized with Sr Marie-Bernard, and offered a simple remedy – she locked the door of the infirmary the following morning. Sr Marie-Bernard enjoyed the unprecedented privacy. 'What a service you performed for me! I rested in true peace. Someone came and knocked. They even turned the knob, but I did not falter. I was so happy in the company of the Good Lord!'[84] In terms of convent life, this action was wrong, on the part of both the novice and the patient. As a cleric who heard Sr Marcella's account concluded: 'to lock the door in this manner, this could only be the idea of a novice, little acquainted with proper ways. The Rule of the Community does not permit either to shut someone out, nor to shut anyone away.'[85] Sr Marie-Bernard herself must have known this, and the next day she said to Sr Marcella ' "Don't lock me in again." I answered: "As you wish." She did not give any reason, and I did not ask.' Even years later, when she recounted these scenes, Sr Marcella did not seem to have repented of her audacity.

When Sr Marie-Bernard could no longer leave her bed, she could not go to the chapel and attend devotions. She pinned holy cards to the curtains of her bed. Her words, and her attitudes, varied. Her devotion and piety were manifest, as were her humour, cynicism and anger. Among the holy cards on her curtain was a picture of the altar at Mass, and Sr Philomena recalled her pointing it out – ' "Masses are celebrated perpetually on one or another parts of the globe, and I unite my prayers with them, especially at night when I am not sleeping." She said this very seriously, but then resumed a playful manner and added: "What annoys me is that little choir-boy who doesn't ring the bell." ' The picture should have shown the bell being rung, as it represented the elevation of the host, and once Sr Marie-Bernard had noticed this, 'he never chimes' became a favourite joke.[86] She took more serious inspiration from her crucifix, and said that: 'When one is in bed one must keep still and consider oneself as being like Our Lord on the cross.'[87]

The chaplain would visit her bedside, and offer words of spiritual comfort. When he told her that she would soon know the delights of paradise 'and contemplate the beauty and glory of Our Lord', she responded with enthusiasm and said that the thought did her good.[88] This was an unusually positive moment. More often, when the chaplain, and others, tried to encourage her by saying that 'heaven is at the end', their pieties weighed on her. She would answer, 'The end is slow to arrive.'[89] She was even more contrary when Abbé Febvre suggested that she should 'offer the sacrifice of her life'. This was a devotion often practised by the Sisters of Nevers, who would pray that their deaths would be accepted as a sacrifice for the good of their religion, their order, or their nation. Sr Marie-Bernard rejected the idea. She spoke up loudly with a rhetorical question: 'What sacrifice? It is no sacrifice to leave this miserable life, where it is so difficult to belong to God.'[90] This comment is a disillusioned echo of the optimistic statement which had been the opening lines of her *Carnet*: 'From this time onward I must belong entirely to God.'[91] It had not been quite so simple, even at St Gildard. Sr Marie-Bernard might also have rejected the suggestion because, in her case, people wanted to believe that she would offer the sacrifice of her life for 'the Church, France and the congregation'.[92] Indeed, after her death it was authoritatively claimed that she had done so. Bernadette had always been inimical to the religious nationalism which flooded French Catholicism at this time. Yet her words 'What sacrifice?' spoken with 'a surprising sharpness', did not have any effect.[93] The idea that she suffered for 'the triumph of the Church and the salvation of France' was a conclusive interpretation of her situation.[94]

The contemplation and interpretation of her pain came to mean a great deal to her audience of clerical admirers, and the people for whom they wrote. Representations of her terminal illness were elaborated through such studied metaphors as a comparison of the dissolution of her skeleton with the raising of the walls of the Grand Basilica at Lourdes (which took place at exactly the same time, in 1877–9). The convent chaplain was to write that: 'The Lord was not content to dwell in her heart as a tabernacle. He wanted a spiritual temple more grand, more rich and more worthy of him, of which the stones were cut and polished by pain and in the midst of which he would never cease to repose with delight.'[95] Sr Marie-Bernard had always had an attitude of pronounced indifference to the redevelopment of the Grotto. Considering this, such flights of fancy, and the daily attitudes which underpinned them, may have irked her. Mgr Forcade, the Bishop of Nevers, came out of the clouds to recall that: 'She did not suffer in an irreproachable manner. Certain impatient gestures, certain vivacities, certain outbursts even, had sometimes astonished and painfully impressed those who cared for her.'[96] This is probably true, although some other witnesses, who were closer to Bernadette and lived within the convent, claimed that her uncertain temper actually improved when she was ill.

As the tumour in her knee grew, it spread an infection through the marrow of her bones. The tuberculous lesions corroded her bone structure amid violent bouts of pain. By 1879, she was immobilized, and needed help in order to turn in the bed. She had developed bedsores, and the infirmarian saw that 'Her poor body is nothing but one wound, there is no more skin on all of the lower half.'[97] A night-nurse was assigned to sleep in the infirmary and assist her when called. A novice, Sr Michel Duhème, was one of those who performed this duty, and received a strong impression from it. 'What a night I passed! ... I could not tell you what I felt, on being present but helpless at the martyrdom of our poor Sister.' Sr Michel described how Sr Marie-Bernard gasped with pain, but did not call for assistance. 'One by one, I heard the hours sound, and when the chimes ceased the same sighs continued ... That is how I passed that terrible night, like someone at the foot of a living crucifix.'[98] Reading this description, one can understand why Sr Marie-Bernard asked that Sr Michel not be sent back for the same duty. ' "I do not want that Sister to look after me, she hasn't slept. I want Sisters who sleep. If I have need for them, I can call." ' [99] Sr Alphonse Guerre, a novice who looked after her during her last weeks, found that she was called several times during the night. Sr Marie-Bernard 'asked me to help turn her in order that she could rest: for her poor body was raw, and one could say that she was resting on wounds. Then we would try this manoeuvre, which was difficult. I would take the foot of her affected leg (she had a knee horribly tumified by the decay of the bones) and I would try to follow the movement of her body, in order that she could turn over at once, without having to move her leg. I can remember that during that interminable night she did not speak one impatient or discontented word.'[100]

At the Mother House, the simple jobs of the infirmary were given to novices. It was these young people, with few skills or status, who carried out the direct nursing of the dying Sister. Novices were strong enough to lift the immobile, humble enough to make beds and empty chamber pots, and unimportant enough to carry out the time-consuming tasks of accompanying an invalid. Sr Marie-Bernard's last social relationships were with these girls, who had always been her favourite members of the community. She still had the status of a visionary, but she was no longer an authority figure; her powers, her religious habit, and even her pretty face had all gone. The indignities of the sickbed had to be endured, and she was undressed by her nurses. 'She was of an extreme reserve and of a remarkable modesty. You could discern her purity in the manner by which she comported herself when, in the infirmary, we gave her the services which her state of health required.'[101]

Many witnesses maintained the custom of describing her beautiful eyes, and radiant gaze, even when referring to her last days. Abbé Febvre drew upon his literary skills when he gave an account of how her eyes 'ordinarily bright and clear, took on a particular expression ... Her gaze became more expressive to the extent that her body became emaciated.'[102] One has the impression that some of the novices who worked in the infirmary strained to be able to dredge up these memories, but failed. 'She was little, dainty, with very small hands. I was not struck as others were by her gaze, perhaps because the curtains of the bed cast her in the shade.'[103] They washed her, fed her, and during the summer of 1878, Sr Marie-Bernard had her last walks, supported on the arm of a novice. The impatient words which she spoke were not directed at the novices. 'She did not complain, neither of her sufferings, nor of her bad nights, nor of the length of her illness, nor of me, who from time to time made blunders.'[104]

In her last weeks, Sr Marie-Bernard burned with a fever, and showed some signs of delirium. She awoke frightened from nightmares, and took a few moments to recognize where she was. Sr Philomena Roques, who was on duty in the infirmary one night, was jolted by a cry from Sr Marie-Bernard: 'Who is there to look after me?' Sr Philomena went to her immediately, and found her forehead running with sweat. She seemed to be 'under the influence of a bad dream which filled her with terror'. Sr Philomena was shocked to hear her patient say ' "I was back there – at Massabielle ..." '[105] Sr Philomena reassured her 'No, dear Sister, you are in your bed.'[106] She found this 'a mystery. Massabielle, the Grotto, ought to have been for Bernadette a souvenir of paradise. How had she been able to change the sight of that place into a nightmare?' Sr Marie-Bernard explained her dream briefly: 'There was a little boy, he was throwing stones in the stream.' It is in the nature of a nightmare that the fear often cannot be described to another person. Psychological interpretations of this dream could be offered, and religious writers have suggested that Bernadette was recalling the scenes of 'false visionaries'. In fact, it is not clear from this description if the boy was throwing stones in the sacred spring, as most writers assume, or if the waterway in question (*torrent* is the word quoted from Bernadette) was the Gave river. Whatever the scene, it frightened the dying woman, and her cries sounded 'as if the stones of the little boy had struck her'.[107]

At this very last stage of her life, Sr Marie-Bernard seems to have returned to Massabielle, but not happily. After so many years of silence, she spoke of the Grotto and the visions without being prompted. One evening she told Sr

Gabrielle that when she had first seen the vision 'I thought that it was the devil.'[108] Possibly, amid her fevers and broken nights, she was haunted by the original Massabielle – not the 'souvenir of paradise' which Sr Philomena assumed it to be, but the dark site of Pyrenean folklore. She was afraid of the approach of evil spirits, and sometimes cried out 'away Satan'. These moments of fear might have been what Mère Éléonore Cassagnes remembered when she said that despite the fact that 'her character was more unified when she was ill – she was more amiable – she also had some rather difficult times when she was dying. She developed some imaginary ideas. [*Elle se mettait un peu en fantaisie.*]'[109] (This could also be interpreted as simply meaning that she had odd crochets.) It is possible that the last visions of St Bernadette were the terrifying deliriums of her deathbed.

The psychological sufferings seem to have faded away again during her last weeks, when she was perfectly lucid, but the physical torment never ceased. Mère Éléonore sounded appalled to recall it: 'her knee enormous, the leg shrunk. Sometimes it took an hour to put her in one position – her face changed, she became like a corpse. She who was very energetic in suffering, she was defeated by the disease... Even when asleep, the slightest movement of her leg would cause her to cry out ... She passed nights without sleep. During the last winter before her death, her feverish cries prevented her companions in the infirmary from sleeping. In her suffering, she shrank away, became nothing.'[110] The photograph taken of Bernadette after her death shows how emaciated her face had become.

She received Extreme Unction (the Sacrament of the Dying) on 28 March. A large number of Sisters gathered in the infirmary in order to participate in the ceremony. Sr Marie-Bernard spoke to them, in 'a strong clear voice which surprised us, on account of her infirmity ... "My dear Mère, I ask your pardon for all the pains which I have caused you in the course of my religious life, and I also ask pardon of my companions for the bad examples which I have given them." She added in an even stronger tone: "And especially for my pride." '[111] She was extremely weak, and this sacrament was administered because she was judged to be at the point of death, but she lingered for a further three weeks.

By Easter of 1879, her life was finally over. The Journal of the Community noted that: 'She is edifying, resigned in the midst of her great sufferings.'[112] Every day, they expected her to die, and she herself said: 'I am ground like a grain of wheat. I would not have believed that one had to suffer so much in order to die.'[113] The Easter ceremonies began on 13 April. Lent was over, and the feast days had begun, but Sr Marie-Bernard had no role any more in either feasting or fasting. Holy Communion was brought to the infirmary, and she said that she had asked God for only ten minutes of peace, in order to meditate after communion 'but He did not wish to grant it'.[114] She still received visitors, although she could hardly respond to them. Sr Bernard Dalias came to the infirmary with a group of Sisters.

> They came in as quietly as they could, in order to spare her fatigue and respect her rest. It was a visit of devotion as much as charity. I was part of

**Plate XV**   Sr Marie-Bernard immediately after her death. © *Ed. A Doucet, Lourdes*

this pilgrimage, but I did not have the strength to keep the same discretion as my companions, who stayed in the doorway ... I went to the foot of her bed, of which the white curtains had been drawn back in order to allow her to breathe more freely; and there, resting on the metal bar, I watched her in silence. She seemed to be dozing, her face was turned toward the wall.

I believe that she had at that moment an impression that someone was near her. I saw her turn her head slightly, open her eyes and look at me. She recognized me at once and let me know it with an expression which I cannot describe, but which I would call a smile of her eyes.

Then, that language of looks seemed, I think, too little expressive, she lifted her arms outside of the covers and extended her hand to me, which I seized to grasp in affection. She accompanied her gesture with these words, which were enough to exhaust her breath:

—Adieu, Bernard. This time, it is really the end ...

As soon as she had gasped these words, I thought of kissing this little hand which I still held and which had performed such great works through the almighty power of God. ... But as soon as I made a gesture toward my lips the invalid herself prevented me, as if she had guessed my intention. Her hand was suddenly withdrawn, and she hid it under the sheet. ... she then resumed her first position in silence, for the retirement of her last hours. She had not noticed the presence of my companions; this gave me the privilege of a personal adieu.[115]

Sr Bernard remembered that she had exclaimed 'Only that!' upon first meeting Bernadette twelve years before. Sr Marie-Bernard had responded happily then, and had immediately shaken hands with her. As Sr Bernard said, their friendship began and ended with a handclasp. Sr Bernard recounted with pride how she had disturbed Bernadette on her deathbed. To her, as to so many others, Sr Marie-Bernard was a privileged being, and there were no limits to their expectations of her. One person who was not at St Gildard was Mère Marie-Thérèse Vauzou. She herself had been ill, and then had been sent to another convent to convalesce. So she and Sr Marie-Bernard were not obliged to go on communicating with each other during the final three weeks.

In complete contrast to Sr Bernard Dalias, there were some people in Sr Marie-Bernard's environment who responded to her with tact and reserve. These very qualities prevented them from joining the ranks of those who boasted of the words and gestures which they wrung out of Bernadette. As she dozed on the bed, another group of Sisters came to the infirmary to look at her. These were newly professed, former novices who had just taken their vows. They were less forward than high-ranking religious, and stayed quietly by the door. But Sr Marie-Bernard saw them, and put out her arm to beckon one over. It was Sr Marcella Poujade, the novice who had once closed the door of the infirmary for her, and had taken her for her last walks in the garden. Sr Marie-Bernard kissed her, in a unique gesture of farewell.

Sr Nathalie Portat, one of the superiors at St Gildard, was a frequent visitor to the bedside, and was known to have an exceptionally close friendship with Sr Marie-Bernard. Yet, probably for this very reason, we know very little about it. Sr Nathalie was in her late fifties when Bernadette died, and she herself lived on until 1908. Despite her long life, she left no testimonial about her relationship with the famous visionary. Sr Nathalie is an elusive presence in the story of Nevers. She had the reputation of being a model religious, and of being sensitive to others. Before she died, Sr Nathalie was asked by Abbé Febvre to write an account of Bernadette's death. She did so, in a 'Black Notebook' which has since been lost.[116] The substance of her account was recorded when it was read to the *Procès* at Nevers. Sr Nathalie's account is unusual. 'One notices that the tone is impersonal, and that there are a lot of ellipses and matters not fully stated.'[117] Sr Nathalie refers to herself, in this account, in the third person as Sr X. Her reticent memoir gives a reflective view of Sr Marie-Bernard's last hours. The other Sisters who were present in the infirmary have also given descriptions of her final moments.

Sr Nathalie visited Sr Marie-Bernard in the evening, and found her in a state of suffering, both physical and emotional. 'I am afraid, she said ... I have received so many graces ... and I have made so little use of them.' Sr Nathalie soothed her, saying 'All the merits of the Heart of Jesus are ours. Offer them to God in repayment of your debts.'[118] The dying woman appeared to be consoled, and thanked her for the thought. But on the following day her distress returned. It was Wednesday 16 April 1879, the day of her death.

Sr Marie-Bernard could no longer bear lying in bed, and asked to be moved to the armchair. The Sisters on duty in the infirmary sprinkled her with holy water, and suggested prayers, because she seemed to be 'in the grip of an inexpressible interior suffering'.[119] They gave Sr Marie-Bernard a crucifix, which she kissed and regarded with love. They pinned it to her breast, as she seemed to want to hold it but was too weak. When Sr Nathalie visited her, Sr Marie-Bernard said, 'Sister, forgive me ... pray for me.'[120] They tried to give her some food at midday, but she could not swallow. Her state of extreme weakness struck Sr Josephine, who thought that it was time to call the infirmarian and ring the bell to summon the community. It was a custom that all the Sisters who could be spared from their duties would gather at a deathbed. Sr Marie-Bernard reclined in the chair, barely breathing, and joined the prayers as well as she could. This continued for about two hours. At 3.00 she was still alive, and the bell rang for devotions. Most of the Sisters left the room to go to the chapel. After the room emptied, she went into her last crisis. While the Sisters recited a Hail Mary she repeated the words 'Holy Mary, Mother of God, pray for me, a poor sinner, a poor sinner ...' Sr Nathalie and Sr Gabrielle sat on either side of her and held her arms. Some minutes afterwards, Sr Marie-Bernard made a gesture to indicate that she wished to drink. She crossed herself, and sipped some cordial from a glass which they offered her. Her head then sank forward, and she died.

# NOTES

1. To Sr Mathilde Pomain, 7 Sept. 1876, *ESB*, no. 177, 436.

2. Sr Basile Lauzeral and Sr Marcelline Durand, *Logia*, Vol. 2, no. 409, 93.

3. René Laurentin, ibid.

4. Sr Saint-Michel Duhème, Guynot, *Contemporains*, 69. Sr Saint-Michel asserts that she remembered this scene distinctly, and that it took place in 1878, some months before Bernadette's death. She would then have been thirty-five years old. But one wonders if this date is mistaken, as by then her leg was badly affected by the tuberculous tumour.

5. Abbé Febvre, interviewed by Père Cros, *ESB*, 515.

6. Claire de Mevolhon, Guynot, *Contemporains*, 79.

7. Forcade, *Notice sur la vie*, 35.

8. Sr Gabrielle de Vigouroux d'Arvieu, *PON*, Sessio LXXXVI, 1015.

9. Sr Vincent d'Eauga (30) *Calendrier, 1861*, 80.

10. Forcade, *Notice sur la vie*, 33.

11. Sr Marie-Bernard quoted Guynot, *Contemporains*, 213.

12. To Mère Ursule, 16 Aug. 1867, *ESB*, no. 89, 252.

13. *ESB*, 461.

14. To Sr Mathilde Pomain, 7 Sept. 1876, *ESB*, no. 177, 436–7.

15. To Sr Victorine Poux, 27 June 1876, *ESB*, no. 171, 428.

16. To her sister Marie, 25 June 1876, *ESB*, no. 163, 422.

17. To her brother Pierre, 7 Oct. 1878, *ESB*, no. 222, 504.

18. Forcade, *Notice sur la vie*, 34.

19. Mère Eléonore Cassagnes quoted, Trochu, *Sainte Bernadette*, 438.

20. *ESB*, 337.

21. Abbé Febvre interviewed by Père Cros, *ESB*, 515.

22. Guynot quoted, Trochu, *Sainte Bernadette*, 533.

23. Jean-Marie Febvre, Guynot, *Contemporains*, 75.

24. Mère Générale, *ESB*, 516.

25. Ibid.

26. Recollection of Chanoine Perreau, quoted, Trochu, *Sainte Bernadette*, 439.

27. Trochu, *Sainte Bernadette*, 440.

28. Ibid.

29. Forcade, *Notice sur la vie*, 33.

30. Une Soeur venue d'Oudan, Guynot, *Contemporains*, 177.

31. To her sister Marie, 28 Apr. 1873, *ESB*, no. 136, 319.

32. Mgr Lelong, *Allocution aux obsèques de Bernadette Soubirous, en religion Soeur Marie-Bernard, le 19 avril 1879* (Nevers 1879), 18.

33. Lasserre, *Sainte Bernadette*, 215. She must have told him this during his final visit, during the affair of the protestation in 1875.

34. Sr Gabrielle de Vigouroux d'Arvieu, *PON*, Sessio LXXXVI, 1015.

35. Sr Philippine Molinéry, *PON*, Sessio CVI, 1200.

36. Ibid., 1203.

37. Sr Victoire Cassou, *PON*, Sessio CV, 1194.

38. Laurentin quoted, introduction, *Témoins*, 9.

39. Père Cros cited, ibid.

40. Père Cros cited, *BVP*, 2. 238.

41. Ibid.

42. The original lists of questions are kept in 'Archives Cros', *AG*. These questions are from 19 and 20 February 1879.

43. Père Sempé's letter, 12 Dec. 1878, *Logia*, 229.

44. Letter from Sr Adélaïde Dons, 30 Jan. 1879, (E) A1 [o] à (39), Archives Cros.

45. Sr Victoire Seurre, *PON*, Sessio XCVIII, 1124.

46. Sr Marie-Josephine Forestier, *PON*, Sessio XII, 181.

47. Père Cros quoted, *BVP*, 2. 258.

48. *ESB*, 469.

49. Ibid.

50. Letter from Sr A. Dons, 3 Mar. 1879, Archives Cros, *AG*.

51. *ESB*, 469.

52. Letter from Père Sempé to Mère Dons, 21 Dec. 1878, *Logia*, 231.

53. Sr Stanislas Tourriol, *RdC*, 35.

54. Sr Joseph Caldairou, *Logia*, no. 525, 198.

55. To Jean-Marie Soubirous, July 1876, *ESB*, no. 172, 429.

56. To Jean-Marie Soubirous, Nov. 1876, *ESB*, no. 181, 443.

57. Ibid.

58. To Pierre Soubirous, 3 Nov. 1876, *ESB*, no. 182, 445.

59. To Jean-Marie Soubirous, end of Feb. 1877, *ESB*, no. 196, 477.

60. To Jean-Marie Soubirous, July 1877, *ESB*, no. 202, 485.

61. To her cousin Lucile Pène, 3 Nov. 1876, *ESB*, no. 184, 447.

62. From Jean-Marie to Sr Marie-Bernard, 23 July 1877, *ESB*, no. 204, 487.

63. Père Ravier, the editor: 'we believe it to be our duty to omit, in discretion, some sentences which concern the family inheritance and which touch too closely upon some people.' *ESB*, 484.

64. Ravier, ibid., 301.

65. To Père Sempé, 17 July 1877, *ESB*, no. 201, 481.

66. From Pierre to Sr Marie-Bernard, 4 Dec. 1877, *ESB*, no. 209, 492. It is not clear what her response to this letter was, or if she did write to her brother-in-law. It is more likely that she would have contacted her sister, Toinette Soubirous.

67. Jean-Marie Soubirous, *PON*, Sessio LVII, 747.

68.   Sr Rosalie Pérasse, Guynot, 103.

69.   To her sister Marie, 28 Apr. 1873, *ESB*, no. 136, 320.

70.   Mère Dons cited, Chronologie des événements, 18 Dec. 1878, *ESB*, 469.

71.   Zola, *Voyages*, 64.

72.   Ibid.

73.   Ibid., 65.

74.   Ibid.

75.   To Mgr Peyramale, 28 Dec. 1878, *ESB*, no. 194, 475.

76.   Memoire Confidentiel communiqué à Monseigneurs Les Evêques de France, 27 Dec. 1877, *AG*, A40.

77.   Ibid.

78.   To Abbé Pomain, 15 Sept. 1877, *ESB*, no. 208, 490.

79.   Reine Basset, *Calendrier 1867*, 94.

80.   To Abbé Pomain, 28 Dec. 1876, *ESB*, no. 193, 473.

81.   Interview with L'Abbé Febvre by Père Cros, *ESB*, 515. These are brief and fragmentary notes, which do not permit that one fully reconstructs the interview.

82.   Interview with Abbé Febvre by Père Cros, *ESB*, no. 235, 515.

83.   Sr Victoire Cassou, *PON*, Sessio CV, 1192.

84.   Sr Marcella Poujade, Guynot, *Contemporains*, 185.

85.   Guynot, ibid.

86.   Mère Philomena Roques, Guynot, *Contemporains*, 86.

87.   Trochu, *Sainte Bernadette*, 544.

88.   Ibid., 546.

89.   Jean-Auguste Perreau, *PON*, Sessio V, 117. She seems to have made the same remark to others.

90.   Notes of Abbé Febvre, *PON*, Sessio CXII, 1267.

91.   Le Carnet de notes intimes, 1873–1874, *PON*, Sessio XCV, 1093.

92.   Sr Marthe du Rais, and other witnesses, affirm that they heard that this was so. *PON*, Sessio XCV, 1093.

93.   Notes of Abbé Febvre, *PON*, Sessio CXII, 1267.

94.   Forcade, *Notice sur la vie*, 33.

95.   Notes of Abbé Febvre, *PON*, Sessio CXII, 1235.

96.   Forcade, *Notice sur la vie*, 35.

97.   Infirmarian quoted by Sr Philomena Roques, *RdC*, 178.

98.   Sr Michel Duhème, Guynot, *Contemporains*, 71.

99.   Sr Michel Duhème, *RdC*, 180.

100.  Sr Alphonse Guerre, Guynot, *Contemporains*, 220.

101.  Sr Philippine Molinéry, *PON*, Sessio CVI, 1209.

102.  Guynot, *Contemporains*, 227.

103. Une soeur venue d'Oudan, Guynot, *Contemporains*, 177.

104. Ibid.

105. Sr Philomena Roques, Guynot, *Contemporains*, 91.

106. Sr Philomena Roques, *RdC*, 178.

107. Sr Philomena Roques, Guynot, *Contemporains*, 91.

108. Sr Gabrielle Vigouroux, *PON*, Sessio LXXXVI, 1010.

109. Mère Éléonore, interview with Père Cros, *ESB*, 517.

110. Ibid., 516.

111. Notes of Abbé Febvre, Trochu, *Sainte Bernadette*, 545.

112. Journal of the Community, *ESB*, 469.

113. Laurentin, *Vie*, 245.

114. Laurentin, *Vie*, 244.

115. Sr Bernard Dalias, *Contemporains*, 98.

116. It is remarkable that such a relic would have been lost, but we are reliably informed that it has been. *Logia*, 272.

117. Abbé Picq quoted, ibid.

118. Sr Nathalie Portat raconte la mort de Sr Marie-Bernard, *ESB*, 513.

119. Ibid.

120. Ibid.

# Conclusion

Confiteántur tibi, Dómine,
ómnia ópera tua
*Et Sancti tui benedícant tibi*
Exsultábunt sancti in glória
*Laetabúntur in cubílibus suis*

Let all your works praise you, Lord

*And let your saints bless you*
Your saints shall rejoice in glory
*They shall rejoice in their resting place*

From Prayers after Mass

It was obvious, even before Bernadette died, that she would eventually be made into a saint. Many Catholic writers have made the point that she was canonized on the basis of her consistently virtuous life, not because she had seen visions. But no-one denies that, without the visions, Bernadette would have lived and died unknown.

After death, Sr Marie-Bernard was dressed again in her religious habit. 'We had no difficulty in doing so,' said Sr Gabrielle de Vigouroux, 'because her body was supple, even though it was more than two hours after her death.'[1] Throughout the evening of 16 April 1879, she was laid out on her bed, and visited by each of the religious at St Gildard. The next day, at about 11am, the body was brought down to the chapel and exposed for public veneration. This was the custom with all Sisters of Nevers, but of course Bernadette's body drew unprecedented crowds. 'It seemed that everyone wanted to compensate themselves for not being able to approach Bernadette during her life.'[2] The news of her death had been generally reported, and queues of visitors formed, despite driving rain, while trains to Nevers were crowded with pilgrims. A file of people moved through the chapel, day and night, while four Sisters kept each corner of the coffin. The Sisters passed objects against the corpse, in order that people could take away relics. Within only one day, the town of Nevers had sold out of rosaries and medals.

The funeral of Bernadette had been arranged for 18 April 1879, but then was delayed, until Saturday 19 April, in order to allow more of the crowds to pass. The corpse remained unchanged in appearance. After her funeral, the coffin was finally closed, and the body removed to the Chapel of St Joseph, an oratory within St Gildard. It had been decided that she would not be in the public graveyard, with the other Sisters of Nevers. A special crypt was prepared, and the coffin was buried on 22 May 1879.

Canonization allows the Church to affirm that a particular member of the faithful is certainly in heaven, that they can intercede for those who pray, and that God has performed miracles through their presence or relics. Unusually, Bernadette was almost considered to be a saint while she was still alive, and

312

had a fervent public before her cause was introduced before the Vatican. However, the church authorities waited until 1909, before beginning the *Procès Ordinaire*. At that time, the Vatican maintained a tradition of prudence in regard to canonization, and always allowed time to pass, and passing enthusiasms to expire, before even looking at any cause.

As a routine part of the *Procès Ordinaire* the body of the prospective saint was exhumed. This is in order to ascertain the place of burial, and to allow for the collection of relics if the cause is approved. In Bernadette's case, when the coffin was opened on 22 September 1909, her body was found intact and incorrupt, although the damp grave had caused her clothes and rosary beads to corrode. This was witnessed by the Bishop of Nevers, the Mayor, several doctors and other assistants.

> We did not sense any odour. The body was covered by the habit of the order, which was soaked in damp. The face, hands and forearms alone were uncovered. The head was resting to the left-hand side, the face was of a matt white; the skin adhered to the muscles and the muscles to the bones. The eyelids covered the eyes ... The hands, crossed at the chest, were perfectly conserved to the fingertips, and still carried a rosary which was rusting away ... The feet were like the hands, and with their nails (one of each fell off when the corpse was washed). After having removed the habit and veil, one could see all the body dry and stiff, with skin like parchment ... The body was so rigid that it could be picked up and turned, during washing, without any difficulty. The lower parts of the body were slightly darkened. That seems to have been because of the carbon which was found, in a rather large quantity, in the coffin.[3]

Another witness to the exhumation also noted that the body was

> completely intact, without odour, almost mummified, covered with some damp patches and a significant amount of salts, which seemed to be calcific salts. The corpse is complete ... the skin has disappeared in some places but it remains in most of the corpse. Some veins are still visible.[4]

The body was washed, and dressed in a new habit, then placed in a new casket. It was exhumed again on 3 April 1919, and found to be unaltered, except that it bore patches of mildew and a layer of crystallized salts.

On 18 April 1925, at the time of the conclusion of the final enquiry (*the Procès Apostolique*), there was a final exhumation. There was some alteration in the appearance of the corpse. The face was darkened and discoloured, the eyes sunken, and the soft tissues of the nose had disappeared. More skin was missing from her lower limbs. It was noted that her right knee, which had been affected by the tumour, was still enlarged. The interior organs showed a remarkable state of preservation, including the liver, which the doctor reported to be still fresh and pliable. The doctor stated that he had wished to

> Open the chest to the neck, in order to take some ribs as relics, and then

313

remove the heart, which must still have existed, but because of the inclination of the trunk to the left arm, it would have been difficult to locate that organ without making large and destructive incisions.[5]

From this account, one understands that the body was rigid to the point of being melded, and that the limbs could not be moved. The rather gruesome medical account from 1925 notes that some small pieces of the flesh of her thighs were removed for relics. The examination and dissection of the body appears insensitive, but all of these actions were taken in a spirit of reverence for saintly relics. Like the autopsy reports prepared for courts in our own time, these were not seen as violations of the body, but as a means of producing necessary facts.

The body was then swathed in bandages except for the hands and face. The firm of Pierre Imans in Paris was contracted to make a light wax mask to cover them, and the body was dressed in the habit of the Sisters of Nevers. A special casket had been made, and installed in the Chapel at St Gildard. Bernadette's body was moved there in August 1925. She had been beatified on 14 June 1925, which meant that she was given the titled of Blessed and approved for veneration. The Vatican canonized her as a saint on 8 December 1933.

The Church does not claim that the incorrupt body of Bernadette is a miracle, in itself:

> It is well known that corpses decompose less in certain kinds of soil and gradually mummify. It should be noted, however, that in the case of Bernadette this mummified state is quite astounding. Her illnesses and the state of her body when she died, the humidity in the vault in the chapel of Saint Joseph (the habit was damp, the rosary rusty and the crucifix had turned green) would all seem to be conducive to disintegration of the flesh. We should be glad, therefore, that Bernadette benefited from a fairly rare biological phenomenon. But this is not a 'miracle' in the strictest sense of the word.[6]

The mystery of incorrupt bodies is not restricted to Catholicism. Many different faiths make such claims for members, and the bodies of some people, who were not known to be saints at all, have been discovered intact when their tombs were opened. One example is the discovery of the body of Katherine Parr, the last wife of Henry VIII. In 1782, nearly two hundred and fifty years after her death, Mr John Lucas found her coffin amid the ruins of the chapel at Sudeley Castle. He opened the coffin and found the body wrapped in six or seven seer cloths. 'The body was entire and uncorrupted, and, cutting through the seer cloths, he found the flesh of one of her arms to be still white and moist. He took a few locks of hair, which was auburn in colour ... '[7] The coffin was unearthed and opened, several further times over the next ten years, and was even vandalized and roughly buried upside-down by a group of drunken men. In 1817 a search for it was again made, but by then nothing but the skeleton remained. A similar story is that of the body of Mary Tudor, sister of Henry VIII, whose coffin was excavated and opened during Victorian times. It was said to be completely intact, and many souvenirs of her hair were taken. There were reports from Renaissance Italy that when antique cemeteries were overbuilt, during the renovation of Rome, some corpses were found intact. They were under tombstones with Latin inscriptions from the time of the Caesars. In most of these cases, the corpses seem to have soon deteriorated when opened to the atmosphere and handled. Despite histories of spontaneous preservation, many of the faithful do see the conservation of Saint Bernadette's body as a miracle of the first order.

In their turn, rationalist critics see the displayed body as a type of fraud, and claim that it must have been embalmed. Turning back to accounts of the original exhumation, they ask: 'Why the carbon in the coffin? What carbon, if not antiseptic carbon powder? Why that "notable" layer of salts covering the corpse? Calcareous salts [salts derived from hard water] it is said, but were they analysed in order to ascertain their nature?' The writer of this text flatly states that the body must have been embalmed, 'but the medical doctors held their silence, not for the glory of science, but the elaboration of the legend'.[8]

These claims were rebutted by Catholic writers, such as Abbé Deroo, who pointed out that the embalming of a body, according to the techniques of the nineteenth century, was a lengthy procedure. It required that the body be immersed in a bath of aluminium sulphate, and other chemicals, for at least three days. There was no time to do this, as Bernadette was on public display between the time of her death and her funeral. Abbé Deroo explained the presence of carbon in the coffin as a 'means employed to slow the putrefaction of a body which cannot be immediately buried ... this is a practice still employed by the religious of the Charity of Nevers, they put a wooden support so that the body is not lying flat against the wood of the coffin, and they add a layer of carbon pieces, because it is absorbent ... Let us state again, this assures only a very short-term conservation.'[9]

Such measures would have been judged necessary while Bernadette was lying in the chapel, because her body was already in a very poor state when she died. Her flesh was decayed by the tuberculosis, and possibly she had gangrene in the pressure sores caused by her immobility. The fragile condition of the corpse was noticed by the Sisters who laid her out, and they were surprised that the body did not show signs of decomposing when it remained on display for several days. If she was lying above a layer of carbon, it was because they expected the corpse to suppurate. The three days during which she was visited by crowds are one of the strongest arguments against the allegation that she was embalmed – there simply was no time to do so. If any treatment was given to the corpse, it would have had to have been afterwards – between her funeral and burial. There was, indeed, a delay in her burial, which is explained by the church authorities as being due to the need to prepare a special tomb within the convent precincts. A rationalist critic might dismiss that as a falsehood, but they would have to concede that an embalming procedure carried out at that time would have been belated, and therefore probably ineffective.

A more pertinent critique of the legendary incorrupt body would stress the fact that it is not truly on display. The face and hands, so often photographed, are wax masks. They are a very light layer, but amount to a representation of the body rather than its genuine appearance. The waxed features were prepared by experts, after viewing photographs and are a composite of her appearance, not simply the impression of the wasted visage of her corpse. Exactly how the body of Bernadette appears cannot be judged by a visit to the chapel of St Gildard. The church authorities justified their decision to cover the face and hands because they thought that the darkening of the skin, and the sunken eyes and nose, would make a painful impression on the faithful. So Bernadette's own corpse was ornamented, in order to provide a 'better' representation of her appearance. Much of her life was spent amid an exchange of ideals and the deliberate creation of images. Like the peasant costume which she wore when living as a young lady, the wax mask is a created reality, expressing what her public is judged to want from her.

The shrine at the chapel is only one way of displaying Bernadette. Since her death, she has also been presented through pictures, biographies, novels and films. These have gone through several fashions. Images of Bernadette, until the end of the 1950s, were continuous with the presentations of her during her life. She was a pattern of Catholic femininity, and an exemplar of a type of piety which favoured sweetness and simplicity over complexity. Titles of biographies, for instance, were *Humble St Bernadette*, *She Met Our Lady*, and *Sublime Shepherdess*.[10] They expressed veneration for Bernadette, but also an almost patronizing admiration for her girlish charm. A more serious work of scholarship, by Père Trochu, was published in 1956, and attempted to relate her life in a fully documented fashion. But this was not typical of Lourdes devotional literature.

Many people knew of Bernadette not through biographies, but through the more twentieth-century medium of film. In 1942, the novel *Song of Bernadette* was published. It was the work of Franz Werfel, an Austrian Jewish refugee who had passed through Lourdes in 1940. Werfel was fascinated by Bernadette's story, and in his words: 'I vowed that if I escaped from this desperate situation ... I would put off all other tasks and sing, as best I could, the song of Bernadette.'[11] Franz Werfel was a fluent writer, secular, poetic and populist. He wrote about religion in a way which celebrated its ideals, and ignored theology and sectarianism. Werfel's work rediscovered the mythic ideal which had existed from the beginning of the Lourdes story. The spring, the young girl, the White Lady, the indomitable people of Lourdes, and the pristine mountain Grotto appeared in all their folkloric splendour.

*Song of Bernadette* was an enormous success, and in 1953 it was made into a Hollywood film. Jennifer Jones played the lead role, and the film, which attracted huge audiences, perpetuated the visionary's image. Films have also been made in the French language. In 1960 Robert Darène directed *Il suffit d'aimer*, an account of Bernadette's life. It was an artistically accomplished film, deliberately austere and produced in black and white. It reclaimed Bernadette for French culture, being in contrast to the Hollywood product, and stylistically related to films about Jeanne d'Arc, peasant life and rural

France. In recent years two further French films, directed by Jean Delannoy, have provided lengthy cinematic biographies. *Bernadette* covered her life in Lourdes, and *La Passion de Bernadette* her last years in Nevers. These two films have the advantage of being filmed on location, and preserving in visual format many details of landscape, costumes and interiors, which go unexplained in texts.

Traditionalist Catholic culture had exhausted itself by the 1960s, and the changes of that decade revolutionized saintliness. The 'girl saints', such as St Bernadette of Lourdes and St Thérèse of Lisieux, were quite suddenly seen as cloying and even puerile. The heroes of the new post-war culture were figures of daring, such as Charles de Foucault and Edith Stein. Catholic writers became interested in anti-authoritarian attitudes, and individualistic figures who were misunderstood by their repressive elders.

Bernadette had always been celebrated for her simplicity, obedience and virtue. She did not easily fit the 1960s spirit of revolt. Even her rural innocence did not quite fit the counter-culture notion of living close to nature – as that of St Francis of Assisi could be made to do. Although the traditional iconography of Bernadette seemed dated, no strong new outline was fashioned to replace it. By contrast, the other famous nineteenth-century French saint, Thérèse of Lisieux, attracted a band of modernist admirers who rebutted the traditional image, rediscovered the original texts of her autobiography, and generally presented a pristine, radical, original Thérèse Martin. A new saint for a new age. The post-1960s St Thérèse was found to have struggled for self-expression, and was empathetic to the oppressed and marginalized. Bernadette, whose lived experiences of poverty were truly oppressive, could not so easily yield a message. Generally, during the period of Vatican II 'renewal', attention toward her diminished. Publications tended to turn to the 'message of Lourdes', and the Virgin Mary, rather than the messenger. The celebration of Marian apparitions was changed. It moved away from ornate ritual, and was given a stronger biblical focus.

Although Bernadette was not a fashion in post-Vatican-II Catholicism, she attracted steady attention from a small number of scholars who worked to present the message of Lourdes in its historical context. In particular, Père Laurentin, Père André Ravier, with the assistance of Sr Marie-Thérèse Bourgeade and Dom Bernard Billet, made painstaking efforts to edit document collections from Lourdes and Nevers. Their excellent works made numerous primary sources accessible. They were motivated by one of the more positive impulses arising from the culture of the 1960s – to look at episodes of Catholic history and present the full story, regardless of inconsistencies, embarrassments and subsequent distortions.

Once the collected writings were edited, it became obvious that many of Bernadette's diary entries, which had been assumed to be her own work, were in fact copied from published texts. 'In discovering the sources for these notes, we do not annul them: on the contrary, we reconstitute, as much as possible, the profound interior life of Sr Marie-Bernard.'[12] (The word profound was unlikely to have been used of Bernadette prior to the 1960s.) The textual research was a mere correction, which did not change anyone's view of

Bernadette. There was no indignant re-evaluation, as had been experienced when the text of Thérèse of Lisieux's biography had proved to be retouched by her Sisters. The truth was, that Bernadette's notebooks, although read and treasured by many pilgrims to Nevers, were not especially important to the overall cult of Our Lady of Lourdes.

When Père Laurentin was working at the archives at St Gildard, he depended upon the expertise of Sr Marie-Thérèse Bourgeade, who was often the sole witness of many customs of the order, which had been discontinued. Convent life was being transformed wholesale. So much so that Bernadette's body is the only one now, at the Convent of St Gildard, that wears the habit.

Time rushed by, Saint Bernadette remained, resting in her casket. She was preserved from change as from decay – to such a degree that the side altar, which holds her casket, is now notably different from the rest of the chapel. The casket of Saint Bernadette, gilded and ornate, retains the style which dominated holy objects during her lifetime. It is an island of old-world Catholicism in an otherwise modernized space. A vase of flowers, and an antique statue of the Virgin Mary, stand nearby. The stained-glass above is an abstract design of bright colours. She lies untouched, before the shifting eyes of thousands of visitors who have never ceased to arrive.

Bernadette would hardly recognize the chapel, if she walked into it now, although it is the same building where she worshipped. The nineteenth-century high altar was once the focal point of the area. It was set into the wall and dominated the view of anyone who entered through the main doors. It has now been removed, along with the three steps which led up to it, and the rails which marked the sanctuary. After several successive changes from the 1970s to the 1990s, the altar space has become a bare white niche, with an unadorned table, and the tabernacle has been removed to the left-hand side of the chapel.

A few remains of the chapel which Bernadette knew are now in the small museum-like area, where visitors see photographs, furniture and heritage items. A piece of the stonework from the communion rails is included, as if it were an ancient relic, rather than an integral part of the nineteenth-century chapel. This annexe to the entrance at St Gildard allows pilgrims to see relevant cultural items, and to buy souvenirs. For most of the twentieth century, St Gildard had no such commercial space, as the Sisters did not see it as compatible with the atmosphere of their convent. However, it was introduced in recent decades, and is a harmonious and well-patronized place. The emphasis, in the contemporary shop, is to provide authentic images and information about Bernadette, and also religious writings about the community and its founder, Père de Laveyne.

The Convent of Saint Gildard is still a house for the Sisters of Nevers, but no longer serves as a novitiate. Entrants to the order live in a smaller house in the public housing area of Nevers – nearer to their work as Sisters of Charity. The convent now functions as a pilgrimage centre, and receives numerous visitors all year around. Some merely pass by in a day, but most make use of the residential facilities, and stay several nights. The atmosphere is cosmopolitan, as people come from many nations to honour the shrine of Saint Bernadette. There are visitors of all types and classes, both individuals and groups, and all are received with true hospitality. Anyone who has stayed at St Gildard must have noticed the kindness, the equality of welcome, and the freedom from commercial concerns. The pilgrimage house does charge for accommodation, but only to meet costs, and makes concessions for pilgrims in need, as well as special provisions for the disabled.

There were two centenaries relating to Bernadette – one, the anniversary of her visions in 1958, and the second, the anniversary of her death in 1979. In 1958, 'the example of Bernadette was still close. Neither the Church, nor the congregation at Nevers, had changed much ... a religious at Nevers led, very nearly, the same life that Bernadette did. She wore the same costume, practised the same customs, recited the same prayers ... If certain rules had been adapted, they remained present in memory. Today, after the consular reforms ... a thousand rules and usages have been swept away.'[13] By the time of the anniversary of her death, in 1979, celebrations deliberately focused upon new liturgical forms, and underplayed the litanies, processions and novenas which had once maintained her fame. Two new biographies were issued, which tried to give a non-sentimental and accurate review of Bernadette's life. These works were informative, and different in tone from Père Trochu's magisterial biography of the 1950s. However, the information in Trochu was not superseded, merely restated in a modernist manner.

Père Laurentin, writing in the early 1970s, commented that at that time, when the customs of traditional Catholicism were being abandoned, they recalled 'a recent past, disgraced and old-fashioned without having the lustre of history'.[14] Another generation has passed since then, and it is the culture of the early 1970s which seems terribly dated, and which has imprinted itself on the liturgical changes introduced during that era. From the perspective of the new century, the culture which predominated during Bernadette's life is more distant, and has recovered some of its charm. Where Saint Bernadette will remain, amid the heritage and the future of Catholicism, is up to her current and future public to determine.

# NOTES

1.  Trochu, *Sainte Bernadette*, 554.

2.  Mère Joséphine Forestier quoted, ibid, 555.

3.  Père André Ravier, *Le corps de sainte Bernadette* (Nevers 1991), 5.

4.  Ibid.

5.  Ibid., 7.

6.  Ibid., 6.

7.  Anthony Martienssen, *Queen Katherine Parr* (London 1975), 245.

8.  Drs Thérèse and Guy Valot, *Lourdes et l'Illusion* (Paris 1956), 24.

9.  Abbé A. Deroo, *Lourdes cité des miracles ou marché d'illusions* (Paris 1956), 76.

10. Yver, *L'Humble Sainte Bernadette*. (Paris 1933). Frances Parkinson Keyes, *Sublime Shepherdess: The Life of Saint Bernadette* (New York 1940). Bernadette Andrews, *She Met Our Lady: the Story of Bernadette*. Catholic Truth Society, nd.

11. Franz Werfel, *Song of Bernadette* (Glasgow 1977; f.p. 1942), 12.

12. Ravier, *Ecrits*, edition of 1961, 339.

13. *Logia*, presentation, 32.

14. Ibid.

# Bibliography

## Document collections

Cros, Léonard, and P. M. Olphe-Galliard, *Lourdes 1858. Témoins de l'événement* Lethielleux, Paris 1958.

Guynot, Ernest, *Bernadette d'après ses contemporains* Éditions de Cerf, Paris 1978.

Hommage à la bienheureuse Bernadette Soubirous, *Revue d'ascétique et de mystique* 10 (1929). Printed testimonies from the Cros archive.

Laurentin, René, et al., eds, *Lourdes. Documents authentiques*, vols 1–7. Lethielleux, Paris 1958–66.

Laurentin, René, and Sr Marie-Thérèse Bourgeade, eds, *Logia de Bernadette. Etude critique de ses paroles de 1866 à 1879*, 3 vols. Lethielleux and Oeuvre de la Grotte, Paris 1971.

Laurentin, René, and P. Roche, eds, *Catherine Labouré et la Médaille Miraculeuse. Documents authentiques 1830–1876* Lethielleux, Paris 1986.

Ravier, André, ed., *Les Écrits de Sainte Bernadette et sa voie spirituelle* Lethielleux, Paris 1980.

Stern, Jean, ed., *La Salette. Documents authentiques*, vols 1 and 2. Desclée de Brouwer, Paris 1980.

Tauriac, J.-M. and J. Aubery, eds, *Procès de Bernadette. Documents authentiques* Librairie des Champs-Élysées, Paris 1958.

## Primary sources

Agos, Baron Louis d', 6 Oct. 1857, 'De la représentation de Marie Immaculée', *Revue de l'art chrétien*, 1 (1857): 511–12.

Alix, Abbé, *Discours pour l'inaguration de la bénédiction solennelle de la statue de la très-sainte vierge dans la Grotte Miraculeuse de Lourdes, 4 avril 1864* M. Bellet, Clermont-Ferrand 1864.

Alix, Abbé, *Une enfante de Marie ou vie d'une jeune pensionnaire* Charles Douniol Libraire, Paris 1854.

Azun de Bernétas, T.-M.-J.-T., *La Grotte des Pyrénées ou manifestation de la*

*Sainte-Vierge à la grotte de Lourdes. Précéde d'une notice sur les Pyrénées* Imprimerie J. P. Larrieu, Tarbes 1861.

De Barandiarán Irizar, Luis, ed., *A View from the Witch's Cave: Folktales of the Pyrenees.* Collected and with a prologue by José Miguel de Barandiarán, translated by Linda White. University of Nevada Press, Reno 1991.

Barbet, Jean, *La Dame plus belle que tout. Naissance, vie et mort de Bernadette Soubirous* Le livre contemporain, Paris 1957 (f.p. 1909).

Barbet, M. A. Fils (avocat), *Bernadette Soubirous. Sa naissance, sa vie sa mort, d'après des documents inédits de la collection de M. Barbet, père* Lescher-Moutouté Imprimeur, Pau 1909.

Bidal, Marie-Joseph, *Bernadette Soubirous et les Événements des Grottes de Lourdes de 1858 à 1873* Lépagnez Libraire, Vesoul 1873.

Boissairie, Dr, *Les Grandes Guérisons de Lourdes* Ancienne Maison Charles Douniol, Paris 1900.

Bordenave, Mère Marie-Thérèse, *Sainte Bernadette. La confidente de l'Immaculée* Couvent St Gildard, Nevers 1978 (f.p.1912).

Bouix, Abbé Dominique, Introduction, *Vie de Marcelline Pauper de congrégation des Soeurs de la Charité de Nevers. Écrite par elle-même* Imp. de Fay, Nevers 1871.

Bouix, P. Marcel, *Une héroine de la charité au XIXe siècle. Élisabeth de Brugelles, perle du midi de la France* Imprimerie Gauthier-Villars, Paris 1875.

Boyer, L'Abbé Eugène, *Une visite à Bernadette et à la Grotte de Lourdes. Précédée de quelques renseignments sur Lourdes et ses environs* Paul Dufour, Tarbes 1866.

Boyer, L'Abbé Eugène, *Notre Dame de Lourdes ou réflexions symboliques et morales sur les apparitions de la Sainte-Vierge à Bernadette Soubirous* Librairie E Lasserre, Bayonne 1868.

Corbin, L'abbé, *L'Apparition de la Sainte-Vierge à la Grotte de Lourdes* Typographie Justin Dupuy & Comp., Bordeaux 1862.

Cordier, Eugène, *Le Droit de famille aux Pyrénées. Barège – Lavedan – Béarn et Pays Basque* Auguste Durand libraire, Paris 1859.

Cordier, Eugène, *Les Légendes des Hautes-Pyrénées. Suivies des lettres de deux abbés contre l'Auteur et de sa réplique* Association Guillaume Mauran, Tarbes 1986 (f.p. Lourdes 1855).

Dauzat-Dembarrère, Pierre, *Des origines politiques de La Grotte de Lourdes* J. M. Cazaux éditeur, Tarbes 1890.

Dozous, Docteur (de Lourdes), *La Grotte de Lourdes, sa fontaine, ses guérisons* Maison de la Bonne Press, Paris 1926 (f.p. 1874).

Estrade, Jean-Baptiste, *Les Apparitions de Lourdes, souvenirs intimes d'un témoin* Imprimerie de la Grotte, Lourdes 1920 (f.p. 1899).

Fedacou, Henri, *Henri Fedacou raconte la vie montagnarde dans un village des Pyrénées au début du siècle*, ed. Georges Buisan, L'association Guillaume Mauran, no. 3, Tarbes 1984.

Forcade, Augustin, *Notice sur la vie de soeur Marie-Bernard (Bernadette de Lourdes)* A. Makaire, Imprimeur de l'archevêché, Aix 1879.

Fourcade, M. l'abbé, *L'Apparition à la Grotte de Lourdes en 1858* J. A. Fouga, Tarbes 1862.

Gentillucci, Emidio, *Le Parfait Légendaire. Vie de la Très-sainte Vierge Marie,* translated by Abbé Alix. Julien Lanier et cie. Librairies, Paris 1856 (f.p. 1848).

L. de M., *Réflexions sur le départ de Nevers de la soeur Dorothée* Nevers 1842.

La Caze, Louis, *Les Libertés provinciales en Béarn* Librairie de A. D. Laine, Paris 1865.

Lagrèze, Gustave Bascle de, *Chronique de la ville et du chateau de Lourdes* Imprimerie de É. Vignancour, Pau 1845.

Lagrèze, Gustave Bascle de, *Etudes sur la révision du code forestier* J.-M. Dossun Typographie, Bagnères-de-Bigorre 1851.

Lagrèze, Gustave Bascle de, *Essai sur la langue et la littérature du Béarn* G. Gounouilhou Imprimeur, Bordeaux 1856.

Lagrèze, Gustave Bascle de, *Les Pèlerinages des Pyrénées* Th. Telmon imprimeur-éditeur, Tarbes 1858.

Lagrèze, Gustave Bascle de, *Le Château de Lourdes et la Grotte de l'Apparition* Th. Telmon imprimeur-éditeur, Tarbes 1875.

Lasserre, Henri, *Notre-Dame de Lourdes* Victor Palmé, Paris 1870.

Lasserre, Henri, *Sainte Bernadette, la voyante de Lourdes. La religieuse - la sainte* Lethielleux éditeur, Paris 1948.

Laurence, Mgr B. S., Évêque de Tarbes, *Lettre pastorale pour le couronnement de la Vierge de Garaison* Th. Telmon, Tarbes 1865.

Lelong, Mgr, *Allocution prononcée par Mgr l'évêque de Nevers dans la chapelle de la maison-mère des Soeurs de Nevers, aux obsèques de Bernadette Soubirous, en religion Sr Marie-Bernard, le 19 avril 1879* Imp. de Faÿ, Nevers n.d.

Marie-Antoine, Père, missionnaire Capucin, *Nos plaies sociales ou mission providentielle de Bernadette* Imprimerie nouvelle J. Parer, Carcassonne 1879.

Mullois, M. l'abbé Isidore, *Cours d'éloquence sacrée populaire, ou essai sur la manière de parler au peuple*, 3 vols. Libraire catholique de J.-L. Paulmier, Paris 1856.

P. M. *La Bergère de Lourdes, Bernadette Soubirous. Sa vie, sa correspondence, sa mort, ses funérailles* La société archéologique du Midi de la France, Toulouse 1880.

Stern, Jean, ed. *La Salette. Documents authentiques* CERF, Paris 1980.

Suberville, M. curé doyen, and M. Duchein, desservant, *Histoire de la chapelle de Garaison* Imprimerie de J.-M. Corne, Toulouse 1836.

Un Ermite en Vacances, *Réponse à une attaque contre Notre-Dame de Lourdes* Chez Coderc, Bordeaux 1870.

Un serviteur de Marie, *La Vision de la jeune fille de Lourdes* V. Poullet Libraire-éditeur, Paris 1858.

Veuillot, Louis, 'La Grotte de Lourdes, 1858', *Mélanges religieux, historiques, politiques et littéraires*, serie 2, tome 4, Gaume frères & J. Duprey Éditeurs, Paris 1860.

Zola, Émile, *Mes voyages. Lourdes, Rome*, Journaux inédits présentés et annotés par René Ternois. Fasquelle Éditeurs, Paris 1958.

### Anonymous printed primary sources

*Calendrier religieux a l'usage des Soeurs de la Charité et Instruction Chrétienne de Nevers* P. Begat, Nevers 1860s–1870s.

*Directoire des Soeurs de la Charité et Instruction Chrétienne de Nevers*, Imprimié par ordre de Monseigneur Dufêtre, évêque de Nevers P. Begat, Nevers 1847.

*Esquisse sur Soeur Marie-Bernard (Bernadette Soubirous) de Lourdes (Hautes-Pyrénées)* Mme Vve Gadola Auteur Éditeur, Lyon 1872.

*Explication des réglements de la congrégation des Soeurs de la Charité et Instruction Chrétienne*, Établie à Nevers par lettres-patentes du 15 septembre 1780, enregistrées au Parlement le 29 décembre, même année, sous l'autorité de Monseigneur l'évêque de Nevers. De l'Imprimerie de la Veuve le Febvre, Nevers 1782.

*Le Trésor spirituel des Soeurs de la Charité et Instruction Chrétienne de Nevers*, Imprimié par ordre de Monseigneur l'Évêque de Nevers. P. Begat, Nevers 1860.

## Secondary sources

Aron, Jean-Paul, ed., *Misérable et glorieuse: La femme du XIX siècle* Fayard, Paris 1980.

Atkinson, Clarissa W., Constance H. Buchanan, and Margaret R. Miles, eds, *Immaculate and Powerful: The Female in Sacred Image and Social Reality* Beacon Press, Boston 1985.

Auclair, Marcelle, *Bernadette* Bloud et Gay éditeurs, Paris 1957.

Baumont, Stéphane, ed., *Histoire de Lourdes* Éditions Privat, Toulouse 1993.

Belleney, Joseph, *Sainte Bernadette. Bergère en Chrétienté* Bonne Presse, Paris 1936.

Berenson, Edward, *Populist Religion and Left-Wing Politics in France*, 1830–1852 Princeton University Press, Princeton 1984.

Bernheimer, Charles, *Figures of Ill Repute, Representing Prostitution in Nineteenth-Century France* Harvard University Press, Harvard 1989.

Boutry, Philippe, and Michel Cinquin, *Deux pèlerinages au XIX siècle. Ars et Paray-le-Monial* Beauchesne, Paris 1980.

Boyer, Marie-France, *The Cult of the Virgin: Offerings, Ornaments and Festivals* Thames & Hudson, London 2000.

Brown, Marvin L., *Louis Veuillot, French Ultramontane Catholic Journalist and Layman 1813–1883* Moore, North Carolina 1977.

Brownstein, Rachel, 'The funeral of the tragic muse', *Yale Review* 81 (1993).

Buzy, D. *Sister Mary of Jesus Crucified* Sands & Co., London 1919.

Campbell, Stuart L., *The Second Empire Revisited: A study of French Historiography* Rutgers University Press, New Jersey 1978.

Carroll, Michael P., 'The Virgin Mary at La Salette and Lourdes: Whom did the children see?' *Journal of the Scientific Study of Religion* 24 (1985): 71.

Carroll, Michael P., *The Cult of the Virgin Mary: Psychological Origins* Princeton University Press, Princeton 1986.

Caulier, Brigitte, *L'Eau et le sacré* Beauchesne, Paris 1990.

Chadefaud, Michel, *Lourdes, un pèlerinage, une ville* Edisud, La Calade 1981.

Chadefaud, Michel, *Aux origines du tourisme dans les pays de l'Adour* Université de Pau, Cahiers de l'Université 1987.

Corbin, Alain, 'Déchristianisation et fidélité aux pratiques archaïques', *Archaïsime et modernité en Limousin au XIXe siècle 1845–1880,* 2 vols. Éditions Marcel Rivière, Paris 1975.

Cros, L.-J.-M., *Histoire de Notre-Dame de Lourdes*, 3 vols. Gabriel Beauchesne éditeur, Paris 1925.

Deery, Mgr Joseph, *Our Lady of Lourdes* Browne & Nolan Ltd., Dublin 1958.

Devlin, Judith, *The Superstitious Mind: French Peasants and the Supernatural in the Nineteenth Century* Yale University Press, New Haven and London 1987.

Dompnier, Marthe, ed., *La Femme dans la société savoyarde* Imprimerie Salomon, Maurienne 1993.

Duhourcau, B., *Guide des Pyrénées mystérieuses* Paris 1985.

Ebel, Eugène, *Soeur Catherine. Notes biographiques sur la mystique lorraine Catherine Filljung 1848–1915* Imprimerie J. Téqui, Paris 1932.

Flament, René (Dr), *Notes médicales sur les souffrances physiques de Bernadette Soubirous* Imprimerie de la Grotte, Lourdes 1967.

Frechin, Georges, and Jean Robert, *Pèlerins et pèlerinages dans les Pyrénées Françaises* Musée Pyrénéen, Lourdes 1975.

Gibson, Ralph, *A Social History of French Catholicism 1789–1914* Routledge, London 1989.

Gough, Austin, *Paris and Rome: The Gallican Church and the Ultramontane Campaign, 1848–1853* Oxford University Press, Oxford 1986.

Gratacos, Isaure, *Fées et gestes, femmes Pyrénéennes: Un statut social exceptionnel en Europe* Privat, Toulouse 1986.

Green, Nicholas, *The Spectacle of Nature: Landscape and Bourgeois Culture in Nineteenth-Century France* Manchester University Press, Manchester 1990.

Harris, Ruth, *Lourdes: Body and Spirit in the Secular Age* Penguin Press, London 1999.

Harrison, Carol E., *The Bourgeois Citizen in Nineteenth-Century France: Gender, Sociability, and the Uses of Emulation* Oxford University Press, Oxford 1999.

Le Hidec, Max, *Les Secrets de la Salette* Nouvelles éditions Latines, Paris 1969.

Katz, Melissa, and Robert A. Orsi, *Divine Mirrors: The Virgin Mary in the Visual Arts* Oxford University Press, Oxford 2001.

Kselman, Thomas A., *Miracles and Prophecies in Nineteenth-Century France* Rutgers University Press, New Jersey 1983.

Laffon, Jean-Baptiste, ed., *Le Diocèse de Tarbes et Lourdes* Letouzey & Ané, Éditeurs, Paris 1971.

Laffon, Jean-Baptiste, ed., *Le Monde religieux Bigourdan (1800–1962)* Éditions oeuvre de la Grotte, Lourdes 1984.

Lafourcade, Pierre, and G. Marsan, *Lourdes autrefois de 1800 à 1930* Éditions Horvath, Paris 1988.

Lanore, M. 'L'art dans la région bigourdane', *Revue des Hautes-Pyrénées* 11 (1906): 336–40.

Laurentin, René, *Lourdes, histoire authentique*, vols 1–6. Lethielleux, Paris 1961–4.

Laurentin, Renè, *Bernadette vous parle*, vols 1 and 2. Lethielleux, Paris 1972.

Laurentin, René, *Vie de Bernadette* Desclée de Brouwer, Alençon 1978.

Laurentin, René, *Visage de Bernadette* Lethielleux, Paris 1978.

Le Clère, Bernard, and Vincent Wright, *Les Préfets du Second Empire* Armand Colin, Paris 1973.

Lerou, Paule, and Roger Lerou, 'La statue, support de la piété populaire', *Cahiers Percherons* 3–4 (1987): 25–40.

McMillan, James, 'Religion and gender in modern France: Some reflections', Frank Tallett and Nicholas Atkin, eds, *Religion, Society and Gender in France since 1789* Hambledon Press, London 1991.

McMillan, James, *France and Women, 1789–1914: Gender, Society and Politics* Routledge, London and New York 2000.

McPhee, Peter, *The Politics of Rural Life: Political Mobilization in the French Countryside 1846–1852* Oxford University Press, Oxford 1992.

Margadant, Ted W., *French Peasants in Revolt: The Insurrection of 1851* Princeton University Press, New Jersey 1979.

Merriman, J. M. 'Demoiselles', in J. M. Merriman, *1830 in France* New Viewpoints, New York, 1975.

Musée Pyrénéen, *La Vie quotidienne dans les Hautes-Pyrénées au temps de Bernadette* Musée Pyrénéen, Lourdes 1979.

Musée Pyrénéen, *Regards neufs sur l'art religieux dans les Hautes-Pyrénées* Musée Pyrénéen, Auch 1981.

Neame, Alan, *The Happening at Lourdes, or the Sociology of the Grotto* Hodder & Stoughton, London 1968.

Parson, Christopher, and Neil McWilliam, ' "Le Paysan de Paris": Alfred Sensier and the myth of rural France', *Oxford Art Journal* 6 (1983): 38–58.

Payne, Howard C., *The Police State of Louis Napoleon Bonaparte 1851–1860* University of Washington Press, Seattle 1966.

Pelikan, Jaroslav, *Mary through the Centuries: Her Place in the History of Culture*. Yale University Press, Yale *c.*1996.

Petitot, R. P. H., *Histoire exacte des apparitions de N. D. de Lourdes à Bernadette* Desclée de Brouwer, Paris 1935.

Price, Roger, 'Techniques of repression: the control of popular protest in mid-nineteenth-century France', *Historical Journal* 25 (1982): 859–87.

Ravier, Xavier, *Le Récit mythologique en Haute-Bigorre* Édisud/Éditions du CNRS, Gap 1986.

Recroix, Xavier, *Les Peintures du narthex de la chapelle de Garaison* Imprimerie Marrimpouey Jeune, Pau 1981.

Recroix, Xavier, 'Un aspect de la piété populaire dans les Pyrénées Centrales: La dévotion Mariale', *Revue de Comminges* 1 (1989): 121–8.

Roberdel, Pierre, *Marie-Julie Jahenny, la stigmatisée de Blain 1850–1941* Éditions Résiac, Montsûrs 1987.

Rogers, Nancy, 'The wasting away of romantic heroines', *Nineteenth-Century French Studies* 11 (1983): 246–55.

Rosapelly, Norbert, *Traditions et coutumes des Hautes-Pyrénées* Société Academique des Hautes-Pyrénées, 1990.

Rosenbaum-Dondaine, Catherine, ed., *L'Image de piété en France 1814–1914* Musée-Galerie de la Seita, Paris 1984.

Rouby, Dr, *La Vérité sur Lourdes* Imprimerie et Lithographie A. Vaubourg, Paris 1910.

Sahlins, Peter, *Forest Rites: The War of the Demoiselles in Nineteenth-Century France* Harvard University Press, Harvard 1994.

Saint Pierre, Michel de, *Bernadette et Lourdes* La table ronde, Paris 1979.

Savart, Claude, 'A la recherche de l'art dit de Saint-Sulpice', *Revue d'histoire de la spiritualité* 52 (1976): 265–82.

Scott, James C., *Weapons of the Weak: Everyday Forms of Peasant Resistance* Yale University Press, New Haven 1985.

Singer, Barnett, *Village Notables in Nineteenth-Century France* State University of New York Press, Albany 1983.

Smith, Bonnie G., *Ladies of the Leisure Class: The Bourgeoises of Northern France in the Nineteenth Century*. Princeton University Press, Princeton c.1981.

Soulet, Jean-François, *Les Pyrénées au XIXe siècle*, 2 vols. Éché, Toulouse 1987.

Tallett, Frank, and Nicholas Atkin, *Catholicism in Britain and France since 1789* Hambledon Press, London 1996.

Thuillier, Guy, *Pour une histoire du quotidien au XIXe siècle en Nivernais* École des hautes études en sciences sociales, Paris 1977.

Trochu, Francis, *Sainte Bernadette: La voyante de Lourdes* Emmanuel Vitte, Lyon 1958.

Valois, Jeanne, 'La fontaine de salut a Rébénacq', *Revue de Pau et du Béarn* 19 (1992): 240–8.

Weber, Eugen, *Peasants into Frenchmen: The Modernization of Rural France 1870–1914* Chatto & Windus, London 1976.

Yver, Colette, *L'Humble Sainte Bernadette* Éditions Spes, Saint-Armand 1933.

Zimdars-Swartz, Sandra, *Encountering Mary: From La Salette to Medjugorje* Princeton University Press, New Jersey 1991.

# Index

Page numbers in *italics* refer to plates.